THE
EIGHTH
WONDER
OF THE
WORLD

THE EIGHTH WONDER OF THE WORLD

THE TRUE STORY OF
ANDRÉ THE GIANT

BERTRAND HÉBERT
AND PAT LAPRADE

Published by ECW Press
665 Gerrard Street East
Toronto, Ontario, Canada M4M 1Y2
416-694-3348 / info@ecwpress.com

Editor for the Press: Michael Holmes
Cover design: Michel Vrana
Cover image: © WWE
Pat Laprade author photo: © Marc Dussault

LIBRARY AND ARCHIVES CANADA CATALOGUING IN PUBLICATION

Title: The eighth wonder of the world : the true story of André the Giant / Bertrand Hébert and Pat Laprade.

Names: Hébert, Bertrand, author. | Laprade, Pat, author.

Description: Includes bibliographical references.

Identifiers: Canadiana (print) 2020017147X
Canadiana (ebook) 20200171488

ISBN 978-1-77041-466-2 (hardcover)
ISBN 978-1-77305-477-3 (PDF)
ISBN 978-1-77305-476-6 (EPUB)

Subjects: LCSH: Andre, the Giant, 1946-1993. | LCSH: Wrestlers—France—Biography. | LCGFT: Biographies.

Classification: LCC GV1196.A53 H47 2020
DDC 796.812092—dc23

The publication of *The Eighth Wonder of the World* has been funded in part by the Government of Canada. *Ce livre est financé en partie par le gouvernement du Canada.* We also acknowledge the contribution of the Government of Ontario through the Ontario Book Publishing Tax Credit, and through Ontario Creates for the marketing of this book.

PRINTED AND BOUND IN CANADA   PRINTING: FRIESENS   5   4   3   2   1

This book is dedicated to Gérald Hébert, Gene Okerlund,
Larry Hennig, Don Leo Jonathan, Michel Dubois, Terry Todd,
Françoise Valois, Jacques Rougeau Sr., René Goulet, and Jackie Wiecz

CONTENTS

FOREWORD BY STAN HANSEN IX

INTRODUCTION XI

CHAPTER 1   A BIG BABY . . .   1

CHAPTER 2   THE BIRTH OF JEAN FERRÉ   13

CHAPTER 3   THE INVASION OF ENGLAND   28

CHAPTER 4   FROM A GIANT TO A MONSTER!   41

CHAPTER 5   A GIANT DISORDER   52

CHAPTER 6   VALOIS, VACHON, CARPENTIER, AND . . . SADDAM   63

CHAPTER 7   TALL TALES: HOW TALL WAS ANDRÉ, REALLY?   75

CHAPTER 8   MONTREAL, WHERE ANDRÉ'S CAREER TOOK OFF   85

CHAPTER 9   AROUND THE WORLD!   96

CHAPTER 10   MATCH OF THE CENTURY, NAME OF THE DECADE   112

CHAPTER 11   IF I CAN MAKE IT THERE, I'LL MAKE IT ANYWHERE   124

CHAPTER 12   TRAVELING TO GREATNESS   135

CHAPTER 13   "NOW PLAYING DEFENSIVE END . . . ANDRÉ THE GIANT!"   147

CHAPTER 14   THREE BOXERS, TWO KINGS, AND ONE BIGFOOT!   158

CHAPTER 15   BATTLE OF THE GIANTS!   179

CHAPTER 16   WHEN ANDRÉ MET HULK   191

CHAPTER 17   TO THE GIANT AMONG US   210

CHAPTER 18   BUSINESS IS BUSINESS   222

CHAPTER 19   A GREAT EXPANSION, BUT NOT FOR ANDRÉ   236

CHAPTER 20   THE WOMEN IN HIS LIFE   250

CHAPTER 21   SPEARHEADING WWF SUCCESS   266

CHAPTER 22   SHOOTING IN JAPAN   283

CHAPTER 23   A GENTLE GIANT!   297

CHAPTER 24   BIGGER, BETTER, BADDER!   310

CHAPTER 25   THE FOUNDATION OF WWE PPVS   325

CHAPTER 26   OFF CAMERA   344

CHAPTER 27   THE END OF AN ERA   356

CHAPTER 28   LIFE AFTER THE WWF   375

CHAPTER 29   A LEGEND IN AND AFTER HIS DEATH   387

CHAPTER 30   A GIANT LEGACY   395

ACKNOWLEDGMENTS   409

REFERENCES   413

FOREWORD

It's my honor to write a foreword about André the Giant. In my opinion, there has been no one in the wrestling business that carved out a spectacular and unique position as André did. No one had an instant influence on the wrestling shows that he performed on more than André. I first met him in the Amarillo territory in 1973. He was just a green "boy" then. If there was an awe moment in my wrestling life, it was when I first met and stood next to André. Even today, it is hard to comprehend the massive size and presence he had in and out of the ring. He was so tall at seven feet and somewhere in the 450 pounds range. Everything about him was just massive. His head was almost so big that you could hardly put a headlock on him. He wore size 22 shoes, I was told. His fist was as big as two of anyone else's. His fingers were as large as big sausages.

There are countless André stories. Most everyone has one and it is unique and told in awe and with respect. You can be sure that there will be numerous stories about him from the wrestling events and also outside of the wrestling business in this book. André not only was a great performer but also was agile for someone his size.

I think that he needed and wanted a life out of the limelight. He longed to be able to live a normal life and not be looked at and noticed constantly. I am sure that it became a huge burden living the life of "André the Giant." He longed for normalcy and privacy that he hardly ever received.

In many ways, I think he enjoyed the wrestlers so much because they treated him as an equal and not as "the giant." I never heard anyone say that André was full of himself or selfish. He just wanted to enjoy life in a normal way.

Personally, I really got to know André in Japan where we ended up working against each other for New Japan Pro Wrestling and Antonio Inoki. The thing that I realized is that André was smart in the ring and also in the wrestling business. He knew his place and the difficulty of being able to wrestle in something other than a "special" type of match. André was always looking for a way to be more than a special attraction. He was smart enough to see that he needed an opponent to work with while in Japan and realized that I was the one. He, for sure, enhanced my career and was also instrumental in making me a top guy in Japan. For this, I am and will always be grateful.

Enjoy this book and read the spectacular and interesting life of a true giant of a man, wrestler, dad, and friend.

STAN HANSEN

INTRODUCTION

The story goes like this . . .

André the Giant is challenging Hulk Hogan for the World Wrestling Federation title. Near the corner of Michigan Highway and Opdyke Road, in a town of 70,000, 30 miles northwest of Detroit, 93,173 people are crammed together to witness one of the biggest pro wrestling matches of all time. The Pontiac Silverdome — home of the NFL's Detroit Lions and the NBA's Detroit Pistons — is the place to be. Much like André, the stadium is the largest of its kind and a great stage for a match like this.

André versus Hogan is the perfect match on the perfect stage. The challenger, from Grenoble in the French Alps, stands seven foot four, weighing 520 pounds. The champion, from Venice Beach, California, is six foot six and 302 pounds. Both are undefeated, and they face each other for the very first time. Will Hogan be able to slam the Giant, let alone beat him? Will the Giant end Hogan's 39-month title reign? This *WrestleMania*, the showcase of the immortals, the third such event organized by Vincent Kennedy McMahon, is the first to reach a worldwide phenomenon level. *WrestleMania III*'s slogan "Bigger, Better, Badder" suits it to a T.

Ever since arriving in North America, André had been the biggest attraction in pro wrestling. Fans have heard that André came from France in the early '70s and, after a brief stint in Canada, went on to rule the wrestling world, managed by the top impresario in the sport, Vincent James McMahon. André was his vision.

A decade later, McMahon's son took over the company, and he chose Hulk Hogan as the future of the business. As the company's history goes, André and Hogan were best friends. André was even part of the celebration when Hogan defeated The Iron Sheik for the WWF World Heavyweight championship at Madison Square Garden in 1984 — he famously poured champagne on Hogan's head.

Since becoming champion, Hogan had defended the title against almost every bad guy in the promotion: Rowdy Roddy Piper, Paul Orndorff, Big John Studd, King Kong Bundy, Jesse Ventura . . . the list goes on and on and on. A couple of times a year, Hulk and André teamed up to face adversity that one man alone could not overcome. André, it seemed, was too much of a novelty to be considered for a championship match; since he had started working for the elder McMahon, seven different wrestlers had won the crown jewel. Hogan was simply the latest to jump ahead of him.

And that is what March 29, 1987, is all about: André being overshadowed by Hogan, not getting the respect he deserves. By the time of the marquee match, fans in the Silverdome have already seen so much: pretty boys Rick Martel and Tom Zenk opened *WrestleMania III* with real vigor; Brutus Beefcake was evicted from the Dream Team, replaced by Dino Bravo; Ricky Steamboat defeated Randy Savage in a match no one will ever forget; and Jim Duggan and Nikolai Volkoff had their own version of the Cold War. Édouard Carpentier, André's old friend from France, is providing commentary in French for André's francophone fans.

The building is rumbling when "Mr. Baseball" Bob Uecker introduces *Entertainment Tonight*'s Mary Hart as the guest timekeeper. With former enemy Bobby "The Brain" Heenan by his side, André comes down the very long walkway from the backstage area to the ring on a motorized cart made to look like a miniature ring. He remains stonily indifferent to the chorus of boos and the debris thrown at him. He enters his battlefield by stepping over the top rope, as he always does. This is the pinnacle of his career.

Backstage, Hogan is nervous. "What if André goes into business for himself? What if he decides he's winning tonight?" If André did, there would be nothing the Hulkster could do to defeat him.

Hogan's "Real American" entrance music finally hits. In better shape than André, he walks from the curtain to the ring, cheered on by the thousands of Hulkamaniacs in attendance.

The tension is real. The two biggest stars of the last decade are in the ring, and everybody in attendance or watching on closed-circuit TV around the world are on the edge of their seats. After just a few seconds, Hogan tries to slam the Giant, something that no one has ever been able to do. But he's denied by André, who covers the champion for a two-and-three-quarter count by referee Joey Marella. After taking the beating of a lifetime, Hogan comes back from the dead, slams André, and hits the leg drop for the one, two, three. Not only did Hogan win the match and keep his title, but he also dealt André his very first defeat.

Or *did* he?

"The Hogan-André match at *WrestleMania III* and the Bret-Shawn match in Montreal in 1997 are the two most important matches in the history of modern wrestling," argues journalist and founder of the *Wrestling Observer Newsletter*, Dave Meltzer.

This match and everything surrounding it were the culmination of every myth and legend ever heard about André coming to a head, on the biggest stage he ever performed on.

André wasn't seven foot four, at any point in his life. He didn't weigh 520 pounds. And he wasn't from Grenoble or even the French Alps. This was not André and Hogan's first match, and André had been lifted off his feet way before Hogan stepped foot in a ring for the first time.

Montreal was more important to André's career than any biography of him has ever revealed. Even the number of people in attendance that night in Pontiac was exaggerated.

However, one thing is true: the magnitude of that encounter was undeniable. Depending on a fan's age and knowledge of pro wrestling at the time, they either loved it or thought it was a poor performance. But everyone agrees that its influence on the future of the WWF is immeasurable. André's health was declining, and it was the right time to officially pass the torch, even though Hulk had already been the star of the WWF for a while. André knew this match would make him a legend beyond his time. In a business where timing is everything, that feud opened the door to so many great things for the WWF as it seemed to expand without limit at the beginning of the PPV era. The André and Hogan feud was, in fact, an important piece of what would come next — so much so that people may still not even realize.

In 1987, the biggest lie about André wasn't his height or his undefeated record. It was that by that time, he had lost so much strength he even had trouble catching a teenage actress in a movie. While photographs showed he could easily lift five women at once — casting him as a real-life mythical being — acromegaly, the ailment that had made him a superstar known around the world, was catching up to him. The body that had made him famous was betraying him in pernicious ways every day. Condemned to be André the Giant 24 hours a day, seven days a week, he was likely depressed — at very least, sad that he couldn't go anywhere without being stared at, pointed at, or touched. He was 40 years old and he knew he wouldn't live to see 50.

From Paris to Montreal, from Tokyo to New York City, he transcended the world of professional wrestling. The Seven Wonders of the World, like the Pyramid of Giza or the Colossus of Rhodes, have something mysterious about them, something mythical, as if sprung from some legend or fairy tale. André's real life and career were the same, clouded by myths and overshadowed by his larger-than-life character and personality.

On March 29, 1987, André probably wasn't the *better*, or even the *badder*, but he was definitely the *bigger* wrestler. Much like *WrestleMania* today, André René Roussimoff was at one point the greatest spectacle in sports entertainment.

He was the Eighth Wonder of the World . . .

CHAPTER 1

A
BIG
BABY . . .

L ike everything else in his life, the origin story of André Roussimoff is anything but simple.

In the late 19th and early 20th century, Europe was beset by major crises and it was within that fraught environment that André's father, Boris Roussimoff Stoeff, was born on March 15, 1907, in Ribaritsa, a small village near the Balkan Mountains in Bulgaria. Bulgaria, home to the larger ethnolinguistic group of the Slavs, was at war less than two years after Roussimoff was born in the First and Second Balkan Wars.

Aligning itself with its western neighbor the kingdom of Serbia, Bulgaria wasn't pleased with how the new territories acquired from the Ottoman Empire were divided. Like a wrestler betraying his tag team partner, Bulgaria turned against Serbia; the two territories had been battling for 500 years. Bulgaria was defeated and lost all the gains it had made in the First Balkan War. Soon after, in 1914, the Austro-Hungarians declared war on Serbia and a year later, Bulgaria also declared war on Serbia to join the central powers of Austria-Hungary, as well as the German and Ottoman empires. After making vital contributions to World War I by occupying Serbia, as well as parts of Romania and Greece, the tide turned. On November 27, 1918, two weeks after the war ended, Bulgaria signed the Treaty of Neuilly-sur-Seine, in which it was required, among other things, to cede to Serbia the territory it had taken over during the war, plus a 990-square-mile territory on its border called the Western Outlands.

Before World War I started, the Roussimoff family had moved to the Outlands, close to the Serbian border. After the treaty, they were no longer living in Bulgaria but in Serbia. To make matters even more complicated, Serbia wasn't Serbia anymore: it was now part of the kingdom of Yugoslavia, a merger between the south Slavic states of Serbia, Slovenia, Croatia, and Montenegro.

Boris Roussimoff had five siblings: three brothers named Todor, Cvetko, and Krum, and two sisters, Vena and Stojna. The family didn't have much money, and with their country at war, education wasn't a priority. When World War I ended, Boris was 11 and he didn't know how to read; he eventually learned how to write a little in Bulgarian. He knew how to count though.

"He was trafficking illegal goods and got caught by the police in 1936," said one of André's nephews, named Boris in honor of his grandfather. "He jumped from the second floor of the police station and was able to escape. From that point on, he was a fugitive. That's how he ended up in France. For 30 years, the family thought he hadn't survived World War II, but in the late 1960s, my grandpa told his story to a Bulgarian in France and that man offered to write a letter to [the Roussimoff] family, and that's how they knew he was alive and well."

To escape, Boris traveled west through Yugoslavia, over northern Italy and the Adriatic Sea before ending his trek in France, a journey of at least 1,500 miles. How he traveled and why he chose France is unknown, but one could guess that he felt France was far enough to be a safe place to start fresh. He settled in Molien, a hamlet that was part of a bigger village called Ussy-sur-Marne, approximately 40 miles northeast of Paris. Boris started working on a farm named Courtablon. One of his coworkers, Mazarek, couldn't stop talking about his sister, Marianne.

Marianne and Mazarek were the children of Antoine and Anne Marasjeck. Marianne was born on January 24, 1910, in the village of Korytnica, Poland (with no less than six villages named Korytnica in Poland, which village it was has been lost to history). After its independence at the end of World War I, Poland was faced with major economic difficulties. Hostile relations with neighbors like Germany and the Soviet Union were a concern; a few years before the invasion of Poland that started World War II, Mazarek had found peace hundreds of miles away in France.

"One day, my grandpa told him to stop talking about her and to bring her there," said Boris, André's nephew. "He did, and my grandpa simply fell in love with her."

Boris rented a house in Molien, less than a 10-minute walk from where he was working. He officially became a French citizen in March 1938, and three months later, he married Marianne. In January 1939, the couple welcomed their first son, Antoine, namesake of Marianne's father. Then came their first daughter, Hélène, in November 1940. However, Boris wasn't there to welcome his second child.

On September 1, 1939, Germany invaded Poland. In the following days, France, the United Kingdom, Australia, New Zealand, South Africa, and Canada declared war on Germany. Sometime during the first few months of 1940, Boris had to join the French forces. In June 1940, Germany won the Battle of France and completed its invasion of the country. Germany seized two million French prisoners of war and sent them to camps in Germany. Boris was among them.

"My dad was taken prisoner in Germany," said Boris's eldest, Antoine. "He tried to escape but didn't succeed. He was freed only when the war ended."

"My mom had to work to make sure my sister and I could eat," Antoine added. "She was picking beets in the fields. I also remember that in Ussy-sur-Marne, there was a castle and that's where the Germans were. One day, I opened our front door and a bomb exploded in Ussy and the blast propelled me to the back of the kitchen. I will always remember that."

By the time World War II ended in 1945, 600,000 French had been killed. Fortunately, Boris was still alive and came back to his family, who were all alive as well. Soon thereafter, Marianne became pregnant again and on May 19, 1946, at 3:10 p.m., she gave birth to her third child, André René Roussimoff.

André was a big baby, weighing six kilos, or a little over 13 pounds. Six kilos is much more than average, even for today. According to Statistics Canada, in 2008, only 0.02 percent of newborns exceeded 5.5 kilos. In 2017, in Merced, California, ABC News reported that a mother gave birth to a 13-pound baby. Jessica Newton, a nurse where the mother delivered, said, "I've worked in labor delivery for about seven years, and the largest baby I've ever seen was a little bit over 10 pounds. So, 13 pounds is a big baby. I've never seen one that big." Even 70 years later, André would still be considered a big baby at birth. Marianne did not deliver him at home, as she had with her first two children, but in a hospital in Coulommiers, a small village next to Ussy-sur-Marne, the closest hospital from their home. "My mother tried to deliver at home, but she was just not able to," explained Antoine. "Our family doctor, Dr. Brecher, told her that she would have to deliver at the hospital."

André's full name was supposed to be André René Roussimoff Stoeff, but the clerk filing the birth certificate misunderstood the information given to him. "The person working at the registry office didn't understand Bulgarian names," said Boris. "My grandpa's full name was Boris Roussimoff Stoeff, with no hyphen. However, [the clerk] took that second last name for my grandpa's first name. That's why on André's birth certificate, my grandpa is referred to as Stoeff Roussimoff, and the name Stoeff is not on André's. Since my grandparents didn't read French, they didn't notice it. Of the five siblings, only my dad, Antoine, the first born, has the full name."

André was barely one day old and there was already an issue with the facts surrounding his life.

André's parents didn't have the time to worry about things like that though. Boris was working on the farm all day and Marianne was busy

ANTOINE ROUSSIMOFF COLLECTION

HÉLÈNE AND ANTOINE, WITH THEIR "BIG" BROTHER ANDRÉ IN THE MIDDLE.

PAT LAPRADE COLLECTION

ANDRÉ'S FAMILY HOUSE IS STILL STANDING TODAY.

ANDRÉ AT ANTOINE'S WEDDING, ON FEBRUARY 29, 1964, WITH THEIR FATHER IN THE BACK.

THE SIGNS OF ACROMEGALY DID NOT SHOW ON ANDRÉ YET.

BEFORE BECOMING A PRO WRESTLER, ANDRÉ WORKED ON A FARM. HERE HE IS, AT THE WHEEL.

at home with three young kids. The couple had also moved — just one house over, as Boris bought the house right next to the one they were renting. In time, he also bought the cow pens next to their house in order to build an extension. Marianne gave birth to two more children, Mauricette in October 1947 and Jacques in May 1950, to complete the Roussimoff family. Given the Bulgarian, Serbian, and Polish origins of the couple, it's worth noting that all five children had French names. The kids also grew up in a French-speaking home. Although Boris could speak Russian, Yugoslav, Polish, Bulgar, and French, the latter was the language in which they raised their children; they had adapted to their new country, language, and reality.

Even though he was bigger than normal, baby André's health was generally good. The only real issue the family noticed was that he started talking late — very late. He was five years old when he started speaking. A year later, he started school in Ussy-sur-Marne, the same school all the Roussimoff children went to. A few years into school, he grew to be the tallest of his classmates, and by the end of his school days, he was said to be a good head taller than the other kids. His hands were also bigger than a normal child's. At recess, when kids played soccer, or football as it is called in Europe, André was asked to be the goaltender. Alone between two trees serving as goalposts, his larger hands were a tool; it was the first time his larger-than-average body helped him with something.

"He really enjoyed stopping the ball," remembered Jacques Poulain, André's childhood friend, whose sister was in the same class as André. "Back then, we never thought he would become a giant."

As a kid, André didn't play many sports. Besides some recreational soccer, he once tried cycling. The Tour de France, which started in 1903, made cycling very popular. One day, there was a 10-kilometer cycling race organized by the local parish. A few hundred meters into it, André's bicycle chain gave up on him. He wanted his classmates to wait for him, but competitive kids being just that, no one did. André was left alone. Was it bad equipment or André's size to blame here? Probably a combination of the two. Equipment not adapted to his size would become another theme of his life.

Boris and Marianne were not a family of means. Still, they made sure their children ate three times a day, mostly chicken, rabbit, and pork, since that was what Boris was breeding. Putting food on the table was a priority, but at Christmas, or at any other time for that matter, there were no toys — the Roussimoff kids would get oranges. And although they had a dog, a cat, and several farm animals, the brothers don't remember having time to play with them. If they had nothing to do, Boris made sure to find them a chore to do around the house.

"I remember that he made us clean the rabbits' cage, the pigs' cage, and we had to store the wood for the winter," recalled the youngest sibling, Jacques. "On some Sundays, we played pétanque [bocce]. Sometimes, we would go horseback riding. But that's the only playing I can remember."

In school, André was an average student. "He was better than me," said Jacques, with a laugh, adding that his big brother's favorite classes were mathematics, geography, and French. According to Poulain, André liked going to school, but the only problem was that school wasn't close to home. The school was in Ussy-sur-Marne, a 30-minute walk each way. This actually brings up another well-known fairy tale.

Famous Irish novelist and playwright and recipient of the 1969 Nobel Prize in Literature Samuel Beckett moved to France in 1937. He had learned French in college and had even done some studies in Paris in the late 1920s. After working as a courier and doing translations for the French Resistance during World War II, he lived in different French towns until he found his way to Molien in 1953. Later in life, he moved to Paris, but kept his house in Molien for writing retreats until he passed away in 1989. As the story goes, 12-year-old André was too big to fit in the local school bus. Boris and Beckett knew each other well, since the former had helped the writer build his house. So, Beckett would drive André back and forth to school in the back of his pick-up truck.

Antoine sets the record straight. "We walked a mile and a half to school every day, all the time," he recalled. "There was no bus. Sometimes, a man or a woman who knew the kids in the village would bring us to school or back home after school. One of those people was Samuel Beckett."

While it's possible that Beckett did pick up André at one point, it's not like it was something specifically done for him. Antoine continues, "And my dad never helped him build his house. I don't understand how people can come up with those stories." Adding to his brother's clarification, Jacques said they did get a bus in his last school year, four years after André had finished school. That said, Antoine raises a good question. How does a story like that spread?

The story first gained worldwide attention as part of Box Brown's graphic novel *André the Giant: Life and Legend*, published in 2014. In his notes, the author wrote that he took the story from Craig Brown's book *One on One*, and that according to Craig Brown, the story was true. The only problem with this claim is that Craig Brown doesn't write about André and Beckett at all in his book. The story actually comes from a conversation between André and actor Cary Elwes (who played Mayor Larry Kline in the third installment of *Stranger Things* on Netflix) on the set of the movie *The Princess Bride*. According to Elwes, André told him that because of his size, he couldn't fit in the bus and that Samuel Beckett drove him to school a few times. Elwes wrote about it in his book. However, the biggest lie in this story is that André, at 12 years old, hadn't started growing to the degree he later did. That only started when André was between 14 and 15 years old. He was bigger than the other kids at 12 but not to the point of being too big to fit in a fictional school bus.

"The most interesting thing I learned about André was that he himself was the primary perpetuator of so much of the mythology," wrote Jason Hehir, director of an HBO documentary on André released in April 2018, on Reddit. "He seemed to revel in his own mythology and shied away from revealing his own truth."

One must not forget the era in which André lived and wrestled. The reality of wrestling was not something wrestlers talked about with non-wrestlers, sometimes not even with their own families. If you had a background story, you had to protect it to the point you would lie to journalists and to other people about your real origins. André wasn't the only one doing so, although it was different for him, since tales like that one became legion, his life story morphing into legend. As former wrestler the late Ray Stevens often told Pat Patterson, "If a story is worth telling, it's worth coloring!" So the legend of Samuel Beckett driving André to school was a tale told by André himself, 30 years later, coloring the facts to make it a better story.

Another legend surrounding André's childhood was that at age 14, due to his abnormal size, he quit school and left Molien for five years. And for the past 30 years, because it was printed in a *Sports Illustrated* 11-page profile on André, it's what most people believe to be fact. It's not.

André did leave school at 14 not because of his size but for the simple reason that in France in 1960, it was only obligatory to attend until the age of 14. Not as mesmerizing, but that does make much more sense. In 1936, France's minister of national education and fine arts Jean Zay, who was imprisoned and then killed by anti-Semitic French militia in 1944, wrote the Zay Bill, an education reform bill that, among other things, extended the schooling age from 13 to 14. In fact, André was almost forced to stay in school two more years. In 1959, the Berthoin Bill increased the mandatory age to 16, but it was only applicable to those who turned 16 after January 1, 1959, and therefore not applicable to André. For French youth of that era, after school finished, they would start to work or study further. The latter option wasn't available to the Roussimoffs. Although he did okay in school, André thought he didn't need more education in order to work on the farm. So André started working.

André didn't start working on the farm with his father right away though. "André started working as an apprentice cabinetmaker," remembered his younger brother Jacques. "The owner of the Courtablon farm, Guy Musnier, the same place where my father was working, asked him if he wanted to come and work there, so he did." His older brother Antoine, who used to work at the farm as well, was off doing his military service. In 1959, when Antoine left for the military, the country was at war with Algeria and 30-month service was mandatory. Antoine left home in January 1959 and came back in June 1961. It's during that time, after André finished school, that he really started to grow. In an interview he gave in 1968, André said that as a young teenager (around 13 or 14 years old), he was six feet tall and 213 pounds.

"André was 14 when he started to grow significantly," said Antoine. "When I came back, he was taller than me . . . about two meters tall [six foot six]. I remember asking my mother what was happening with him and she didn't know. She didn't understand why he was growing so fast." Jacques, who was 10 at the time, remembered that when André was 14, he was not quite as tall as his dad, but that a year later, he was close to six foot six.

"My mother went to see Dr. Brecher," continued Antoine. "But the doctor told her that it was normal. He didn't find anything wrong with him. And my father was not worried about that." Here's another tale that André himself perpetuated: when asked if other family members were also tall, André used to say that his grandfather was eight feet tall, remembering a story told many times by his dad. His brother Antoine remembered the story differently. "My father was not worried about André's growth because he always told us the story that his grandmother was very tall, so it wasn't a surprise to him," said Antoine. So who was it: André's grandfather or great-grandmother who was very tall?

Thanks to Antoine's son, Boris, the truth can finally be known. Boris is the only family member who went to Serbia and Bulgaria to meet the family there and to learn more about them. "It was my dad and uncle's great-grandfather, so Boris's grandfather, who was very tall," Boris revealed. "His name was Ivanko and he passed away at 106 years old."

When you take a look at the family, it's obvious that there's something in the genes. Both Antoine and Jacques, like their father, have big and thick hands. One of Antoine's granddaughters is six feet tall, one of his grandsons is close to that at only 13 years old, and a cousin on his father's side is also very tall. Boris was six feet tall and André's nephew Boris is six foot two. Although acromegaly was already known by the medical community at the time, André wasn't showing any pronounced sign of it yet. It is also possible that the family doctor didn't recognize the symptoms, that it wasn't in his field of expertise. In any case, André was 15 and he was close to six foot six.

He worked on the farm for a few years — riding tractors, laboring in the fields, harvesting, and carrying 220-pound bags of grain. Still living at his parents' house, he then went to work in La Ferté-sous-Jouarre, another small village, four miles east of Molien and Ussy-sur-Marne. There he worked in a factory with grinders and delivered goods to restock small groceries. André was happy working there and met his first girlfriend, Josée, whom he dated for less than two years. He also played some recreational football when he was 18 for his hometown, Ussy-sur-Marne, against other nearby villages St-Jean and Changis. He was center-forward but didn't play for long. A farmer had offered a pair of football shoes to every player except for André, because he didn't have a pair that would fit him. So André played in a pair of military boot covers, used by soldiers to prevent their boots from getting wet. At the time, finding clothes for André was not a problem compared to finding shoes, which had to be custom-made. Around the same time, he was also asked to play rugby, very popular in France as well, but he had no interest, just like he had no interest in basketball.

As fate would have it, it was during his time in La Ferté-sous-Jouarre that André met a man who would change his life. At 18, without knowing it, he was about to take the most important step in his life. And he would never look back.

CHAPTER 2

THE BIRTH OF JEAN FERRÉ

n the late 19th and early 20th centuries, Paris, France, was the center of Greco-Roman wrestling. In fact, the Greco-Roman style of wrestling was a French creation, but the name Greco-Roman was an invention for the rest of the continent that resented the French. The style of wrestling was first known as "la lutte Française" around 1840. The very first French wrestler to make a name for himself was André Christol, who started as a teenager in the 1860s. He first wrestled for Claude-Eugene Rossignol-Rollin, who had been the main promoter in France since 1852. Nicknamed the "French Demon," Christol wrestled in Europe and North America and main-evented the first show held at the Gilmore's Garden, before it was renamed Madison Square Garden, in New York City in 1875. Three years later, like many Frenchmen after him, he came to Montreal, the biggest French-speaking city in America, to wrestle. "He is credited with being the first man to introduce the French Hug, which appears to be a move a couple of you may have heard of . . . the Bear Hug," wrote wrestling historian Jimmy Wheeler. Although he was only five foot five and 150 pounds, he won a version of the World Greco-Roman championship in 1875.

Around the time he retired, an impressive young wrestler emerged on the scene. Nicknamed "The Colossal" and "The European Giant" because he was six foot four and 260 pounds, Paul Pons started wrestling in 1888. The local French wrestling scene had a down period between 1891 and 1894, but Pons's feud with outsiders like the Terrible Turk and Nikolai Petroff made wrestling interesting again. In 1898, André de Lucenski, the director of the *Journal des Sports*, created the first World Greco-Roman Heavyweight Championship tournament at the Casino de Paris. That tournament was a preview of what the European wrestling scene looked like for the next two decades. During those years, the stages of the Montesquieu Theater, Casino de Paris, the Apollo, the Hippodrome, and Folies Bergère in France saw major European tournaments featuring the greatest stars of the Greco-Roman world. It was in Paris that the great George Hackenschmidt won a world championship tournament, beating Constant le Boucher in the final on December 27, 1901. Pons won the tournament on multiple occasions, and other Frenchmen, like Laurent le Beaucairois and Raoul le Boucher, did as well. Pons also wrestled in New York City and in Montreal, drawing a good crowd in the latter, again due to the French connection. However, by the 1920s, the World War and the resulting high taxes almost killed wrestling as a major sport in Paris. Pons died in 1915, and with the main star of the past 15 to 20 years gone, pro wrestling in France as a whole suffered the same fate.

It took a trio of Olympic medalists to revive pro wrestling, or "catch" as they call it in France. Born in 1902, Henri Deglane won the gold medal in the heavyweight division at the 1924 Paris Olympics. He was the first Frenchman to ever win gold in wrestling, and it made him a national hero. With very little action for a wrestler in France, Deglane left for North America at the end of 1927. Following in the footsteps of guys like Christol, Pons, and Emile Maupas, Deglane became a huge star in Montreal, helping the territory bounce back. He also won Paul Bowser's AWA World title in what later was dubbed the first Montreal Screwjob; that made him the first man to ever win an Olympic gold medal in wrestling and a world professional wrestling title. In September

1933, Deglane and another Frenchman, Raoul Paoli, whom he had met in the United States, opened a wrestling promotion in France. Paoli, born in 1887, was a several-time French heavyweight champion in amateur wrestling and boxing, had won a bronze medal at the 1900 Paris Olympics in rowing, had participated in five Olympic Games, and had played for the French national rugby team. Paoli was the promoter and matchmaker, and Deglane was the top star. The latter didn't come home alone: he returned with his manager and the man who had acted as his policeman when he wrestled for Bowser, Dan Koloff. Koloff used his connections to assist them in bringing talent over, as well as getting a couple of their top young wrestlers dates in North America. In the ring, Koloff was the number-two star. By the end of 1933, Charles Rigoulot, the final piece of the puzzle, joined the promotion. Rigoulot had also won a gold medal for France in the 1924 Olympics in weightlifting. Paoli recruited him and he quickly became the second-most popular local star, behind Deglane. With Paoli, Deglane, Rigoulot, and Koloff, pro wrestling in France saw a huge revival, bringing back memories of when Pons was performing. It wasn't strange to see the promotion filling the 17,000-seat Vel' d'Hiv (also called Palais des Sports) on a regular basis.

Obviously, with World War II, wrestling saw a down period until the mid-1940s, but in 1946, Deglane was still regarded as the kingpin, followed closely by Rigoulot and one of his trainees, Félix Miquet. Deglane retired in 1950, but Paoli kept promoting until he died in March 1960. Wrestling was popular on television — it had been broadcast at least once, sometimes even twice a week on RTF since 1952, the main TV station in France — and the attractive territory was now up for grabs. Accordingly, the 1960s saw many wrestling promoters sharing the territory and the television exposure.

Alex Goldstein, Maurice Durand, Roger Delaporte, and the duo of Robert Lageat and Étienne Siry became the main promoters. Even if the territory wasn't built like the National Wrestling Alliance — an organization overseeing all the promotions — these promoters often exchanged talent and only recognized one national champion. At the same time, RTF (and then ORTF in 1964) aired matches from all of them, so they were battling for that exposure too.

In 1965, while André was working at La Ferté-sous-Jouarre, he met Robert Lageat. Lageat, born on May 9, 1911, in Paris, was a former boxer who had started wrestling in the 1930s under the name of Alexandre Lageat. His son, Jacques, was also wrestling, as Jacky Corn. Retired from the ring, Robert Lageat became one of Paoli's assistants with Alex Goldstein, who was the man behind the idea of l'Ange Blanc (the White Angel), perhaps the most popular wrestler in France's history. L'Ange Blanc's feud with le Bourreau de Béthune (Béthune's Hangman) in the 1960s is still remembered. At the start of the first full season after Paoli's passing, Lageat had already split from Paoli and started out on his own, becoming the promoter of the Fédération Française de Catch Professionnel (the French Professional Wrestling Federation, or FFCP). He then partnered with a boxing promoter, Étienne Siry.

"They all had names for their promotions, but we'd never use them, we would use their personal names," explained second-generation grappler and promoter Marc Mercier. "We'd say that we wrestled for Durand or Delaporte or Lageat. They were known to the public as matchmakers."

With wrestling a hot product, promoters were always looking for the newest star. Lageat met André by chance when he was in La Ferté-sous-Jouarre. He immediately saw money in André's size and offered to train him in Paris. André had never been a wrestling fan growing up. To begin with, the family couldn't afford a television set. Since Boris and Marianne didn't know how to read, there were no newspapers at home. Since André didn't watch wrestling or read about wrestling, he had never had a favorite wrestler and never dreamed of becoming a pro wrestler. He had seen a show or two around town with his brother Jacques, but no more than that. But André had never really liked his jobs, whether at the farm or not. He was always trying to find a better job, one that would pay him more or that he'd enjoy more. And that's probably the biggest advantage wrestling had for him. It would allow him to travel and meet people, and it was an opportunity to make more money. In addition to that, Paris was less than an hour from Molien, a relatively short trip to come back home whenever needed.

André got his driver's license at 18. His first car was an old Renault 4CV, once the bestselling car in France. Sometimes, André would have fun with the small car: as he was getting out of it, he would pretend to be stuck, half of his body inside and the other half outside. When people started staring, he would try to stand up straight and lift his car a little. It was a prelude to all the pranks he later played and the seed for the many stories of him lifting cars. His brother Jacques remembered that André had lifted a Peugeot 404, just enough for Jacques to change the tire. In Montreal years later, wrestler Luke Williams saw him flip a Volkswagen Beetle on its side, something many others, true or not, have said they saw him do as well.

André decided to go to Paris to try this wrestling thing, but he wasn't the first Roussimoff to move away from home. Both his sisters had already gone to work in a Paris butcher shop. Antoine had left to get married in 1964, so only André and Jacques were left at the family home. He didn't ask for his parents' approval or advice. "We were managing ourselves," Jacques said. "Our parents never said anything; it was only normal for them that we moved on with our lives."

André started training at 22 rue des Martyrs. The building was close to l'Élysée-Montmartre, a 3,000-seat venue owned at the time by Roger Delaporte; it had started showcasing pro wrestling in 1936. The training facility was 20 minutes away from le Palais de la Mutualité (usually referred to as la Mutualité), which was a smaller venue most often used by Lageat and Siry; Siry used to stage his boxing events there. In other words, André was training right in the middle of Paris's wrestling scene. André's trainer was a former wrestler by the name of Michel Saulnier. The difference between André and his trainer was noticeable: Saulnier was a small man, not only compared to André. He was a former French champion, winning in 1955 in the 52-kilogram (114-pound) category, and he had turned pro in 1957 after failing to represent his country at the 1956 Melbourne Olympics.

"Robert Lageat had found and bought a hall," explained former wrestler Claude Roca. "When it was time to find himself a trainer, he offered the job to Guy Mercier and, of course, to Michel Saulnier. The 22 rue des Martyrs became a mythic place where all the aspiring wrestlers wanted to get trained." The training facility also served as the business office for Lageat and Siry.

Saulnier was in his mid-30s and still wrestling on the local scene when he trained André. Other trainees at the same time included Gilbert Wehrle and Daniel Dubail, who became one of the most popular wrestlers in France in the late '60s and the 1970s under the name of Albéric d'Éricourt, le Petit Prince (the Little Prince).

"Ferré [as André came to be known] trained for about a year," remembered Wehrle. "It wasn't easy to find people to train with." Words echoed by Lageat's promotional program in February 1966 for a show at the Palais des Sports in Toulouse. The preceding month, in what is probably the very first reference to André in any wrestling-related magazine, the writer explained, "Soon, we will be able to witness two phenoms who will perform in the ring of the Palais des Sports, two extraordinary local wrestlers, who, between the two of them, are the most astonishing contrast of what the French technique can produce in wrestling: the lightweight Albéric d'Éricourt and the giant, Jean Ferré (19 years old — 2m. 09 — 135kg)." That's six foot nine and 300 pounds.

The program went on to say that matchmakers would have a hard time finding André an opponent and that the same thing could be said for the diminutive d'Érincourt, who was only five foot two and 120 pounds. As would be the case throughout his career, André was now said to be "2m. 10" and 140 kilograms, a centimeter and five kilograms more than the previous month. Even then, no one could agree on his height. To account for the change, it was added that the doctors of the FFCP had seen him and said he was not done growing. It would be surprising if such a medical test had actually been done, especially since the next line mentioned his lumberjack background, which was 100 percent made up.

A YOUNG MAN STARTING HIS CAREER, WITH WRESTLER CHÉRI BIBI.

ONE OF ANDRÉ'S EARLY PROMO SHOTS IN FRANCE.

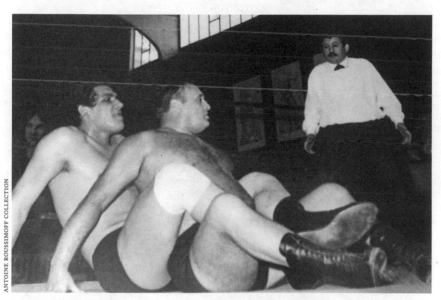

ANDRÉ USING THE SWEET SCIENCE ON FUTURE MENTOR FRANK VALOIS.

ABOVE: EVEN BEFORE SMARTPHONES, EVERYONE WANTED TO TAKE A PICTURE OF ANDRÉ.

LEFT: ANDRÉ WAS ALWAYS POPULAR WITH THE LADIES, EVEN AT THE BEACH!

HIS VERY FIRST MOVIE: *CASSE-TÊTE CHINOIS POUR LE JUDOKA.*

It was also mentioned that André could be the one to replace strongman Charles Rigoulot, who had passed away in 1962.

In some of the earliest known recorded footage of André in a wrestling ring, he is seen training with smaller wrestlers, notably the Prince. Like any other wrestler, he had to learn how to bump and all the basics of pro wrestling. Although he was tall, he wasn't big and Lageat made sure to let André know. "Jean said he was 140 kilograms," remembered Wehrle. "'My little boy,' said Lageat, 'you're not really heavy.' The next day, Jean arrived at the venue with some chocolate bars. He was eating so many of them."

André trained for most of 1965, and life wasn't easy. Money was always an issue since he was not making a dime while he was learning the ropes. He told his brother Jacques that sometimes he slept in a metro station, having nowhere else to go. He ended up doing a couple of different jobs, including helping with warehouse and industrial moves in Paris, hauling machinery throughout the city. As the fairy tale goes, he was already living in Paris doing that when Lageat saw him for the first time, which is not accurate. He had moved to Paris to become a wrestler. Another job he worked, because of his size, was as a doorman for bars and clubs. This job eventually led to another . . .

The training facilities, as well as the Élysée-Montmartre, were in a neighborhood called Pigalle. It's Paris's version of a red-light district, where many bars, clubs, cabarets, and adult shows are located. The world-famous Moulin Rouge is the area's main attraction to this day. This was where prostitutes were hanging out, and André befriended some of them.

"Frank Valois told me what he was doing over there," recalled former wrestler and promoter Paul Vachon. "The story is that since the wrestling building was in Pigalle, he hung around that district. Prostitution was out in the open, and the prostitutes would use him for protection, paying him to be their bodyguard. That's really the story about it."

André trained and finally made his debut in January 1966. Another legend about him was that he was hanging out with some wrestlers, and one day, one of them got injured and they asked André, who supposedly had never wrestled before, to replace him and that's how his career got started. Whether or not he replaced an injured wrestler for his first match is unknown, but the rest of that legend is certainly untrue.

Contrary to what has been often reported, he didn't start using the name Jean Ferré in Montreal. It was the name he used from the get-go in France. In fact, he never used any other name while in France other than Jean or Géant (Giant) Ferré. The names "Monster Eiffel Tower" or "Monsieur Eiffel Tower" were nothing more than nicknames used by New Zealand historian and journalist Dave Cameron in one of André's first big features in a wrestling magazine. But he never officially used either name as a wrestler or even in promoting a match. The name Jean Ferré was given to him in honor of a French folk hero. In 1359, during the Hundred Years' War between England and France, a peasant from Rivecourt by the name of Georges Ijlopon, but known as le Grand Ferré, defended a castle that the English were trying to seize. According to the story, Ferré, a lumberjack known for being a strongman, killed 85 of his adversaries with only an ax. That feat was taught in schools in France and sometimes in Quebec until the 1960s. His backstory had nothing to do with the legend of Paul Bunyan, which many Americans tried to stick to André's legend. Nevertheless, in his first televised interview, André Roussimoff became the lumberjack, Jean Ferré.

André made his official debut on January 25, 1966, in Rouen, 85 miles northwest of Paris. He opened the show, defeating Ted Lamar, a five-foot-nine, 200-pound veteran, a solid worker whose real name was Albert Lafeuille and who had started wrestling in the 1950s. Two days later, in Amiens, 100 miles north of Paris, he beat Yves Amor, real name René Rousselin, another veteran who had started in the late '50s and was well known for his beard. For the very first time, André was pitted against another big man, as Amor was about six foot five and 240 pounds.

A wrestling promoter can't have a giant in his stable without trying to make him a star. In short order, André was publicized and shown on television. On Friday, February 11, 1966, matches were televised from the Léo-Lagrange Hall in Stains, just outside of Paris. A deal was made between Lageat, Siry, and matchmaker Maurice Durand for André to be on that show. That is the earliest existing known footage of André. He wore a dark robe with "Jean Ferré France" written on the back. He was announced at two meters 15 (close to seven foot one) and 150 kilos (330 pounds). The most interesting note from that footage is that he was already entering the ring by stepping over the top rope, a move he brought with him to North America.

The very next day, André was showcased in his first televised interview to publicize his debut in Paris on the 13th at Palais de la Mutualité. Playing up the Grand Ferré reference, the clip started with André chopping wood in the forest, wearing a lumberjack shirt. He doesn't seem to show major signs of acromegaly yet. That said, he looks to be already bending a little from the shoulders and the neck. He isn't standing upright, like when you want to show how tall a person is. An interviewer comes in and asks André how old he is and how tall, certainly not the first and definitely not the last time he would get that question. He answers that he is 19 and that he measures two meters 10, which is six foot nine. Not even a month in and there were discrepancies regarding his height, as he was announced as seven foot one the day before.

Another interesting thing from that interview is André saying that he doesn't drink wine. "Oh no. Never. Only milk!" he told the viewers. André was very lean at the time — a tall lean lumberjack who only drank milk was a more suitable image for an athlete. Although he had started to drink alcohol before he was even 18, he was nowhere close to a heavy drinker. Then, in an attempt at a cheesy segue between the woods and pro wrestling, André is asked if he was focusing his life on being a lumberjack, to which he responded that it wasn't the case anymore, he was now trying to get into pro wrestling. Of course, no one knew at the time that André had been training for so long already and that he had never been a lumberjack. The footage then moves to the wrestling ring at the training facility where André was learning the ropes. There, he makes a point of weighing in at 308 pounds, having a 44-size neck and 16-size feet. In the ring, they have him work out with a trainee, believe it or not, doing leg scissors. So yes, in one of his earliest televised moments, André is in the ring, sitting on his butt, applying leg scissors to his opponent's waist! He then stands up for the interview and he keeps talking with his head down. Evidently, he wasn't produced at all! He wasn't told how to stand to look even taller or anything like it. His promo skills were below average, and one could already predict that he would not become Mad Dog Vachon on the mic. When he gets back to the wrestling part of the interview, he works with le Petit Prince, a smart move since André looks even more like a giant in comparison. Dubail, a former gymnast, tries to climb on André, but the latter just throws him off like a bag of potatoes to the other side of the ring. It is a great way of showing off André, much better than trying to make him look like a scientific wrestler. He then concludes the interview by saying he would make his debut the next day at la Mutualité. He did, and in impressive fashion. On February 13, 1966, he defeated Yves Amor in his very first match in Paris.

André wrestled sporadically throughout the rest of the year. In the fall of 1966, he wrestled a man called Spartacus, nicknamed the "young giant." In some places, André was hailed as the biggest attraction of the season. However, his most important match was on November 20, when he battled French-Canadian Frank Valois in Paris. The match itself was not significant; the importance came from the role Valois would play a few years later, when he took André under his wing and became his biggest advocate.

André wrestled more in the following year. Although he worked with some of the same faces he had in 1966, such as Spartacus, Valois, and Lamar, he also started wrestling against the likes of Gaby Calderon, André Bollet, and Jack de Lassartesse. These three were among the top 10 wrestlers in France at the time. Bollet was a well-known veteran who made a killing teaming with Roger Delaporte, and Lassartesse was perhaps the best heel of his era in France. Born January 21, 1928, in Bern, Switzerland, Lassartesse, whose real name was Édouard Probst, was six foot four and 250 pounds and had started wrestling in 1953. Known as the "Ring Aristocrat," he portrayed an arrogant but good-looking heel, with bleached blond hair, who considered himself above everybody else. Because he could speak German, English, and French, when he went to the United States to work for Vince McMahon in the late 1950s, he became Ludwig Von Krupp, a German, since heel Germans were still getting heat post–World War II. He also wrestled under the name René Lassartesse. The Lassartesse name was well known in France going back· to the early Greco-Roman tournaments at the beginning of the century, which featured Gabriel Lassartesse. Jack de Lassartesse became one of André's biggest rivals in Europe, and upon returning to Europe from North America in 1959, he bought a small plane to travel to shows and André flew with him from time to time.

"Lassartesse told a story about once doing a show where the ring was set up on a platform in a lake," wrote Dave Meltzer. "Wrestlers would get rowed to the ring for their matches, and the gimmick was to get easy pops by throwing opponents into the lake. Lassartesse said that Ferré told him that he didn't know how to swim, so not to throw him in the lake. So, of course, he did. Ferré freaked out in the water, as he really didn't know how to swim. Security had to save him." (In fact, no one in André's family knew how to swim.) Lassartesse wrestled full-time until 1986. He trained many wrestlers, including NXT trainer Robbie Brookside, and died on December 12, 2018, at the age of 90.

As a giant of a man in the wrestling world, André was getting more and more attention. Furthermore, Lassartesse advised him on the subject. "He was everybody's darling in France and anyone could touch him," said Lassartesse, who believed it could hurt André's aura. "I often told him it was not good. When he came back from Canada, he was completely different and did not settle for the people anymore." It wasn't uncommon for a French wrestler to be used in a movie; Lino Ventura, Charles Rigoulot, Robert Duranton, and Roger Delaporte all had appeared in at least one film. It was no surprise when André made his debut as an actor in 1967. Author Ernie Clerk had published a series of 20 spy novels about a judoka between 1961 and 1971; one of them, *Casse-tête chinois: le judoka dans l'enfer* (*Chinese Puzzle: The Judoka in Hell*) published in 1965, became a movie called *Casse-tête chinois pour le judoka* (*Chinese Puzzle for the Judoka*), a sequel to *Le Judoka agent secret* (*Secret Agent Judoka*). Directed by Maurice Labro, the film featured André in a very limited role; he fought the movie's hero. The 104-minute movie was first released in West Germany on December 22, 1967, then in France on February 9, 1968, and finally in Italy on June 23, 1968.

"It was usually not very difficult for me, I just played my own role," André confided to the *Journal de Montréal* about the experience. Funnily enough, his mother never saw the movie, because André's character dies in it.

Three weeks before the release of the movie in France, fans saw André wrestle in his biggest match to date. Broadcast on January 20, 1968, from la Mutualité, André squared off against French heavyweight champion Franz Van Buyten. The 29-year-old Belgian wrestler, whose real name is Francis Van Buyten, had started wrestling in the 1960s. He was known for his pencil mustache and also wrestled as Ivan Buyten. His son Daniel became one of the best Belgian football players of the 2000s, playing in two World Cups.

"When I was in France, André called me Pompidou, after the French president at the time," recalled Gerard Ethifier, a French-speaking wrestler from Martinique, who also wrestled under the names Gerry Morrow and Jiro Inazuma. "He and his buddy Ivan Buyten would come to the dorm where the Japanese guys stayed and yell 'Pompidou'! And we would go drinking. He looked after me, and it prompted me in Japan to always change with the foreign guys, pick up some English, that kind of thing."

André's match was a real extravaganza. He arrived with the French flag, Van Buyten with the flag of his native Belgium. Even the national anthems from both countries were played. Before the match, many great French wrestlers were presented to the crowd, such as André Drapp, Gilbert Leduc, and Jack de Lassartesse, who, playing his gimmick, touched with disdain the material of the giant's trapper jacket and refused to shake his hand. Also presented to both the live and the

TV crowd was Maria Minh, who played with André in *Casse-tête chinois pour le judoka*. André was announced at 140 kilos, which is 308 pounds, 92 more than his opponent. Besides using a bear hug and a body slam, he worked a completely different kind of match than North American fans would see him in just a few years later, but it was a typical match for him at this stage of his career. He worked a lot on the mat, doing some technical wrestling; he took a hip toss, head scissors, and he exchanged some European forearms. One thing never changed though. After a few high spots, André had blown up. On commentary, the announcer was selling André's hands as if they were big frying pans. After three back breakers and a body slam, André won his most important match up to that point — and became champion. As funny as it sounds, the belt didn't fit around his waist. Still, it was undeniable: France had a new wrestling hero.

André was different then not only in his move set but also in his look. It might be hard to believe for those who only saw him in the 1970s and 1980s, but in 1968 André was muscular: biceps, pecs, and big muscular legs. His wrestling was much more scientific, mixed with some brawling, head butts, and full nelsons. He sold when on the mat and was quite fast getting back to his feet. Even if his cardio was not the best, he was actually doing 15- to 20-minute matches. On television, he was presented as a lumberjack who had never lost; that part, at the time, was true.

Winning the heavyweight title and acting in a movie meant André was on his way to becoming a household name in 1968. After just a few years in the business, he was intriguing more and more promoters.

And the best was yet to come.

CHAPTER 3

THE INVASION OF ENGLAND

André was wrestling throughout France, from the north to the south. When he started making some money, he replaced his Renault 4CV with something a little better, an Opel Admiral. "He was a good driver," said his brother Jacques. "The wrestlers used to carpool when they were on the road. Often, he was the one driving. He liked to drive. He liked traveling." On one occasion, after a match, he was in a terrible accident. "It was late at night, something like two a.m.," remembered Jacques. "He was coming back from giving a lift to some other wrestlers. A guy on a moped ran a red light and André hit him. The guy died. Thankfully, André had not been drinking." This tragedy left a mark on André. "I'm the one who picked him up after. He was in shock," continued Jacques. "I told him he should get back behind the wheel as soon as possible if he didn't want to remain traumatized. Police investigation cleared André on any wrong doing."

Although he had been driving throughout France, André had never wrestled outside its borders.

The principality of Monaco — famous in North America thanks to Grace Kelly marrying Prince Rainier of Monaco — is a constitutional monarchy located in the southeast part of France, between the city of Nice and the frontier of Italy, on the shore of the Mediterranean Sea. France took control of it in 1860, but in 1918, after World War I, its authority was limited. This meant that Monaco kept its independence; however, it had to exercise its sovereign rights in perfect conformity with the political, military, naval, and economic interests of France. It only made sense for André to wrestle there for his first match "outside" of France, especially since Monaco's primary language is French. On August 18, 1967, he made his debut at the Rainier III Nautical Stadium against André Bollet. It was a one-and-done foray; André kept wrestling in France for the rest of 1967 and 1968.

That latter year wasn't special for him only because of the movie release and the championship opportunity. It was also the year when English-speaking fans would become aware of him. *The Ring Wrestling* was one of few wrestling magazines back in 1968. Stanley Weston ran the *Wrestling Revue* and had just started *Inside Wrestling*. Norman Kietzer had the *Wrestling News*. And then there was *The Ring Wrestling*, which was first published in 1963 by Nat Fleischer. *The Ring* was different from the other magazines in that it covered much more women's wrestling and the European scene than did its competition. Covering the European wrestling scene was a journalist by the name of Michel Bézy. The Frenchman was involved in wrestling for 31 years, mainly as a journalist. He had his own wrestling magazine in France, and he was the main contact for magazines on the other side of the Atlantic. It only made sense that he was the first one to write about André, and *The Ring Wrestling* was certainly the obvious choice. "The current sensation in male wrestling is a former woodcutter, Jean Ferré, a young giant, powerful, weighing around 280," wrote Bézy in a compliment-filled piece in the February 1968 issue. "Right now he needs more coaching. He is getting it. Within a year this young man, now 19, from the woods around la Ferté-sous-Jouarre, will dominate the European grappling situation."

To spike even more interest in him, Bézy ranked him at number three in his France monthly ranking, behind André Bollet but ahead of

French mat legends such as l'Ange Blanc, Robert Duranton, and Jack de Lassartesse. Ranked under the name of "Giant Ferré," it was the first time that an American wrestling magazine featured André. Moreover, Bézy was right. Well within that year, André took over the wrestling scene.

With more and more exposure from both wrestling and movie people, André's prominence grew, and he was soon noticed outside of France. The nearest and most important wrestling scene at the time was in the United Kingdom. Like pretty much everywhere else in Europe, in the U.K. in the late 1800s, Greco-Roman wrestling reigned, with Tom Cannon being the top British star. However, the outbreak of World War I put a stop to that, and wrestling didn't make a comeback in the U.K. until the 1930s. By the time it did, it was more about catch-as-catch-can wrestling; with an already established amateur style called Lancashire catch-as-catch-can, it made for something unique. It's that style that influenced wrestler Billy Joyce in the 1930s. Twenty years later, he opened a gym called the Snake Pit, where he trained future catch legends such as Karl Gotch, Bert Assirati, and Billy Robinson.

After pro wrestling was banned in the late 1930s because of World War II, it came back in the second half of the 1940s, this time with a new set of rules, known as the Mountevans rules. Matches consisted of rounds, as in boxing, and a disqualification was an automatic win in a best-of-three-falls match. A few years later, in 1952, a cartel of wrestling promoters founded Joint Promotions to rule the territory, similar to what the National Wrestling Alliance had done four years earlier in North America. They were the keepers of the Mountevans rules.

"Joint was comprised of various promoters, including Dale-Martin Promotions, Best-Wryton, George de Relwyskow (pronounced Rellwisco) and his partner Arthur Green, and a promotion run by the Crabtree family," said Scotland's wrestling historian Bradley Craig. Around the same time, in 1955, wrestling started airing on television on ITV, but only became a weekly show in 1960. Five years later, in 1965, wrestling was broadcast on *World of Sport*, similar to ABC's *Wide World of Sports* in the U.S., every Saturday afternoon. "Due to popularity, pro wrestling was heavily featured as a weekly segment in a prime 3:45/4 p.m. to 5 p.m. slot before the football results," added Craig.

André made his debut in the U.K. working in Paisley, Scotland, on May 22, 1969, against Wild Angus, using the same moniker he had in France, Jean Ferré. Angus, whose real name was Frank Hoy, was a six-foot-three, 250-pound wrestler from Northern Ireland but billed from Scotland; his look was similar to the one Bruiser Brody later sported. Working as a blue-eye (a babyface, or good guy, in U.K. wrestling lingo), André was victorious in his first encounter. The next day, he headed to St. Albans, England, some 400 miles south of Paisley. There, he wrestled against Jim Hussey, a great worker who was only five foot six but wide, said to be a good opponent for André. (Hussey's son, Mark, who had just turned 18, had already wrestled for two years by then. Wrestling as Mark "Rollerball" Rocco, he ended up working as Black Tiger in Japan a decade later.) The match between André and Jim Hussey was taped for television, the only time an André match aired in the U.K. in 1969. The next day on TV, the fans saw André win by KO, meaning a match won outright when the opponent was knocked out (wrestling rules were still flirting with boxing rules). At the time, between six and eight million fans were watching wrestling on Saturday afternoons.

Throughout his time in England, André stayed with the St. Clairs, a wrestling family through and through. Francis Gregory had wrestled from the 1930s to the 1960s under the name of Francis St. Clair Gregory, on top of being a Cornish wrestler and a rugby player. On Wednesday, November 9, 1955, he participated in the very first televised wrestling match on ITV. Wrestling was broadcast on the BBC in the late 1930s, but only around 30,000 homes had TV at the time. By 1955, most households had TV, mainly thanks to the televised coronation of Queen Elizabeth II two years earlier. ITV was just a few months old when wrestling started on the station. Francis's two sons, Roy and Tony, also wrestled.

"My brother brought [André] to our house because he had met him in France the year before," remembered Tony St. Clair. "He had already been booked in England by a promoter who saw him in a small town, before meeting my brother, and [André] told him he was going to England for two or three months. My brother invited him to our house. My parents had a pub in Manchester. It was the beginning of a lifelong friendship."

Tony had just started wrestling in 1967, so the two of them found a likeness in each other. "He was good, he was fit, flexible, and he was very light for his size," Tony added. "There was no fat on him at all. We got along great because I was just starting as well, so we were at the same level." André wrestled there until the end of July, facing a who's who list of British wrestlers. He impressed a lot of people, including Tony himself. "Of course, I saw potential in him," he said. "Anybody with that size who could move like him had potential."

Less than a week in, on May 28, André got to wrestle in one of England's most legendary venues, the Royal Albert Hall. In 1969, the territory was dominated by middleweight wrestlers such as "Mr. TV" Jackie Pallo; Mick McManus, a Hall of Famer and the most famous wrestler in U.K. history; Les Kellett; and George Kidd.

Although heavyweight wrestlers were usually billed on top, Billy Robinson, who had won the British Heavyweight title in 1967, was spending more time outside of the U.K. than at home. In 1968, the champion was on TV only once. Still, it was better than 1969, when he didn't appear at all on national TV. Rightfully, the title was stripped from Robinson the following year.

So when André was wrestling in the U.K., the great work from the middleweight division dominated the territory. In both 1967 and 1968, the biggest ratings on ITV were the middleweights over the heavyweights, thanks to their dynamic style and showmanship.

Regardless, André wrestled against the top heavyweights who were in the U.K. Former heavyweight champions like "Rocky" Albert Wall, Gwyn Davies (who was six foot five), and the Giant Scot, Ian Campbell. He also wrestled other top heavyweights the nation had to offer, such as Steve Veidor, John Cox, and Hans Streiger. Cox's memories of wrestling André are not fond. "He was a huge guy, and you couldn't really do much with him," he said in the book *Have a Good Week . . . Till Next Week.*

"You tried to do something with him, almost like being on with [Giant] Haystacks, you've got to try and do something, knowing full well that you're not going to succeed."

For the Royal Albert Hall show, he was pitted against another heavyweight, local "Big" Bruno Elrington, billed as six foot five and 20 stone (280 pounds). As in France, André was billed as six foot 10, sometimes during his time in the U.K. as six foot 11. The Frenchman defeated Big Bruno. "André being in a heavyweight match in the undercard was great exposure for him," said Craig. "But on that first tour, he also got the opportunity to polish his skills against some of the finest technical wrestlers that the U.K. had to offer."

It's also in England that André suffered his first loss in a singles match. After victories in cities like Bristol, Norwich, and London, his streak ended in Hanley, England. On June 7, 1969, at the Victoria Hall, he was pitted against one of the biggest household names in U.K. wrestling history, Kendo Nagasaki.

Born Brian Stevens on October 19, 1941, in England, Stevens was adopted and his family changed his name to Peter Thornley. Thornley, who started wrestling at the age of 23 in November 1964, became Nagasaki in and out the ring. Known for years to protect his character like no one else, Thornley published his autobiography in 2018, and when he talked about his wrestling character, he used the third person, as if Kendo Nagasaki was another person. The Nagasaki gimmick was that of a masked Japanese samurai warrior. Considered edgy and dangerous, he did not appear on TV before 1971, since promoters were hesitant because of his violent ring nature. Nevertheless, he was a local star and enjoyed an undefeated streak of his own.

According to Thornley, André pulled him aside before their match and said, "Look, I've come here to learn how to wrestle, I don't know a lot about it — if I'm clumsy, forgive me, and please don't hurt me!" Throughout his life, André always tried to stay away from confrontation.

So on that date, the six-foot-one 250-pounder Nagasaki defeated André, by technical knockout, the giant's first loss ever in a one-on-one match. "I now knew that making a fool of an inexperienced wrestler made for a bad show — he had to look like he might be able to beat Kendo, and physically Jean Ferré certainly did, so I did my best to work with him," wrote Thornley in his book. The pair wrestled two more times before the end of 1969, and on both occasions, André lost. He was defeated in the rematch clean and in the third bout by disqualification.

Looking back, it shouldn't surprise anyone. "Hanley was Kendo's hometown," said Tony St. Clair. "Kendo had a lot of power in the office. He very rarely lost. Since it was his hometown, it would make sense he asked to be over. And it doesn't surprise me that André never won a match against him. Kendo was more interested in his career than the business." Tony himself wrestled André a few times, thanks to one of his mentors, Max Crabtree. The Crabtrees were another well-known wrestling family in the U.K. The patriarch, Shirley Crabtree, was a former wrestler and his two sons were also involved with pro wrestling. Shirley Jr., billed as six foot six and 375 pounds, became one of U.K.'s biggest stars under the name of Big Daddy, but by 1969 he had wound down his schedule, so he didn't wrestle André, in what would have been a true battle of the giants. Shirley's other son, Max, also wrestled but was mainly working as a promoter in Scotland. At six foot one and 180 pounds, Tony could make André look good. André got along very well with the St. Clair family. He was drinking more than he had been the previous year, but not as much as he later would. "The first day he came down to the pub, my mother was amazed. She hadn't seen anybody like him before," Tony remembered, laughing. "Using broken English, I asked him if he wanted breakfast.

"Yes.

"Coffee?

"No.

"Tea

"No.

"Beer?

"Yes. Light beer. Blond.

WRESTLING WITH TONY ST. CLAIR, WHILE TOURING THE U.K.

ARTHUR GREEN WAS ONE OF THE PROMOTERS WHO BROUGHT ANDRÉ TO THE U.K.

ANDRÉ WRESTLED UNDER HIS REAL NAME REPRESENTING BULGARIA IN SOUTH AFRICA.

"He had eight pints of beer and eight sandwiches with bacon for his first breakfast. My mother couldn't believe it!"

That said, he was drinking and eating in moderation compared to what Tony later saw. At the end of July, André went back to France for a month before coming back in mid-September. At that time, European wrestlers could only wrestle 40 times in England before going elsewhere. Not necessarily 40 days, but 40 times. This was to protect English wrestlers from an influx of European wrestlers. He stayed through October, left again, and then came back one last time in December 1969. In between tours, he started performing in other European countries like West Germany, Austria, Belgium, Spain, and Luxembourg, where he quickly became the number one attraction. On every tour, he stayed with the St. Clairs. When he was booked at the same time as Tony, the two would drive together. If alone, André would travel by train. A young, tall, and somewhat lean guy like André would undoubtedly be getting his way with the ladies, but according to Tony, it was not the case. "He was an attraction for the ladies but always went home with me," said Tony, who called André either Jean or John. "He was stuck to my back with glue. We would never separate. So I don't think he dated any women, because he went home with me every night."

Perhaps because of the language barrier, André was still a shy man, and not only with women. Nevertheless, he was not the man he would become when he moved to America. At this time, André was quite laid-back and didn't play pranks. He didn't drink before shows. He was a happy-go-lucky type of guy, and great to be around. There were various charity shows in England then, as well as football and cricket games between wrestlers and celebrities, and although André did not himself play, he would always go with Tony. That's one thing that never changed: he liked to be around the boys.

As in France, André traveled the country from south to north, east to west, something not every outsider was doing; they usually only wrestled in the south of England. Wrestling six times a week leads to loads of road stories. There's one Tony will always remember.

"One day, André and I were driving to a show about 50 miles from Manchester. I had a rather small car and about 20 miles out of Southport, the town we were to work in, I had a breakdown, a loss of oil. So I called the breakdown service, and they sent a truck to pick up the car. The truck only had limited seats, one for the driver and one passenger, so André sat in the car as it got loaded onto the truck. We were then driven to the show, passing astounded fans on the way. It made good conversation for the wrestlers for weeks."

According to Tony, André's English was non-existent at first, but it got to the point where it was passable. The St. Clairs helped him with that. He could formulate a sentence and order food, but that was about it. Several U.K. wrestlers were also touring in France and knew some French, enough to help André when needed. A funny story happened in Montrose, Scotland, which actually made the front page of the local newspaper. André had defeated Tony Orford, over whom he had a significant weight advantage. After his match, he wanted to explain to the crowd that it should have been a no-contest because he thought the weight advantage was unfair. Since he didn't know how to explain that to the crowd, he asked a lady who spoke both languages to translate for him. As a true blue-eye, it got him a run of applause. He was so beloved in Montrose that they declared him the town's Holiday Giant!

"Between matches, André immersed himself in the nation's culture, showing a clear interest in local customs and history," said Craig. "He visited the fishing villages and also the Snake Pit and Billy Robinson's gym."

Surprisingly though, André was not the drawing card one would think. He was never brought back to television after his first match in England; his loss to Nagasaki happened before it should have and hurt his push. "You know, he started to job more on the second tour, as his aura of invincibility was shattered to the British crowds after he lost to Kendo Nagasaki in a match that was highly publicized by the U.K. wrestling magazines like *Ringsport* and *The Wrestler*," stated Craig. "I do know that on some of the cards he slipped down the bill."

"I don't think he was a drawing card because the business in most towns was either every second week or monthly, and the business didn't change in numbers much from one show to the next," said Tony St. Clair, adding that André did work a lot of main events.

Aside from the losses to Nagasaki, his record shows losses by disqualification in 1969 to Mr. Universe John Lees in July; to British, European, and World Mid-Heavyweight champion Mike Marino in September; and the same month to Roy St. Clair, although that might have been a favor to the family. From the eight matches he had on his last tour in December, he was good for two draws, five losses by disqualification, and one clean loss, the latter against Andy Robin, who was a huge regional star in Scotland (his later main claim to fame was as the owner of a wrestling bear). To say Joint Promotions had given up on André is an understatement. It's not like André was making that much money either compared to what was coming. According to St. Clair, who himself earned eight pounds a show at the time, André was making around 25 to 30 pounds a show, plus his travel and hotel costs. Based on six shows a week, 52 weeks a year, it was a few thousand pounds more than the average salary in the U.K. at the time, or a little less than $19,000 U.S.

Before going back to England for his last tour, André wrestled in East London, South Africa, and his presence made the news all over the world — but not because of his wrestling. According to the Associated Press report from December 3, 1969, "When a seven-foot-tall Bulgarian wrestler André Roussimoff visited South Africa, the Grand Hotel found it had no beds large enough for him. So hotel owner Peter Morris called another hotel and borrowed a special bed that was built for ex-president C.R. Swart, who is six-foot-seven." Situations like that became frequent for André. "My greatest problems as a giant are clothes, I suppose. I can't pick them up in a bargain basement," said André, who ended up wearing no less than size five or six XL shirts. "Everything has to be tailored to my measure. And beds, on the road. One bed isn't enough. I have to stick two beds together. Otherwise, my legs dangle."

Speaking of Africa, the Giant toured there a few times during that period. Professional wrestling on the African continent mostly occurred either completely to the north, in countries like Morocco, Tunisia and Algeria, the three African countries closest to France and all places where André worked before coming to America, or completely to the south, in cities such as East London, Port Elizabeth, Cape Town, and Johannesburg in South Africa. Former amateur wrestler Johan Daniël Hefer had been the promoter in South Africa since 1947 and was known for bringing several European wrestlers there. André was not advertised as a Frenchman in South Africa, nor even known as Jean Ferré, but as a Bulgarian named André Roussimoff. Although wrestling was popular in South Africa in the late 1960s thanks to the popularity of local star Jan Wilkens, André had not enjoyed his time. "I wouldn't go back there, not even for a million," he told the *Journal de Montréal*, referring to all the violence due to apartheid. "I've seen some disturbing things. There were mornings when I got up and wondered if what I had seen the night before was real." As for Wilkens — a strong six-foot-five, 280-pound man — it is said that he and André really came to blows at some point and that Wilkens did not have the better of it. However, since the wrestling archives from South Africa are almost non-existent, André's adventures, both in and out the arena, are hard to verify.

Unfortunately, December 1969 was the last time Tony St. Clair and André saw each other before the 1980s, when St. Clair got booked for New Japan Pro Wrestling. However, that was, and still is, the nature of the business. One can be very close to someone else for a year, and then not see them for 10 years. Time would show that André never forgot where he came from and the friends he made in pro wrestling. He wrestled his last match in England on December 17, teaming again with frequent partner that month Gargantua (Jim Moran, six foot six) in a duo dubbed the Goliaths, and lost against Davies and Wall. He did not return to England for close to 20 years. That said, though the United Kingdom didn't want André anymore, another country did. André's life was about to change.

CHAPTER 4

FROM A GIANT TO A MONSTER!

By the late 1960s, André was established in France, had won a major title, and had wrestled outside the country. Before leaving for England, however, André had wrestled in what was one of the most important matches of his early career. And he wasn't even supposed to be in it. Four days before making his debut in the U.K., on May 18, 1969, André teamed with Ivan Strogoff in Paris against two Japanese wrestlers, Toyonobori and Strong Kobayashi. Traveling with the two wrestlers was Isao Yoshihara, president of the International Wrestling Enterprise (IWE).

At the time, the IWE was the second-biggest wrestling organization in Japan, behind Japan Pro Wrestling, better known by fans as the Japanese Wrestling Alliance (JWA). Rikidozan had started JWA back in February 1954 but was stabbed in a yakuza revenge plot in a nightclub on December 8, 1963; he died seven days later from his wounds. Michiharu Sadano (who wrestled as Toyonobori) was considered by many to be the second-biggest star in Japan behind Rikidozan; he became the group's new president. However, JWA was never the same, and less than three years later, on January 5, 1966, JWA announced Toyonobori's resignation.

Newspapers reported that Toyonobori had embezzled 20 million yen (around $55,500 U.S.) from JWA. Junzo Hasegawa became the company's next, and last, president.

Following his departure, Toyonobori went to Hawaii and convinced Kanji "Antonio" Inoki, who would become a legendary opponent for André, to join him in a new venture back in Japan. He promised him he'd become his biggest star. Inoki had been wrestling in the U.S. for quite a while; it was standard at the time, and still is, for a Japanese wrestler to be trained and start his career in Japan and then to gain experience in the U.S. before returning to Japan as a bigger star. On April 23, 1966, Toyonobori and Inoki announced the creation of Tokyo Pro-Wrestling and they held their first show on October 12, 1966, with Inoki defeating Johnny Valentine by count-out. It was in this promotion that Inoki first became a major star. However, JWA stood in the way, and they really played hardball. Attendance was poor and the new group often had to cancel shows.

In the meantime, another promotion was getting started. Isao Yoshihara was a former judo champion who had started wrestling in 1955. Since he was a light heavyweight, he was mostly used as a preliminary guy on big shows, wrestling in one of the first couple of matches. He made it to the final of the tournament to crown the first light heavyweight champion in Tokyo on October 23, 1956, and then ended up winning the title on October 19, 1960. As champion, he had a series of matches against Inoki, winning most of them. After losing the belt, he was mainly used as a mid-card guy to put over the next generation of superstars like Kintaro Ohki, Shohei Baba, and Inoki. Yoshihara stopped wrestling at the end of 1964 and became an office employee for JWA. Because he was having constant problems with the treasurer of the company, Kokichi Endo, he quit his position as chairman of the JWA business department on October 6, 1966. On October 24, at the Haneda airport in Tokyo, Yoshihara and wrestler Hiro Matsuda, one of his closest friends, announced the creation of the International Wrestling Enterprise, better known in Japan as the Kokusai promotion. Matsuda had started with JWA in 1957 but had a falling out with Rikidozan and had left Japan to wrestle in America in April 1960. In 1966, he wrestled in Japan for the first time in almost six years. Yoshihara used to be like an older brother to him and was the individual behind his return; Matsuda became his business partner in this new promotion.

IWE's first card, on January 5, 1967, was a combined show with Tokyo Pro, and it represented the first real threat to JWA. However, this association didn't last long. By the end of 1966, Toyonobori and Inoki had split and Inoki decided to work with Yoshihara and Matsuda instead. But in April 1967, JWA lured Inoki back, and Tokyo Pro folded soon after. Most of its wrestlers joined the IWE, including Toyonobori who had not worked with IWE when Inoki was with the company.

JWA's answer to this threat was massive. In early August, JWA officially became a member of the National Wrestling Alliance, and on August 14, it ran a huge show at the Osaka Baseball Stadium, with Baba and NWA world champion Gene Kiniski wrestling a 65-minute draw in front of 25,720 fans, a crowd 10 times the size of what the IWE drew in the same city that same night. IWE couldn't compete with the NWA or with Inoki and Baba, the two biggest stars in the country, teaming together, and it ultimately folded as JWA easily won its first war.

Yoshihara was put aside by a new investor, Hiroshi Iwata, who, with the backing of the Tokyo Broadcasting System (TBS) for a TV deal, announced the reopening of the promotion, this time with Great Togo as the head booker. Togo had been the head booker for JWA until Rikidozan died and the new partners fired him. According to Japanese historian Haruo Yamaguchi, "this hurt Hiro Matsuda's pride so badly that he split off from the company he founded."

This lasted until Togo told six Americans not to show up to a show in February 1968 because they were not going to be adequately paid by the office. In fact, Togo had been exposed by Yoshihara for taking a bigger cut than he should have when booking outside talent and he was let go over this. After that debacle, Yoshihara was back in charge. Yoshihara decided to concentrate his efforts on some local young guys like Tsuneharu "Thunder" Sugiyama, Kiyomasa "Great" Kusatsu, Masao

"Rusher" Kimura, Shozo "Strong" Kobayashi, and Sueo "Mighty" Inoue, alongside veteran Toyonobori. Without the backing of the NWA and because of the sour experience with some Americans, he went to another continent, Europe, to book gaijins (foreigners). Using promoter George de Relwyskow from the U.K. as booker, he started getting an influx of English wrestlers, naming his first two tours "Japan versus Europe series" and "Japanese & British champion series." It's during that second tour, in April and May 1968, that Billy Robinson made his debut in Japan. Throughout that year, guys like Wild Angus, Sky Hi Lee and George Gordienko (two Canadians wrestling in England), Lord Alfred Hayes, Kendo Nagasaki, and Jim Hussey traveled to Japan to work for the IWE. Since Yoshihara had good relations with European promotions, he created a partnership with French promoter Roger Delaporte and founded the International Wrestling Alliance (IWA), because international is bigger than national! In November 1968, the first IWA World Series was presented in Japan, and the following month, Robinson defeated Toyonobori to win this round-robin tournament. He was recognized as the IWA World Heavyweight champion. Yoshihara was clearly building the company around him.

Five months later, on May 18, 1969, in Paris, the IWA tag team titles were created at l'Élysée-Montmartre. "The IWA singles title was held in Japan, so the tag team championship match was held in Paris," explained historian and author Koji Miyamoto, regarding the relationship between the two promoters. That match ended up being important for the IWE, for many different reasons, but even more so for André. Toyonobori and Strong Kobayashi was the team selected by the IWE and Yoshihara himself decided to make the trip to Paris. "They were scheduled to wrestle Ivan Strogoff and Roger Delaporte that night," wrote Yoshihara in a special edition program on André in Japan. "But Roger was replaced by Jean Ferré at the last moment."

Approximately two years after his debut, André had left the stable of Lageat and Siry in order to start working for Delaporte. He always kept a good relationship with Lageat though, and went to see him at his bar every time he could. While it's not known why Delaporte left his spot to André, an educated guess would be that since he was the promoter, and over 40 years old, he preferred to give his role to a young gun. He knew that putting André in that match would elevate him and give him an opportunity to one day wrestle in Japan. Thus, André teamed with Strogoff, a Belgian wrestler, whose nickname was Egghead because he was bald. He had a good build at 315 pounds and had wrestled throughout Europe. The two Japanese wrestlers won the match and the titles, but the biggest winner was André. Although Yoshihara had already heard of André, it was the first time he'd seen him live and André made such an impression on him that it changed his career forever.

"I've known Ferré's name since March 1968, when I first contacted George de Relwyskow," Yoshihara recalled. "He said, 'There is a giant in Paris. I will send him for you maybe next year.' George sent all U.K. wrestlers first, so French wrestlers were sent to me later, in 1969. He sent me André Bollet and Robert Gastel first in February 1969. They were so-so. I was not so impressed. Then I went to Paris in May. *Wow!* Very impressed. He was taller than Giant Baba and could move faster than Baba." While in Paris, Yoshihara met with Umenosuke Sato, a Japanese wrestler who was working in Europe and living in Paris, better known by his wrestling name Kiyomigawa. He was one of the first wrestlers to join Rikidozan's promotion in 1954.

"Yoshihara met Kiyomigawa and then asked him to become booker for IWE," said Miyamoto. "Until that time, de Relwyskow did all the booking by himself. Yoshihara asked George whether it was okay for him to let Kiyomigawa do the task. George said it was okay. Starting from then, Kiyomigawa was booker for IWE when Yoshihara needed wrestlers from Europe." Frank Valois, André Saadeh, and Jean Saadeh (Lebanese wrestlers working in France since the country was under the control of France for 20 years) also joined Bollet and Gastel in Japan by the end of the year.

André was leaving for the United Kingdom, however, so Japan was not a priority. He finished his last shows in the U.K., spent the holidays at home, and, on January 3, 1970, made his debut in Japan for Yoshihara's IWE.

When André started wrestling for IWE, pro wrestling was very popular in Japan. The company had a television show every Wednesday night at 7 p.m. on TBS. There was a real war in Japan as JWA was on Nippon Television Network Corporation (NTV) and NET (today's TV Asahi). Two years earlier, during its debut, IWE had done a 26 rating with Lou Thesz defeating Great Kusatsu, while JWA drew a 48 rating the exact same night with Giant Baba beating The Crusher in what was one of the biggest nights in Japanese wrestling television history.

However, the money wasn't in ratings but in house shows. And to draw fans to a house show, you needed attractions, men and women who could make someone leave their home and put down their money. Aside from a few exceptions, an outsider is usually a heel in Japan. But to Yoshihara, Jean Ferré — the name André had used everywhere up to that point — wasn't heel enough. He needed to find a name that would fit this seven-foot, 390-pound giant. And he found one: Monster Roussimoff!

Roussimoff is self-explanatory. By definition, a "monster" is an animal of abnormal form, a threatening force, and large for its kind. In the context of pro wrestling, it fit André like a big glove. At the time, in Japan especially, Godzilla, the big monster taking over Japan, was a huge hit; there were already 10 movies made by 1970. Monster Roussimoff could be the big giant taking over puroresu (pro wrestling) in Japan, another box office attraction. IWE was celebrating its third anniversary in January 1970, and although there was a war between the promotion and JWA, it was still considered the number two promotion, mainly due to the fact the two biggest stars, Baba and Inoki, were still working for the company Rikidozan had created. But the year didn't start well for the promotion. One of their biggest stars, Toyonobori, announced his retirement at the young age of 38.

"Toyonobori's sloppy way of living caused him to retire prematurely," wrote Yamaguchi. "He even missed the farewell match IWE prepared for him." Billy Robinson was still the champion, but Toyonobori's retirement left an empty spot as he was tag team champion with Strong Kobayashi, the wrestler the promotion was building up.

EVEN THOUGH VERNE GAGNE MET ANDRÉ IN 1970, HE DIDN'T SEE HIS POTENTIAL THEN.

②ジャック・クレイボーン（東南アジア代表）178cm 108kg

　昨年の第3回ビッグ・サマー、ダイナマイト両シリーズにかけて活躍したおなじみの黒人正統派テクニシャン。41年11月にはエディ・モレアの名で来日しており、これが3回目の来日である。

　クレイボーンはここ4〜5年、東南アジアをホーム・リングとしているが、昨10月、日本を去ってからは久しぶりにフランス・マット界にカム・バックし、エリーゼ・モンマルトのメーン・イベンターとして、2月中旬まで、人気を一身に集めていた。しかし天性陽気な性格のクレイボーンは、冬のヨーロッパ・マット界はやはり肌に合わなかったとみえ、ふたたび東南アジアに帰り、"もっとも好きな国"日本にやってきたもの。

　黒豹のようなしなやかな体を生かした千変万化の変り身、バネの利いたドロップ・キック、天性の頭突き、恐怖のパイル・ドライバーと、見せるプロレスのだいご味を満喫させるスリリングなファイトを展開するクレイボーンは、まことに日本人の好みにズバリのレスラーである。

フランス代表
モンスター・ロシモフ
MONSTER ROUSSIMOFF

世界1の巨人レスラー
2m18cm

ALREADY A FEATURED ATTRACTION ON HIS FIRST JAPANESE TOUR.

Aside from André, the gaijins during his first tour were Quasimodo (Victor Castilla) from Spain, Michael Nador from Hungry, Bad Boy Shields (Bull Bullinski) from the U.S., and Enrique Edo from Spain. There's an interesting story regarding Edo. At the time, the story of Yoshihara going to Paris and seeing André wrestle wasn't the one told to the fans. The fans were told that Edo was the one who discovered André. In the tour's program, it said that Edo was told by lumberjacks that André was very strong, and he asked him to do pro wrestling. Edo was wrestling throughout Europe and André was billed as a lumberjack in France, but one could ask what one has to do with the other.

Koji Miyamoto came up with an explanation. "Enrique Edo's wife was George de Relwyskow's daughter," he explained. "To help put over Edo, they created a story in the program for the 'Challenge series' where Edo was the one who discovered André in the mountains, between Spain and France, where he was a lumberjack."

It's a made-up story using real details. The Pyrenees are a range of mountains that form a natural border between Spain and France. And, of course, de Relwyskow and Yoshihara were friends from the time they were working together, and the U.K. promoter probably asked for a favor to help his son-in-law. It was Edo's second tour in Japan. He was wrestling in France when André broke into the business and he was actually on the card in Paris when André wrestled for the IWA tag team titles the year before. Unfortunately, the André story was the only good thing for Edo: he lost his eight matches on that tour. He left IWE in mid-January and never wrestled in Japan again.

In that same program, André was billed as "2m18," eight centimeters taller than Sky Hi Lee. In fact, for most of his career Lee was billed as the tallest wrestler ever, either at six foot eight or nine. Born Robert Leedy in Toronto, Ontario, his name was a play on Sky Low Low, the famous midget wrestler from Quebec. The comparisons of Sky Hi Lee to André were normal in Japan since Sky Hi Lee had done two tours there, one in 1958 and one more recently in 1968. He also wrestled in England in the 1960s. In Japan especially, one didn't need to be that tall. Data shows that worldwide, the average man in his thirties in 1970 was 162.6 cm, which is five foot three. The average in France was five foot six, and five foot eight in the U.S. Leedy was one foot taller than that — so one can imagine how André quickly became the center of attention.

André's highlight on that first tour was winning the IWA tag team titles, which had been left vacant when Toyonobori retired, on January 18 with Michael Nador in front of 5,000 fans in Fukuoka. The team defeated Great Kusatsu and Thunder Sugiyama. They then lost the titles at the end of the tour, as was the norm at the time, to the same team on February 11. Aside from the tag team championship, the biggest feud André had was with Strong Kobayashi. Actually, the event program promoted André as the biggest attraction and questioned whether Kobayashi would be able to beat him. Out of the 20 matches they each had, they wrestled each other seven times, including three singles. André was not protected at all in that first tour. Not only did André never defeat Kobayashi, in his fifth match, he wrestled him one on one and lost the second fall by submission with a Boston crab, as all main events were two-out-of-three falls. In other matches, André got pinned by Kobayashi, as well as by Sugiyama and Kusatsu. And, of course, Kobayashi body slammed him. Clearly, Yoshihara was trying to get his guys over more than a first-time outsider. Nevertheless, André was on TV every week with a rating of 20, or with 10 million people watching, which was a much bigger audience than he had ever been exposed to in France.

"No one had seen someone bigger than Giant Baba at the time," recalled Miyamoto. "Baba was the tallest wrestler in the world for the fans in Japan, before Roussimoff came in. That's one of the reasons why the ratings for his first tour were better, and the crowds too."

At least André was victorious in his very first match, in Okayama, as he teamed with Quasimodo against two locals. He teamed six more times with him, in tag team or six-man matches, including his debut in Tokyo at the Metropolitan Gym on February 6 in front of 3,000 fans, in a losing effort. Quasimodo was a Spanish wrestler named Victor Castilla, who had wrestled in France, the U.K., and in the U.S. among other places. His Hunchback of Notre-Dame gimmick came with the outfit and a bell. What's interesting about Castilla teaming with André is that Quasimodo may have suffered from acromegaly. He had a huge cyst in the back of his bald head and a disproportioned body, especially his face and jaw.

Did André learn about his condition on this first trip to the land of the rising sun? It's a question people have been asking for a very long time, and there may finally be an answer.

CHAPTER 5

A GIANT DISORDER

cromegaly is not something you see every day. As of 2018, only 0.0005 percent of the population has the hormonal disorder, which most commonly develops between the age of 30 and 40. It was first diagnosed in 1886 by Frenchman Dr. Pierre Marie, who described the different symptoms for the first time. The name "acromegaly" comes from the Greek words for "extremities" (*acro*) and "great" (*megaly*) because one of the most common symptoms of this condition is an abnormal growth of the hands and feet. According to acromegaly.org, "untreated acromegaly results in marked bony and soft tissue changes including an altered facial appearance (frontal bossing, prognathism), enlargement of the hands and feet, sleep apnea, and carpal tunnel syndrome. More serious problems may include accelerated cardiovascular disease, hypertension, diabetes mellitus, and possibly an increased risk of colon cancer. If the tumor develops before bone growth is completed in adolescence, the result will be gigantism." Other symptoms include enlargement of the jaw, spreading teeth, enlarging tongue, arthritis, tiredness, fatigue, depression, impotence, heart enlargement, and headaches. Those familiar with André recognize most of these symptoms.

In fact, already in 1968, André sometimes wrestled with a bandage on his knee. Gigantism is the most obvious symptom of acromegaly but importantly is not the disorder itself. Since in André's case acromegaly started before puberty, he grew in height first. Later his bones became larger and thicker since they couldn't grow longer, and this was especially apparent in his extremities — his head, hands, and feet. The space between his teeth also gradually increased. Less-known symptoms experienced by André were excessive sweat, projecting eyebrows, and back problems. Because of when he developed acromegaly, André was, in a strange sense, able to take advantage of it, since being so tall at a young age provided him the opportunity to become a wrestler.

When did André become aware of his condition?

One thing is for sure: he didn't learn about his condition in the 1960s. The family believes that he was never diagnosed in France. Their family doctor never mentioned it. The rumor has always been that André was aware of acromegaly since his first trip to Japan. Even though he was still living in France at the time, André, like every Roussimoff, was very private about his personal life. Both Jacques and Antoine only learned years later that he had acromegaly.

The 2018 HBO documentary *André the Giant* suggested that he didn't know about the disorder before meeting Dr. Harris Yett in 1981 for a broken ankle, based on the interview Dr. Yett gave. According to Yett, an orthopedic surgeon at Beth Israel Hospital (now called the Beth Israel Deaconess Medical Center) in Boston, Massachusetts, he told André about it, and André told him he didn't know he had acromegaly. Then again, in that same interview, Dr. Yett doesn't recall André being surprised by the news, which is somewhat startling. Perhaps André, who by that time had spent a decade lying, or embellishing the truth, about so many things regarding his past, kayfabed the doctor. If he already knew about his condition but pretended not to, the lack of surprise makes sense. Or perhaps he decided to no-sell the news and that's why he didn't look surprised. People process serious medical news differently — from surprise to quiet resignation.

Contrary to Dr. Yett's understanding, there are those who attest that André knew about his condition well before. According to Paul Vachon, his promoter in Montreal in the early '70s, André knew when he arrived in North America. "I think he knew how bad acromegaly was, as he told me that he wouldn't live to be very old," remembered Vachon. "I remember having that discussion with him, during the Grand Prix days. I am thinking, by the way he lived his life, he knew at the time." André didn't drink as much when he was still living in Europe, and the consensus among his friends was that part of why he drank heavily later was because André knew he wouldn't live long; so, he lived life to its fullest. And he'd have to be aware of his condition to know he wouldn't live long.

"When he was coming to IWE, we always had nice beers together on the road," remembered Heigo "Animal" Hamaguchi, who was a prelim guy on André's first tour. "He liked our [IWE] president, Mr. Yoshihara. He invited him into our beer tables. I remember he was drinking an average of 10 bottles of beer. He was 24, 25 then. One time, Enrique Edo fainted after he drank five bottles, then André carried his body to the hotel room. Funny. He was such a nice guy. I never had bad experiences with him."

Then there is Paul Leduc, another friend of André from his time in Montreal. The former wrestler goes a little deeper into the situation. "I've seen the Giant become emotional with me. Sometimes, when he was drinking too much, and we were only the two of us, his mood would change, as if he was depressed or something, and then he would cry like a little boy," said Leduc, who befriended André between 1972 and 1975. "When he was in that mood, he would start to talk about his condition. André used to say that he knew he wasn't normal, he knew he would die at a young age, he saw the changes in his body, like one of his heels getting thicker. He had read about his condition, and it was like a relief for him to talk about it." Even if those brief moments didn't happen often, and the words "acromegaly" or "gigantism" were never used, it was enough for Paul to understand what André was talking about.

André had met Michelle Léon, who also came from France, while she was working in a Montreal restaurant called La Crêpe Bretonne. "He would complain to me about [how] the Windsor Hotel could not provide king beds to him," she recalled. "He would tell me, 'One day, Michelle, I will go unexpectedly.' But he would never further discuss his condition with me." André knew he wasn't a normal man, he knew his body was changing, he knew he was going to die young. It would be a massive coincidence if he didn't already know about his condition.

Finally, there is Jackie McAuley, who took care of André's ranch later in life, along with her late husband, Frenchy. Jackie said André told her he knew about the disease a long time ago. "He told me he went to see a doctor in Japan, on his very first trip over there in 1970, and that he was diagnosed with the disease," recalled Jackie.

Later in life, André developed fluid congestion around his heart. He went to see a doctor near his ranch in Ellerbe, North Carolina. The fluid was drained and sent to Duke University Hospital in Durham, North Carolina, for some tests; the results came back, and André was told he had acromegaly. "He told the doctors he knew. He said he had known since 1970," revealed Jackie.

What sent André to see a doctor in Japan? Wrestlers tried to avoid those visits as much as possible, fearful of finding something that would prevent them from working. Back in those days, no work meant no money. That's where Quasimodo may have come into the equation. Did he go because he saw Quasimodo's cyst, or maybe it was Quasimodo telling André about his own condition that encouraged him to go see a doctor? Or if Quasimodo didn't have acromegaly or didn't talk about it to André, was it the doctor at the matches, who knew enough about the disorder to talk to André about it? Or did André have a minor injury that necessitated a trip to the doctor? Unfortunately, the truth about this is most likely lost forever. But it seems likely that André found out about his condition in January 1970 in Japan.

However, André never had surgery. And it wasn't because it was too late for him. Today, the tumor near the pituitary gland that is secreting growth hormone beyond normal levels can be removed, usually after puberty, and this saves the patient from developing more symptoms later in life, as André did. Again according to acromegaly.org, "long-term cure of acromegaly after transsphenoidal surgery is seen in approximately 80-85% or patients with microadenomas (tumours less than 1 cm in size) and in approximately 50-60% of patients with macroadenomas (tumours greater than 1cm)." In the 1970s and 1980s, the surgery was a little more complicated, and the recuperation longer, than it is today but the condition has been treatable since at least 1967.

Why didn't André have the surgery that could have extended or even saved his life?

Was it because the odds of a long-term cure were too slim considering the size of his tumor? Doesn't seem like it, since no doctor ever identified the size of his tumor, as far as is known. Was it because in Japan, he was not told about a possible operation? Perhaps he didn't completely understand the implications of surgery since it was explained to him through a translator or in English, a language he was still struggling with at the time. Medical terms can be a struggle for anyone. It was his first trip to Japan, and he didn't have a translator, like Frank Valois, to speak French with him. Or it could have come down to his beliefs about surgery. "In Japan, he was told he could be operated on," recalled Jackie. "But he said that God had made him that way and he wasn't going to change that."

By 1981, the situation should have been different. Dr. Yett knew as soon as he saw his famous patient that he was suffering from acromegaly. As a precaution before administering anesthesia to treat the broken ankle that brought André in to see him, Dr. Yett got all the testing done to confirm his diagnosis, working with Dr. Johanna A. Pallotta, an endocrinologist. This was probably the first time André went through all the testing and got an official diagnosis he could fully understand. With Dr. Yett, no translation was necessary; André got the truth straight from the doctor. In the 2018 HBO documentary, Dr. Yett remembered André's answer all too well: "He decided he didn't want treatment at that time because he thought it would interfere with his career as a wrestler."

ANDRÉ'S SIZE WAS ALWAYS IMPRESSIVE, ESPECIALLY COMPARED TO A YOUNG CHILD.

PAUL WIGHT, BETTER KNOWN AS THE BIG SHOW, STARTED HIS CAREER AS THE GIANT, THE "SON" OF ANDRÉ.

But since his ankle was broken, the timing would have been perfect. He would not have lost any more time from the road than that injury would have required. Momentum for the ever pressing construction of his legend would have resumed quickly. But when someone gets this type of surgery, the risk of diabetes grows. André would have had to change his diet and drinking habits. So maybe that's the reason: he didn't see himself changing his habits.

According to Jackie, he was at peace with his size and that he was still growing. She said he thought it was what made him, the reason why he was who he was — a successful professional wrestler, an attraction who was touring the world — and he had no intention of changing that. In that regard, he was ill-informed, or he didn't understand the treatment properly. With surgery, André would have kept his height and most of his body mass. The operation would have stunted the further growth of his body and his heart and added years to his life.

However, he was who he was, and nothing was going to change that. André loved being with the boys too much and was never ready to quit, which perhaps he feared would happen if he had surgery. Françoise Valois, Frank's daughter, who knew him well, said that he never had anyone around him to tell him to take it easy for a few months or to think about himself first. Still, it's hard to understand why someone would choose death over retirement.

André wasn't the first or the last pro wrestler with acromegaly. "The French Angel" Maurice Tillet, born in 1903 in Russia to French parents, noticed at 19 years old that his feet, hands, and head were getting thicker. He went to see a doctor and was diagnosed with acromegaly. He developed the disorder after his body had grown; he was only five foot nine. He became a wrestler in 1937 and wrestled all over the world. It is said that he was the inspiration for the character design of Shrek. Tillet passed away at age 50 from cardiomegaly, a result of the disorder. Paul Wight, better known to the wrestling world as The Big Show, also suffered from acromegaly; as with André, Wight grew to be very tall, between six foot ten and seven foot one depending on what report you believe. He underwent surgery in 1991 at age 19, after being diagnosed while in college. The surgery removed the tumor and with it the life-threatening side effects of the condition. And if André had been afraid to lose his giant look, Wight is the living proof it would not have happened.

"The pituitary gland is located under the front lobe of the brain. If you were to go straight through the nose and straight through the ear where those two lines intersect, that's where the pituitary gland is — in that bone pocket, so it's basically brain surgery," Wight said in an interview with Hot 97. "They have to go in, chip out that little pocket of bone, with a laser, cut the tumor and hopefully not damage the pituitary gland because the pituitary gland runs so many senses: your eye moisture, tear ducts, nasal passages, and your testosterone . . . it's like a governor for so many things in your body. That surgery sometimes, if not done properly, can damage other things so then you're on medication the rest of your life just to try and be normal. So I got really lucky and everything turned out great. One of the bad side effects to acromegaly is it leads to diabetes and a lot of things if not corrected, so I got lucky with it. I still have to pay attention to it." Wight started wrestling three years after his surgery and is still active to this day.

Of course, if the complications of the surgery had been presented to André back in 1970, it would have been a little scary. And who better than Wight to know how André was feeling when he was given the news about his condition. "It really hit me right in the stomach hard because I always just thought I was blessed, I never thought of it as an abnormality," he said in his WWE documentary. "You won't probably live past your 40s if you don't get this fixed," he added in an interview with Steve Austin. "When you're 19 or 20, you think your mid-40s are a long time away. Well, bam, here I am now and I still want more out of life." Wight has now outlived André; he turned 47 in February 2019.

In 2012, Dalip Singh Rana, better known as the Great Khali, was diagnosed with acromegaly by WWE's wellness program, and he had the surgery at age 39. He had started wrestling in 2000 and is still wrestling part-time. He is reported to be seven foot one. Others who had the condition include boxer and wrestler Primo Carnera; wrestler Paul Cesar da "Giant" Silva of the WWF Oddities stable fame, who came out to André's music when he was in New Japan and Pride; mixed martial artist Antônio "Bigfoot" Silva, who had surgery twice, after another growth developed; WWE's Lars Sullivan, who had the surgery but continues to grow; and Jorge "Giant" Gonzales, who was seven foot seven. The latter never had the surgery and unfortunately passed away in his 40s from diabetes caused by acromegaly.

The effects of acromegaly help someone become an attraction in an entertainment business like professional wrestling. Tillet was an attraction because of it, as he was even dubbed as the world's ugliest man. Carnera benefited from it. And since 1993, every giant has been compared to André, and every wrestling promoter wants the next André the Giant on their roster. Gonzales, who wrestled from 1989 to 1995, is considered to be the second-tallest pro wrestler in history, only behind Canada's Édouard Beaupré, who was eight foot two but only wrestled one match. André doesn't rank in the top 10 tallest wrestlers of all time, although most ahead of him on that list didn't have a long career, let alone a career like André's.

"Gonzalez never became the attraction they hoped for," wrote Meltzer. "The difference is that André had a certain look of power, with the giant chest, back, butt, and thighs. Gonzalez was actually thicker than most seven-footers who played basketball and wrestled at about 405 pounds and was in condition at that weight, but he never could portray being dangerous or scary when riled, which was the main key to André's success. In hindsight, what a lot of people never understood about André is that his height was only a small part of his attraction. The major parts were his girth at that height and that he was scary, looked like the strongest man in the world, understood how to portray being dangerous, and people believed he was the toughest of everyone, he was always protected until the end of his career, and he also understood how to work."

No one is as closely associated with André as The Big Show. But Wight didn't see the resemblance between them before watching the HBO documentary. "I didn't realize how much my life really parallels

André's," he said to Austin. "But when I saw André getting into airports, and everyone staring, and not being able to fit in hotels, not being able to fit in cars, and what he went through on a day-to-day basis, or the fact that wherever he went he was the spectacle. And I understand that."

By 1970, when André first learned of his condition, his body was starting to undergo radical changes. In a match in France in October, he wasn't as lean as he was just a couple of years prior. Only nine months after his trip to Japan, he had already gained weight from drinking and eating, and his body began showing more signs of the disorder. André was slowly transforming himself into what people would remember him for. And this ultimate change was going to happen not in Europe but in North America.

CHAPTER 6

VALOIS, VACHON, CARPENTIER, AND . . . SADDAM

Upon returning from his first tour in Japan, André began to find himself in a better position, in terms of the politics of wrestling. He was a big star in France, and working for IWE was the best thing that had ever happened to him. Japan was the first country outside of France where he became a superstar. He was in that good of a position he could do pretty much anything he wanted.

"When I went to Paris in 1970, I was ordered to wrestle for the opposition group of the main one of Roger Delaporte, for Siry," remembered Mighty Inoue, who wrestled against André in 1970. "There was this place near Bois de Boulogne where we met before going to the matches, and André was there sometimes. When he saw me, he asked me who I was working for, I told him, and he told me, 'He's no good. You have to come working for Roger.' So I moved. My boss, Kiyomigawa, was a little bit upset, but he said, 'Okay, if André said so.' According to the other wrestlers, in my original group, the payoffs were terrible. André was so nice. Since we were working for the same group, we often drank together."

André continued to wrestle in France until a big opportunity came up. Adnan Alkaissy — most wrestling fans remember him as General

Adnan, alongside Sgt. Slaughter, in their feud with Hulk Hogan in 1991 — had started wrestling professionally in 1959 and worked under different aliases, including Billy White Wolf, an "Indian chief." Ten years after his debut in North America, Alkaissy decided to return home to Baghdad, Iraq, for a vacation. On his way there, he made a stop in England in December 1969, where he wrestled for a few months. That's where he met André for the very first time. "I told him I was going back to Baghdad and asked him if he would like to come over one day," remembered Alkaissy. "He said yes right away!"

Upon returning to Baghdad, Alkaissy met with an old friend from junior high school, none other than Saddam Hussein. In 1968, Hussein was one of the leaders of the 17 July Revolution, which brought the Iraqi Regional Branch of the Arab Socialist Ba'ath Party to power. When Alkaissy came back home, Hussein was vice-president of the Revolutionary Command Council, a position he held until 1979, when he became president of Iraq. Alkaissy's wrestling success was known in his native country, and Hussein met with Alkaissy and told him he was the newest national hero. "We are going to take care of you," Alkaissy recalled Saddam saying. "We are not asking you to do this. We are expecting you to do this. This is home. You are staying." Alkaissy had no choice but to stay.

He started promoting matches, usually a one-match showdown between an outsider and himself, with the national hero going over. The first outsider brought in was Canada's George Gordienko, but others included Scottish wrestler Ian Campbell and USA's Bob Roop. For the 50th anniversary of the activation of the Iraqi Army, a national holiday, the government hyped up Army Day like never before. Money was no object. Foreign dignitaries from all over the world were invited. Alkaissy wanted a bigger man and brought in André. The match was scheduled for January 6, 1971, the day of the holiday, and André was brought in a week before to do some promotional appearances.

"I put him up at the Sahara Hotel, and they had to have a bed custom made for him," recalled Alkaissy in his book. "I got a really big

Mercedes for him too, along with four armed guards. He couldn't believe it. I remember he went shopping one day and wound up having a pair of shoes custom-made at this ritzy show store in downtown Baghdad. They were so in awe of the guy's feet that they made an extra pair of his size 24 shoes to display in their front window. The shoes remained in the window for years."

The match was a best-of-three-falls. Alkaissy planned to win the first one by DQ, lose the second, and win the decisive fall. But just before the match, Saddam, who had become a fan of pro wrestling but didn't know it was scripted, met with him.

"Be victorious, Adnan; we are all counting on you. Be victorious," Alkaissy remembered Saddam saying. "This guy is big, but he is a pussy. I know that you can beat him. If he hurts you in any way, he is going to get this." And Saddam lifted his coat and showed Alkaissy a solid gold, British-made gun. "I will put every bullet in there in his fat head and send him back to France in a pine box."

The pep talk scared Alkaissy into changing his booking to win the second fall, not knowing if Saddam would understand the concept of a best-of-three-falls match . . . He even body slammed the Giant in the second fall. The match sold out the Al-Shaab Stadium, with thousands turned away. Every prominent member of the government, every ambassador in the country, was in attendance. It was a big deal. As it is custom there, when Alkaissy won, a thousand Iraqi commandos shot their rifles in the sky to celebrate their hero's victory. André didn't know what was happening, if he was getting shot at or something. "He sat down, rolled outside, and hid underneath the ring," said Alkaissy. "He was almost in tears."

The show was the most successful ever promoted by Alkaissy. He asked André to stay one more week, and they had a rematch in the city of Kut, two hours south of Baghdad. André was paid $10,000 for that second match, but most importantly, he was promised he would not be shot at this time! André eventually met with Saddam, and the latter told him to lose some weight if he wanted to succeed in pro wrestling.

André remembered the fear he had when he went there. "The hotel was approximately one mile from where the show was being held," recalled André in an interview with Pierre Nadeau on Channel 3 in Montreal. "I entered the place in a Mercedes with two police cars in front and one behind. There were policemen sitting on top of their vehicles firing shots with machine guns. Even if they were blank shots, it would be the last time I went to Iraq!"

Alkaissy made a fortune with those matches, but as the situation changed in Iraq, he was ultimately told to go back to the United States, as it would be safer for him there. Saddam didn't need him anymore. When Alkaissy saw the Giant again in America in the mid-1970s, André remembered him well. "He told me he had enjoyed the matches in Iraq," said Alkaissy. "I thought he was more experienced; his timing was better than when we wrestled together. He had just a few years under his belt at the time."

André returned to France but just for a short while, as he had another tour in Japan scheduled to start March 31, 1971. It's during that tour that André became a star in Japan because he won the third IWA World Series. He was also better protected this time around, not getting pinned or losing as often. Physically, he came in a lot heavier; at almost 400 pounds, he had gained 30 to 40 pounds. The World Series was a round-robin tournament with a scoring system. Three wrestlers were left in the final — Billy Robinson, Karl Gotch, and André — and the matches were best-of-three-falls. Robinson and André finished in a draw, Gotch and André each scored a pin before drawing the third fall, and Gotch and Robinson did the same thing in their final encounter. Because he had the highest score, André won the tournament. It's worth noting that Robinson had won the first two tournaments and was a big name in Japan. In the four matches the two had against each other, three ended up being reported as a draw, and the other one was specified as a 30-minute time limit draw. As in his first tour in Japan, André often worked 30- to 40-minute matches. Although Robinson didn't defeat him, he did body slam André on that tour. Gotch, a former Olympian, was also a huge name at the time. André and Gotch wrestled three times, each having a win and a loss to go with one draw. But what is remembered most is that Gotch not only body slammed André, he impressively applied his patented move, a German suplex, on him (the clip is available on YouTube). Gotch is also known to have stood up for the Giant and made sure he was properly booked. In return, André was said to be very modest with Robinson and Gotch, since he was still green in comparison to the veterans.

André really came into his own during that tour. That's when he became truly hated as a heel. "André's gimmick in Japan was that he hated Japanese people," said Miyamoto. "He also would never talk in Japan." He also started using a new finishing move. Until then, André was lifting his opponents by the neck to finish his matches. But it wasn't catching on. "His neck-hanging move was weak because he could not stretch his arms," wrote journalist Hideo Usagawa. "Ernie Ladd, Big Bill Miller, they could stretch their arms straight when they did that move. But André could not." He used his new finishing move for the first time on May 7 when he beat Buster Matthews, a native of Lac-Saint-Jean, Quebec later known as Gilles "The Fish" Poisson. The finish of the match was a piledriver but not a regular one. It was a kneeling reverse piledriver, where André lifted his opponent, turned him upside-down (similar to a scoop slam lift), then lowered his opponent (so that his opponent's head would hang between his knees), and finally, André then fell to his knees, driving his opponent's head into the mat. If that sounds like a Tombstone Piledriver, you're right — it was indeed a Tombstone Piledriver. Though commonly believed that Dynamite Kid invented the move, it was used in England in the 1960s by Jackie Pallo, who called it the Head Drop. And while The Undertaker popularized the move and the name in the 1990s, the name "tombstone" was already being used when André was in Japan. André pinned Strong Kobayashi in 1972, and in a video of the match, you can clearly hear the Japanese announcer say, "Tombstone Driver!" on several occasions.

After he finished his tour on May 25, André went back to France for a few days and got ready for a trip that would change his life forever. He was going to Montreal.

Between 1939 and 1963, Eddie Quinn was the top promoter in Montreal. In the second half of 1963, the best wrestler in the history of the territory, Yvon Robert, started his own promotion, running a few shows at the Montreal Forum in the summer of 1963, although he mainly used the Paul-Sauvé Arena. His promotion didn't last long since Robert had no TV, and ultimately it closed in November 1964. When Robert's protégé Johnny Rougeau started his own wrestling company, his first move was to get TV. To do so, he took Quinn's master tape, which Robert had inherited at Quinn's death in December 1964, without asking Robert's permission or offering him a partnership, and went to Channel 10 to pitch his new show, which he got.

All Star Wrestling began running shows in 1965, and in 1966 they debuted on TV. They got the rights to promote cards at the Montreal Forum and were the only ones to have a license from the Montreal Athletic Commission (MAC). On paper, the promoter was Bob Langevin, but secretly Johnny Rougeau was pulling the strings. At the time, according to the rules of the MAC, a promoter was not allowed to also wrestle.

At this point, the relationship between Robert and Rougeau fell into disarray, with Robert angry that Rougeau had not included him in this new venture, even though he'd helped him when he started and booked him on his shows in the years prior. On the other hand, some speculate that Robert owed him money from the shows he had wrestled on. Whatever the case may be, the animosity lasted for many years. Robert and Rougeau didn't want to work together. Robert refereed matches occasionally because the fans were asking for him and he didn't want to disappoint them, and Rougeau knew what Robert could bring to the gate. But when Robert's son, Yvon Robert Jr., got into the business, he didn't want him to wrestle for Rougeau. That's why in 1971, the elder

LE GÉANT JEAN · FÉRRÉ
AU JAPON

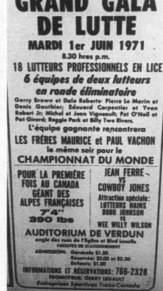

GRAND GALA DE LUTTE

MARDI 1er JUIN 1971
8.30 hres p.m.

18 LUTTEURS PROFESSIONNELS EN LICE
*6 équipes de deux lutteurs
en ronde éliminatoire*

Gerry Brown et Dale Roberts· Pierre Le Marin et
Denis Gauthier; Édouard Carpentier et Yvon
Robert Jr; Michel et Jean Vigneault; Pat O'Neil et
Pat Girard; Reggie Park et Billy Two Rivers.

L'équipe gagnante rencontrera

LES FRÈRES MAURICE et PAUL VACHON
le même soir pour le
CHAMPIONNAT DU MONDE

| POUR LA PREMIÈRE FOIS AU CANADA GÉANT DES ALPES FRANÇAISES 7'4" 390 lbs | JEAN FERRÉ vs COWBOY JONES Attraction spéciale: LUTTEURS NAINS BOBO JOHNSON vs WEE WILLY WILSON |

AUDITORIUM DE VERDUN
angle des rues de l'Église et Blvd Lasalle
FACILITÉS DE STATIONNEMENT

ADMISSION: Générale $3.50
Réservées $2.00 et $2.50
Enfants $1.00

INFORMATIONS ET RÉSERVATIONS: 766-2328
PROMOTEUR: GERRY LEGAULT
Entreprises Sportives Trans-Canada

ANDRÉ WITH THE TRADITIONAL JAPANESE SASH RIBBON IN ONE OF HIS EARLY TOURS FOR IWE.

MONTREAL NEWSPAPER HYPING ANDRÉ'S UPCOMING DEBUT.

ANDRÉ PLAYING CARDS WITH BILLY ROBINSON (ON HIS LEFT), KARL GOTCH (IN FRONT OF HIM), AND MAGNA CLEMENTE.

ANDRÉ WAS USING THE TOMBSTONE PILEDRIVER WHEN THE UNDERTAKER WAS JUST A KID.

KOJI MIYAMOTO

Robert went to Minneapolis to meet with Mad Dog Vachon and asked him to come back to Montreal, be his own boss, and create opposition to All Star Wrestling. The irony in this is that, several years earlier, Robert had chosen Rougeau to be his heir apparent instead of another young Quebec wrestler, such as Vachon.

So in 1971, a group consisting of Yvon Robert Sr., wrestlers Édouard Carpentier (who was tired of being used more as an announcer than a wrestler for All Star) and Maurice Vachon, promoters Lucien Grégoire and Gerry Legault, and lawyer Michel Awada started their own wrestling promotion under the banner of les Entreprises Sportives Transcanada (later renamed les Entreprises Sportives Grand Prix).

Starting in May, the group did some spot shows outside of Montreal. Maurice and Paul Vachon gave their notice to Verne Gagne and the American Wrestling Association, then lost the tag team title on May 15, after being champions for most of the past two years. On May 20 and May 27, they promoted two shows at the Maurice Richard Arena in Montreal, both serving as TV tapings for CFCF-12, the biggest private English TV station in town. The list of talent was quite impressive, as everyone wanted to work for a promotion that Maurice Vachon partly owned. Verne Gagne, Strong Kobayashi, Don and Johnny Fargo, the Hollywood Blonds, Larry Hennig, Hercules Cortez, Red Bastien, and many more wrestled on either or both shows. Carpentier main-evented both, wrestling Gagne on the first show and Kobayashi on the second. CFCF-12 decided to sign the promotion based on the quality of the matches. During that time, promoter Gerry Legault, who promoted Maurice's first pro match, decided to get out of the business and sold his shares to Paul Vachon, Maurice's brother, and "The Butcher" also became Grand Prix's promoter. Legault stayed as a local promoter for a few weeks before ultimately leaving the company.

That all led up to June 1, 1971. The date is important for two reasons. First, the company was making its debut at the Verdun Auditorium, where it would run on a weekly basis. Since the group didn't have a license with the Montreal Athletic Commission, it couldn't run Montreal every week. Verdun is now a borough of Montreal, located on the Island of Montreal, three miles west of the Montreal Forum, but in 1971, it was a town of its own, meaning the athletic commission did not regulate it. Paul could actually wrestle there every week, and Paul's sister, Vivian, who had started wrestling a couple of years before, could too — Montreal didn't allow women's wrestling at the time.

June 1 is an important date for another reason: it was the debut of André in North America.

Fernand Levis Valois was 45 years old when he met André for the first time in France, in 1966. Valois had started training at 15 under the guidance of Yvon Robert, Eugene Tremblay, and Emile Maupas and got his start two years later in 1939. After he wrestled in Quebec, Eddie Quinn sent him to Boston to work for Paul Bowser and that's when he got the name Frank, which was easier for English-speaking fans to remember than Fernand. Then, in 1949, the great French wrestler Felix Miquet invited him to France. Valois was supposed to stay there for three months, but he ended up staying for three years. He came back in 1952 to start a family. Five years later, he was on the road again, going back to France, before wrestling mainly in Texas, North Carolina, Florida, and Ontario, Canada. He brought his family back to Quebec in 1966, before going back to Europe on a more regular basis. He became a huge star in France but also wrestled a lot in Austria and Germany. He was such a star in France that he was asked to be an actor in movies and plays. In the summer of 1968, he was shooting a movie called *The Brain*, filmed in both French and English, with famous French actor Jean-Paul Belmondo. In December 1968, he played a wrestler in a play called *Rabelais at l'Élysée-Montmartre*. In November 1970, he played in *La promesse de l'aube* with Melina Mercouri, a movie directed by Jules Dassin, father of famous French singer Joe Dassin. It was also during that time that he became a bodyguard for both Georges Pompidou and Charles de Gaulle, presidents of the French Republic.

Valois knew Maurice Vachon from their days in Texas, and he knew Paul Vachon from when they had teamed in France in 1965. He also knew Carpentier from his time in France. So it was only normal for Valois to tell his friends about this giant of a man he had met in Paris. Although both Paul and Maurice wrestled for the IWE in Japan in February and March 1971, they hadn't yet heard about André. "Frank Valois had told us that there was this giant in France and that if we didn't send someone for him, we were fucking nuts," recalled Paul. "It was the first time I ever heard of the Giant. You have to take into consideration that news didn't travel as fast then."

As for Carpentier, he first saw André when he toured in France in early 1966 — not in 1964 like he often claimed, as André was not wrestling then. Among Grand Prix owners, Carpentier was selected to go back to France since he was the only one in the promotion who knew André. So he went to France in March 1971 and met with André to ask him to join the Grand Prix promotion. They even had a match against each other on March 21 in Paris. However, Carpentier had left Rougeau's promotion to be used on top by Grand Prix. Having another Frenchman in his way, who was legitimately one foot taller than him, wasn't something he particularly liked. In the world of wrestling, Carpentier's ego was well known. But for the benefit of this new organization, he understood that André was a game changer. "After I had dropped his name and vital statistics to everybody, my partners all agreed — except that Carpentier did so rather reluctantly," said Paul. "He had been for years the big French drawing card and he was thinking, rightly so, that a big attraction like André would steal his thunder." It's also worth noting that Carpentier never told Johnny Rougeau about the Giant when he was still working for All Star.

André came back from Japan and wrestled in what would be his last match in France, in Savigny-en-Sancerre, 120 miles south of Paris, on May 30, against long time foe Jack de Lassartesse. With some perspective, it was a smart move for André since the wrestling scene in France began to fall off just a couple of years later. He had the chance to wrestle there during what was called "les Trente Glorieuses" (the Glorious 30), meaning the 30 years where wrestling in France was exceptionally hot. However, it was time for André to move on, and moving on meant flying to Montreal, Quebec, Canada. Paul Vachon still remembers writing a $600 check for his plane ticket. André was not the first French wrestler to make the trip: Paul Pons, Emile Maupas, Henri Deglane, and Édouard Carpentier all came to Montreal and took advantage of the French-speaking connection they had with local fans. Montreal and the province of Quebec were a perfect fit for André, since his English was still way below average. With close to five million people speaking French, he could feel at home. Plus, Montreal and Quebec City were widely known for their European feel, especially in the old districts, built by French settlers back in the 17th century.

The very first ad for the June 1 show at the Verdun Auditorium hyped up a huge event with a one-night tag team tournament where the winners would face Maurice and Paul Vachon for the titles. Just above that, it said that for the first time in Canada, there would be a seven-foot-four, 390-pound giant from the French Alps by the name of Jean Ferré, who would wrestle Cowboy Jones.

The French Alps and seven foot four were to become quite common in André's career and life. However, they were just the beginning of so many more tall tales to come.

CHAPTER 7

TALL TALES: HOW TALL WAS ANDRÉ, REALLY?

C uriously, André's height was never sold with an over-the-top number while he was in France, the U.K., or Japan. He *was* promoted as a giant, and his height was the subject of every interview. But the figure mentioned was, give or take, his real height, something we don't see too often in the realm of pro wrestling. Most of the time, in sports like hockey or baseball, someone's height and weight are legit numbers. (Let alone where someone is from or other details of their background.) In wrestling, people are a little bit looser with the facts, to say the least. If someone is 285 pounds, he might suddenly gain 15 and be billed at 300. If another is from Berwyn, Illinois, you can bet he's going to be announced as from Chicago. If someone looks like another wrestler, he might become his brother or his cousin. And let's not even get into French-Canadians playing Russians or Hawaiians portraying Japanese nationals.

In the very first TV interview André did in January 1966, he said he was two meters 10. (France uses the international system of units: meters, centimeters, and kilograms.) Two meters 10 is six foot 10. A poster from September 1966 listed him as "2m08," which is kind of funny to think that someone would intentionally lowball the giant's height. Was it that or a simple mistake? We'll never know. As years went by, French posters increased his height slightly: he was two meters 12 (six foot 11.5) by 1968. On the poster from his last show in France before coming to Montreal in 1971, his height is two meters 14, which is just over seven feet. However, those were wrestling posters — the same posters that stated André was still 20 years old in 1969. And it's not like André was measured before each match.

On the very few French broadcasts available online, his height varies even more. According to the announcers in February 1966, he was two meters 15 (half an inch over seven feet); in 1968, he was two meters 11 (six foot 11); and in October 1970, he was two meters 14 (just over seven feet). And no, he wasn't still growing anymore at age 24. Unlike in modern-day American football or baseball, there was no media guide with the heights and weights of all the wrestlers for the announcers to refer to. The details came from the promoter in the territory where a wrestler was working.

The confusion with André's height actually started before he had his first match, and promoter Robert Lageat is maybe the one to blame. "Lageat had a two-meter pocket measuring tape," recalled Gilbert Wehrle. "Michel Saulnier climbed on Claude Ledoux's shoulders to measure him. And Jean was taller than the measuring tape. Many centimeters taller. So Lageat decided that Jean's height was two meters 12. Since Lageat was the boss, no one argued with him." However, Lageat didn't even follow his own declaration. In his first program that featured André, in January 1966, he was announced at two meters 9 and the following month, he had grown to two meters 10!

Adding to the legend, there is Tony St. Clair's story. The wrestler was present in 1969 when André's height was measured in England. "He was seven foot one, with his wrestling shoes on," remembered St. Clair. Those shoes were not as thick as wrestling boots are today, adding only about an inch to his real height. That brings his height to about seven feet, or two meters 14.

ANDRÉ AND PROMOTER TONY MULÉ, ON ANDRÉ'S FIRST DAY IN MONTREAL.

REFEREE ANDRÉ ROY AND HIS WIFE, GHISLAINE, WERE THERE AS WELL TO WELCOME ANDRÉ.

If the wrestling world couldn't agree, what about his own family?

His brothers never asked André about his height, and he was never measured at home. They both said when interviewed that he was two meters 18 but later said the number came from wrestling magazines or posters. The only official document where his height was mentioned was on his French passport (he never became an American or Canadian citizen) and it said two meters 18, which is a little under seven foot two. When he worked in Japan, in 1970, he was billed as two meters 18. Former wrestler Paul Leduc remembered measuring André when working for Grand Prix in 1972 and said he was barely seven feet tall.

"In 1976, when André had his famous boxer versus wrestler match at Shea Stadium against Chuck Wepner on the undercard of the Muhammad Ali versus Antonio Inoki fiasco, legitimate sportswriters who took notice of André for the first time estimated him at six nine," wrote Dave Meltzer when André passed away. "Basketball players who met him generally also estimated his height at around six nine, although he was proportioned completely different than any six nine man around with relatively short legs, a long torso, and huge head; their estimates could have been deceptive."

Then there is the famous photo with basketball player Wilt Chamberlain and actor Arnold Schwarzenegger on the set of *Conan the Destroyer* in 1983 in which Chamberlain, who stands at seven foot one, appears to be a few inches taller than André. Then again, there was more than one picture taken, and in others, the difference is not as noticeable.

By 1976, gravity had already taken its toll on his aching spine and lower back, which shrunk a little. In fact, according to the University of California, a human being will not lose more than an inch or two as they grow older. Someone can get shorter because the cartilage between his joints wears out. One of acromegaly's symptoms is osteoporosis, and that, or any bone disease for that matter, can accentuate the loss of height. Add to that the wear and tear André put on his body from pro wrestling. While André was never officially diagnosed with osteoporosis, chances are he was suffering from it, as it makes bone fractures occur more easily than expected. It's not surprising to learn that in his later years André did fracture his ankle simply by getting out of bed. In André's *Montreal Gazette* obituary, it was mentioned that André was measured upon his death at six foot 10, corresponding to a loss of two inches, which is within the parameters the studies established.

No wonder he started sporting an afro in the 1970s. Not only was it in style at the time, but it gave André the appearance of being a few inches taller. Basketball players and athletes, in general, were getting taller as years went by, and Vince McMahon Sr. was known to reprimand André anytime he took a picture with an athlete who was taller, as he wanted to protect the legend of André being the tallest athlete in the world. There's one story told by many WWF wrestlers: basketball player Manute Bol, who played in the late 1980s to early 1990s and was listed at seven foot seven, wanted to meet with André, but André was rushed out of the arena to avoid the height comparison. A famous photo from 1972 in Japan shows Don Leo Jonathan in wrestling boots beside André, who is barefoot. While many experts cite this as evidence that André wasn't seven feet tall, if you take a close look at the photo, you can see that André's head is bending forward a little, and his shoulders are too, while Jonathan is standing up straight. With Jonathan at six foot six, André must have been a four or five inches taller, therefore closer to seven feet.

One of the conclusions we can make is that having a consistent height for André was not seen as a priority in France. For the last 45 years, in Canada and the U.S., André's height was listed as seven foot four, with the occasional seven foot five or even six. Although his height was put on every poster and in almost every interview he did in Europe, whether he was six foot 11 or seven foot one didn't seem to matter. He was a giant, and that's what they were pushing. Perhaps rightfully so, since the average height in France in 1970 was five foot seven. The attraction was the "Giant" Jean Ferré, not his exact height.

In his HBO documentary, Jason Hehir tried to solve the mystery of André's height but was unable to. "We asked it of everybody," he said in an interview with Kevin Iole of Yahoo Sports. "And pretty much everybody just lied. Vince said, 'I don't know if he was seven foot four, but for sure he was seven feet.' He just mumbled about it. The reality of it is that we tried pretty hard to track down any sort of official document that would have an official measurement. We had some of his state wrestling licenses, but it was clear that he, or whoever his handler was, was just scrawling numbers down on a piece of paper and perpetuating the myth that this guy was anywhere from seven feet to seven feet four and anywhere from 380 to 520 [pounds]."

With all that said, the bottom line is this: to the best of anyone's knowledge, André never talked about his real height, there is no medical record showing it, and his family doesn't know more than the wrestling people who have tried to figure it out. That said, we can make an assumption and believe that he was, at one point in his life, a real seven-footer.

When it was time to make an ad for his first appearance in Montreal, no one could text André or send him an email to get his stats. Even calling from Montreal to Paris wasn't an easy task back then. Promoters, especially the Vachons, knew he was around seven feet tall and were too smart not to take advantage of that.

At that time, one of the biggest sports stars was Lew Alcindor, who played basketball in Milwaukee. The Milwaukee Bucks were the hottest thing in town, having won 66 games, including a 20-win streak. At only 24, in his second season, Alcindor won the scoring title and was named MVP for both the regular season and the playoffs. Plus, at seven foot two, he was the tallest player in the game. On April 30, thanks to Alcindor, the Bucks won the NBA championship in Baltimore after sweeping the Bullets. Coincidentally, that same night at the Milwaukee Auditorium, Verne Gagne's AWA had a sell-out show with the Vachon brothers winning a best-of-three-falls match against Wilbur Snyder and Bull Bullinski. The very next day, Alcindor publicly announced his conversion to Islam and changed his name to Kareem Abdul-Jabbar. On May 15, in the same arena where the Bucks played, Maurice and Paul lost the tag team titles to Red Bastien and Hercules Cortez in front of 10,271 fans, on their way back to Montreal. Since Abdul-Jabbar had started playing with the Bucks in 1969, the Vachons had wrestled in Milwaukee more than 20 times. They both liked to watch the news and keep themselves informed and were well aware of Abdul-Jabbar's success — and height. It only made sense that when the Vachons debuted André, they billed him at seven foot four, making André the tallest athlete in all of North America. "Seven foot four sounded good. We couldn't say seven foot nine," recalled Paul Vachon.

While his exact height is hard to pin down, it's easier to understand why André suddenly hailed from the French Alps upon his arrival in Montreal. Stretching across eight countries, the Alps are the highest and most extensive mountain chain in Europe. With André being a mountain of a man, it was easy to make the connection. Incidentally, there were some 8x10s sold of André looking bigger than the French Alps behind him. As his character developed, he was announced as from Grenoble, a well-known city in France that had hosted the 1968 Winter Olympic Games and was nicknamed the "Capital of the Alps." Especially for the French-Canadians in Montreal and in the province of Quebec, Grenoble resonated, and the Winter Games there were the first to be shown on TV live and in color. A Frenchman, Jean-Claude Killy, was crowned the king of the Games with three gold medals in alpine skiing. A year before André's debut in Montreal, the city had been selected to host the upcoming 1976 Summer Olympic Games. With Grenoble being the latest host city, it was something Montreal fans could relate to.

Regarding André's weight, there's no story behind its fluctuation. In France in the late 1960s, he was promoted at different weights: 135, 140, and 144 kilograms but most frequently at 140, which translates to 309 pounds. In 1971, just prior to coming to Montreal, he was promoted at 174 kilograms (384 pounds), which could have been his real weight or close to it. Between then and March 1973, he was billed anywhere between 400 and 460 pounds. In New Zealand in 1972, he was billed as 35 stones, which is 490 pounds, a number completely exaggerated, even for wrestling. It's not like he was put on a scale every week; the figure was merely conjured up by the promoter he was working for, and as his real weight increased, his fake weight increased accordingly.

But enough with the tale of the tape. Let's talk about the name, Jean Ferré or le Géant Jean Ferré. It was the name he had used everywhere but in Japan and South Africa. More people knew about the Great Ferré's story in France than in Quebec, but Quebecers knew another of André's namesakes, the popular singer Léo Ferré. Indeed, he was one of the most popular French singers of his era and had performed a lot in Montreal especially in the 1960s and '70s, as most of France's biggest artists did. But Léo Ferré was special and considered an immortal. (He's so well known on this side of the Atlantic that in 2016, there was a celebration in Montreal to commemorate what would have been his 100th birthday.) Although the Vachons' promotion didn't go as far as to say that they were related, as with Édouard Carpentier and famous French boxer Georges Carpentier, the name Jean Ferré would be connected to Léo Ferré for fans in Montreal.

There was also another legend told to the fans in Montreal upon André's arrival. A lot of wrestlers are given a new background story when coming into a new territory. Whether it was Mad Dog Vachon coming from Algeria, or Kane being the long-lost half-brother of The Undertaker, such a story often gave a little something extra for the fans to care about. André was too much of an attraction to have an ordinary background story. He had to have *more* than one. So as one of the stories went, Édouard Carpentier was driving in the French Alps when a colossal redwood tree fell in front of him and blocked the road. Carpentier wasn't able to move the tree, but out of the woods came a giant, the biggest man he'd ever seen. He grabbed the tree and threw it away like it was nothing. Carpentier and André became friends and eventually Carpentier brought André to wrestle in Montreal. Another story was that André, at l'Élysée-Montmartre, went to see Carpentier, told him he wanted to wrestle, and asked him to train him. Carpentier told him there were wrestling schools in Paris, but André said that no one wanted to train him. So Carpentier trained him and eventually brought him to Montreal.

Of course, none of this really happened. But those stories were told by Carpentier himself, so it was hard for the press not to believe them. As much as Carpentier was reluctant to bring André over, once André became a huge name, suddenly *he* had made André. He had discovered him, trained him, and brought him to Montreal and New York.

What is true, however, is that Carpentier picked André up at Dorval airport with Yvon Robert Jr. and local promoter Tony Mule on May 31, 1971. They brought him to a restaurant and then to his hotel, the Windsor, in downtown Montreal, the same hotel where the National Hockey League had been created in 1917. André would live there for close to a year before getting his own apartment. The idea behind those first tall tales was to get fans in seats in Verdun on June 1, when André was scheduled to wrestle against Cowboy Jones. But like André, Cowboy Jones wasn't who the fans thought he was. Jones wasn't a cowboy. He wasn't even a Jones. But he was André's first opponent in North America.

CHAPTER 8

MONTREAL, WHERE ANDRÉ'S CAREER TOOK OFF

O
n the afternoon of June 1, in the hallway of the Verdun Auditorium, Cowboy Jones saw his opponent in person for the very first time. "André was signing autographs, and some fans were telling me I still had time to leave the building and run away," remembered Jones. "He was so tall; it was something to see."

Jones was, in fact, Alexandre Lépine, a six-foot-two, 245-pound journeyman who had been trained by Tony Lanza and started wrestling in 1963. He had previously wrestled under a hood as one of the Green Hornets. He worked his first match for Lucien Grégoire, the one putting the matches together for Grand Prix; Grégoire remembered Jones and thought he would be the right opponent to put over the Giant. "I remembered Carpentier telling me about the Giant coming to Montreal," Jones recalled. "I had seen pictures of him at the office. I asked what kind of person he was and had been told he was a very good guy. Grégoire told me I didn't need to be scared. He wasn't coming here to injure anyone." According to Jones, the match went well, about seven or eight minutes long, and André was not dangerous at all and in full control of what he was doing in the ring.

The next day, *La Presse*, a prominent French newspaper in Montreal, ran a picture of André. This is notable because unlike the two other popular newspapers of the era, *La Presse* didn't cover pro wrestling as much. The results were not mentioned; they only printed a picture of André and Jones with the caption: "The monster has no mercy! The French wrestler Jean Ferré, from the French Alps, measuring more than 7 feet, weighing around 380 pounds, is a good attraction for professional wrestling. He made his debut at the Verdun Auditorium, last night, against Cowboy Jones. He showed no mercy for his opponent."

It was André's first match in North America, and it was also very special for Jones. And true to who André was, he would never forget Jones. "It's always been a huge honor to have been his first opponent," said Jones, who celebrated his 80th birthday in 2019. "I have very fond memories of that match and his time in Montreal. In the mid-1980s, four or five years after I retired, I went to the Forum and wanted to say hi to Jean, but the security guy didn't want to let me pass. I told him to tell the Giant that Cowboy Jones was there to see him. Jean had overheard the conversation and told the guy, 'Let him pass; he's my dear friend!'"

The *La Presse* photo was the first picture of André to appear in a Montreal newspaper, but it certainly wouldn't be the last. It was the start of a loving relationship with the fans in the province of Quebec. And the timing was right, both on a sports and political level. The province was emerging from the Quiet Revolution, a period where French-Canadians had stood up for themselves for the first time in a very long time. In 1970, Montreal had been named the host of the 1976 Summer Olympics, a first in Canada. In 1971, the Montreal Canadiens had won the Stanley Cup; the Montreal Alouettes were the best team in Canadian football; the best junior hockey player in the country, Guy Lafleur, was about to start his career as a Montreal Canadien, replacing the great Jean Béliveau, who had just retired; and harness racing driver Hervé Filion was doing so great on the tracks that, by the end of the year, he won the Lou Marsh Trophy, an annual award presented to Canada's top athlete.

In pro wrestling, All Star Wrestling wasn't what it used to be. It was still going strong, but the crowds were not as big as in 1968 or 1969. Moreover, its attendance numbers were slowly declining. And to top it all off, Johnny Rougeau, who was named wrestler of the year in Quebec by *La Presse* in 1970, was on his last legs and retired on August 2, 1971, in order to take care of his junior hockey team. Since pro wrestling always did well at the box office and on television in the territory — better than almost any other sport except for hockey — there was a place for Grand Prix Wrestling to take and an open spot for a new top star to emerge.

André had a busy schedule. After his debut on June 1, he started touring the province. Again, the timing was good since it was easier for wrestling promotions in Quebec to book arenas during summertime, when there was no hockey. Riding with Paul Vachon or Cowboy Jones, he wrestled in Jonquière, Pont-Rouge, and Shawinigan during his first week before coming back to Verdun on June 8, logging a total of 620 miles. "He could drive, but he'd rather have somebody else do the driving since he could drink more, explained Paul Leduc. "He wasn't a fool. He didn't want to risk being arrested and causing the promotion some problems." Paul Vachon wrestled André and put him over in Jonquière. "I just wanted to show the talent it could be done," remembered Vachon. "People were afraid to get hurt."

In Pont-Rouge, André wrestled in his first handicap match. For some reason, France didn't care for treating him like a giant, which infuriated Paul Vachon when he was told about it in recent years. "It doesn't take a brain to figure this out," Vachon said. So not only did they not play up his tall stature, but there weren't any handicap matches recorded during his time in the country. His first two-on-one match was against Michel Vigneault, later known as Michel Martel (Rick's brother), and Jean Vigneault (John Walsh).

"Making him work with two opponents in a handicap match was Grégoire's idea," explained Vachon. "He had seen a wrestler called The Blimp against two, three, or even four guys. That guy weighed more than 500 pounds. He was an attraction just like André." Lucien Grégoire had been in the wrestling business since the end of the 1920s. He knew everyone and had seen everything, twice. Almost blind after getting into a car accident while traveling with Carpentier, he had started as a wrestler but by the early 1970s had been a promoter for 30 years. Grégoire had seen Martin "The Blimp" Levy during his heyday in the 1930s and 1940s. Billed as the largest wrestler in the world, Levy was such an attraction that he was featured in various national magazines and newspapers in the U.S.

For the rest of June, André didn't wrestle in any singles matches. He worked in several handicap matches, mainly against Martel and Vigneault. He also worked with others like Fernand Fréchette and Pat Girard (who had trained Ronnie and Terry Garvin), as well the Hollywood Blonds, Dale Roberts and Jerry Brown, and André won all of those contests. He was also put in a couple of battle royals; on June 29, he teamed with Édouard Carpentier for the very first time against Maurice and Paul Vachon. Clearly, the Giant was protected as he was still kind of green, especially in terms of the North American style, which was different than European- or Japanese-style wrestling. Not only were the matches different for André, but the culture and the food were different too.

"I had a big car, a convertible Cadillac," remembered Jones, "so he sat in the back seat, all by himself, drinking beer and eating cheese puffs, something he didn't have in France at the time. He could drink 12 beers between Chicoutimi and Quebec City, which was a two- or three-hour drive."

The arrival of André coincided with the debut of Grand Prix Wrestling on local television. The TV deal with Channel 12 started on Saturday, June 19, in English, at 3 p.m. The group was lucky enough to be unopposed that afternoon as all the French-language stations were airing election results of a top political party's leader. *On the Mat*, All Star Wrestling's show, wasn't broadcast that week. At the time, Saturday was a big wrestling day in Montreal. *On the Mat* aired at 4 p.m. on Channel 10 and *NWA All Star Wrestling* (from the Northwest Wrestling Promotions run by Sandor Kovacs, Gene Kiniski, and Don Owen) was on at 2:30 p.m. on Channel 8. However, Vancouver-based wrestling was never a threat to any of the local groups, mainly because the promotion didn't have French-Canadian wrestlers and Channel 12 had better viewership than Channel 8.

After being undefeated during his first month, André finally suffered his first loss. Not by disqualification or count-out — but not clean either. On July 1, he wrestled against the Hollywood Blonds at the Palais des Sports in Jonquière, Quebec. Near the end of the match, André was about to get the win, when Gilles "The Fish" Poisson interfered in favor of the Blonds. The referee, who had been thrown out of the ring earlier and didn't see the interference, got back in, and he had no other choice than to count to three, as both Brown and Roberts were on top of the Giant. There were only 400 people in attendance at the venue, and with news not traveling like it does today, it didn't affect André's standing at all. The reason behind the loss was to create a regional program between Poisson and the Giant going forward.

Poisson had started wrestling in 1969 after Mad Dog Vachon sent him to Calgary to work for Stu Hart. He then wrestled in Portland and Japan. When Grand Prix started, Poisson, who had yet to wrestle in his home province, was brought back by his mentor. He was built up as a strongman, since he'd done weightlifting when he was younger. He knew André from their IWE tour back in May. In the return match the following week, André lost again versus Poisson, this time by disqualification, after hitting the referee and not stopping his attack on Poisson. That was a finish often used by Grand Prix to protect the Giant. He was always a babyface but would lose his cool against heels if they were cheating or using some kind of shenanigans. He was the one standing tall at the end of the match, but in the record books, it was a loss.

His first feud outside of Montreal was against Poisson, and his first in Verdun was against The Professional. The Pro was a masked wrestler by the name of Doug Gilbert. From Omaha, Nebraska, he had a good look at six foot one and 275 pounds. A Georgia wrestling mainstay, he had also worked for Verne Gagne and wrestled against Mad Dog Vachon quite a few times by the end of the 1960s. The Vachons brought him in to feud with the Giant.

On July 6, André wrestled in a battle royal. Once there was only him and The Professional left in the ring, they simultaneously eliminated themselves. The following week, they wrestled in a singles match won by The Pro via count-out in front of 3,700 fans. It was André's first defeat in Montreal, but the fans understood he hadn't been pinned and wanted to see more of him. On July 20, André teamed with Carpentier and Reggie Parks to beat the team of The Pro and the Vachon brothers, in front of a crowd of 4,700. Finally, on July 27, in a best-of-three-falls match, the Giant again lost his cool and hit the referee before being disqualified. The attendance was 5,227 — proof that André was a draw. In one of those matches, Gilbert body slammed him, something Paul Vachon didn't agree with. "I told André when he got here, 'I know your style, I have wrestled in France,'" remembered Vachon. "'I don't want you to do that. Don't go down on dropkicks and don't let anyone body slam you, unless it's me.' But I said that as a joke!" After that match with Gilbert, Paul went to see André in the locker room.

"Why did you let him pick you up and body slam you?"

"I wanted to make him look good."

"Don't do that again."

"Okay, boss."

If you've ever read anything about André, "boss" is a term he really liked. It wasn't something he said in England or Japan, but he started using it while working for Grand Prix —and Paul Vachon was the very first one he called "boss," since technically Vachon *was* his boss! Meeting so many workers, even if he had a good memory, it was easier to call everyone, or at least everyone he liked, "boss" instead of remembering everyone's name. That said, he didn't like to be called "boss." It was a one-way greeting!

In July, tragedy hit the territory. On July 12, Yvon Robert — arguably the best wrestler in the history of Quebec — died of a heart attack at the age of 56. Even though André hadn't known him well, he visited Robert at his home just before he died. In fact, Yvon Robert Jr. and one of his best friends, Tony Mule, quickly became friends with André. The trio

EDOUARD CARPENTIER, YVON ROBERT JR., AND ANDRÉ WERE PROMOTED AS THE THREE MUSKETEERS IN MONTREAL.

ANDRÉ WITH SOME OF HIS MONTREAL FRIENDS: CARPENTIER, MULÉ, ROBERT JR., AND PAUL LEDUC.

ONE OF THE FIRST PROMO SHOTS IN MONTREAL FOR GRAND PRIX WRESTLING.

ANDRÉ AND CARPENTIER BOTH ATTENDED YVON ROBERT SR.'S FUNERAL.

ANDRÉ STARTED WRESTLING IN HANDICAP MATCHES IN THE PROVINCE OF QUEBEC; HERE AGAINST THE GREEN HORNETS.

was together at Robert's home. He also went to the funeral along with pretty much everyone involved in the business. Robert was said to have been impressed with the Giant. (Yvon Robert Jr. inherited his father's shares in the company.)

Just a few days before that last match against The Professional, André had made his official debut in the United States for the American Wrestling Association, a promotion in the Midwest run by Verne Gagne and Wally Karbo. Gagne was a former amateur wrestler who was an alternate at the 1948 Olympic Games, which Vachon and Carpentier also attended. Annoyed with being overlooked for the NWA World title, Gagne formed his own promotion in 1960.

The AWA and the IWE had a working relationship that started in 1970 with Gagne's first match for IWE, on February 3, 1970, in Hiroshima, when he wrestled Strong Kobayashi. Coincidently, this was the first time that Gagne saw the Giant, as he was on the same card, teaming with Michael Nador against Thunder Sugiyama and Great Kusatsu. Many people thought that because of the relationship between AWA and IWE, Verne's introduction to André, and Verne's friendship with the Vachons, he was the reason André started wrestling in Canada and then in Minneapolis. However, that's not the case at all.

When Verne saw André in Japan, he didn't see money in him as a wrestler, but he did think he could make it as a boxer. While Verne Gagne himself never promoted boxing, the parent company of the AWA, the Minneapolis Boxing and Wrestling Club, which he co-owned with Karbo, did. "The office did sporadically promote boxing cards but didn't concentrate on that end of the business to any degree," recalled AWA historian George Schire. "However in the mid-1960s, Verne Gagne trained with and managed a young boxer named Ron Marsh. During this brief time, they promoted some local boxing cards featuring Marsh with Gagne in his corner. After that short run, boxing was not a focus anymore." The heavyweight boxing division was not doing great in early 1970. Muhammad Ali was still serving a suspension for refusing to be drafted into the armed forces during the Vietnam War, and

Jimmy Ellis, who was the heavyweight champion, hadn't fought in over 18 months. In André, Gagne must have seen another Primo Carnera, a very well-known boxer-turned-wrestler from the 1930s, who was billed as the tallest boxer ever. Coincidentally, there's always been talk about Carnera having acromegaly and André was often compared to him both in Europe and North America. But André was just not interested in boxing. Contrary to what is sometimes reported, he had never boxed and didn't intend to. He wanted to stick with wrestling. "Verne never told us about the Giant before he came here," confirmed Paul Vachon. In fact, the Vachons were the ones who sent André to Verne.

The Vachons had a few dates for Verne in June 1971, doing return matches with Cortez and Bastien. As they were discussing their new promotion, they spoke about the Giant and got him booked the following month. Just like that, the Vachons and Grand Prix became André's first booking agents in North America. Any promoter who wanted to book André, except for Japan, had to go through them. And they never took a percentage.

On July 24, 1971, at the Minneapolis Auditorium, André was scheduled for his first booking in the United States. Because his English was so bad, Édouard Carpentier went along to help the Giant; this was before Frank Valois became his official handler and traveling partner. There was an angle where Bull Bullinski was going to find himself a partner against the team of "Pretty Boy" Larry Hennig and "Luscious" Lars Anderson. "The week before the July 24 card, Bullinski was asked by TV announcer Marty O'Neill who his partner would be, and Bull answered only by saying 'Ferré,' and then he walked off the interview area," remembered Schire. "The following week, on the 24th, André debuted and was introduced as 'André Russimoff.' But truth be told, André's debut was overshadowed."

After a show in Winnipeg, Canada, on Friday, July 23, where Nick Bockwinkel defeated Hercules Cortez by disqualification, the challenger and his tag team partner, Red Bastien, left to go back to Minneapolis. They had to pick up André at the Minneapolis airport early in the morning of the 24th, and 450 miles separated the two cities. Born Alfonso Carlos Chicharro on July 7, 1932, in San Sebastián, in northern Spain, 14 miles from France's border, Cortez had wrestled against André in France in the 1960s and he spoke French, which made him the perfect choice to pick André up. At 6:30 a.m., Cortez and Bastien were on Highway 52, just an hour away from Minneapolis, near Waite Park, north of St. Cloud, when their car overturned and crashed. Cortez, who was driving, was killed. Bastien survived, only sustaining a leg injury.

"I talked to Red Bastien many times about the accident, and he told me that Hercules had fallen asleep at the wheel and lost control of the car," recalled Schire. "When the car overturned, Cortez was thrown from the car and Red was shoved down on the floor between the front seat and the dash. Neither was wearing seat belts, which were still not mandatory in those days." Cortez was supposed to wrestle Bockwinkel that night with the winner facing Gagne for the title. He was replaced by Gagne himself. Not the best atmosphere to make a debut in a new territory. In the program following that match, André was billed as seven foot five and 400 pounds, taller than Wilt Chamberlain and Lew Alcindor. He was referred as both "Rousimoff" and "Russimoff" (as with his height and weight varying, his name was written so many different ways, especially as André wrestled more in the U.S.). After coming back to Quebec, he wrestled the following week, on July 31, in Milwaukee, billed as Jean Ferré, teaming again with Bullinski against Hennig and Anderson. Paul Vachon was the one traveling with him this time.

It was his last match before going back to France. According to Jones, André's mother was ill, and he had some personal affairs he needed to address. It must have been a last-minute ordeal to leave as he was scheduled and advertised to wrestle in Trois-Rivières on August 16. But when André came back, it was for good.

CHAPTER 9

AROUND THE WORLD!

Grand Prix was beginning to be a serious threat to All Star Wrestling. For the new promotion to be a real player, however, it needed three things: a wrestling TV show in French, since more than 80 percent of the six million people in Quebec were francophones; a license from the Montreal Athletic Commission; and dates at the biggest indoor venue in the province, the famous Montreal Forum. The journey to those objectives started in the summer of 1971, when Michel Longtin, a friend of Yvon Robert Jr. who became Maurice Vachon's business manager, suggested that the group meet with Jean Brisson, a local wrestling promoter and radio and TV announcer in Rimouski, 330 miles northeast of Montreal. Paul Vachon led that group and met with one of the bosses of the CJBR-TV station, Jacques Brillant.

"He said it would be impossible to [record television] there because his station was just a small affiliate of a company called Telemedia," remembered Paul Vachon. "And the parent station was in Sherbrooke. He said his station didn't have the mobile setup needed to go on location to tape a wrestling show or the facilities to do one at the station. But the station in Sherbrooke would be perfect for that. They had a specially built studio with built-in bleachers that could hold 250 people."

So the very same day, Vachon drove 300 miles to Sherbrooke and met with Fernand Corbeil, the station's manager. For a lofty $4,500, the station agreed to do a three-show taping every three weeks and to air the show on Sunday mornings at 11 a.m., right after mass, replacing a religion-themed show. According to Vachon, he proposed the time slot, remembering that Verne Gagne's AWA was doing great ratings in Milwaukee because it aired when kids could watch the show. The reach of the Sherbrooke station meant it could be seen in Montreal, the primary market. On Sunday, September 5, 1971, Grand Prix Wrestling aired on Channel 7 at 11 a.m. for the very first time. A week later, they were on Channel 4 in Quebec City, replacing All Star Wrestling's *On the Mat* because, according to what Corbeil told Vachon, the station's manager didn't like Johnny Rougeau. The promotion was now the only one to have both French and English broadcasts in the province. One objective down . . . two to go.

October was a month of many debuts for André. Not only did he debut on French-language TV, but he also made his first appearances in both Quebec City and Toronto. The Queen City was an important step in André's career since the card drew 16,000 fans, the biggest crowd André had wrestled in front of at the time. Grand Prix was taking care of André. On that show, which was main-evented by Tiger Jeet Singh and the Sheik, Maurice and Paul Vachon and Yvon Robert Jr. were also wrestling, which meant that André wasn't left in a new English-speaking town all by himself. Frank Tunney was the promoter, and as difficult as it is to understand, he was not doing much with André, not promoting him like the Giant he was. André wrestled under the name Jean Ferré but wasn't advertised much. He was just a name on the card, in small characters, with his height and weight. All the publicity was around the Sheik, since he was the hottest ticket in town, with his undefeated streak at the Maple Leaf Gardens that had started in February 1969. André wrestled there four times between October 1971 and January 1972, always in front of big crowds; he won every match and then disappeared from the city for almost two years. Shortly after his first trip to Toronto, André went back to the U.S. but not for the AWA. Because the state of Vermont shares a border with the province of Quebec and it's near where the Vachons grew up, Grand Prix promoted a show in Burlington. Using the name "Giant" Jean Ferré, André even met with the mayor, who tried to compare the size of his hand with André's hand. Vermont ended up being a regular stop for the group.

In the meantime, Paul Vachon was working hard to achieve his promotion's goals. The Montreal Athletic Commission didn't want to give Grand Prix Wrestling a license until they were able to secure dates at the Forum, and in a catch-22 situation, the Forum didn't want to give any dates to Grand Prix before it got a license. Retired from the ring but still in charge of his promotion, Johnny Rougeau didn't like having any opposition, and he had found a way to make his influence felt with the athletic commission. Since wrestling is always about timing, when Grand Prix was starting, former captain and Montreal Canadiens legend Jean Béliveau retired and took on the job of vice-president and director of public relations for the Canadiens. When Paul Vachon realized that the MAC was protecting Johnny Rougeau's promotion, he went to meet with Béliveau, whom he knew, and Béliveau got him dates at the Montreal Forum. The MAC had no other choice but to allow Grand Prix to promote shows in Montreal. The first show was scheduled on December 15, 1971. It was the first time Paul Vachon was featured as a promoter in the newspaper's ads. To make sure it was a great night, the Vachons called their friends and stacked the card: Carpentier against Dick the Bruiser; Mad Dog Vachon versus Verne Gagne; Baron von Raschke teaming with Blackjack Mulligan; plus Don Leo Jonathan, René Goulet in his debut for Grand Prix, and many others. There were eight matches in total, and André made his debut at the Montreal Forum against Ivan Koloff, a slap in the face for All Star since the Rougeaus had come up with the Russian gimmick for Koloff several years prior. Moreover, Koloff and Johnny Rougeau held the record for the biggest wrestling attendance at the Forum from November 1968. Now well connected with the front office, Grand Prix's event was even advertised during the hockey games at the Forum the week prior. Unfortunately for Grand Prix, a mix of rain and snow hit the city that day, and only 5,311 fans attended.

Attendance in Quebec City at the Coliseum, on the other hand, was growing. After the group's debut on September 26 with 7,000 fans, it drew 7,000 more in November and 9,200 in December, the latter two shows featuring André in the main event. The December show was the first time André teamed with Édouard Carpentier in Quebec City to face the Vachon brothers. The same pair-up had happened only once before, on June 29, in Verdun but it would happen a lot in the following years. Although Carpentier had points in the company, he wasn't always easy to work with, and sometimes he put his own business ahead of the company's interests. He had left Rougeau to become relevant again in the ring and was now seeing another Frenchman get all the attention. The best thing he could do was to stick to André like glue. However, André and Carpentier versus the Vachons saw the four biggest names in the company working together. Plus, André and Carpentier were a natural team since they were both from France.

"At the beginning, we were careful in front of Jean not to talk about Carpentier," remembered Paul Leduc. "But it's like the Giant realized it and started to keep a distance from Carpentier." Added Paul Vachon, "I wouldn't call André a friend of Carpentier since, like all of us, he wasn't too fond of him."

In the HBO documentary, Shane McMahon says, "André started very small. He started in small towns performing in front of 10 people, 100 people, 300 people, and by the time he made it to my grandfather's territory, which was the northeast, then you had made it all the way to the big time." But that's a completely false narrative. Montreal, Quebec City, Minneapolis, Toronto, Paris, and Tokyo were no small towns and André wrestled regularly in front of thousands of fans in 1971 and 1972.

Before the end of the year, André made another debut, this time in Detroit, Michigan. Detroit had been the Sheik's town ever since he acquired a promotion there in the mid-1960s, producing shows at the Cobo Arena. But 1971 seemed to be a good year to start an opposition in the established territory, and Dick the Bruiser and Wilbur Snyder began their own promotion using the Detroit Red Wings' home, the Olympia. Because Bruiser was close to the Vachons, he asked for André for his holiday special on December 27. What's notable about that appearance is the name he was given: the Polish Giant! This was coming off the heels of a campaign to reduce anti-Polish jokes in the U.S. in the fall of 1971. Detroit was chosen as the target city since they had one of the largest Polish-American populations in the United States at an estimated 400,000. Playing on André's mother's heritage, it was only fitting to have a giant hero from Poland. He was billed at seven foot four and 460 pounds (again demonstrating that his advertised weight wasn't consistent at all).

Another thing that helped the Giant's career was Paul Vachon syndicating his television show. Thanks to him, and because CFCF didn't own Grand Prix tapes, Grand Prix TV was broadcasted from coast to coast in Canada. If he wanted to run a show one day in another province, his promotion would have already been exposed to fans. And since the money was in house shows and not TV ratings, he wasn't ruffling the feathers of the other promoters running in Canada like Frank Tunney in Toronto, Verne Gagne in Winnipeg, Stu Hart in Calgary, or Gene Kiniski in Vancouver. As a matter of fact, Kiniski and Tunney had also done the same thing. But not every promotion was doing so. For example, All Star Wrestling's tapes in Montreal didn't belong to the Rougeaus but to Channel 10. So Rougeau's wrestling could be seen across the province of Quebec, but there was no reason for Channel 10 to send the tapes to another province. That said, aside from Ottawa and Cornwall, Ontario; Plattsburgh, New York; and Burlington, Vermont; Grand Prix never extended to the west or the east. Before André had started wrestling across the country, he had already been seen everywhere.

By the end of 1971, the war between Grand Prix and All Star was in full swing, analogous to, in many ways, the famed Monday Night Wars between WCW and WWF in the 1990s. Talent switched sides, got better payoffs, and more than a million fans watched each show. In 1972, the rivalry reached its highest point, and even the newspapers started covering it. Eventually, it became personal. "Where were they when Bob and I were building this business back in 1965, 1966, and 1967?" said Johnny Rougeau to the *Montreal Gazette*. "Now that it's profitable, they want to come in and take over." To which Paul Vachon answered, "They didn't pay us enough," talking about the time both Vachons were working for Rougeau. "We had to exile ourselves to make a living." But even in 1971, All Star Wrestling started to respond to Grand Prix and especially its tallest star. When André came back from France, his first match was scheduled on Tuesday, October 5, in Verdun against Paul Vachon. That very same day, All Star made an announcement in the newspapers: the following Monday the group would present the first battle royal in the history of the Montreal Forum. A battle royal was among André's specialties since arriving in Montreal, so the timing of the maneuver was clearly to counter André's return. If just a few fans were going to save their dollars to go to the Forum instead of the Auditorium, it would be mission accomplished. André had become a threat to All Star. "The popularity of Jean Ferré was *the* thing that made this feud," said Gilles Poisson.

On that same October 5 card, former Montreal territory two-time champion Don Leo Jonathan made his return to Montreal. Jonathan, who had wrestled regularly in Montreal back in the 1950s, was coming back after five years. He made his debut for Grand Prix on the promotion's first card at the Coliseum in Quebec City on September 26. "I was working in New Brunswick for Emile Duprée during the summer when Paul Vachon contacted me," the "Mormon Giant" remembered. "He needed someone to work with André. He had no one of his stature to work with him. I had heard of André, but I hadn't seen him yet."

Upon his return, Jonathan was pitted against Carpentier in the main event in a best-of-three-falls match. With the match tied at one each, André saw his friend in trouble and came to the rescue of Carpentier, therefore disqualifying Carpentier. Jonathan won the match, laying the groundwork for the feud between the two behemoths. On November 23, still in Verdun, André was appointed as special referee for a match between Jonathan and Blackjack Mulligan. It was a slow build, but Vachon and Grégoire wanted to take their time. Grand Prix returned to the Forum on January 12. The Giant won his match, but it wasn't his biggest contribution to the show. The main event was a rematch between Jonathan and Carpentier, this time for Carpentier's title. Near the end, in a replay of what happened in October, André intervened in favor of his friend and fellow countryman. He attacked Jonathan and threw him to the outside. The champion was disqualified. Even though Jonathan won the match, he had just lost his chance of winning the title since a title cannot change hands on a DQ or a count-out. The show drew 11,187 fans, the biggest crowd in the short history of the promotion.

At the same time, Paul Vachon was getting more and more calls about André. Verne wanted him back . . . Bruiser wanted him back in Detroit . . .

André was known by a variety of names when he wasn't in the Montreal territory. Upon returning to Detroit in January, he was called "The Polish Giant" Rousanoff. A week later in Minneapolis, he was André, the Giant Frenchman (the closest thing to André the Giant he was called at the time). Detroit especially had a real struggle with his last name. In the early 1970s, when a newspaper published an article in the lead-up to a card, or when it reported the results afterward, there wasn't always a journalist reporting from the scene. Most of the time, the promoter or someone in his organization dictated news releases over the phone to someone at the news desk at the local paper. (For this reason, many of these news items weren't signed.) In such press releases taken down over the phone and even in the promotion's posters, accuracy wasn't too important: Rousanoff, Rosimov, Rosanoff, Rusinoff — everything but the correct spelling.

There was so much demand for André that he left the territory for the whole month of February and then again for a two-month tour in Japan at the end of March. He also worked in Ottawa, Canada's capital;

Grand Prix had decided to take over this abandoned wrestling town. Montreal's Eddie Quinn had run the town during his day, then Toronto's Frank Tunney ran it in the 1960s. But since 1968, no promoter was putting on regular shows there, Johnny Rougeau favoring Hull, Quebec, just on the other side of the river separating Ontario and Quebec. Grand Prix brought wrestling back to Ottawa on January 31 and put most of its publicity efforts into André and his match with Paul Vachon. The card drew a respectable 3,700 fans. The next night in Verdun, they did an injury angle where Poisson and his friend Zarinoff Leboeuf attacked André with chairs, providing the fans with a reason why André would miss the next month of action.

Steve Rickard was a wrestler who also promoted in New Zealand. He was a friend of the Vachons and had wrestled for Grand Prix during his Canadian and American tours in the summer and fall of 1971, including a match against André in Toronto in November. Rickard asked Grand Prix about bringing André on tour in New Zealand. Rickard already knew about André prior to his time with Grand Prix. Back in 1969 when the Giant was wrestling in England, New Zealander journalist Dave Cameron was on assignment there. When he saw André, he immediately wrote to Rickard. Rickard told him to get his address and see if he could come over. Unfortunately, Cameron was not able to catch André before he ended his stay there. So when Rickard was in Montreal, he didn't miss his opportunity. "He's the biggest man I've ever seen in my life, the only true giant I've set eyes upon," Rickard told the *New Zealand Sports Digest* back in 1972. "When I first saw him, it looked like the side of a building was coming toward me!" Over there, André was compared in height to Sky Hi Lee and in weight to Emile Czaja, a Hungarian native wrestling under the name of King Kong, who mostly wrestled in Asia and Oceania and who was sold as being more than 400 pounds. André wrestled in all the main cities like Auckland, Christchurch, and Wellington. The latter was Rickard's town, and his All Star Pro-Wrestling was the biggest promotion in the country at the time. Billed as "The Giant" Jean Ferré, André was a big hit at the box office. He wrestled in singles matches, tag team matches, and even three-on-two handicap matches mostly against locals, including Rickard himself. In Wellington, Rickard, who had a station wagon, was André's driver. He had the back seat removed and installed a mattress so André could stretch out on the road.

One of the most famous stories about André's time in New Zealand happened at a Chinese restaurant. "He started off with a plateful of scallops, tossing them back like a handful of peanuts," described Cameron. "Two bowls of soup were followed by his first order of pork chow mein. Chinese food fills most people quickly, but André ordered seconds of chow mein and then ripped into a large rump steak with French fries, onions, eggs, and tomatoes. Peaches and ice cream came next, the lot washed down with two bottles of Coca Cola and two cups of coffee."

Another story involved a game of pool. "Locals in the hotel invited me to participate in a game of pool," recalled writer John Mancer, who was asked to take care of André in the city of Palmerston North. "Jean indicated that he did not play but was content to watch. I potted a ball and left the white at the other end of the table. I searched for the jigger, but Jean indicated that I should take up my stance in the usual manner. Then, without so much as a grunt, he lifted me clean off my feet by one hand on the seat of my trousers and the other on my neck. There I was able to play my 'aerial' shot as he held me over the table! Both feet off the ground is a penalty in pool playing, but none of my opponents bothered to protest. They were doubled up with laughter at our tableau."

André stayed in New Zealand for two weeks and enjoyed his time with the Kiwis. "It is natural that a man of his proportions is regarded as a freak, but he said he found New Zealanders, on the whole, took him into their homes and were more friendly than any other nationalities he has encountered around the world," wrote Mancer. Before coming back to Montreal, André gave himself a little vacation as he spent a few days in Tahiti, a part of the French Polynesia which in 1972 was fully controlled by France. He then continued his way from Tahiti to the United States' west coast, literally traveling around the world.

MONSTER ROSHIMOFU

EVEN IN JAPAN, THE SPELLING WAS AN ISSUE.

EARLY ON IN THE UNITED STATES, NO ONE SEEMED TO UNDERSTAND HOW TO SPELL HIS NAME.

ANDRÉ LIKED TO PLAY RIBS . . . AND BE ON THE RECEIVING END TOO!

ANDRÉ HOLDING THE MONTREAL EXPOS' JOHN STROHMAYER, JOE GILBERT, WHILE MIKE TORREZ TRIES SOME KUNG-FU.

WHEN THE AIRLINE LOST ANDRÉ'S GEAR IN JAPAN, NO ONE HAD A PAIR OF BOOTS THAT FIT.

His first match back was supposed to be in Ottawa on March 9, but what was said to be flight problems coming from the west coast kept André from performing alongside Carpentier against the Vachons. It was reported that 24 of the 3,400 fans in attendance asked for a refund. The previous show, without André, had drawn 2,000 fans. On his first match back, on March 14 in Verdun, the main event of André and Carpentier against Mad Dog Vachon and Don Leo Jonathan drew a sell-out crowd of 5,000 people, with many being turned away, the biggest crowd yet at the Auditorium. The feud between André and Jonathan kept going. In the third and final fall of the match, André, pissed off because he had lost the second fall, threw some hard punches to Jonathan's nose, making him bleed. Vachon came to the rescue, and the match was called a no-contest. A week later, on March 20, Grand Prix held its biggest show ever, when 15,232 fans showed up to the Coliseum in Quebec City to see the Vachons fighting Carpentier and André. The very same night at the Forum, All Star drew a little over 10,000. André was really moving numbers.

"I have seen fathers bringing their sons to see the Giant. They weren't wrestling fans, they had never been to the matches, but they wanted to bring their sons to see the Giant. Everyone wanted a piece of him, even Channel 10, where All Star aired," recalled Paul Leduc. "I do think he was a great help in accelerating the whole process," said Paul Vachon. "It gave us something no one else had, especially All Star. He was great to help develop business since every town wanted to feature the Giant."

And Vachon brings up a good point. All Star was losing momentum and didn't have a novelty like the Giant. "First of all, you need to know that Johnny Rougeau was mad at his right-hand man, Bob Langevin," revealed Paul Leduc. "Bob knew about André before he came to Grand Prix but never told Johnny about him. He was a good friend of Frank Valois and had met the Giant in France. When the Giant was here working for Grand Prix, they would have dinner together on Crescent Street. Johnny didn't know about that, but I knew!" Speaking for All Star

Wrestling, Jacques Rougeau Sr. blamed the people behind Grand Prix more than the Giant for how hard the new promotion hit them.

"The creation of Grand Prix really hurt us because they had so many contacts in the U.S., they were able to get very good wrestlers," recalled Rougeau Sr. "We never tried to sign the Giant away from Grand Prix. He was close to Frank Valois and Valois was close to the Grand Prix people, so we would have tried for nothing."

André was named rookie of the year in 1971 by the *Victory Sports Series Wrestling* magazine, one of Stanley Weston's magazines. Not even taking into consideration what André did in Japan that year, the magazine based its choice on the impact he had in Montreal, calling him "perhaps the greatest French grappler since Édouard Carpentier" in the four-page story, the first big article he had in an American wrestling magazine.

To counter André's effect, Johnny had a plan of his own. "Johnny was telling me he had two guys who would make the fans forget about the Giant," remembered Gino Brito. "He was talking about the McGuire twins." Billy and Benny McGuire (their real surname was McCrary) were twin brothers who had started wrestling in 1972 and who were known for being very heavy. The Guinness World Records confirmed in November 1978 they were the world's heaviest twins, with a combined weight of 1,466 pounds. But they were not known to be good in the ring. "Johnny and I didn't always see eye to eye and I told him he didn't know what he was talking about," continued Brito. "I told him they were just a one-and-done gimmick and that the Giant, with his agility, had the potential to draw money." And Brito was right. The twins never drew a dime for Rougeau. Ironically, after the death of Billy in 1979, Benny would occasionally team with André.

The Coliseum was going to be Grand Prix's stronghold, even more so than the Forum, and Grand Prix was gaining more and more ground over All Star, even surpassing it at some points. The Leduc brothers had left All Star for Grand Prix in February 1972, and with guys like Jonathan, Billy Two Rivers, Carpentier, the Vachons, the lady wrestlers including Vivian Vachon, and André, they had the momentum going for them. Grand Prix was just about ready to take the lead in the province of Quebec.

Montreal wasn't the only place where André's momentum built. He left for Japan at the end of March 1972 for an eight-week tour. When André arrived, his luggage had not. So for his first match of the tour against Don Leo Jonathan, a 20-minute draw, André borrowed tights from Thunder Sugiyama, who was only five foot 10 but 275 pounds, and André wrestled barefoot for the first and only time. The line-up of wrestlers working during that tour was a good one, including someone André was feuding with in Canada.

"Nineteen seventy-two was amazing," remembered Koji Miyamoto. "Roussimoff, Don Leo Jonathan, Baron von Raschke, George Gordienko, Horst Hoffman — unbelievable roster." It was the fourth edition of the IWA World Series, and fans and experts didn't know who would win. "Maybe Jonathan, maybe Gordienko, maybe Hoffman, but Roussimoff went to the final," explained Miyamoto. For the second consecutive year, André had made it to the final of the tournament. The story wasn't whom he defeated to get there but whom he would face in the main event. In 1971, Strong Kobayashi had missed the tournament because he was working in the United States for the AWA. But in 1972 he had come back to his native land and picked back up where he had left off in 1970 on André's first tour in the country. They wrestled one another a ridiculous number of times, mostly in tag team action. Most of those matches saw André win the second fall by pinning Kobayashi, with Kobayashi coming back to win the third fall with his submission move, the Boston Crab. And, of course, Kobayashi body slammed him again. However, in the final, André was protected. He won the first fall with his Tombstone but was then disqualified and counted out, in a 37-minute match. Kobayashi, after losing in the finals against Billy Robinson in 1970, became the first Japanese competitor to win the tournament. Yoshihara was without a doubt building the company around him. André had become the second outsider to make it to the final two years in a row, and he participated in some classic matches during the tour.

"His peak in Japan was 1972," said Miyamoto. "He had a 20-minute draw against Jonathan and a 23-minute match against Baron von Raschke. Those were great matches. That's when he hit his peak, in my opinion. Even if people didn't know wrestling, they knew Roussimoff. The next day, they would say, 'Did you see Roussimoff last night?'" He had become water-cooler talk.

During that tour, André rekindled his friendship with French promoter Roger Delaporte and made sure to help another friend, Mighty Inoue, one more time. "In April 1972, André invited me to Montreal, Canada," said Inoue in a Japanese wrestling program. "I went there. My partner was Mitsu Arakawa. He was a bad man. He treated me bad. But that was not a failure on the part of André. He tried to help me in Montreal." Inoue only stayed from May to October before going back to Japan.

Around that time, André finally moved into his own apartment in Montreal, on the corner of Sherbrooke and Berri. Lucien Grégoire got him the place: he lived in the same apartment building. It was the perfect home for André because it was almost like a hideout. The apartment was on the 17th floor and had a huge 35-foot balcony, where André could get some fresh air with an incredible scenic view of Mount Royal. He had a king-sized bed, and at its foot, a double bed was placed the other way around to create a bed long enough for him. It was an identical set-up to what he had at the Windsor. Later, he got a round bed large enough for him. But the real asset of the apartment was the location. It was not accessible like a regular house, and André never had to leave by the main entrance. The building, still in existence today, connects with the Sherbrooke metro station, and from there, André could get to Grand Prix's office at the old Palais du Commerce. He was in such high demand that interviews were being conducted at the office and not at André's place. Also, there was a tavern on the bottom floor of the apartment building, which he could access without going outside. Downtown Montreal is known for its Underground City — its many underground connections between buildings. So André could go out on his balcony without being disturbed, and he could go to the office or have a beer without having to go outside, which was very practical during the cold Montreal winters. Since everyone wanted to see him or talk to him, it was almost like the perfect home, his own cave, adapted to his reality. "That's why we chose that place. Yvon Robert Jr. had something to do with it as well," recalled Paul Vachon. However, soon enough, André was inviting some of his friends to his apartment for dinners and parties.

While André had been away in Japan, Paul Vachon and Grand Prix had been busy preparing their biggest show ever — one that would make or break them. They were about to leave their mark on the history of Quebec wrestling. And André would be a big part of it.

CHAPTER 10

MATCH OF THE CENTURY, NAME OF THE DECADE

Grand Prix had gained momentum in its war with All Star, but that didn't mean they could rest on their laurels. The group had won Quebec City, but the Montreal Forum was not going to be easy to conquer. Since running the arena for the first time, Grand Prix had held three more Forum shows, drawing an average of 12,780 fans. The latter two events didn't have André on the card since he was abroad. In the other corner, All Star was not doing well at the Forum. Since December 1971, All Star's attendance was on the downslope. The group drew 14,900 fans in December 1971, 10,284 in March 1972, then 9,588 in April and 7,783 on May 15, for an average of 9,218 fans. It was time for Grand Prix to hit hard and fast.

Grand Prix needed to put that last nail in All Star's coffin and the main event to do it was easy to book: Jean Ferré versus Don Leo Jonathan, on May 31, 1972, at the Forum, exactly one year after André's arrival in Montreal. It was a feud they had been building for a long time. "Jonathan was happy to work with the Giant," explained Paul Vachon. "They had good chemistry, so it made sense. We had a good feeling about it from the start." However, the right match doesn't necessarily make for a good crowd. So Grand Prix made a deal with Channel 12 which gave them a percentage of the gate in return for seemingly endless commercials for the match. "It came out three or four times an hour with an action-packed 20-man battle royal announcement that included André the Giant, [with] all the other 19 wrestlers trying without success to throw the Giant over the top rope," wrote Vachon in his memoirs. "That commercial came with such regularity that for me it was embarrassing."

The match also needed a name that fans would remember. Inspired by the previous year's match between Muhammad Ali and Joe Frazier, which was called the Fight of the Century, they called it the Match of the Century, a catchy phrase good in both languages as in French it became le Combat du Siècle. But Vachon and his crew were not done yet. "Also for about eight weekly television programs of Grand Prix Wrestling, whenever anybody had an interview to talk about their upcoming matches, I had them comment about the Match of the Century, and everybody would say they would not miss it for the world," recalled Paul Vachon. In the newspapers, there was also a tale of the tape, with both opponents' stats such as height, weight, age, and much more. The Giant was billed at his regular seven foot four, 402 pounds, while the "Mormon Giant" was sold at six foot seven and 305 pounds. This was more than enough to make people want to see this match live. Ticket prices were increased. At the Forum show in April, general admission tickets were $2, while reserved seats were $3 to $5. For the Match of the Century, general admission was $3 and reserved seats were $5 to $10.

André versus Jonathan was the match everyone wanted to see, but the rest of the card was solid. Édouard Carpentier and Yvon Robert Jr. were up against Maurice Vachon and Rapapapotski (the usual replacement in Montreal, since Paul Vachon as the promoter couldn't wrestle), the Leduc brothers versus Baron von Raschke and Black Jack Mulligan, Gilles "The Fish" Poisson and Zarinoff Leboeuf against the Hollywood Blonds. Also booked were Billy Two Rivers and Johnny War Eagle against Mitsu Arakawa and Mighty Inoue, Tarzan Tyler against René

Goulet, Jackie Wiecz versus Ricco Garcia, and Reggie Parks against The Destroyer for a total of eight matches.

Of course, the match was hyped as the first time André had to wrestle someone almost his size. It was far from the truth, but it was the first singles match between the two in Montreal, and as in any other territory at the time, if it didn't happen in Montreal, it had never happened at all. Now that everything had been done to promote the contest, the match had to deliver.

The match had a slow build and was a clean bout — for the most part. An interesting fact is that in that match, the Giant was body slammed for the very first time inside the Forum. Then Jonathan hit André with a knee in the mid-section and rammed his head into the steel ring post. As André started bleeding, Jonathan kept punching him with his closed fists, until the referee, Omer Marchessault, told him to stop. André came back to life and snapped. He ran toward Jonathan and wrapped his huge hands around his neck, strangling his opponent. He did that four times, and on the last occasion, the referee had no other choice but to ring the bell. André had lost by disqualification — but André refused to let go, and it took all of the locker room to separate André from his victim. The perfect finish to set up a rematch. The show drew 16,164.

"The angle had worked very well, better than we expected," recalled Don Leo Jonathan. Almost three weeks later, in Quebec City, André and Jonathan had their first rematch. Curiously, the match didn't draw well. Only 8,000 showed up. And even though the first match took place in Montreal, it was still built up in Quebec City. The Sunday before the Match of the Century, André had made his return in the province after his tour in Japan by refereeing a match between Carpentier and Maurice Vachon. The match, in front of 10,000 fans, was a bloody mess in which André and Jonathan both interfered. On June 5, a tag match between André and Carpentier against Vachon and Jonathan only drew 8,000 fans. It was announced the next day that Quebec City would have its own version of the Match of the Century and that ticket prices would not be increased, a sign of appreciation to the fans there. While the

TONY LANZA

PAUL VACHON IS KEEPING THE PEACE BETWEEN ANDRÉ AND DON LEO JONATHAN BEFORE THE
MATCH OF THE CENTURY.

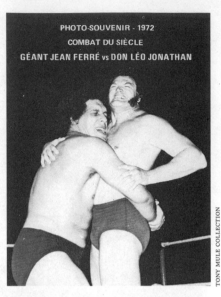

THE TALE OF THE TAPE IS STILL TELLING THE STORY OF THAT MATCH.

THE MATCH THAT HELPED HIM GET BOOKED IN NEW YORK.

ANDRÉ AND HIS BOSS, PAUL VACHON, IN CHICAGO, THE FIRST TIME HE WAS CALLED ANDRÉ THE GIANT.

match didn't draw half of what it did in Montreal, it was a nasty affair. The ropes broke, and in all the pandemonium the match caused, both André and Jonathan used them as a weapon. André won by disqualification this time, leaving the series one-all. History would show that Quebec City worked better with the Vachons-Leducs feud on top, followed by André-Jonathan.

In the meantime, All Star Wrestling finally found the key to large attendance at the Forum: the return of Johnny Rougeau. A year after retiring to take care of his junior hockey team, Rougeau was back. It was summertime, and junior hockey was on break. On June 12, Rougeau and the Sheik drew 15,000 fans to the Forum. Nevertheless, Grand Prix came back to the Forum two weeks later and drew nearly 13,000 fans for a double main event consisting of Carpentier against Maurice Vachon, and André with Yvon Robert Jr. versus Blackjack Mulligan and Jonathan. Then, on July 3 in Quebec City, not only was the crowd much larger, but the 15,000 fans in attendance witnessed something no one expected to see: André on a stretcher! The main event was a six-man tag between the Vachons and Jonathan against André, Carpentier, and Robert Jr. Attacked in the third fall by the three heels, André was left lying in the ring and then stretchered to the back. The next day, the newspapers had photos of André looking weak and beat up for the very first time. To add to the drama, it was said that he was brought to the nearest hospital. The rematch 10 days later drew 16,000 fans, the biggest crowd at the Coliseum (and today's second-biggest ever). These two shows were the first of eight consecutive 13,000-plus crowds in Quebec City. Even the rematch between Johnny Rougeau and the Sheik in Quebec City could not compare to the success Grand Prix had there. While the main Grand Prix feud was between the two sets of brothers (Vachons and Leducs), André was always prominently featured, whether it was a handicap match against the Hollywood Blonds or a six-man tag with his two favorite partners Carpentier and Robert Jr. versus Jonathan, Mulligan, and le Bourreau de Mongolie (Mongolian Executioner). In what would be a constant throughout his career, André never forgot his roots and his friends. Always looking for a big opponent, André brought The Executioner to Grand Prix. The so-called Mongolian was, in fact, Jean-Louis Breston, a six-foot-four 375-pounder from Belgium, who had worked with André (under the name Jean-Pierre Bustin) in France and in other countries in Europe.

If Grand Prix had taken over Quebec City decisively, back in Montreal, the return of Johnny Rougeau was giving them trouble. A month after his comeback, Johnny decided to run Jarry Park Stadium, home of the Montreal Expos. Stadium shows at the old Delorimier Stadium had been a big hit for Eddie Quinn years earlier, and Rougeau wanted to capitalize on his own momentum. And he did. On July 17, he drew 26,237 fans, the biggest wrestling crowd in the history of the province at the time, with the three Rougeaus on top: Johnny versus Abdullah the Butcher, Jacques versus the Sheik, and Raymond versus Don Serrano. A little more than two weeks later, Grand Prix fired back with the rematch between André and Jonathan. Since every promoter wanted the rematch of the Match of the Century, following the success of the first one, it was only natural Montreal and its Forum got it too.

"I got communications from all over the world, promoters wanting to book that match in their territories," wrote Paul Vachon in his book. In Ottawa, Grand Prix's third-biggest town, the feud between André and Jonathan spiked the attendance. On July 10, André teaming with Carpentier against Jonathan and Poisson drew 7,600 fans, an attendance record at the Civic Centre. Two weeks later, André and Jonathan drew 7,900 at the local football stadium.

On Wednesday, August 2, the rematch was scheduled at the Forum. Prices were back to normal, between $2 and $5, and the fans responded well, with 20,347 paying to attend. It was the biggest Forum wrestling crowd since a 1968 match between Johnny Rougeau and Ivan Koloff. When the Forum closed in 1996, it was still the fourth-biggest wrestling audience in the history of the venue. To the surprise of many, Jonathan won, this time clean. But after the match, a bloodied André lost all restraint and hit not one, not two, but three piledrivers on his opponent. The piledriver, the same move he used in Japan, was somewhat controversial because André had injured someone with it a few weeks prior.

On June 13, in between the two matches with Jonathan, André faced veteran wrestler Tarzan "The Boot" Tyler in Verdun. Tyler debuted in the late 1950s and had been around the block, including a run as WWWF tag team champion. At 45 years old and close to 300 pounds, he was back in Montreal for the first time in more than a decade. During the match, André was about to apply his finishing maneuver to Tyler, but the sweat on his hands and on his opponent's body made him drop Tyler on his head. For real.

André was not always easy to work with. You had to compensate for the size difference in everything you were doing. While someone like Gilles Poisson considered him to be a safe opponent, on the other hand, "Hangman" Neil Guay, another Quebecer, had a couple of incidents with André, similar to Tyler's, including one severe concussion. On both occasions, he blamed André's drinking. Either way, being in the ring with the Giant could be risky. "Sometimes, it was dangerous working with him," concluded Guay on the subject.

So many stories came out of that incident, from Tyler missing close to a year to André no longer using the piledriver. The reality is Tyler severely injured his neck. So much so that he had to cancel an IWE tour in Japan that was to begin on June 25. Although he wasn't out of action for anything like a year, he didn't wrestle in Montreal for a long time after the incident. He returned from his injury in August in Louisiana, and that's where he finished the year. In 1973, he wrestled in Atlanta; went to Japan alongside other Grand Prix wrestlers such as Mad Dog Vachon, Carpentier, and Poisson; and finally made his comeback in Montreal in September 1973. That's how the story of his year-long recovery was born. Because he only returned to Montreal a year later, in an era where news didn't travel like it does today, he was effectively out of action for 12 months. Tyler continued to wrestle until the early 1980s, when he became a manager in Montreal. He died in a car accident on Christmas

Eve, 1985. It should be noted that there's no record of him ever wrestling the Giant again.

"There was no animosity between the two," said Gino Brito. "Tyler was never the same after that, in the sense he didn't take big bumps, but at the same time, he was getting older." As for André, he kept using his piledriver, although later in the 1970s, he mostly used a boot to the face, followed by a splash as a finisher.

A month after the successful Forum event, Grand Prix came back with the third installment of the Ferré-Jonathan trilogy. The original idea wasn't to do three matches. That said, by the time the second match happened, the third one was already in preparation. To help promote the match, Grand Prix aired the first two on its broadcast in the weeks preceding the event. Yet, on September 7, 12,000 fans saw André's sole win in the series, a small crowd compared to the first two. A press conference at the Labatt Brewery was also organized the day before the event, to announce Wladek "Killer" Kowalski's big return to the Montreal Forum. "Killer" was the nickname he received when he ripped Yukon Eric's ear at the Forum in 1952. "It was my idea," said Paul Vachon. "Kowalski was the best heel in Canada." But it was too little too late. While hockey's Summit Series between Canada and U.S.S.R was getting a lot of attention from media and fans, drawing millions of people on television, another reason might also explain the smaller crowd. André had spent pretty much all of his summer of 1972 in the province of Quebec, mainly working against Jonathan in different kinds of matches, and it was becoming a negative rather than a positive for Grand Prix.

"The more he was getting booked in Quebec, the more his reach was shrinking," explained Paul Leduc. "You could have brought Elvis Presley here for a year and a half in the same venue, and you would have burned him out. The territory was too small; there wasn't enough population. You could do 10 different matches between the Leducs and the Vachons, but you couldn't do that with the Giant."

Still, he continued to primarily work for Grand Prix into 1973, with the only exceptions being matches he worked for the AWA or Dick the

Bruiser either in Chicago or Indianapolis. Chicago was where the event that changed the course of André's history in North America occurred: there, for the very first time, he was billed as André the Giant.

The Chicago Wrestling Club Inc., owned by Verne Gagne, Wilbur Snyder, and Dick the Bruiser, held a show on September 1 at Soldier Field, the newest home of the Chicago Bears. It was André's first time in the Windy City. Bruiser, who had booked him in Detroit, didn't want to use the Polish Giant name.

"Dick the Bruiser called to ask me about the Giant," remembered Paul Vachon. "He wanted to bring him to Chicago, and after we managed the financial side of things, he asked me about his name. I told him that it was le Géant Ferré. He seemed surprised and asked me, 'What do you really call him?' I told him that it was the name, le Géant Ferré. He asked me what it meant, and I told him that it simply meant Giant Ferré." It's important to mention here that Ferré in English can sound a lot like "fairy" instead of "feh-ray," as it is in French. "Bruiser laughed, saying we couldn't call him the 'giant fairy'! He asked me about his first name, and I told him it was André. He then said that he would call him André the Giant. As it happened, I went with the Giant to Chicago, and his very first match under the name André the Giant took place on September 1, 1972, in a handicap contest against Larry Hennig and me."

But wait, this is an André story, so it's not as simple as that sounds. Over the years, many have reported that this match actually happened on January 9, not September 1. The error resides in how the dates are written in French or English. In English, a date is typically written month/day/year. In French, it's usually the opposite, day/month/year. Therefore, the first of September (09/01), or 01/09 in French, becomes the ninth of January in some records. Also, according to Richard Vicek, who wrote Dick the Bruiser's biography, the Chicago Wrestling Club didn't advertise shows in newspapers. So, there are no advertising clippings for the show with André the Giant on the bill in circulation. In the *Wrestling Monthly* magazine report of the show, André was called André "Rousimoff" or "The Giant." Perhaps this is an indication that he was called André the Giant in the arena that night. In the October issue of the *Chicago Wrestling* program, he was only called "The Giant." In October, in Green Bay, Wisconsin, a Verne Gagne AWA town, the newspaper referred to him as "André (The Giant) Roussimoff." However, in the fall of 1972, whether it was in Minneapolis, Detroit, or Indianapolis, he was never referred to as "André the Giant," at least not in any newspaper. Yet, the story holds enough ground to likely be true. Also, Paul Vachon never wavered on the story and he was there that night. When asked, Larry Hennig didn't remember that particular match, let alone what name André used.

From all reports, people thought André was very impressive in his Chicago debut. At one point, after he threw Hennig in the corner, the third rope broke, giving the illusion that André's strength was even more incredible. But according to Vachon himself, he had made a mistake during the match. "Larry was really impressed with André's size," recalled Vachon. "To rib him a little, I bet him I was going to slam him. Larry laughed at me and took the bet. In the ring, I told André in French, 'I bet my partner I could body slam you.' He laughed out loud, and he said, 'Yes, boss.'" Fatefully, Vachon had made a joke to André upon his arrival in Montreal, telling him not to get slammed by anyone but him. Soon enough, Vachon would regret it. "It was a mistake," admitted Vachon. "Later on, I felt like a fool for letting my personal feelings get in the way of what we could do with him. It didn't help business and proved nothing. That said, it didn't seem to affect things as they would build his career on the body slam." Actually, in the match, André didn't sell the body slam, got right back on his feet, and gave Paul a body slam of his own.

Meanwhile, All Star Wrestling held a second show at Jarry Park Stadium but only drew 11,703 fans. The promotion was no longer using the Forum as much, and when they did, they drew poorly compared to Grand Prix. Slowly but surely, Grand Prix was transitioning its programming to center on a feud between André and another big man, Killer Kowalski. However, it didn't draw as well as Jonathan. Both main events at the Forum in November finished short of 10,000 fans. Still, 1972 was a hell of a year for Grand Prix. The group firmly established itself as number one in Quebec. Grand Prix ran 19 shows at the Coliseum compared to four for All Star, and 13 at the Forum compared to seven, and that's including the two shows at Jarry. Of those 32 shows, more than half had André in one of the main events, and they drew close to 400,000 fans.

It was a breakout year for André. In the province of Quebec, he truly became a superstar who was able to transcend the world of professional wrestling. He was a guest on many talk shows, even played in sitcoms, and hung out with local celebrities. He was talked about regularly in the TV listings and in the tabloids. Internationally, he landed his first magazine covers, the August 1972 edition of the *Wrestling Monthly* and the October 1972 edition of *Inside Wrestling*. In addition to that, he was the third-biggest draw in the entire world, only behind the Sheik and Pedro Morales, and ahead of legends like Dory Funk Jr., Killer Kowalski, and Bruno Sammartino.

Although his matches with Jonathan were the most seen of the year, according to some, they weren't necessarily the best. "The Giant and Jonathan were protecting each other in the match," said Paul Leduc. "He had much better matches that year with Maurice." Yet the rivalry between Jonathan and André was the Giant's highlight of the year. It was his first real program in North America and the match every promoter wanted to have. It put André on the wrestling map, more than he actually thought, and eventually opened doors for him.

"I ended up working with André everywhere," recalled Jonathan. "We wrestled in Texas, New Mexico, Washington State, Vancouver, Japan, and France. I would have liked to work with him in New York, but it never happened."

It's interesting that Jonathan mentioned New York. By that point, André had wrestled around the globe, but New York, just a six-hour drive from his new home in Montreal, hadn't been checked off his list . . . yet.

CHAPTER 11

IF I CAN MAKE IT THERE, I'LL MAKE IT ANYWHERE

Grand Prix had become known as a great wrestling promotion, especially after its breakthrough year of 1972. But internally, it was reportedly a mess. As the saying goes, too many cooks spoil the broth. You had the Vachon brothers on one side, and Yvon Robert Jr. and Édouard Carpentier on the other. It got to the point where Maurice Vachon was happy when his towns were doing better than Carpentier's, or vice versa, even though it was all the same money. André, who never liked disputes, was put in a position he didn't ask for. Although Carpentier was trying to stick to André's success as much as he could, André was much closer to Maurice.

"He never traveled with Carpentier," remembered Paul Leduc. "He didn't like Lucien Grégoire either because he made him feel like he was a circus animal or an alien. His real dear friend in the office was Maurice."

On some occasions, the miscommunications between the shareholders put the company in trouble. Some other times, as luck would have it, good things arose from the disputes. Around this time, promoter Abe Ford had proposed selling the Boston and New England wrestling territory to Grand Prix. Paul Vachon saw this as a great opportunity

— he had already considered expanding the organization outside of Quebec. He was all for striking a deal on the spot. Ford's asking price was $100,000, and Grand Prix had the cash on hand. But Yvon Robert Jr. countered there was no need to rush things. He wanted the Grand Prix partners to go over Ford's offer with a fine-tooth comb. As it turned out, he was right to be cautious: Ford didn't actually own the territory he was proposing to sell. Boston and New England actually belonged to Vince McMahon Sr. To smooth things out between WWWF and Grand Prix, McMahon invited the Vachon brothers down to New York to wrestle and to resolve the misunderstanding. The Vachons wrestled in Madison Square Garden on January 15, 1973, while Paul worked on forging a strong relationship with McMahon. That night, the Vachons and McMahon talked about the Giant. Vince Sr. had heard about André from the feud he had with Don Leo Jonathan in Montreal. The Vachons told him he should book André in his territory, even proposing that Vince should book him all over the country. McMahon was interested and made sure to bring André in shortly.

"We knew we couldn't use him full-time forever," admitted Paul Vachon. "Early on, he was still a novelty, and we could get away with it. It was much better to use him as an attraction as McMahon did. That's why we let him go because there was not much more we could do with him after he had been in Montreal a few years."

In addition to that, McMahon's territory was much larger than Grand Prix, as was its population. On March 24, 1973, André made his official debut for the World Wide Wrestling Federation in Philadelphia. You may have read that Carpentier, Valois, or Verne Gagne brought André to New York, but it was Paul and Maurice. Also, you may read that André's first match for McMahon was in 1972. The error comes from two different sources. On newspapers.com, there is an article from the *Lowell Sun* about André visiting the Boston Bruins locker room, dated January 2, 1973, which would mean André's visit was at the very end of 1972. But when you take a good look at the article, the date on the website is wrong, the actual newspaper says November 19, 1973. First problem solved. The second problem comes from early research done on André by fans and historians. They reported on some online messages boards that André had wrestled in White Plains, New York, on October 24, 1972. Yet, when you look at the advertising for the show, it says Wednesday, October 24. The problem is that in 1972, October 24 was a Tuesday. But it was a Wednesday in 1973. André didn't wrestle there in 1972, but in 1973, which makes more sense. Nothing is ever easy trying to figure out André's career!

Nevertheless, André started on March 24 at the old Philadelphia Arena in a handicap match against Vincente "Bull" Pometti and none other than his old friend from Paris, Frank Valois. Valois was still working in Europe and Africa, when the Giant had made his way to Montreal. Valois came back in the summer of 1972 and immediately joined Grand Prix. "The Giant told me six months before that my dad was coming back home," recalled Frank's daughter Françoise. "I hadn't seen my dad for five or six years."

André made his debut in the mecca of pro wrestling, Madison Square Garden in Manhattan, New York. MSG, the home of the New York Knicks and New York Rangers, is a mythical arena and was and still is a venue that every wrestler dreams about. In this case, MSG and its tenant, Vince McMahon's WWWF, were just as pleased to announce the arrival of André. At the February 26 show, there were posters hung on the walls advertising André's upcoming first appearance the following month, on March 26. The same poster hung at the Boston Garden the same day, announcing his presence for March 31. On the poster, in bold capital letters is the name André the Giant, probably the very first time McMahon used the name he would make popular worldwide. A sign there was some kind of transition between Grand Prix and WWWF, the photos used on the poster were the ones from Grand Prix, where you see André with Carpentier and Robert Jr. On the poster, he is billed as seven foot four and 424 pounds. For the March show, André was shown on the back of the monthly program. The story compared him to other tall guys. It said he was bigger than Primo Carnera and Gorilla Monsoon and taller than basketball players Wilt Chamberlain, Kareem Abdul-Jabbar, and Artis Gilmore. It also added that he had been recommended to McMahon by Carpentier and Valois — which is likely why some stories had them, or one of them, as integral to getting André to New York. Since the Vachons had brokered the deal, they were invited to be on the card as well, and they were put over the team of Curtis Iaukea and Louie Tillet. Valois also wrestled, losing against New Zealander Tony Garea, who also worked the Philadelphia show two nights earlier. "I had met André in New Zealand when he came to work there," recalled Garea. "I remember telling him, 'I'm going to the United States to wrestle this year, maybe I'll see you there.' I wasn't sure if he would ever remember me. So we were in Philadelphia, and he walked to the locker room, he spotted me and he walked right over and said, 'Hi Tony, how are you?' Oh man, he remembered me!"

As for André, he was pitted against Buddy Wolfe, a big guy at six foot one and 260 pounds, trained by Verne Gagne but with only a few years of experience. (Wolfe soon become the Vachons' brother-in-law, marrying their sister Vivian.) The match didn't last long, and Wolfe did a good job selling for André. The Giant had the advantage for most of the match, showing off his power by lifting Wolfe and sitting him on the top rope and also using some European uppercuts. The finish came with André hitting a body slam that turned into a backbreaker, followed by a big splash as Wolfe was lying on his back in the middle of the ring. After 7:46, André had won his first match at MSG in front of 19,000 fans. On March 31, André finished his first run for McMahon, working at the Boston Garden in front of 15,600 fans. After defeating Pometti, André wrestled in a battle royal, where, surprisingly, he was eliminated after everyone ganged up on him. Of course, Valois was working the show and the Leduc brothers were as well. When McMahon booked the Giant, the Vachons made sure some of their other guys also got booked. That's why Valois, the Leducs, and the Vachons themselves worked the territory that week.

And a week was all it took for Vince McMahon Sr. to offer a contract to André, to become André's agent. McMahon called Paul Vachon following that first week and made the deal. Grand Prix never received or asked for any money from that transaction. The only thing they got from the deal was that they didn't have to pay McMahon a percentage when booking the giant they had brought to North America. And they had one other condition: Frank Valois had to travel with André, as his road manager. If Grand Prix was to lose André, the people behind it wanted the best for him and wanted to protect him as much as they could. André's English wasn't good enough for him to travel alone and he needed someone to help him on the road. André and Valois had known each other for a long time, and Valois was a smart choice to accompany André for other reasons as well: he spoke English, French, and Quebec's French. Just as England's English is often quite unlike America's, France's French is different than Quebec's. The accent is different, and some expressions and words are as well. "Jean had to adapt to Quebec's French when he arrived here," said Paul Leduc. "Sometimes he would tell me, 'Paul, I do not understand!'" Plus, even though Valois was over 50 years old, he was still able to lace up his boots and get in the ring if André needed an opponent or if someone on the card needed to be replaced. McMahon, in fact, dealt with Valois most of the time he had dates for his newest protégé. McMahon booked André like the NWA booked its world champions, getting a percentage every time another promoter used his services. He was booked alike, but he was never used like the NWA champion, coming into a territory to make the local champion into an equal. That was not his role. It wasn't unheard of in pro wrestling for a promoter to take a percentage out of someone's booking. Eddie Quinn did the same thing with Carpentier when the latter first arrived in Montreal in 1956. McMahon himself had previously done it with guys like Antonino Rocca, Ricki Starr, and Bearcat Wright. The only difference between Rocca and André was the number of dates Vince needed him in his territory.

"McMahon made a fortune booking André elsewhere, whereas Rocca was more valuable to him in the NYC region because of the tremendous Hispanic audience," reflected wrestling historian Tim Hornbaker. It also kept the Giant fresh in McMahon's territory. Even

ANDRÉ ROUSSIMOFF, YOUNG AND READY TO CONQUER THE WORLD.

KARL GOTCH HAD A LOT OF RESPECT FOR ANDRÉ; THEY'RE SEEN HERE WHEN ANDRÉ WON THE IWA WORLD SERIES IN 1971.

ANDRÉ BATTLES DON LEO JONATHAN IN JAPAN IN 1972, BEFORE THEIR MATCH OF THE CENTURY IN MONTREAL.

THE UNDISPUTED "KING OF THE BATTLE ROYALS."

ANDRÉ VISITED THE BOSTON BRUINS LOCKER ROOM A FEW TIMES; HERE WITH TERRY O'REILLY AND NHL HOFAMER BOBBY ORR.

GRAND PRIX WRESTLING, REPRESENTED HERE BY FRANK VALOIS AND YVON ROBERT JR., HAD A GIANT OF A CAKE MADE ON ANDRÉ'S BIRTHDAY.

ANDRÉ WITH ANOTHER BIG MAN FROM MONTREAL, JOS LEDUC, WHO LOOKS LIKE A SMALL MAN NEXT TO HIM.

PAT PATTERSON, RENÉ GOULET, AND ANDRÉ HANGING OUT BACKSTAGE IN JAPAN.

SOME WOULD SAY VINCE MCMAHON SR. WAS LIKE A FATHER FIGURE FOR ANDRÉ.

ONE OF ANDRÉ'S SIGNATURE POSES: LIFTING SEVERAL WOMEN.

FRANK VALOIS WAS ALWAYS AROUND IN ANDRÉ'S EARLY DAYS ON THE ROAD.

ANDRÉ AND KILLER KOWALSKI HAD MANY ENCOUNTERS OVER THE YEARS.

WHEN BOXING MEETS WRESTLING: CHUCK WEPNER AND ANDRÉ IN 1976.

THE GREATEST OF ALL TIME, MUHAMMAD ALI, AND THE EIGHTH WONDER OF THE WORLD, ANDRÉ THE GIANT.

ANDRÉ VS. BRUNO SAMMARTINO: A MATCH THAT NEVER WAS.

ONE OF THE MOST ICONIC PICTURES OF ANDRÉ AS BIG FOOT WITH ACTOR LEE MAJORS.

IN JAPAN, ANDRÉ COULD NEVER FIND ANYTHING TRULY SUITABLE FOR HIS SIZE.

BEYOND HIS HEIGHT, ANDRÉ'S PROPORTIONS WERE WHAT MADE HIM A GIANT.

ANDRÉ AT HIS BROTHER'S WEDDING. FROM LEFT TO RIGHT: JACQUES, MAURICETTE, HÉLÈNE, AND ANTOINE.

ANDRÉ'S RELATIONSHIP WITH VINCE MCMAHON JR. HAD ITS UPS AND DOWNS OVER THE YEARS.

AS YEARS WENT BY, ANDRÉ KEPT TRANSFORMING BECAUSE OF ACROMEGALY.

though it was bigger than Grand Prix's, he couldn't book André every month at the Garden, or in any other town. By loaning him for a week or two to another promoter, he was still making money without hurting the popularity of the Giant in his territory. It was a win-win situation for everyone involved. McMahon was making money; André was too, plus he could travel a lot more and meet new friends; and the promoters using him could make more money at the gate because of the attraction André was. Sometimes, if McMahon wanted a wrestler from another territory, he would call the promoter, ask about the guy he wanted, and in the conversation offer a choice of dates for the Giant. In retrospect, this is something Paul Vachon and Grand Prix should have done. "I had thought about signing the Giant exclusively," revealed Paul Vachon for the first time in a 2019 interview. "But I thought he would have been in a better position with McMahon. The best thing for him, really, was to be booked by the biggest booking office in the world. And I don't regret it."

André kept splitting his time between the WWWF and Grand Prix. He was back at MSG in April in front of a sell-out crowd of more than 20,000 fans. Although he was the main attraction, the main event of the card was WWWF champion Pedro Morales against Don Leo Jonathan. It was Jonathan's return to New York; he had not wrestled there in 17 years. And although the timing of it suggested he was brought in to wrestle André at some point, that match never happened, aside from a tag team bout at MSG a year later. Perhaps McMahon didn't want to redo what had already been done or thought the feud between the two had run its course.

Since it was summertime, André worked for the two territories that benefit the most from hockey's off-season, Quebec and the Maritimes. In New Brunswick, he was so hot that he was receiving three times his guaranteed pay by promoter Emile Duprée. The summer of 1973 was also when Grand Prix decided to respond to All Star's big show from the year before. They decided to book Jarry Park Stadium on July 14, almost a year to the date after the All Star show. The end result was a success. Mad Dog Vachon versus Killer Kowalski in the main event drew the biggest wrestling crowd ever recorded in the province of Quebec, with 29,127 fans

— a record that has yet to be broken. For André, things were a little more difficult. He was scheduled to wrestle Gilles "The Fish" Poisson, one of his most frequent opponents outside of Montreal. They had wrestled each other once at the Forum, a year earlier. Grand Prix had Poisson doing handicap matches on television for a number of weeks in preparation for the big confrontation built as the Giant against the Giant Killer.

"The Giant was very busy and would not come back to Montreal until the day before the show," wrote Paul Vachon. "We were okay with that, but the night of the show the athletic commission informed us that the Giant could not wrestle because his $1,500 license had expired. So I said, 'So what? Sell him another one.'

"For years, they had been giving out licenses to new wrestlers the night of the matches, renewals too. But for the Giant, that night they said no. 'Furthermore, since we have been hounding you for weeks that the Giant's license had expired and needed to be renewed, you cannot say to the crowd that the Giant cannot wrestle because of the athletic commission. If you do, we will cancel your promoter's license.'"

It was always thought, obviously never proved though, that All Star had something to do with the athletic commission's decision. Nevertheless, André and Poisson were both told to go to the ring, not to touch each other, and the ring announcer simply told the crowd that for a reason beyond Grand Prix's control, the match could not be held. Although the crowd was disappointed, the big draw of the card was Vachon and Kowalski, so no one asked for their money back. A month later, on August 11, Grand Prix ran a second show at Jarry, exactly like All Star did the year before, and the result was similar. All Star had only drawn 11,703 fans, less than half of what it had in July 1972. Grand Prix, with Mad Dog Vachon against Don Leo Jonathan, drew 12,383. That time around, André was able to work the show, his very first big stadium show, as he faced Professor Toru Tanaka, the same opponent he had encountered his second time at MSG. It also marked the last time Grand Prix drew more than 10,000 people on its own — there were so many problems behind the scenes that the company was struggling.

ANDRÉ LIKED TO RIDE A BIKE AS A KID AND GOT TO DO IT AGAIN WITH PAUL LEDUC.

IF YOU CAN MAKE IT TO THE MSG, YOU CAN MAKE IT ANYWHERE!

Géant JEAN FERRE. 7 pieds 4 pouces, des Alpes Françaises. 408 livres

ANDRÉ WAS CRUSHING HIS OPPONENTS.

ANDRÉ WITH FRANK VALOIS' DAUGHTERS: MICHELE AND FRANCOISE.

The Leducs had left in the spring. The Vachons were a few months away from selling their shares to promoter Tony Mule. And André would soon be gone too. He finished his dates in Quebec, which bridged him to the fall. On October 2, he wrestled at the Montreal Forum for the last time for almost two years, subbing for Bruno Sammartino alongside Carpentier against Poisson and Kowalski. To show how bad the situation was, the show only drew 6,000 fans. A week later, he wrestled his last show for Grand Prix, a six-man tag with Carpentier and the newly babyface Don Leo Jonathan against the Hollywood Blonds and Chuck O'Connor, a Kowalski trainee, who ended up being one of André's biggest rivals years later as Big John Studd.

Until the end of the year, André mostly wrestled for McMahon, touring his territory from Bangor, Maine, to Baltimore, Maryland, teaming more often than not with Chief Jay Strongbow. Although he was traveling with Frank Valois, the two of them were not always alone on the road.

"Some of the guys were saying, 'Who's going to drive with him?' They were a little bit discouraged because of his size, being in their car," recalled Tony Garea. "I told André to come with me. So Frank and André drove with me the first couple of years. I had a Ford LTD, it was a big car, and he fit in the front seat. I used him as my bartender: he opened my beers!"

Vince McMahon had sent André to Verne Gagne in September, but just for a day of taping. The first real territory McMahon sent André to was Texas, where he worked for two weeks in December. Frank Valois was not only there to make arrangements for him and wrestle from time to time, he was also taking care of interviews with reporters and journalists since André still struggled with English. And the story told in the *Austin American-Statesman* newspaper is just one example of what kind of job Valois was doing, perpetuating the many tales that would follow André for years to come. "Mr. Giant is on his first United States tour after wrestling in Europe for the last several years," wrote reporter Roy Mark. "We didn't come to the United States earlier because we didn't feel he was ready," answered Valois, who, according to Mark, didn't even turn to André to ask him anything. Of course, he already knew what to say, including the tale that he had yet to lose a match.

André closed out the year in Toronto, where he was featured in the main event for the very first time against another wrestler who had "never lost" — at least in Toronto. His match with the Sheik ended in a double count-out in less than three minutes in front of another sell-out crowd of 18,000 fans. The Sheik was wrestling's biggest draw at the time, and while André didn't have a year like he had in 1972, mainly because Grand Prix was winding down, he soon made up for lost time.

Almost as quickly as it began, André found himself at the end of a phase of his career. All Star Wrestling was back on track, and Grand Prix was, already, almost a thing of the past. The two companies produced joint shows in the first few months of 1974, but neither André nor the Vachons participated, depriving the fans of dream matches. Although Montreal was his home and where he continued to live when not on the road, André's days of wrestling full time in the province were over, and he didn't come back as a regular until the start of the new decade. Even then, it was not the same. Montreal and Grand Prix allowed André to become a well-known attraction throughout North America. They opened the doors to his Hall of Fame career. And even if he would always be known as Jean Ferré in Montreal, he was now André the Giant to the rest of the world; larger than life, he was the Eighth Wonder of the World . . .

CHAPTER 12

TRAVELING TO GREATNESS

Always trying to promote André in fresh ways, Vince McMahon Sr. adopted the expression "Eighth Wonder of the World" and by the start of 1974, the American press was using it regularly. In fact, Grand Prix Wrestling's ring announcer Fernand Ste-Marie had come up with the phrase for the promotion's English television shows and, like the name André the Giant itself, it was made way more popular by McMahon and his crew. It became so associated with André that 25 years later, woman wrestler Chyna was dubbed the ninth wonder of the world — because the number eight was already taken. Interestingly, André was not the only pro wrestler associated with the phrase, as Bobo Brazil and Pampero Firpo were called the same thing at some point in each of their careers. But the "Eighth Wonder of the World" really stuck with André. It became part of his gimmick, almost synonymous with his name. Another thing that McMahon wanted to refine was André's wrestling style. Gone were the days of dropkicks, something Paul Vachon tried to make him abandon as well. McMahon wanted him to wrestle like a giant. "André was doing dropkicks when he was up there in Montreal," explained Vince Jr. "Even though he could, why let him do dropkicks? He was very agile, very quick. I wouldn't say he had a lot of speed, but God he was quick."

With a new nickname and after working in new towns, new states, and new territories, André soon left for Japan, where he had not wrestled since 1972. The two biggest stars working for JWA in the late 1960s were Antonio Inoki and Shohei "Giant" Baba. As a tag team known as the B-I Cannon, they won the NWA International tag team title four times between 1967 and 1971. In singles competition, Baba was the more popular of the two. However, Inoki was growing as a singles draw, leading to an increase in television revenue that allowed the company to sign another TV deal. The promotion was already televised on the NTV network, and the new deal was with NET TV. To mollify NTV, JWA gave the station Baba exclusively, while NET got Inoki — it was akin to the brand split the WWE made decades later. Still, unhappy with how JWA was doing business and convinced it was doomed to fail, Inoki was arranging a coup alongside Baba. Many wrestlers were not happy with JWA management, Yoshinosato and Kokichi Endo, accusing them of managing the company for their benefit only. Wrestler Umanosuke Ueda suspected Inoki had been preparing a coup and ratted him out to the office. Inoki and Baba lost their tag team title to the Funk brothers on December 7, 1971, and on the 9th, Ioki was replaced in the main event spot against NWA World Heavyweight champion Dory Funk Jr. He was fired a few days later, while JWA convinced Baba to stay with the company. In January 1972, Inoki announced he was starting a new company called New Japan Pro Wrestling and held his first show in March. In August, Baba finally left JWA, and in October, he opened his own company as well, called All Japan Pro Wrestling. By April 1973, JWA had closed, leaving Japan with three major promotions: NJPW, AJPW, and IWE.

In 1974, Inoki, who didn't have access to NWA wrestlers since Baba was the one with the strongest relationship with the alliance, had to make deals for other performers. He liked André a lot and knew his value. "Inoki and his booker, Hisashi Shinma, had started to negotiate with McMahon to get André in August 1973 through [Los Angeles promoter] Mike LeBell," revealed Koji Miyamoto. "So it was a long negotiation, but Vince McMahon, in order to fulfill his working relationship with New Japan, sent André in 1974. Even Vince Sr. came to Japan for the very first time on that same tour. Then he sent a few top guys to every tour, but André was the first big one from Vince Sr. to New Japan." In the following years, guys like Stan Stasiak, Nikolai Volkoff, and Freddie Blassie (already a huge star in Japan) were sent to Inoki. It was the start of a long-term relationship between the two companies that grew stronger and stronger over the years. And although McMahon was part of the NWA, he was treated differently by then NWA president Sam Muchnick. He could do pretty much anything but proclaim the WWWF title as the World title. That's also why someone like AWA's owner, Verne Gagne, was able to work MSG in the early 1970s. "I think McMahon wielded an incredible amount of power and had great respect within the NWA," said Tim Hornbaker, the historian who has chronicled the inner workings of both the NWA and the WWF. "Even if he was doing something at odds with what other promoters were doing, I think it would have been overlooked to some degree. Also, McMahon was already booking André out to other NWA members. So it was financially smarter to work with him than drum up a grievance based on his other dealings."

So André, with Frank Valois, left for Japan for a four-week tour. It was the first time he was working under the moniker André the Giant in Japan, rather than Monster Roussimoff, and the first time he was working for New Japan. Aside from working tag team and handicap matches, the highlight of the tour was André's first singles match with Inoki himself. Near the end of the match, Valois, who was in the Giant's corner, pulled Inoki's left leg when they were battling in the corner and Inoki fell down on his back. Still a heel despite the name change, André covered him right away and got the pinfall in the 20-minute match. It wasn't surprising to see Inoki put over a foreigner the first time around. He had done the same against Karl Gotch, Tiger Jeet Singh, and John Tolos, although the latter two were by disqualification.

"For me, he is the strongest and toughest rival in the ring," Inoki said in a Japanese magazine. "But I could feel he accumulated basic wrestling skills in Europe, when he was in France. He knew a lot of skills that I learned from Karl Gotch when I was young. Basic skills are important, but most giant wrestlers are lacking in that regard. André is an exception I'd say."

That match near the end of the tour was the first step to an even bigger match. The very next night, Inoki teamed with Seiji Sakaguchi against André and Australian wrestler Lord Jonathan Boyd. That match led to a double main event on the last day of the tour. André was pitted against Sakaguchi. It was the first time these two had met in singles competition, and it was a big deal. Sakaguchi and Kintaro Ohki were the last two stars JWA had after Baba and Inoki left the company. However, as JWA was falling in popularity, Sakaguchi wanted to merge with New Japan, something Ohki didn't want. So in March 1973, Sakaguchi left JWA to join Inoki's promotion and ended up being very influential behind the scenes. Around the same time, NET started airing New Japan instead of JWA, marking New Japan's first TV deal.

At six foot five and 280 pounds, Sakaguchi was the right size for André. "I was a very big guy for a Japanese, but for André, I was just a medium-sized boy," Sakaguchi once said. In the other main event, Inoki was facing someone André knew pretty well, none other than Strong Kobayashi. In February 1974, unhappy with IWE's management staff, Kobayashi left the company and made arrangements to wrestle Inoki, since Inoki's gimmick was that he was willing to fight anyone. A big matchup between two Japanese wrestlers was something of a rarity back then. Usually, the top local stars were facing the outsiders. The match was dubbed "The Duel on Ganryu-Jima," reminding fans of an ancient battle between two sword masters from the 17th century. The double main event paid off and drew 16,500 fans to the old Sumo Hall, Kuramae Kokugikan, in Tokyo, the biggest New Japan crowd at the time.

André returned to North America and continued his routine, working different towns and different states through the spring, until going

ANTONIO INOKI IS NOT LETTING ANDRÉ TAKE ADVANTAGE OF HIS HEIGHT.

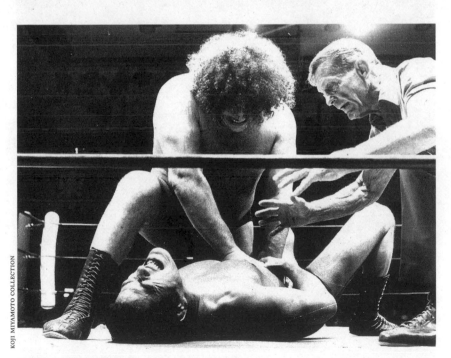

ANDRÉ AND INOKI WRESTLED MANY TIMES IN JAPAN.

ROGER BAKER

THE SHEIK AND ANDRÉ WRESTLED EACH OTHER A LOT IN THE 1970S.

back to Japan in June. But it wasn't for Inoki. Around that time, IWE lost its biggest star in Kobayashi, and the group also lost its TV deal with TBS. Trying to compete with New Japan, Yoshihara worked some joint shows with Baba, but that didn't last long. Somehow, André heard about IWE having a hard time and wanted to help. It didn't matter that IWE was competition to New Japan: André had enough influence to pull off working for competitors. And it's not like André working for IWE was going to turn its business upside down. Inoki wasn't going to risk losing André over that.

"My promotion was in big trouble after Strong Kobayashi suddenly jumped to New Japan," recalled Yoshihara. "André heard that fact somewhere, then called me from Montreal to hear about the actual situation from me directly. I was so surprised by what he did. In June 1974, for only five days, he came to IWE after a two-year absence. My money offer to him was not much, but he refused to take the pay. He said, 'I became a big star thanks to you. It is my time to pay you back.' André was such a nice guy." This generosity was trademark André. He never forgot who was there for him in his life and career. So André returned to Japan with Valois on June 25; he left again on July 2. He worked exclusively with IWE's top guys: Mighty Inoue, Animal Hamaguchi, and Rusher Kimura. But it meant the world to Yoshihara.

"After I came back to Japan though I wrestled him once in Hokkaido," remembered Inoue. "He took two or three of my moves. I mean, the timing on the bumps was hard because of his size, but he was very eager to work to his opponent's strengths. More European than American in that sense; Americans went right at you from the bell, but Europeans would take a few moves and shine their opponents first."

During that time, Kobayashi had left for North America after his match with Inoki but was brought back on December 12, 1974. That day was the last of another Japan tour for André, and Inoki wanted to recreate what had worked so well earlier that year: a match with Kobayashi. Just underneath the main event, André worked a tag match with Sakaguchi on the opposite team. The event drew a solid 10,000 fans. Following that show, Inoki and his crew left for a two-day tour in Brazil. Inoki had lived in Brazil with his family for a few years when he was a teenager, at the end of the 1950s. He was, in fact, discovered there by Rikidozan, who brought him back to his native Japan. On December 15, 1974, Inoki wrestled André to a double count-out at the Pacaembu Stadium in São Paulo in front of a reported 21,000 fans, the biggest crowd André had wrestled for. Brazil is still a market WWE is trying to break into today and it is the birthplace of some of the best mixed martial artists. Of course, such an accomplishment needed to be celebrated . . .

"André went to drink with Inoki and Sakaguchi only one time, it's when they went to Brazil together," remembered Peter Takahashi, a referee for New Japan who accompanied André many times after the matches. "Tony Charles and Abe Jacobs were there with them. André drank about 20 beers, Inoki had about 15. Inoki gave up eventually!"

But for André, 1974 wasn't only about Japan. At the beginning of the year, he resumed his feud with the Sheik in Toronto. On February 10, 16,000 fans saw André losing his mind after Sheik brought a foreign object into the match. The Giant not only hit the referee but threatened his corner man, Frank Valois. The double disqualification affair only lasted four minutes. A week later, 14,000 fans witnessed a rare loss for André. It was sold as a death match, but in reality, it was more like a last man standing match, where the first competitor not to get up by the count of 10 lost. After a three-minute bout, Sheik threw fire in André's face, and André couldn't get up in time. Even if the record states a loss, it wasn't what we would call a clean loss. Nevertheless, it was in Toronto, where the Sheik was a big hit at the box office and on a victory streak since February 1969 at Maple Leaf Gardens. Therefore his protection prevailed over André's. Six months later, on August 11, the Sheik punched the referee and was disqualified. It was enough for the press to run the headline "The Sheik Unbeaten Streak Is Over," and so was the feud between the two. They had another match the following week, but the paid crowds for the last two matches were not as strong the first three.

From one garden to another, André only wrestled three times in Madison Square Garden in 1974, proof that Vince McMahon Sr. didn't want to overexpose him to his regulars. Since the last time André worked there, Bruno Sammartino had regained his championship and André was pretty much working underneath Sammartino's title defense. André started a short rivalry with Killer Kowalski after the latter was on the losing end of a feud with Bruno for his title. He defeated Kowalski by count-out, and in October, André and Victor Rivera beat Kowalski and another longtime foe of André, Strong Kobayashi. While the main program was Bruno and Chief Jay Strongbow against the Valiant brothers, André and Kowalski certainly contributed to both sell-outs.

Other big matches for André that year included a lights out match against Bill Watts in Atlanta, facing Ox Baker for the WWA title in Indianapolis, and a six-man match in Philadelphia, teaming with Bruno and Haystacks Calhoun against Kowalski and the Valiant brothers. He also wrestled another big man, Ernie Ladd, for the very first time. Before he turned to wrestling, Ladd was a football all-star and is a member of the San Diego (now Los Angeles) Chargers' Hall of Fame. "The Big Cat" was one of the top heels in the business, and at six foot nine and 315 pounds, he was one of the few guys who could challenge André in size. The match happened on August 9 in Los Angeles and ended up with a double disqualification. However, the story of André's presence in L.A. wasn't only about that match. The night before, he was invited on *The Tonight Show*. The famous late-night talk show, hosted by Johnny Carson at the time, was one of the most popular programs on TV. Unfortunately, Carson was off that night, but "Rat Pack" member Joey Bishop, one of Carson's most frequent replacements, was the guest host. It was André's first appearance on the show, and with no surprise, his size was the talk of the interview, with Bishop comparing his hand to André's. André wasn't the first wrestler to appear on the show. In the

1960s, Antonino Rocca, Lou Thesz, and the Great Antonio all made *Tonight Show* appearances. But in the 1970s, it was rare that a wrestler made it to the guest list. "In the 1970s, when wrestlers never received any mainstream publicity — it was almost like there was a law against it — André was the lone exception," wrote Meltzer. "Everyone was watching *The Tonight Show* back then. When someone was on the show, everyone talked about it the next day."

That same year, André wrestled in Australia for the first time, working for World Championship Wrestling, but not the Jim Barnett version. Indeed, Barnett had left the company he created in 1964 at the beginning of 1974, having sold controlling interest to Tony Kolonie. Unfortunately, Kolonie had no knowledge of wrestling, and the promotion never again lived up to its reputation as the best wrestling promotion in the world. That said, Kolonie was the first promoter to bring André to the land down under. As with everywhere else, André was a big hit, selling out the Hordern Pavillon. On his first tour in November 1974, newspapers in Sydney reported he was cheered more than the last time Frank Sinatra was in town. He was such a sensation at the box office and so popular with the fans that he would travel there every other year, coming back in 1976 and 1978. Some of his matches with Brute Bernard, a French-Canadian who was a big star in Australia, are still well remembered by the fans and by the people in the business as well.

"André was part of the biggest riot I've seen," recalled WWE Hall of Famer J.J. Dillon. "It was in Australia. We were running Sydney on the Friday, Melbourne on the Saturday, staying all week and then finishing back to Sydney and Melbourne. We had André for a week. He wrestled Brute Bernard in Sydney, and I was managing Brute. André had Brute in a bear hug, and I came into the ring and hit André with my shoe. André fell down, and when he got back up, he was bleeding. People got so mad at us that they started to throw chairs. I got a chair on the back, and Brute got one behind his head. We finally got out of there and I convinced Brute we should go see a doctor because he was bleeding badly. When the doctor saw him he said, 'Oh my God, what did they do to you?' He had 10 stitches . . . The next night we were supposed to do he and me against André, and sure enough, Brute did the match."

The Giant was getting so much attention that at one point he had to get out of town, to Tea Gardens, 136 miles northeast of Sydney. There, he was staying with Kangaroo Kennedy, a retired wrestler, who set André up on a mattress on the floor so he could be comfortable. By 1978, WCW was on its last legs. At the time it was reported that there was a lack of national interest in pro wrestling in Australia, and GTV-9, unable to match Channel 7's *World of Sport*, decided to pull the plug on the promotion after airing the show for 14 years. The network was also in a bidding war over cricket, a very popular sport in Australia, and it is believed that the time slot wrestling had, weekend midday, was needed for that. Ron Miller, a big local star who had been wrestling since 1964 and who had toured in the U.S. with his partner Larry O'Dea as the Australians in the early 1970s, was the head booker of the promotion. He was friends with André from his previous tours in Australia and brought him back, not knowing it would near to the very last taping of WCW on the Nine Network. On December 8, 1978, André and Miller won the Austra-Asian tag team titles in Sydney, the main tag titles of WCW, defeating the team of Ox Baker and Butcher Brannigan. Two days later, in Melbourne, the promotion taped its last show. André was part of two interviews, one with Miller and King Curtis and the other with Miller only. They were promoting a cage match between André, Miller, and Curtis (who would be replaced by O'Dea) against Baker, Brannigan, and Bulldog Brower. In one of the interviews, André mentioned it would be his first cage match — and for once, he was telling the truth. The TV show aired on Saturday, December 16, and the same night, André's team was victorious in the cage. By the end of the month, the promotion folded and André, four years after his debut for WCW, ended up being its last tag team champion.

Thanks in part to the feud with the Sheik and with Inoki, André ended 1974 as the fifth-biggest draw in the world, a list he was often on during his career. If that wasn't impressive enough, he was also featured in the Guinness World Records book but not for what you'd think . . .

He wasn't the tallest or biggest pro wrestler but the highest-paid wrestler in the world, with documented earnings of over $400,000 in 1974. Of course, he ended up earning more than that in the following years, and later his record was beaten. However, it's still a sign that André's career, with Vince McMahon, was only growing. He was literally the biggest wrestling star in the world. In 1974 alone, he had worked in 26 states, one district, three Canadian provinces, and five different countries. He was traveling all over the world, making more money than ever before. And it was just the beginning for André the Giant.

CHAPTER 13

"NOW PLAYING DEFENSIVE END . . . ANDRÉ THE GIANT!"

T raveling as much he was, André wasn't spending much time in Vince Sr.'s territory. In the mid-'70s, Vince didn't really need André in New York. He had Bruno Sammartino as his world champion and he alone was enough to draw huge in Vince's core towns and especially at the Garden. André only averaged three MSG shows per year from 1975 to 1979, less than half as many as Bruno did during that same time period. André was worth way more money to Vince being booked around the world, and McMahon understood that from the get-go.

The year 1975 began with a big win for the Giant. On January 17, he was victorious in the seventh annual Los Angeles battle royal at the Olympic Auditorium. Inspired by Roy Shire's annual battle royal at the Cow Palace in San Francisco, which had become an enormous draw, Mike LeBell, L.A.'s promoter, adopted a similar formula. Battle royals were one of André's more often used gimmick matches, and he would win the San Francisco staple in 1977 in front of 14,350 fans and then in 1980 became the only wrestler to win the L.A.'s event twice. A few years prior, when Paul Boesch did his first two-ring battle royal on January 4, 1974, in Houston, André had been the last man standing. Clearly, there's something about battle royals in January . . . In 1975, André participated in all three of those battle royals and won two in front of between 10,000 and 13,000 fans each. He really was the master of this type of match, and Boesch was very complimentary about his in-ring skills. "He displayed the agility of a junior heavyweight and had the coordination of a basketball player," he wrote in his book. "Out of the ring, he was an affable, congenial giant who enjoyed the nomadic life he led and appreciated the giant-sized purses that came his way." During his time in California in 1975, André also did a photo shoot at Disneyland, posing with Goofy and Minnie Mouse, apparently having a wonderful time, although he didn't fit on any roller coaster. The man behind that publicity stunt was Mike LeBell, who had sent the Olympic Auditorium's photographer Theo Ehret to Disney with André. That would not be the only publicity stunt André participated in that year.

In 1975, he reconnected with old friends as he worked a New Japan program with his old foe from IWE, Strong Kobayashi. However, it was Kobayashi's time to return the favor, and the Giant won all the matches, including two bouts by pinfall. He wasn't Monster Roussimoff anymore, and André the Giant didn't lose as much. Still in Japan, André also teamed with "The Professional" Doug Gilbert, with whom he had one of his first feuds in Montreal back in 1971. He also wrestled against his first "boss," Paul "The Butcher" Vachon quite a few times, including once at the Garden in New York City, André's first visit there in 1975.

He also returned to Quebec City for the first time since 1973. After Grand Prix folded, a spinoff from the promotion opened in January 1975, as Don Leo Jonathan started Grand Circuit with his friend and businessman Fred Major and Killer Kowalski. It didn't last long and was never a real threat to All Star Wrestling; it shut down by the spring of 1976. But before it failed, in August 1975, the group brought the Giant back home to wrestle Kowalski, drawing a mere 3,400 fans. The territory was dying and All Star, not Grand Circuit, was on top by that point. That's why four months later Johnny Rougeau called Vince McMahon and asked for the Giant, setting up the first time André worked for the Rougeaus in la belle province. The show in Quebec City didn't draw well — only 2,000 fans paid for tickets. All Star was never as popular as Grand Prix in Quebec City. The event was supposed to mark Argentina Rocca's return to the province after several years, but Rocca didn't show up. André worked with the Sheik, managed by Eddie "The Brain" Creatchman, on top, but the best-of-three-falls match only lasted two minutes, with André declared the winner. Fans and reporters were not happy with Rocca's absence and André's in-ring cup of tea presence. All Star redeemed itself a couple of months later in Montreal.

André was brought back to main-event on February 16, 1976, against none other than Abdullah the Butcher — a rare match between the two. They had faced off twice the year before in Georgia and this was their third known singles match. In 1974, when Grand Prix and All Star promoted their joint shows, that would have been a dream match fans would have loved to see. Also helped by the three Rougeaus — Johnny, Jacques Sr., and Raymond teaming together — the show drew 11,000 fans to the Forum, a rare 10,000-plus crowd in those lean years. Working, as always, as Jean Ferré in Montreal, André was still a draw, and this showing was proof that the poor attendance in Quebec City wasn't his doing. Two months later, on April 5, All Star brought him back. André worked against Ivan Koloff, the same opponent he had on his very first match at the Forum back in 1971. They drew another 10,000 fans. It was All Star's last event at the Forum. Knowing they weren't going to get a renewal on their TV deal, Johnny and his partners sold the company on May 26, 1976. By the end of the year, it no longer existed. It was the end of an era in Montreal, and André was the last man to main-event a Forum wrestling event for six years.

Although he hadn't wrestled in Montreal since 1973, it was still André's home. Every time he had a few days off, he would go back to his apartment, which Valois took care of — making sure the rent and the bills were getting paid. While in Montreal, André befriended a well-known photographer by the name of André "Toto" Gingras, who was working for the *Journal de Montréal*, the town's biggest newspaper. Toto and André were friends to the point that the former would not go to bed until he knew André was back home. During the 1970s, André also befriended a famous hockey player from the Montreal Canadiens, future Hockey Hall of Famer Guy Lafleur. They may not have been close, but they often saw each other late at night in the same bars. "When the Giant was going out in Montreal, he would sometimes meet with Guy Lafleur, and he once did to him what he also once did to me and Tommy Rich: he got Lafleur out of the bar, holding him in his arms," remembered Rick Martel, laughing. "Lafleur thought he could drink, but no one drank like André. André liked Lafleur and talked about him fondly." Although he wasn't known to be a hockey fan, André befriended another hockey player, Boston Bruins legend Bobby Orr. As mentioned earlier, on November 19, 1973, the *Lowell Sun* reported that André had visited the Bruins locker room the previous evening, when the Bruins were playing the Atlanta Flames. The Bruins won the game, their sixth consecutive victory, so the atmosphere on that Saturday night was pretty relaxed. When the journalists came in the locker room, only one player was there, defensemen Darryl Edestrand. When asked where the rest of team was, he answered, "In the trainers' room with some monster!" What's also interesting about that article is that André is said to be six foot eight and 300 pounds. Without a doubt, the piece was never approved by Vince McMahon . . .

It was that night that the famous picture of André holding players Carol Vadnais and Bobby Orr in his arms was taken. It wasn't the only time André visited the Bruins locker room, as other pictures with guys like Phil Esposito, Terry O'Reilly, and even one with Orr and his agent, Alan Eagleson, can be found online. Introduced to the team by French-Canadian player Carol Vadnais, who had met André while playing on the west coast, André hung with the players on different occasions. One time, Orr, Vadnais, Esposito, and André went for drinks at a bar that had an indoor swimming pool. "At one o'clock, the manager came and asked us all to leave," wrote Phil Esposito in his memoir.

EVEN THOUGH HIS DAYS WITH GRAND PRIX WERE OVER, IN 1976 ANDRÉ RETURNED TO MONTRÉAL FOR ALL STAR WRESTLING.

A PICTURE WITH ANDRÉ WAS ALWAYS A MUST, EVEN FOR MINNIE MOUSE AT DISNEYLAND.

BORIS ROUSSIMOFF COLLECTION

"We were all together, and Bobby Orr said something to André, and André picked the guy up and threw him into the swimming pool! The cops came, and we left."

Orr's relationship with the Giant developed from there, and according to former minor hockey player Paul Henry, André used to stay at Orr's place when he was in Boston. "Bobby's dad often told the story of seeing André get out of Bobby's jacuzzi naked," Henry told wrestling journalist Greg Oliver. "That always led to the other person asking what André's dick was like. The first telling, Doug was apparently outside and said, 'It wasn't that long,' then paused, as a tanker trunk rumbled by, 'but it was about *that* thick!'" As Ric Flair said in the HBO documentary, "He wears a size 24 ring, baby, what else can I tell ya. And he's wearing a size 24 shoe, what else do you wanna know?" Jim Ross, at a time when he was making $25 to $40 a night working for Bill Watts, was offered $100 by a woman to take a picture of André's penis in the shower. But JR was too scared to do it. And it's not like André wasn't aware of it. There was and would always be a certain fascination surrounding the size of André's penis, from both women and men. Esposito and Vadnais once hooked André up with a woman they knew and managed to sneak into the room to witness the scene. Even in his most private moments, André was never left alone. Another Bruins player whom André befriended was Derek Sanderson, who owned a bar in Boston. "We were having so much fun," recalled André to *La Presse* in 1982. "Sanderson would often call me up because he didn't like football players, and they would always go to the bar."

It's likely that no one ever considered putting André on a pair of skates and offering him a contract to play hockey. Football, however, was another story. And rightfully so. At the time, the tallest player in the game was Ed "Too Tall" Jones, who was listed as six foot nine. Morris Stroud, who retired in 1974 after only five seasons, was six foot 10, while in the 1960s, Richard Sligh, at seven feet, played only eight games as a defensive tackle. To this day, he's the only seven-footer to have ever played pro football. And those guys were all between 250 and

300 pounds. André, billed as seven foot four and 400-plus pounds, was seen as someone who would wreak havoc on the defensive line.

As the story goes, the Washington Redskins were interested in signing André as a defensive end. After all, many great football players transitioned pretty well to the squared circle, so why not the other way? Years before Bill Goldberg or Steve "Mongo" McMichael, guys like Gus Sonnenberg, Bronko Nagurski, Leo Nomellini, Ernie Ladd, and Wahoo McDaniel left the gridiron for wrestling. Coached by George Allen, Washington was one of the best teams in the National Football League but had lost two years in a row in the NFC divisional game. André could have been the answer to spark the team. Although he wasn't the owner, Allen had a lot of influence and had complete personnel control. Known to be quite eccentric, he could be compared to a George Steinbrenner. He once traded the same draft pick to several teams. It was his idea to let President Richard Nixon call a play for the team during the 1971 playoffs. And he liked to spend money. The team president, Edward Bennett Williams, used to say, "George was given an unlimited budget and he exceeded it!"

So it came as no surprise when a press conference was held on July 8, 1975, at Duke Zeibert's restaurant in Washington, DC, to announce the team was interested in André. Tim Temerario, the team's director of personnel, said that four months before, Coach Allen, who was not at the news conference, said he was looking for "something unusual" for his defensive unit, such as a seven-footer who could move. Temerario then contacted Vince McMahon about the possibility.

"We're interested in him," said Temerario, as reported by UPI. "But there are problems, such as his heavy wrestling schedule and the fact he makes so much money from it. However, nothing is impossible," adding he wasn't expecting André at training camp. Both United Press International and the Associated Press ran the story, and it made news everywhere. Adding to that were photos taken of André lifting Washington's future number one quarterback Joe Theismann with one arm. Training camp started five days later, on July 13, in Carlisle,

Pennsylvania. André was wrestling that day — and the following days, as a matter of fact. On July 28, he was wrestling at the Capital Centre in Landover, Maryland, just outside Washington, where the Washington Bullets and Capitals were playing. The day of the show, an ad was published in a local newspaper of André with a drawing of Theismann in between his hands like he was some kind of a puppet, and the ad read, "André the Giant is 7'4" tall, weighs 444 pounds, and can destroy people with his hands, his feet, his elbows, his shoulders, and his breath. And that's why the Redskins want him."

Of course, none of that was true.

The press conference was real, but everything behind it was not. Vincent Kennedy McMahon confirmed it to writer Michael Krugman. "It was really just publicity, and everybody went along with it," he revealed. "There were some guys who had no idea that we were just having fun, that thought, 'Oh my God, can you imagine what this guy would do? André would be like half of the line.' André had no intention of trying out for football. He was making too much money in wrestling."

A good old publicity stunt by Vince Sr. — in a town where he once had his office — that's all it was. And it worked. Newspapers all over the country reported it. According to a longtime trainer, Allen had seen André at a promotional event and really considered giving him a shot. From there, the idea for the publicity stunt was fashioned. Allen was also the right guy for this, as fans would believe he could get that kind of idea. The reason given for the team not signing André was also logical, as the average NFL salary back then was $56,000. They could not have matched his wrestling salary. By September, the rumor had grown. Really grown. Bob Chick, *St. Petersburg Evening Independent* sports editor, wrote that some people were saying André had made it to the camp and left after a day or two. He wrote that even an assistant in the team's publicity office thought it was true. That was pro wrestling at its finest, creating an illusion and suspension of disbelief. Even *Sports Illustrated*, in 1982, published this: "According to Joe Blair, public relations director of the Redskins, there was talk about giving André a tryout in 1976, but it never happened. André told [*SI*'s Terry] Todd that he chose not to risk his wrestling career — he was making more money than any lineman was earning at the time — by taking time off for a trial in a sport in which he had no guarantee of success and no previous experience." Decades later, you can even find some people on forums and message boards saying André played or trained with the team.

Even George "The Animal" Steele had his own version of the story, saying Washington really wanted to sign André. "And because I was a football coach and had played a little bit, Vince Sr. said, 'Jim, what do you think about this idea?' I said, 'I think it's absolutely ridiculous. First of all, if you take André the Giant — as big and strong as he is — and stuck him in front of me, with his hands in the air waving or something, I'd take his knee out. I said first of all, I think you're making a mockery of the game. And he's outstretched, he can't protect himself, I'd cripple him. And I said every guy in the NFL would do that. He has no business doing that.' I don't know if you know that or not, but they had made the offer, and it almost went to signing, and that's why they didn't do it. Because it wasn't the right thing to do for André, for wrestling, and really for football."

A great story, sure, but again not a true one.

What McMahon didn't know at the time was that the story would become bigger and bigger as years went by, in part because of the photo with Theismann. The quarterback became a superstar, leading his team to back-to-back Super Bowls in 1982 and 1983, winning the first one and losing the second but being named the game's MVP. While Theismann was busy winning the Super Bowl, Allen had left the team in 1977 and was hired by the Montreal Alouettes of the Canadian Football League as president and chief operating manager in 1982. However, he quit three months later. Washington wasn't the first football team linked to André. Back in 1972, in Montreal, the Alouettes were also interested — but the team here actually tried to sign him. In April 1972, the team added

Jean Ferré to its negotiation list as a non-import since he was French, a good thing for the team since the number of imports was more limited than non-imports. J.I. Albrecht, the club's general manager, sent a telex and spoke to the secretary-treasurer of the CFL about it. He had seen the Giant on TV and was amazed by him. His public relations director knew Lucien Grégoire and asked for the permission to speak with André. They tried to convince him, but when André told them he was making $3,000 a week wrestling, they lost interest.

Hanging out with hockey players and getting approached to play football — not bad for someone who had never really played sports, other than some recreational soccer. But when you think you have heard it all, here comes the World Bellyflop and Cannonball Diving championship! A man by the name of Tom Butler, the promotion manager of the Bayshore Inn in Vancouver, British Columbia, had an idea for the opening of its pool in 1975: the World Bellyflop and Cannonball Diving Championship. Butler wanted to attract publicity for the hotel and sent out invitations to some celebrities, including former football players; all-time great Gene Kiniski, who was a huge star in Vancouver; André; and B.C.'s Richard "Butts" Giraud, a former football player who had also wrestled in B.C. and in the U.K. Football players and wrestlers were the perfect contestants since one of the few rules was that you had to be at least 250 pounds. So on May 17, 1975, 26 participants took part in the judged contest. Giraud finished first and Kiniski took fourth. Since André didn't know how to swim, he was disqualified. The only lifeguard was a 98-pound girl who didn't want to have to rescue a 400-pound giant . . .

"He never actually tried a bellyflop, but I think he would have broken the board," said Butts, who ended up winning the championship four times. "Those boards weren't made for him, even though they had brought in special boards just to handle all the weight."

After football and bellyflops, what other sport would make sense for André? Boxing, of course. And although the stakes were higher, would the contest be real?

CHAPTER 14

THREE BOXERS, TWO KINGS, AND ONE BIGFOOT!

itting a boxer against a pro wrestler was, and still is, something that every promoter gets excited about. Whether it's Floyd Mayweather against The Big Show or Braun Strowman against Tyson Fury, somehow, it always piques a certain interest. In 1976, André was by far the best-known pro wrestler in the world and one of the sport's biggest draws. But he wasn't as known or as popular as Muhammad Ali. Between 1972 and 1975, Ali had been named fighter of the year three times. On top of this, he was a closed-circuit box office giant. Before pay-per-views, boxing telecasts were broadcast to a number of venues, either theaters or arenas, where fans paid for tickets to watch the live telecast of the fight. One couldn't stay home and watch a fight like we can today. Those viewings became more popular in the 1960s and 1970s because of Ali's fights, and boxing promoters became rich because of them. As the most famous athlete of his era, wrestling promoters spent years trying to come up with an angle that would feature Ali in a mixed match. Promoters tried in 1965 with then NWA champion Lou Thesz, but it didn't work. Ten years later, Vince McMahon Sr. and Bruno Sammartino attempted it again, but Ali's representatives told them he wanted $6 million. Ali was a big wrestling fan and was influenced by Gorgeous George's and Freddie Blassie's promos. The fight would, of course, have been a work and Sammartino went so far as to issue a challenge, while McMahon was trying to get other major wrestling promoters to raise the necessary funds by doing a national closed-circuit event. They all rejected the idea, thinking it would only profit McMahon and Sammartino. New Japan and NET TV heard about the $6 million and told the Ali clan they would do it. Antonio Inoki was always trying to upstage Giant Baba in their territorial rivalry. "In a heated wrestling war built around the two big stars, beating Ali would put Inoki on a level Baba couldn't touch," wrote Meltzer in the *Wrestling Observer Newsletter*. "In doing so, New Japan would overcome its connection disadvantages and most likely, by virtue of having the biggest star, be the number one group in Japan."

On March 25, the fight was officially announced at a press conference held at the Plaza Hotel in New York City. Ali, Inoki, and André were all there. Inoki was sold as the heavyweight champion in Japan and a karate expert. They announced the match to be held in Tokyo on June 25, and a companion wrestler-boxer bout at Shea Stadium in New York with André against either Jerry Quarry, Oscar Bonavena, or Henry Clark. That match would precede the Ali-Inoki match on closed-circuit. During the press conference, Ali asked André, "You think you can beat me up?" to which the Giant answered, "I could beat you up and throw you out of this building." A series of photos were taken at that press conference where Ali compared his hand to André's and put André's fist next to Ali's face.

Quarry, Bonavena, and Clark were all top 10 heavyweight contenders the year before. Quarry, six feet tall, seemed to be the leading candidate for the match. Twice voted the most popular boxer in the late 1960s, the future Hall of Famer had lost twice to Ali, as well as recent losses to former champions Joe Frazier and Ken Norton. After the fight with Norton in March 1975, he had announced his retirement. He was a big-enough name for the fight to spike interest, but it didn't work out. He only returned to fighting in late 1977. Bonavena, only five foot 11, had also lost versus Ali but was in the midst of a seven-win streak. Quarry and Bonavena were the first two guys Ali fought after returning from his suspension in 1970. Bonavena was still being talked about as a possible opponent for André in April, but he wasn't picked. On May 22, about a month before the event, Bonavena was murdered. Finally, Clark was the tallest of the three and the California state champion, but the promoters had other plans for him.

Chuck Wepner was scheduled to fight Johnny Clohessy, whom Wepner had beat a few years before, in a high school gym in New York on May 7. On April 29, it was reported that Clohessy had been replaced by Tommy Sheehan (11–16–1). The very next day, a bigger announcement was made. Chuck Wepner had been chosen to face André the Giant at Shea Stadium. Wepner, then the New Jersey state heavyweight champion, still fought against Sheenan, a calculated risk since Sheenan with 11–16–1 wasn't considered a threat. And he wasn't. Wepner beat him in 1:01 of the first round. Although a worked fight, the Shea Stadium bout would be a much bigger deal than some high school gym.

In an interview with Canadian sportswriter Jim Taylor on May 11, Frank Valois said, "It had to be a big name [for the match with André]. First it was Jerry Quarry, which was fine, but that fell through. When they said Wepner, we said okay, because he fought Ali once and he is known."

Wepner had fought Ali a year prior, on March 24, 1975, in Cleveland. Ali was a fighting champ — he had racked up 18 fights in four years prior to facing Wepner. His latest fight, against heavyweight champion George Foreman in Kinshasa, Zaire, was when he introduced his rope-a-dope strategy of letting his opponent tire himself out. The fight with Wepner, billed as "Give the White Guy a Break," was Wepner's biggest test ever. Ali's clan wanted to fight a white boxer, and Wepner was the only one in the top 10 at the time. He had grown up and learned how to fight in the streets of Bayonne, New Jersey. Known as the "Bayonne Bleeder," because of the ease with which he got cut in the ring, he had started his professional career in 1964 and had a few feature bouts against guys like Buster Mathis, a young Foreman, and Sonny Liston in his very last fight — all of which Wepner lost. A 40-to-1 underdog against the champ, all Wepner wanted to do was go the distance to prove the boxing world wrong. He was actually 19 seconds from his goal when he was TKO'd but not before sending Ali to the floor in the ninth round. He was actually the fourth, and the last boxer, to send Ali to the canvas. That fight was the inspiration for Sylvester Stallone's movie *Rocky*.

"At a theater in Los Angeles, struggling actor Sylvester Stallone watched the Ali-Wepner fight and promptly went home and banged out the script for a little movie called *Rocky*," Eric Raskin wrote on ESPN.com in 2011. "It wasn't based on a true story — not directly. But it was inspired by and borrowed heavily from a true story. By the time the movie was released on Dec. 3, 1976, word had spread that Wepner was Stallone's muse, and Wepner basked in the glory of hearing his first name chanted in the New York theater where he watched the film."

When the fight with André came around, that fact was not known yet, but still Wepner was a big enough name — he had been on *The Mike Douglas Show*, among others — and a big enough man at six foot five to go against the Giant.

"The original idea was for three boxer versus wrestler fights, with Ali versus Inoki from Tokyo, André the Giant versus Chuck Wepner from Shea Stadium in New York, and NWA world champion Terry Funk versus Henry Clark," wrote Meltzer. The Funk-Clark fight fell through after Clark got beaten by Earnie Shavers in Paris, France, three days after the press conference.

In the U.S, the main promoters were boxing's Bob Arum and Vince McMahon Sr. In order to draw a bigger crowd, the plan was to hold matches at Shea Stadium, along with the Ali-Inoki fight from Japan via closed-circuit on giant screens. McMahon wanted all the other promoters to do the same. He had given Fred Blassie to Ali to work as his "manager," which made sense because Blassie was well known and respected in the U.S. and Japan, as well as an excellent talker. But wrestling promoters being what they are, the idea of pushing somebody else's promotion and talent wasn't well received.

"In most cases, the promoters pushed their own talent," added Meltzer. "Clips of Inoki beating Ruska (for the Real World Martial Arts Championship), Ali doing interviews, Fred Blassie doing interviews, and André doing interviews were sent to all the major promoters. Most gave the event only a nominal push."

Still, most of the larger wrestling territories ran with the idea. Houston, Indianapolis, Dallas, Los Angeles, and San Francisco (where local matches took place after the two featured bouts because of the time difference), Detroit, Tallahassee, Calgary, Atlanta, Chicago, New York, and Tokyo (on the 26th in Japan) all had a local card before the two main events. In Montreal, André's home, the territory had just started what would be a dark period: the two main fights were shown through CCTV at the Verdun Auditorium, but no local matches were added, and the attendance was poor. Of those showcasing matches, only Atlanta with Jack Brisco against Dory Funk Jr., Chicago with Verne Gagne versus Nick Bockwinkel, and of course Tokyo and New York drew at least 10,000 fans. The biggest was at Shea Stadium since not only was André's match featured live but so was a rematch featuring Sammartino and Stan Hansen. Two months prior, they had faced each other at the Garden, and Hansen accidentally dropped Bruno on top of his head. Sammartino, who could have been paralyzed, came back sooner than he should have (thanks to McMahon's insistence) and wrestled Hansen in a 10-minute match, squeezed between the André fight and the Ali fight. In Flushing, New York, 32,897 fans showed up — more than double what the Nippon Budokan drew for Ali and Inoki. Neither of the wrestler versus boxer contests were match of the year material, to say the least.

In Tokyo, what was supposed to be a work turned out to be a shoot: Ali, who was supposed to lose, had a change of heart; Inoki didn't want to job either. The only solution, at least the only one everyone agreed upon, was to do a shoot — or legit — fight. Refereed by Mike LeBell's brother, "Judo" Gene LeBell, a former wrestler who became a stuntman in Hollywood and later trained Ronda Rousey, the fight was terrible. There was a whole set of rules that didn't allow them to fight as they wanted. So Inoki spent most of the 15 rounds on his back, landing 78 kicks to Ali's legs, while the boxer only landed six punches. They went to the judges, and it came back as a draw. "In those days, there was no kickboxing in the U.S., let alone MMA," Meltzer wrote. "Nobody understood leg kicks. In Japan, they didn't really understand it either. Watching the fight today, while still a terrible fight, Inoki clearly won."

In New York, the crowd left happy because they had seen Sammartino win his match. As far as André and Wepner, it was more of a farce than anything else, even if it was a work. The rules were that André could do anything a wrestler would normally do and Wepner could do anything a boxer would normally do, including fighting with gloves. If Wepner touched the ropes, he would get a clean break. Well, for the first two rounds, that's what happened. Every time André got a hold on Wepner, the boxer grabbed the ropes. The fans even booed the contest, announced on CCTV by Vince McMahon Jr. and Argentina Rocca, who quite frankly didn't say much. Finally, the Giant pressed Wepner over his head and threw him over the top rope. The finish was botched as Wepner didn't know how to take a bump outside the ring and tried to slow down his fall by grabbing the top rope. He fell awkwardly on the apron and then bounced on the field, where he was counted out at 1:17 of the third round. Over the years, many media outlets have treated the match as if it was a shoot. André never talked about the scripted aspect of that night. "Look, boss, the boxer-wrestler business is almost a joke," André told Terry Todd of *Sports Illustrated*. "After all, a man may hit me a couple of times, but if I cut the ring off and close in, what can he do after I put my hands on him? The boxer has no chance since he can't even wrestle in a clinch because of his gloves." Wepner had conflicting statements on the bout, until just recently. "We met at a hotel, and we practiced some of the moves, because it is, you know, show business," he told David Onda in a 2017 interview. "I talked them into letting him just throw me out of the ring, and then I don't make it back in. And that's what he did." Right after the match, a melee started outside the ring between Gorilla Monsoon, who was in André's corner with Frank Valois, and Wepner's cornermen. Monsoon was accused of giving a boot to Wepner as he was on the ground. As soon as it started, Valois rushed to the ring to make sure to raise André's hand and to keep him away from that. But the brawl came back into the ring, with Wepner and André going at it for real this time. One of Wepner's seconds threw a punch at André's shoulder and broke two fingers. According to Wepner, it wasn't a work anymore.

"I was like what the hell is going on here?" Wepner told John Gross for his book *Ali vs. Inoki.* "It got very heated. Some of the wrestlers were jumping into the ring. Gorilla Monsoon was throwing guys around like rag dolls. It got heated and was finally broken up. I didn't want to get involved. We were in there to put on a show and give them a good time. A real fight over this? It was crazy." Meltzer wrote, "There was a post-match brawl that looked like a wrestling pull-apart riot that evidently had some real moments."

There were about 250,000 tickets sold in over 100 closed-circuit venues. It was considered a bomb. In Japan though, the fight was seen by approximately 60 million viewers total. The Inoki-Ali fight was shown on TV with a 45-minute delay from noon to 1:30 p.m. locally. But later that night, at 7:30 p.m., NET TV aired the André-Wepner fight, followed by a replay of Ali and Inoki and then Willem Ruska against Don Fargo from Los Angeles. The evening presentation drew between 27 and 29 million people.

The aftermath of all this was different for the four men. Ali had a busy 1976. Including the fight with Inoki, he had four fights in the span of five months. And just before that, he had been in a war with Joe Frazier in the Philippines. "Ali was never the same as a boxer," wrote Meltzer. "Whether it was the Frazier 'Thrilla in Manila' fight, the long-term wear-and-tear, the kidney problems, or the leg damage he took in this fight, or a combination of everything, he was a different fighter when he stepped into the ring with Norton [in September of 1976]."

CHUCK WEPNER WAS NOT GOING TO MAKE IT EASY ON ANDRÉ.

PLAYING CARDS WITH HIS FRIENDS WAS AS IMPORTANT AS WRESTLING FOR ANDRÉ; HERE WITH PAT PATTERSON.

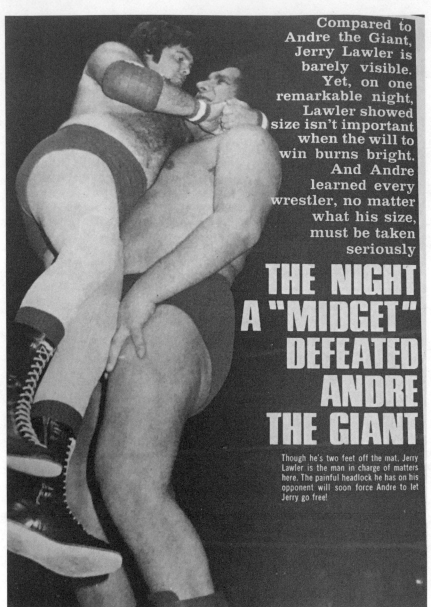

Compared to Andre the Giant, Jerry Lawler is barely visible. Yet, on one remarkable night, Lawler showed size isn't important when the will to win burns bright. And Andre learned every wrestler, no matter what his size, must be taken seriously

THE NIGHT A "MIDGET" DEFEATED ANDRE THE GIANT

Though he's two feet off the mat, Jerry Lawler is the man in charge of matters here. The painful headlock he has on his opponent will soon force Andre to let Jerry go free!

THE WRESTLER

DID JERRY LAWLER REALLY BEAT ANDRÉ? *THE WRESTLER* MAGAZINE SEEMED TO THINK SO.

Inoki continued his quest to be the best mixed martial arts fighter (although that term was not coined until 1989). He had 20 mixed martial arts worked matches, losing only his last. He had created the Real World Martial Arts championship in February 1976, in preparation for the Ali fight, fighting a match with Willem Ruska, a two-time judo Olympic gold medalist. On October 7, he was ready to defend it once again. His opponent was the winner of the other boxer versus wrestler extravaganza, André the Giant. Inoki won by referee stoppage in front of 10,500 fans. A year later, he defended it against Wepner in Japan, winning the contest in the sixth round. So, if this were some kind of a round-robin tournament, Inoki would be 2–0–1, Ali 1–0–1, André 1–1–0, and Wepner 0–3–0. The only match that never happened was Ali versus André, even if it was the match McMahon had wanted from the beginning. "I don't think Ali's people were ever interested again," said Meltzer. "The Inoki thing wasn't the success they hoped for, and Ali got a lot of bad [publicity] on the first one." As the working relationship between McMahon and Inoki grew, McMahon awarded Inoki with the WWWF World Martial Arts championship in December 1978 upon Inoki's return to the Garden after three years. The Inoki-Ali fight, although considered a joke for many years, is seen nowadays by many as the first televised MMA fight.

Wepner was never able to capitalize on the Ali and André fights. After the latter, he lost four of his next six fights, before retiring in 1978. In recent years, a documentary as well as a movie based on his story were made, in which the André fight was featured, and Wepner became known as the "real Rocky."

It was not the only time that André competed against someone wearing boxing gloves. A year later, on September 23, 1977, André had a boxing match against none other than Gorilla Monsoon at the Roberto Clemente Stadium in San Juan, Puerto Rico. Monsoon owned stock in Puerto Rico at the time, with Carlos Colón and Victor Jovica. The match, refereed by former boxing heavyweight champion Jersey Joe Walcott, who was working a lot as a wrestling referee, was a work, of course. The 18,000 fans went nuts when André KO'd a heel Monsoon in the third round, and Verne Gagne's fantasy was becoming real at last. Monsoon was also involved in the Inoki-Ali match, as he gave an airplane spin to Ali on television to help build the match with Inoki, making him the only man to wrestle with Ali and box with André.

And as for André, it was just another step to stardom. In fact, 1976 had started on another high note, with his Hollywood debut. With its labor union, it was a good way for a wrestler to get insurance. In January 1974, a television series called *The Six Million Dollar Man* debuted on ABC. Starring Lee Majors, the show was about NASA astronaut Colonel Steve (not Stone Cold) Austin, who was injured in a plane crash and had to be rebuilt in a $6,000,000 operation. His right arm, both legs, and left eye were replaced with bionic implants to increase his abilities beyond normal, helping him in his new role as a secret agent. Based on a Martin Caidin novel titled *Cyborg*, the science-fiction action series was one of the most popular of the 1970s. Season three of the show featured a two-part episode called "The Secret of Bigfoot." Bigfoot, or the Sasquatch, is the legendary North American ape-like creature that's about six foot nine, muscular, and covered in dark hair . . . With those casting notes, who better than a Giant to play the mythical creature? "We looked around at who could've filled those shoes, and there weren't too many other seven-and-a-half-foot-tall guys around," remembered writer and producer Kenneth Johnson, who also created *The Bionic Woman* (a spinoff of *The Six Million Dollar Man*) and *V*.

Wearing prosthetic makeup and a fur-covered bodysuit, André as Bigfoot had a memorable fight scene with Majors, in which the hero ripped off Bigfoot's right arm, revealing that the creature was, in fact, some kind of a robot controlled by aliens.

"It was a great part of the show. And I loved working with André," said Majors in an interview with *Vanity Fair*. "He was really a gentle giant. Such a sweetheart. I remember doing a fight with him, he'd pick me up and throw me like 10 yards. And then he was supposed to come after me, jump up in the air, and land right on top of me.

"I distinctly remember lying there on the ground and I've got the sun in my eyes," Majors continued. "I know he's running toward me but I can't see anything. And then this big cloud appears over me, just blocks out the sun, and I know it's him crashing down on me. I flinch, waiting for the crush. But you know what? The guy never touched me. It looked so realistic on the show, but I didn't feel a thing. That's what you get with a professional wrestler. He knew what he was doing. It takes more talent to jump on somebody without hurting them than it does to actually break their ribs."

A television set can be a lot like a wrestling dressing room, with pranks and jokes being played among the people working there. "I remember him sitting in 90-degree weather and he drank a case of beer within an hour and he never went to the bathroom either," revealed Majors in the DVD extras of the series. "We could not figure that out. The next day, it's a practical joke, maybe I shouldn't say it. Someone has some diuretic and we put it in one of his beers. He still drank the case and still didn't go to the bathroom!" In catering, André made sure to leave an impression on the crew while feeding his legend, as he was eating eggs by the dozen for breakfast, multiple steaks for lunch, and a whole chicken for dinner. That two-parter is still one of the most popular episodes among fans of the series and a favorite of Lee Majors himself. The two episodes were released as a theatrical film in Europe, Mexico, and South America, adding to the popularity of Andre's Bigfoot character.

Unfortunately, when Johnson wanted to bring back the Bigfoot character later that year, André didn't want to do it, and the production used *The Addams Family*'s Ted Cassidy. "André likes to travel, wrestle, drink beer, and live the good life," wrote Gene LeBell in his book. "He couldn't stand waiting around a back lot all day in a big ape suit. The producers of the show made sure that they didn't kill off the Bigfoot creature that André played. The show with André as the Sasquatch was such a success that they wanted him to do it again. They asked me if he would work cheaper. I asked André and he said that he wouldn't do it for fifty thousand . . . they actually offered him fifty thousand, but André was unmoved. 'I won't do it,' he said. 'I just won't do it. I don't need the money and I don't like it.'" André didn't leave the set before plaster casts of André's size 24 foot were made to be used as Bigfoot's footprint, with the heel of the cast being extended by a few inches. As a trivia note, in the 1977 pilot of *The Incredible Hulk*, developed for television by Kenneth Johnson, there is a big footprint from the Hulk — it was the second one cast by André.

To André's peers and contemporaries, this kind of thing must have seemed quite the accomplishment — that world was simply out of reach for them. Many remembered André being very proud and having good memories from working with guest star Stefanie Powers. "He was sweet on Stefanie Powers and told me he had spent an evening with her," remembered former AWA champion Rick Martel, who was friends with André. "Some wrestlers didn't take it easy on him. They were teasing him about the fact that ripping his arm off might be a good wrestling gimmick to even the odds. But André would always laugh."

This appearance also brought him back to the forefront in France where people had been slowly forgetting about Jean Ferré. "When we were kids, we told the other kids our uncle was a giant," recalled his nephew Boris, "but until *The Six Million Dollar Man* aired on television in France, on TF1 in 1980, people didn't know about his career in the USA."

The story was so big that the wrestling world had to spin it too: a photo of André as Bigfoot and Lee Majors was used on the cover of the *Inside Wrestling* issue for May 1976. That picture was sold to fans in many territories André worked. Lee Majors still sells it today at fan conventions. In 2013–14, the Bigfoot character was brought back in a comic book based on the series. André's presence in the show truly left a mark on the imagination of a whole generation of television viewers worldwide.

Of course, it wasn't the first or last time André made the cover of a wrestling magazine. His image was featured frequently, because he helped sell magazines. That said, sometimes, his picture didn't even need to be on the cover for a tale to be told . . .

A year later, Jerry "The King" Lawler was trying everything in his power to make the cover of a pro wrestling magazine. Since he wasn't wrestling in a big territory like New York or Chicago, he was continually passed over. Lawler had shares in a new wrestling company mainly owned by Jerry Jarrett in Memphis, Tennessee. In early 1977, Jarrett (who decades later co-founded TNA, now Impact Wrestling) and Nashville promoter Nick Gulas had severed ties, and Jarrett was working on a power play to take over the entire territory. He opened his promotion in March, and shortly after, he brought André in for a short run. One of his towns was Louisville, Kentucky, and on April 5, on his third card in the home of Muhammad Ali, André was booked against Lawler. It wasn't André's first appearance in town, but it was his first singles match.

It seems like any other André match, right? But it's what happened next that is interesting and worthy of a tale. Photos of the match were sent to journalist Bill Apter in New York. At the time, Apter was working for Stanley Weston on many of his publications. He liked the photos of the match, and Lawler's wish was finally going to come true. He had made the cover. A photo of him and André featured the tagline: "The night a 'midget' defeated André the Giant." The five-page story of the match described it as Lawler, said to be five foot six, using his quickness and small stature to surprise the Giant. Near the end of the match, Lawler lifted the Giant by the waist and, with almost supernatural strength, was able to throw him over the top rope to the concrete. André was not able to get back in the ring before the 10-count. The story had quotes from Lawler saying it was the biggest thrill of his life and that he was fighting for all the small people out there. It also had quotes from André saying he didn't understand what happened, that Lawler seemed to be everywhere and was always slipping away. And it ends with "Jerry Lawler amazingly defeated André the Giant. No one can take that victory away from him." Shocking story. André losing by count out didn't happen often, especially not against someone who wasn't yet the national star he would become. But since it's an André the Giant story, nothing is as it seems.

Thanks to Jim Cornette and the spiral notebook in which he took note of every result in Louisville, here's what really went on. "Lawler was in his element here, bumping like a ping pong ball for the world's largest athlete," wrote Cornette. "Finally Phil Hickerson and Dennis Condrey ran in to help and Lawler was DQ'd, and Rocky Johnson came in to even the odds." What? So André actually won the match by DQ? How could it be? How could the magazine and Apter be reporting otherwise?

For the younger readers, wrestling magazines in the 1970s were the internet before there was such a thing. They let a fan in Los Angeles know what was going on in New York, and vice-versa. And like the internet today, there was plenty of fake news, exaggeration, and rumors, usually written to sell more magazines. The magazines were usually protecting kayfabe and wrote pieces to enhance the storylines the different promoters were working on. If a story needed a quote from someone, no problem. The writer made one up. Especially in the case of Bill Apter, wrestlers trusted him enough to let him do that. If social media today is all about likes and followers, wrestling magazines were all about selling copies. André defeating Lawler by DQ isn't much of a story. But André losing to Lawler, six feet in reality but smaller for the sake of that story, then you have a headline that moves copies. It was a win-win for Lawler and the magazine, right?

Thanks to *Pro Wrestling Illustrated*'s archives, we were able to uncover another lie.

Even if Lawler has written that "the whole deal was great to me because I finally made it on the cover of the magazine," the reality is different. The magazine mentioned by Lawler and others was *Wrestling Superstars*, but in reality, it was *The Wrestler*. In its August 1977 issue, the guys on the cover were Superstar Billy Graham and Bruno Sammartino; Graham had won the WWWF title at the end of April and magazines usually hit newsstands a few months after any particular event. But if you look closely, on the bottom left corner, just above the barcode, it says, "A 'Midget' Defeated André the Giant." Inside was the five-page story, including a full-page picture of André and Lawler, but still, Lawler didn't make the cover. In his defense, he ended up doing just fine later on, becoming a much bigger star on a broader stage in the 1980s.

End of story, right? Not quite.

The piece didn't please everyone. While André couldn't care less about what was said in the wrestling mags, Vince McMahon did. It was still a kayfabe world, with promoters trying to make professional wrestling look real. Protecting your star, especially one promoted around the country as being undefeated, was very important, and the magazines were very influential in those days. McMahon didn't want fans to think André could be defeated by someone reportedly so small. More importantly, he was sending André to all those promoters with the one condition that André couldn't lose. And although André did lose a few matches by disqualification, or in tag matches where he wasn't involved in the finish, he couldn't lose a singles match; that would look weak. Of course, the article inside the magazine explained it was a count-out finish, but the cover tagline made it seem like André had been defeated. Vince McMahon was unhappy. Four months later, at the NWA convention in Las Vegas, where all the promoters met annually to discuss business, McMahon brought up the magazine and this story.

"He's one of the biggest attractions in this business, and he needs to be protected," McMahon claimed at the meeting. "Not only did someone beat André the Giant, a midget beat André the Giant!" To Bill Apter privately on the phone, McMahon said, "How could you run this without checking with me? It's horrible and unforgivable," he said. "You've ruined everything!" In a weird twist, Jerry Jarrett remembered in his book that Lawler had won the match by DQ, and when McMahon called him, he told him he didn't know that DQ finishes weren't allowed. Odd considering it wasn't the finish at all. Anyway. Back at the convention, Terry Funk, always trying to stir up some shit, asked McMahon, "Well, Vince, who was that little bastard who beat André?" Of course, he knew the answer. Everyone started laughing but McMahon. Lawler pinned the blame on Apter. And, of course, McMahon had spoken to Apter when the magazine hit the newsstand, and Apter told him that Lawler had sent the pictures and that Lawler and the photographer, Mike Shields, told him André had lost by count-out. There was enough heat drawn by McMahon that Apter and Lawler didn't speak for two years. To make it up to McMahon, magazine owner Weston and his crew put André on the cover of the *Wrestling 1977 Annual* with the headline "André the Giant: Wrestling's Only Undefeated Superstar." True or false, everyone was happy.

Where André was concerned, things like this happened all the time. Some people even had a little fun with myth-making. "I used to say to people that André has 82 teeth," said Vince Jr. "And they believed it. You know, I said, yeah, and it's kinda like when you see his teeth, they're not real big but they're like rows of teeth like a shark behind him!" Larry Hennig was another one who added to the stories. "Hennig told me, 'You know he's got two hearts and two rows of teeth,'" recalled Ric Flair. "And I believed him . . . Every time André talked to me, I'd be looking for that second row of teeth. I said he couldn't have two rows of teeth — I could never see them. The two hearts I believed forever!" There are so many myths and stretched truths surrounding him. Being the first to body slam André was another achievement many wrestlers liked to claim. By 1977, André had been body slammed in Europe, Japan, Montreal, and Chicago, among other places. Still, Hogan body slamming André to win their *WrestleMania III* match was sold as the first time ever, and that bothered another King.

Before he became "King" Harley Race in 1986 with the WWF, the Missouri native had won the NWA World Heavyweight title a total of eight times. André, on the other hand, didn't need a title to get over. Some say a championship belt is a gimmick; André's gimmick was his size, and a belt wasn't going to do anything more for him. Plus, who could beat him? For most of his career, he was promoted as undefeated. Losing a championship match didn't fit that angle. As the Giant himself once said, "There are many champions, but there is only one André!" Who could argue with that? That's why he never got a lot of championship matches, especially in the National Wrestling Alliance. His first NWA title match was on March 10, 1976, in Miami Beach against Terry Funk. And like most title matches that involved André, the champ lost by DQ. Disqualifications or count-outs were the smart finishes in those circumstances because they protected both the title holder and the Giant.

Harley Race was the NWA champion André faced the most. Their first encounter was in Calgary, Alberta, on July 15, 1977, during the Calgary Stampede. Known as "The Greatest Outdoor Show on Earth," the Stampede is an annual rodeo, exhibition, and festival held every July. At the time, Stu Hart, Bret's father, held very popular wrestling shows during the week-long festivities, and usually, the NWA champion would come to defend the title. On that date, André got his second-ever NWA title match.

While André didn't win the title, it was said to be his greatest Stampede performance. André was making tons of money, and Stampede week was a good example of that. He had wrestled four times during that tour and made $1,550. Race, the NWA champion, wrestled eight matches and only made $1,000. The year prior, André had made $2,433 for seven matches; McMahon's bookie fees were $650. Both André and McMahon were making money. André really liked going to Calgary at that time of the year, and neither the wrestling nor the money were the sole reasons. "It was written into his contract that four bottles of red wine be left in his dressing room, the contents of which would be swishing in his belly by the time he entered the ring," wrote Heath McCoy in *Pain and Passion: The History of Stampede Wrestling*. Women were another reason — one woman in particular. Swedish actress and exotic dancer Babette Bardot was very popular in the 1970s. Billed as "44-24-38," she made appearances on many talk shows. In 1973, Stu Hart named her Miss Stampede Wrestling, and she became a staple of the annual event. Among her duties was greeting the world champion or an attraction like André. She caught André's eye to the point that every time she was in town, André refused to wrestle unless she was there, even if Hart needed him elsewhere. When André liked you, he *really* liked you . . .

One way André demonstrated that he liked and respected you as a fellow wrestler was by letting you body slam him. Although he had wrestled Race a few times before, the first time Race slammed him was on October 13, 1978, in Houston, Texas. Photos of the feat were taken, but according to Race, he and André convinced the photographer not to publish them since the Giant had a gimmick in which he was offering $25,000 to anyone who could actually do it, and André didn't want that to end. Race really believed he was the very first man to do it. In his 2004 book, he wrote, "I achieved something no one else had ever done, although I didn't get credit for it until years later." Race is referring to after *WrestleMania III*, when a photo from the 1978 match was published in a wrestling magazine to let readers know André *had* been body slammed before and by Race. By the time of *WrestleMania III*, the Weston publications, also known as Apter mags, had been banned from shooting photos ringside and from reporting on WWF; WWF had its own magazine that exclusively covered its matches. So publishing a photo of André getting slammed was a way to take a shot at McMahon.

Race was someone André highly respected. Known for his natural strength, Race was a real tough guy. "The only two men in the world that André the Giant feared were Meng [Haku] and Harley Race," Bobby "The Brain" Heenan once said. But for 21 days between 1977 and 1981, Race wore the 10 pounds of NWA gold. He wrestled against André in about a dozen title defenses. The two of them really clicked in the ring, and their matches pulled big crowds. On New Year's Day 1979, in Atlanta at the Omni, their match drew 12,300, alongside a tag team match between the Funks and the Brisco brothers. The following week in Houston, they drew 11,000. You can watch the match online and it's a great performance by both men. André is really working — he performed double-arm suplexes, was agile in the ring, had good balance, and didn't need the ropes to stand up. His ability to sell is showcased here too: his facial expressions are great, as is the way he articulates pain.

"The André the Giant I knew in the late '70s and early '80s could throw suplexes and get up and down off the mat with relative ease — which made his matches that much more entertaining to watch," wrote Bob Backlund in his book. Both Ric Flair and Jerry Lawler agree. When André was selling for someone, he made him look good. His generosity could extend to the ring, and he had the ability to make the star he was working with look like a million bucks. In the Houston match, Race body slammed him again, directly on the concrete. However, this time, a photo never made the magazines.

André might have feared guys like Race and Haku, but it was nothing compared to the fear of driving with Smith Hart. After the 1979 Stampede Week shows, Stu's sons Smith and Bret had to drive André to the airport. His original flight had been canceled, but Smith found another one. The problem was that the flight was leaving in 20 minutes and the airport was 40 minutes away from André's hotel. As he got in the car, André told Smith, "I'll never make it, boss." However, Smith was determined to get him there.

"Smith drove like an absolute lunatic at speeds in excess of a hundred miles per hour through city traffic," wrote Bret in his book. "We made the sharp curve into the airport with the speedometer pinned and the car tilted up on two wheels, a hair's breadth away from careening forty feet down off the elevated departure ramp! My yell was drowned out by André's loud roar. When we screeched to a stop, André, his big eyes bulging out of his head, was about to explode." André was one pissed-off giant, and according to Bret, he was so mad that he didn't speak to Bret for six years.

The late 1970s saw André enjoying his peak in popularity and demand. He was known everywhere he went. Back home, in Montreal, he became a partner in an established downtown restaurant. Le Pichet was a French cuisine restaurant and bar located at 2155 Mackay. It had opened in 1976, and every time André was home, he would go there to eat and drink. He became friends with the owner, Hans Dungbluth. "One day, Hans told Jean that it would be cheaper for him if he became a partner," recalled John Dzafarov, who was the public relations guy for the restaurant and who was well known on the club scene. So André became a partner in 1977. André didn't need money from the restaurant, he was making enough from wrestling, but it was a good business opportunity for Dungbluth who could benefit from André's partnership and the free publicity he would bring. Another partner was entertainer and actress Denise Filiatrault. Newspapers, tabloids, and magazines all talked about André's restaurant, but it was never all his. For André, it was a place to treat his friends. "I went to eat there many times," remembered Gino Brito. "He was very proud of it and was inviting us all the time. I don't think he ever made any money with it though. He went there to eat and drink; the rest didn't really matter to him. He would tell me, 'Even when I'm not there, it's on me.' I never went without him though. I didn't want to look cheap. When we were going, he wouldn't even let us tip the waitress!" It was the same for Édouard Carpentier. "He never let me pay for a meal," he said. "If he knew you, you couldn't pay for anything." His partnership in the restaurant lasted until the mid-1980s, when it was sold.

But the 1970s were far from over. There were more states to see. More provinces to wrestle in. And most importantly, more battles to win.

CHAPTER 15

BATTLE OF THE GIANTS!

ndré rarely took much time off. He was such an attraction: everyone wanted to book him. But at the end of July 1977, he did schedule some personal time: to see his younger brother Jacques marry his bride, Mauricette. Jacques was probably the sibling he was closest to, and André was not going to miss the big day for all the money in the world. He flew back to France a couple of days before the July 30 wedding. His family was delighted to see him. "It was such a nice day," remembered André's sister-in-law Hortense. "Everyone was happy. It was a very nice wedding!" To Jacques, it meant even more. Not only did André come to his wedding, but André's wedding gift was to pay for Jacques and Mauricette's honeymoon in Canada. Jacques and his wife got to see André team up with Haystacks Calhoun against Don Kent, Frank Stanley, and Chris Tolos in Toronto during the honeymoon. Certainly not André's finest moment in the ring, but that didn't matter to Jacques. "It's one of the best memories of my life," he said.

Earlier in 1977, André had visited a place he had never been: Hawaii. Always a very popular destination for wrestlers, Hawaii is the perfect stop between the west coast and Japan or Australia, so many wrestlers would stop there for a week or two and enjoy a nice working vacation. You could be at the gym in the morning, at the beach all day, and wrestle only a few times a week. In the early 1960s, wrestler Ed Francis bought the territory and rebranded the promotion as 50th State Big Time Wrestling. He did well through the '60s and early '70s, until the Civic Auditorium in Honolulu closed down in 1974. For three years, Francis didn't run a single show in Hawaii. But he came back in 1977 and held a return show on June 22 at the Neal Blaisdell Arena, formerly known as the Honolulu International Center. For his big comeback, Francis and his booker, Lord James Blears, promoted a Texas Battle Royal with the "King of the Battle Royals" himself, André the Giant. The stacked card also included Tosh Togo, John Tolos, Gene Kiniski, and Ed's sons, Russ and Billy. Russ was an NFL player with the New England Patriots and on the verge of becoming an all-star. The other big name brought to the show was another giant, Shohei "Giant" Baba. Baba worked the battle royal, and for the very first time, he and André shared the ring together, though they didn't touch each other. André won the match by eliminating his good friend Billy White Wolf and then throwing Tolos over the top rope. The show was a big success with a near-capacity crowd of 7,600 fans. During his time there, André saw singer Dick Jensen perform. When André stood up after being introduced to the crowd, he blocked the spotlights aimed at the stage. It wasn't always easy being tall. That said, it had its perks. While there, he also went to a night club where he asked the bouncer, a six foot four, 275-pound guy, if he had to pay a cover charge, to which the doorman simply answered, "Aloha!" and let André in.

"I was coming back from Australia and New Zealand in 1977 and decided I would stop in Honolulu for a short vacation," recalled Quebec City native Rick Martel, who had first met André in Atlanta in '76. "I was reading the newspaper and I realized there was wrestling that night. I went to the desk and asked if they knew where the wrestlers were staying. They were at the Ambassador. I asked for André and, lucky me, he was there." The two friends made a plan for the night, but then André invited him to come to the venue for Ed Francis's meeting. Martel didn't feel comfortable since it wasn't a territory he was working at the time. But you couldn't say no to the Giant. "You're already in the business, you're not a mark, you're coming. Period. Then we'll go eat." André made the presentation and told the promoter that Martel should be booked there. "And sure enough, the following year, I was booked!" concluded Martel. André always had a sweet spot in his heart for French-Canadians.

On his way back to New York, André stopped in Los Angeles, where Valois alerted the media about something that had happened a few weeks earlier. Coming back from a tour in Japan, where André wrestled his usual opponents Inoki, Sakaguchi, and Kobayashi, he had stayed at the Gala Hotel in Los Angeles. André always traveled with only one suitcase, which usually contained his wrestling boots, some clothes, and money. While his suitcase was in a storage room, it was stolen. Newspapers from all over the country picked up the UPI article. It was reported that the suitcase contained $7,700 in cash from his tour in Japan. The article also joked about how the shoes and clothes wouldn't fit the thief and added that the robber surely hoped the police would find him before André did. Even when he was the victim of a burglary, his size was talked about. Unfortunately, the story didn't say if the thief was ever arrested.

The late 1970s were full of other surprises. Up until then, André would never lose and never win a title. In Japan, he only wrestled for the New Japan promotion. Well, that wasn't the case anymore.

Knoxville, Tennessee, was where Ronnie Garvin reigned in 1978. Known as "The One Man Gang," he had a gimmick that compares to "Stone Cold" Steve Austin's: Garvin was a tough S.O.B. who could fight more than one man and always stood tall in the end. Since the start of 1978, Garvin was in a feud with Roy Lee Welch. He had already defeated Jos Leduc, and he had broken Welch's arm. André was coming in, so the storyline was that Garvin said he could beat Welch, who had his arm in a cast, and whomever Welch picked as a partner in a handicap match.

On March 5, Welch showed up and announced his partner: André the Giant. Welch chose the man who was usually on the *other* side of a two-against-one match — the king of the handicap matches. How could he lose? Garvin first eliminated Welch to face André one on one. The Giant sold for Garvin like he was getting a pounding. And to the bafflement of everyone in attendance, Garvin beat André. Clean. In the middle of the ring. *What?* Was this another fairy tale or exaggerated story?

Thankfully, Knoxville wrestling historian David Williamson had the answers: "Top heel Garvin beat the stew out of André and actually pinned him. André sold like crazy for Ronnie. André and Ronnie had been friends for years, and André agreed to put Ronnie over in Knoxville, on the agreement that the pin on André wouldn't be taped or televised."

The man himself, Ronnie Garvin, remembered it well. "We were friends. We knew each other from Florida and North Carolina. We would speak French, you know," recalled Garvin, who was born in Montreal. "At the end of the match, André came charging in the corner, and I ducked, so André ran hard in the corner, took a few steps backward, and fell on his back. I immediately covered him. One, two, and as the referee counted three, André bench pressed me over the top rope. Technically he'd been disqualified, but it was too late: the referee had counted to three."

It was the perfect finish to protect the Giant. "André wanted to do the job," explained Garvin. "He saw how over I was there and he wanted to put me over more to help me. It wasn't approved by McMahon or anyone. And if it wasn't for technology, only we and the people in the arena that night would have known. He was the greatest guy."

Garvin is right. Can you imagine this today, in the world of instant social media news? It would have spread all over the world in a heartbeat. But at the time, because it wasn't televised, taped, or reported in a wrestling magazine, it was almost as if it never happened.

When André wasn't too busy being a good friend, he wrestled a healthy number of title holders. Aside from his NWA matches against Race, he wrestled with Nick Bockwinkel for the AWA's championship, against the Sheik for the NWA U.S. title (the old U.S. title from the 1950s in Chicago), and for the WWWF tag team titles with Chief Jay Strongbow. If there was one André could win, it was a tag team championship, because André's partner could always later lose a match and the title without hurting André's undefeated streak. In wrestling, if you're not the one on your team getting pinned or submitted, you technically didn't lose. As mentioned, André had won the tag team titles in Australia in December. However, that was not his only tag title won that month. On Christmas Day 1978, André and Dusty Rhodes worked in New Orleans for promoter Leroy McGuirk, as part of a tournament to crown the new NWA United States tag team champions. After defeating two other teams, André and Dusty made it to the finals against the team of Stan Hansen and Ernie Ladd. At the Superdome in front of 15,900 enthusiastic fans, André and Dusty won the match and the title. Their reign was short lived though, as André's schedule didn't allow him to stay in any one territory for long. He was there to draw a house and to get a big pop on Christmas night. Rhodes defended the titles with the Spoiler (Don Jardine) and lost exactly a month later.

Dusty and André had known each other a long time. They had faced one another in tag team matches for the AWA back in 1972 and then in Florida when Dusty was still a heel. But those days paled in comparison to the nights the two would spend in New Orleans. At the time, you'd still find many French-speaking people there, and when André could speak his native language, he was happy. One night, André and Dusty were drunk on Bourbon Street and André brought Dusty to his favorite bordello, run by a French woman André knew. It was raining, and as they were climbing the stairs to the second floor, lightning struck and the electricity went out. Suddenly, Dusty felt something warm on his leg.

"Ah shit, the rain," Dusty remembered. "A slow, low laughter came from the Giant — next came uncontrollable laughter . . . what I thought was rain from the roof was nothing more than him pissing on my leg. The fucking Giant had just pissed on 'The American Dream' in a French bordello in New Orleans, Louisiana! It was a great rib!"

Always the ribber, some of André's pranks were funnier than others . . . or at least less harmful. "This one time we were in New Orleans and they had a show at the Superdome, Dusty's mom had joined us for the trip," remembered Michelle Runnels, Dusty's second wife and mother of wrestler Cody Rhodes. "Well, at 3 a.m. André called our room and told Dusty that Lee Majors and Farrah Fawcett were down at the bar and wanted to meet him. So Dusty not only gets up and gets dressed, but he wakes me up and then calls his mom's room to wake her up so all of us could go down and meet them. When we went down to the bar, it was deserted except for a cleaning woman vacuuming. André loved to rib Dusty."

Any time a promoter could book a match between André and another big man, they invariably would. Two huge men fighting almost always engaged the fans. For André, sometimes that meant a confrontation with Bobo Brazil in a battle royal since the two of them were babyfaces, and other times it was a big one-on-one match against someone like Blackjack Mulligan or Bruiser Brody. Brody was someone André typically wrestled in Texas. "Brody had great respect for André, for both his ability to make money and working with André. He liked him, and I don't know if 'feared' him is the right word, but he was a pretty brave guy, and he made it clear that there was no way he'd ever test André. I guess he respected him," said Dave Meltzer, who was a friend to Brody. "It's too bad that politically their paths never crossed in Japan because as over as Brody was there, I think he and André would have been like Stan Hansen and André and probably would have been one of the best matches of André's career."

André wrestled Mulligan, whose real name was Bob Windham, the father of Barry Windham and grandfather of WWE's Bo Dallas and Bray Wyatt, for the first time back in the Grand Prix days at the end of 1971. Although he was billed as six foot nine, in reality he was closer to six foot six. After that first encounter, they crossed paths both in and out of the ring many times. One time, in the late 1970s, after the matches in Amarillo, Texas, André and Mulligan were playing cribbage with Dick

GEORGE NAPOLITANO

ANDRÉ AND DUSTY RHODES WERE GOOD FRIENDS; HERE WITH MEXICAN LEGEND MIL MÁSCARAS.

ANDRÉ BECAME FRIENDS WITH A LOT OF QUEBEC WRESTLERS; RICK MARTEL WAS ONE OF THEM.

Murdoch and Manny Fernandez at Fernandez's home. Everyone was drunk, and André and Mulligan got into an argument. Mulligan actually punched André and they started to brawl. No one really knows who won or how the fight ended, but it caused $1,800 worth of damage. It wasn't the only time that André and the big Texan went at it. Another time, André threw Mulligan right through a wall in a motel, into the next room — which was occupied. Their most notorious brawl happened in Virginia Beach. André and Mulligan were again with Murdoch and a young Ric Flair this time. Mulligan, known for his short temper, told Murdoch to watch him, as he sucker-punched the Giant. André got up, grabbed both Mulligan and Murdoch by their shirts, and dragged them to the beach and into the ocean, threatening to drown them. His intention, of course, wasn't really to murder them, just to scare them. And as the story goes, it worked. Meanwhile, Flair walked away from the scene, hoping André wouldn't touch him. "We all got back to the bar and started drinking again!" said Flair.

Although he was a draw everywhere, including in New York, André likely missed the chance to have the biggest match of his career at that point, because of Vince Sr. At the end of the 1970s, after Bruno Sammartino had lost the title, he wanted to work with André. But baby-face versus babyface matches were rarely booked in that era. The match pitting Bruno and Pedro Morales at the first Showdown at Shea in 1972 might explain why. The show was expected to draw 40,000 people but only drew 22,508. McMahon likely didn't feel it would ever work. "It's a really great 'What if?'" said Meltzer. "Bruno's suggestion included him losing, which he never did in those days. I think it would have drawn big, because of the idea of Bruno versus André, on paper . . . nothing could be bigger. But it's still face versus face and long-term Vince never wanted anyone beating Bruno. Bruno had this almost mythical presence and beating André was unthinkable for Vince at that time. Because of André, the time limit draw wouldn't have worked well and a double count-out would have been the likely finish, but that would have been flat, and made people want a rematch, and they'd never do it twice. Perhaps a record-breaking opportunity was missed."

An opportunity might have been missed with Bruno, but it wasn't with Ernie Ladd. Since he hailed from Louisiana, he was a big draw in New Orleans. Earlier in 1978, on April 1, a double main event of NWA champion Harley Race against Rhodes and André facing Ladd drew 20,102 fans to the Superdome. The gate of $100,435 was the biggest in Louisiana to date. A lot of their matches were dubbed "Battle of the Giants," a name also used for some of André's other matches. A few months later, Ladd and André had a match at MSG that drew 18,000 spectators.

"What made [André] special is he learned that he could control an audience and bring them back again," Ladd once said. "Many people could draw an audience the first time and then never get them back to the arena. He could draw them over and over." While true to an extent, it was still possible for André to be overexposed in a territory. It's for that same reason that he didn't remain tag team champions with Dusty for too long.

Another big man who didn't wrestle André but tagged with him a few times was Haystacks Calhoun. One of wrestling's biggest attraction of the 1950s and 1960s, Calhoun was an extremely large country boy, billed as six foot four and more than 600 pounds. One time, they went to dinner together. "There was a place next to the arena, which was one of those all-you-can-eat-for-two-dollars joints," André said in an interview, recalling one of his favorite stories. "When Haystacks and I walked in, you could see the waitress almost faint. About 30 seconds later, the manager comes out, takes a peek at us, and shakes his head and goes back to the kitchen. Haystacks and I decided to tie on a real big feed that night and the waitresses were hysterical. They told us the manager was tearing his hair out and practically in tears. But we felt bad, since we must've eaten about $25 worth of food for $4. After it was over, we told him we'd pay for the regular price instead of the all-you-can-eat price. He thanked us for that and told us two more like us could put him out of business." The generosity of André was almost limitless — and he would prove it again and again.

By the summer of 1979, IWE had fallen to the number three promotion in Japan. And it had been five years since André returned to help out his friend Isao Yoshihara. "He was so busy, but he heard IWE was not doing so well financially, and he asked Vince to let him go to IWE to help me," recalled Yoshihara. "Vince had a contract with New Japan, but André had a lot of power and could bypass that contract. Still, Inoki had to say yes for that." And he did. Again, as in 1974, alienating André wasn't worth the trouble. So sure enough, André worked a week-long tour for IWE, teaming with Alexis Smirnoff and Calhoun, wrestling mostly against his friend Mighty Inoue. "My company, IWE, folded in August 1981 due to bankruptcy. But my memory of André is still vivid. He was one of the best guys," concluded Yoshihara.

Typically, André worked for New Japan once a year, occasionally twice, for a two-week tour. In 1978 though, things were different. The very first Madison Square Garden series, a round-robin tournament demonstrating the strong relationship between Inoki's group and Vince McMahon's WWWF, was something special and kept André in Japan for a whole month. Taking inspiration from the World League tournament, it in turn inspired the biggest wrestling tournament in the world today, the G1 Climax. It was an interesting event for André as he wrestled against New Japan's young gun, Tatsumi Fujinami, for the first time. The two had met in the U.S. when Fujinami was sent there to learn the business, like every other young Japanese wrestler.

"I was in the North Carolina area when I was young, back in 1976, 1977," remembered Fujinami, who, like André, ended up in the WWE Hall of Fame. "André knew I was sent by Inoki, so he was very nice to me in the dressing room. I told him that I had been in Germany before I went to North Carolina, so we chatted a lot about German memories. Talking about promoter Gustl Kaiser, German wrestlers, and, of course, German beers. He mentioned the very hard mats in Europe and said in terms of 'quality of the ring, Japan is the best.' For such a big man, good ring quality was most important, needless to say."

André made it to the final of the tournament, losing to Inoki by count-out. Two days later, on June 1, the double main event of André against Sakaguchi and the double title match between National Wrestling Federation champion Inoki and WWWF champion Bob Backlund drew 13,000 fans. Backlund had started working for McMahon at the very end of 1976, and this was his first Japanese tour — and the start of a good friendship between him and André. The night before, they had teamed together for the first time against Inoki and Sakaguchi.

"The formula when you were André's tag team partner was always the same — get in a few moves at the beginning, take the heat from your opponent for a while, tease an inability to tag André in for a while longer until you had the crowd at its peak, then tag André in, and let him clean house and take it home," wrote Backlund.

André spent the last weeks of the decade working a two-week tour for Verne Gagne and then went to Germany, where he rekindled his feud with an old friend, Jack de Lassartesse. Thanks to markets like New York, Atlanta, St. Louis, Houston, Chicago, Winnipeg, Boston, and Greensboro, the last two years of the decade had seen André as one of the top six biggest drawing cards, usually only behind the NWA or WWWF champion. In the *Pro Wrestling Illustrated* awards, he was voted the most popular wrestler in 1977 and was the runner-up in '78 and '79, behind his good friend Dusty Rhodes. The new decade would be very different: a new home, a new road manager, and a new position mixed with injuries, pain, and more fame. The 1980s gave André a new reality, both personally and professionally. Nothing is forever, and the Giant knew that better than almost anyone.

CHAPTER 16

WHEN ANDRÉ MET HULK

André was clearly fond of Montreal, as it offered a way to connect with his French roots. It was the North American city that felt most like home, in spirit and language at least. Only one other place could compare to the tranquility and anonymity of Molien — Ellerbe in Richmond County, North Carolina.

Over the years, André had befriended a French-Canadian wrestler-turned-referee by the name of Aimé Bernard. Bernard was born June 20, 1936, in a small village with less than a thousand people, St-Alphonse-de-Caplan, in the easternmost part of the province of Quebec, 500 miles from Montreal. He was the last of 16 children. He lost both of his parents by the time he was 11; not getting along with his sister and brother-in-law who were running the house, he left with his brother Roland to work in construction in British Columbia. That's where he learned to speak English, and that's where he was taught the ropes. He was known, of course, as "Frenchy" — a nickname a lot of Quebecers get outside of Quebec. Frenchy became his de facto first name: his 2013 obituary didn't even mention his real first name. While he was wrestling in Washington State, he shattered his ankle, and so he started managing.

He was small enough for the job. He mainly managed in the Gulf Coast territory, working as Monsieur Frenchy Bernard and managing guys like Gorgeous George Jr., whom he had met in Vancouver; Rip Tyler; The Liberator; The Spoiler; Bobby Shane; and the Mysterious Medic. While in Pensacola, Florida, he met Jackie Hester. The two lost touch when Jackie moved to Louisiana. She met someone else in June and the two married in August. On the day of her wedding, Frenchy called her and asked what she was doing. It was a call that changed both of their destinies. By early January, she was back in Florida with Frenchy. She divorced her husband and in the summer of 1977, Jackie married Bernard. They lived in a cabin in Quebec, while Frenchy renewed his legal papers to work in the United States, and then they moved to Tampa, Florida, where Frenchy started refereeing and worked setting up the ring.

A few years before marrying Jackie, Frenchy had been promoting in Baton Rouge, Louisiana. That's where he met André for the first time. "A promoter told me about this new guy coming in, this great big guy. All of a sudden I looked at the door and hell, I seen the body but I couldn't see no head," he told journalist Dave Stubbs. From that point on, every time they saw each other, they played cribbage, and like many other Quebecers in the business, André and Frenchy became friends. It was easier for André to express himself in French, and every time he could make a new friend out of a French-speaking guy, he would. In 1980, after an argument with Dusty Rhodes about a non-wrestling matter, Frenchy was fired from the Tampa promotion.

"Frenchy was a little tough son of a bitch," recalled Mike Graham. "He walked right out of the Sportatorium in Florida and challenged a guy who had heckled him in the ring to come and fight him. Remember Frenchy was 135 pounds. The guy signed a release and I was going to referee the match. I saw something on the mat, and it all happened in a split second, but the guy started screaming at the top of his lungs. Frenchy had bit his ear off! I DQ'd Frenchy and told the guy to get out. Frenchy kept the ear for two weeks and showed it to people. *He was André's bodyguard!*"

In the late 1970s, a bunch of Quebec wrestlers were working in North Carolina. Guys like René Goulet, Dino Bravo, and Ronnie Garvin. Bravo's girlfriend at the time, Denise, had a daughter named Diane and she met a guy from Ellerbe who had built a house there. Sure enough, André liked it so much he bought the 3,500-square-foot, three-story house and the 46-acre land around it. Since he was almost never home, he asked Ray Stevens and his wife, who lived nearby, to check in on his place from time to time. Somehow André had heard about Frenchy being fired. "I met André in his New York hotel room, and he told me and Jackie to move out to the house," Bernard told Stubbs. "He loved Jackie. She could do no wrong in his eyes. I didn't have any money, so he gave me a big pile of bills, about $9,000, that I had to stuff down my boots and into my shirt. I went out to the place and started fixing it up." So Frenchy — who had stopped working in the business after the Rhodes incident — and Jackie moved there in August 1980 and stayed there for the next 15 years.

It was a generous arrangement, although it did help André to have someone to take care of the house. However, André's generosity to Frenchy didn't stop there. A few years after they had moved in, Frenchy rented a few acres of the farmland just next to André's in order to raise cattle and run his horses. Realizing Frenchy loved the land so much, André bought the ranch up the road, which was 80 acres. The two properties did not connect, so André bought a strip of land to connect the house to the ranch. They named it the AFJ ranch, for André, Frenchy, and Jackie. "André would buy me a new truck every two years, whether I needed it or not," Bernard continued. "Sometimes I wouldn't even know about it. Ford would just show up and put it in the yard."

The new decade saw change for André: he would reach the pinnacle of his fame and drawing power with the expansion of the World Wrestling Federation (they had dropped "Wide" in 1979), but before that happened, André went back to Montreal. The territory had been basically dead since the demise of All Star and Grand Prix, and André had rarely wrestled in Montreal since 1976. Even though he loved having fun and playing cards with his colleagues before a show, André liked making money too.

It afforded him the ability to be generous with his people. In that era, in order to make more than a regular payoff, some wrestlers were offered to buy shares in a local office, as a way to prepare for when their career in the ring came to an end. For André, that opportunity was about to knock.

Jack Britton, a wrestler-turned-promoter famous for running the wrestling midgets booking office, had taken over the Montreal and Quebec territory in 1977. But he was losing an average of $2,000 to $3,000 every Monday night running the Paul Sauvé Arena. The promotion could not afford to run any other city and it had no television to help it get out of its financial rut. However, on February 11, 1980, Britton's promotion held a show that was not only profitable but also drew 2,000 people, twice as many as usual. The show featured Pat Patterson and Lou Albano in the main event. Both of them had name-recognition in Montreal, because WWF's television reached Montreal airwaves through the ABC Burlington, Vermont, station. Sadly though, Jack Britton passed away the night before, on February 10, at the age of 63. His son Gino Brito was left in control of a territory that reached from the outskirts of the Maritime provinces to most of northern Ontario and the entire province of Quebec, but it couldn't draw enough in Montreal to jumpstart the business and achieve its full potential.

Per show, the rent at the Paul Sauvé Arena was $1,800, publicity was between $500 to $1,000, plus paying office employees and talents; the promotion needed houses of $6,000 to $7,000 just to break even. Gino Brito spent two days with the company's accountant, Jos Bélanger, trying to figure out his options and not end up in the same situation his father had found himself in. Brito didn't want to make the same mistakes and decided to request a meeting with Vince McMahon Sr. to help him get the ball rolling and open more towns. Brito knew McMahon pretty well, as he had worked for him a few years prior as Louis Cerdan, winning the WWWF tag team titles in the 1970s. It was a smart call, as McMahon had a solution for him.

Just a year or two prior, Frank Valois, who was in his late 50s, found that the wear and tear of the road was taking its toll. Around

1978–1979, he stopped going on the road with André — not by choice. Vince McMahon replaced Valois with Arnold Skaaland, also a former wrestler. Skaaland had started wrestling in 1946 and retired in 1978. By 1973, he was wrestling sporadically and had started managing Bruno Sammartino when the latter won the WWWF title from Stan Stasiak. Then, in 1978, soon after Bob Backlund won that same title, Skaaland became his manager as well. In both 1978 and 1979, Skaaland won PWI's manager of the year award. Vince Sr. decided to assign Skaaland to André, an obvious choice, since Skaaland knew everyone in the business and was a close lieutenant who had shares in the company. It was the biggest change in André's life and career since he had signed with McMahon. He had known Valois for a very long time and had traveled the world with him for years. But business is business and there was nothing André could do to change things. That said, Skaaland was four years younger than Valois, and truth be told, André didn't need as much assistance in talking to reporters by this time. His English — though it never became great — was good enough to get by. So Skaaland only traveled with André when he was working in McMahon's territory and in Japan, where Skaaland also played André's heel manager. The two of them got along well though: Skaaland liked to drink almost as much as the Giant. "The only one who could follow André at the bar to some degree was Skaaland," recalled Brito. "They would have shots and they would motivate themselves to keep going."

Taking Valois off the road didn't mean that Vince didn't appreciate him anymore. He made sure Valois was taken care of. "Vince Sr. was looking to place Frank Valois somewhere," revealed Gino Brito. "It was a loyal family. Vince saw Montreal as an opportunity for Frank to stay involved in the business." Vince Sr. told Brito that Frank Valois was looking to go back home, and since André was still close to Valois, he also joined the adventure. Gino offered them 40 percent of the business, and a deal was made for André and Valois to each buy 20 percent of the Montreal office. Whether he liked it or not, André was now the boss, for real. Still, he was an invisible boss — the partners agreed that it was best that the Giant be a silent partner. They also agreed that he shouldn't act any differently with the other wrestlers. He was one of the boys, and that never changed. The locker room was a safe zone for him, a place where no one would do a double take when they saw him — very different from what he endured on the street, in hotel lobbies, or at the airport. He was not going to put that in jeopardy by bossing anyone around.

Valois was named president and was the promoter on record; Brito appointed himself vice-president. Brito wasn't ready to hang up his boots yet, and the Montreal Athletic Commission, which was still regulating wrestling, didn't allow promoters to wrestle. Therefore, Valois was the obvious choice. The company was named Varoussac Promotions: "Va" for Valois, "Rouss" for Roussimoff and "Ac" for Acocella, Gino's real last name. At the time, André was charging $1,500 per match; multiply that by approximately 300 matches a year and you get André's yearly salary, estimated at around $500,000 by *Sports Illustrated*. As a shareholder, he was getting 5 percent of the profit the company made. He was getting his payoff, without any middle person handling his money and without McMahon taking a cut for the use of André in Montreal. That's the deal Vince McMahon, Gino Brito, and André had made. Back then, $500,000 was a lot of money but it wasn't enough to make him the highest paid athlete of that time. André was making four to six times what an average baseball, basketball, or football player earned and more than 20 times what the U.S. average household income was, but he was way behind Muhammad Ali, who made eight million for his October 1980 fight against Larry Holmes, and Houston Astros pitcher Nolan Ryan, who was making a million a year.

André was now a wrestling promoter and his involvement, even as a silent partner, helped the company in many different ways. Gino Brito received investment money from Capitol Wrestling Corporation Ltd., the parent company of the WWF, to the tune of $75,000 U.S, a little more than $85,000 Canadian at the time. He was never told how Valois and André cut a deal with Vince Sr., but one can safely assume that was money already owed to them or an upfront on upcoming bookings.

THE FIRST RIVALRY BETWEEN ANDRÉ AND HULK HOGAN HAD A DIFFERENT OUTCOME THAN IN 1987.

GINO BRITO WAS A FRIEND AND BUSINESS PARTNER TO ANDRÉ.

IN MONTREAL, ANDRÉ WAS ALWAYS KNOWN AS "LE GÉANT" JEAN FERRÉ.

ANDRÉ WAS MAKING THE COVER OF EVERY WRESTLING MAGAZINE, INCLUDING THOSE IN THE PROVINCE OF QUEBEC.

André was never treated like any other wrestler by the New York office. Here's another example: When André was in Montreal, or anywhere else for that matter, he wasn't one to worry about what he spent. One time, Brito had to call Phil Zacko, who had shares in Capitol Wrestling, to figure out what to do when he needed to front money to the Giant. Zacko told him to stay put, that someone who knew what to do would call him back in 10 minutes.

McMahon Sr. himself called right back and asked to speak with Gino privately: "Listen, it's just between you and me. The Giant, no matter what he needs, be it $1,000 or even 2,000, you give him whatever he wants. Don't worry about it. You don't have to clear it with me, but don't talk about this with nobody and we will pay you back."

It didn't happen every night, but from that moment on, Gino would always carry extra cash, just in case. Some nights, he was carrying so much money that he would stop drinking early to remain sober, feeling the pressure of carrying so much money around. When needed, he would sneak to the restroom, roll up 20 $100 bills, and then discretely slip them into André's hand back at the bar. He would later tell Vince Sr. how much, and sure enough, he would get a check refunding him, no questions asked. Some people in the company thought the expense of bringing André to town was counterproductive, but Gino always insisted that the prestige of having André the Giant was an investment in the business. André was such a drawing card that he could appeal outside of the regular fan base and bring media attention the promotion couldn't buy. Having André the Giant as a partner also helped build a strong relationship between the Montreal and New York offices. In the original agreement, on top of paying the talent he was using from New York, Brito was supposed to pay a percentage of the house when using New York talent, but McMahon didn't enforce that clause in the early days because he knew how hard it was for them to break even. As a matter of fact, before Varoussac got television in December 1980, the group had already used up all the money invested in the company. Brito had to go back to McMahon.

"He told me to take on one of his friends, Moshe Solow, as a part-ner," remembered Brito. "I didn't know the guy. He was from Boston and wanted to put some money in wrestling. I always thought it was someone who Vince owed a favor. I sold him some of my shares but made sure to always keep at least 51 percent of the business. It gave us the money to eventually launch our TV show. But Solow didn't stay long, not even a year. We weren't really talking to him. He didn't understand the business and never had anything to say. So he wanted to leave, and I bought his shares back."

Even if Vince Sr. was good to Brito, Valois, and André, it didn't mean he wasn't looking after his investment. And in this particular deal, his investment wasn't cash money but André himself. In his memoir *Accepted*, Pat Patterson recalled that Vince Sr. specifically wanted Pat to work in Montreal to make sure André's business was well taken care of. During that first year, McMahon also got involved in André's bookings in Montreal, choosing programs based on what he was doing with him on his television shows. And that's when Hulk Hogan came in play.

Jack Brisco was a former two-time NWA champion and part owner of the Florida territory. His promoter was Eddie Graham. One night, in 1977, some of his friends forced him to go out with them to see a band play at a local Tampa bar, the Imperial Room. When Jack arrived, he quickly noticed the bassist, a six-foot-seven good-looking guy with tons of muscles. His name was Terry Bollea. Not only was he a musician, but he had also played little league baseball and high school football, and looked like he had been in the gym all his life. Brisco made a point to speak with him and asked if he had ever thought of being a professional wrestler. Bollea said that he was a huge wrestling fan; becoming a pro wrestler was his dream. So Brisco arranged a meeting for his new friend at the Sportatorium in Tampa the very next day. He introduced him to Graham and head trainer Yasuhiro Kojima, better known as Hiro Matsuda. The latter had quite a reputation as a trainer. Over the years, he trained guys like Brian Blair, Ron Simmons, and Lex Luger. Known to be stiff, especially with rookies, he accidentally either twisted or broke Bollea's ankle, depending on who you talk to, during one training session. Bollea's very first match in front of an audience was against Matsuda, but his first against someone other than his trainer was against Brian Blair.

"I will remember that match forever," said Blair. "We were told to do a 15-minute draw. So Terry and I paced ourselves, and at one point, I saw Pat Patterson and all the heels coming out the curtains and Jack Brisco and all the babyfaces doing the same thing. I told Terry that we must have been doing well since everyone was out there to watch the match. Then just a few minutes before 15 minutes, business started to pick up. One-two kick out, one-two kick out. We gave everything we had in the last few minutes. And that's when the ring announcer said, '15 minutes gone, 15 minutes remaining!' That's when we understood we'd been pranked. Pat Patterson had changed the timing of the match and 'forgot' to let us know! The rest of the match was so bad. We had nothing left in the tank. That's why I will never forget it!" It was a rib André would have appreciated . . .

Bollea started touring the territory, working either as Super Destroyer or under his real name. However, after a few months, he quit because he wasn't making enough money. But the itch came back. Bollea had befriended "Superstar" Billy Graham, and he gave him a call to see if he could get hooked outside Tampa. Graham sent him to Southeastern Championship Wrestling (SECW) and their booker, a French-Canadian named Louie Tillet. The territory covered northern Florida, southern Alabama, and eastern Tennessee. There, Tillet renamed him Terry "The Hulk" Boulder. The name came from Lou Ferrigno's *The Incredible Hulk*, a huge TV sensation at the time. From there, Bollea went to Memphis, Tennessee, and worked for Jerry Jarrett and Jerry Lawler.

According to Jimmy Hart, while in Memphis, Bollea asked Lawler to sign him to a contract to manage him, essentially the same kind of deal that Vince Sr. had with André. Hart urged Lawler to do it. Hart wrote in his book that Lawler's response was, "That guy will never draw

you a dime in professional wrestling. He doesn't have what it takes."
After that, Bollea went to Georgia, under the name of Sterling Golden,
before getting matches with the WWF, thanks again to Jack Brisco,
who put Bollea in touch with Vince McMahon Sr. Bollea made his
WWF debut as "The Incredible" Hulk Hogan at the November 13,
1979, TV taping. The surname Hogan was added because Vince Sr.
wanted an Irish-American hero. He already had Sammartino for the
Italian-Americans, Morales for the Puerto Ricans, and current champion Backlund sounded more Swedish than American. Smart move:
most of the Irish-Americans in the United States lived in McMahon's
territory. Two months later, on December 12, Hogan made his MSG
debut against Ted DiBiase. As they say, the rest is history. He finished his dates in Georgia and Tennessee and started full-time for the
McMahons, as a heel.

Although in both 1980 and 1987, fans were told they were seeing the
first encounter between André and Hogan, that was untrue. They had
first met in the squared circle in 1977. But it wasn't in a packed stadium
— it was a high school gymnasium in Gainesville, Florida. An inauspi-
cious first meeting. Hogan, then wrestling as the Super Destroyer, and
André were in a battle royal, which was won, of course, by the Giant. By
the time Hogan was full-time in New York, he had wrestled André in
singles matches four times, as well as in a few tag team matches and even
in an arm-wrestling contest.

The arm-wrestling contest is important since it led to the first significant match between Hogan and André. Shortly after Hogan started
with SECW, he was matched with André. Their first singles match was
in Pensacola, Florida, on April 26, 1979. Shortly after, in May 1979, in
Dothan, Alabama, they had an arm-wrestling contest that ended with
the interference of Billy Spears, who was managing Hogan (then wrestling as Boulder). The following attack by Hogan left André bleeding in
the ring. That angle set up a match between Hogan and André that sold
out the 5,000-seat Houston County Farm Center in Dothan. "Their
match in Dothan, Alabama, was the match that put Hulk Hogan on the

map," said Dave Meltzer. "I mean, at least to the southeast promoters. They were like, 'Oh my god, he can draw money.'"

In New York, Hogan, managed by Freddie Blassie, was sold as a muscle monster who called himself the king of pro wrestling. So it was no surprise that he was scoring wins by DQ or count-out against champions like Tito Santana, Pat Patterson, and even Bob Backlund. When he lost, it was never by pin or submission. Although some Hogan-André matches ended by DQ or count-out as well, the only one who could have a clean win against Hogan was André — on house shows though, never on TV. Their first WWF singles match was at a house show in Binghamton, New York, on March 28, 1980. Eight days later, in Baltimore, they main-evented their first 10,000-plus crowd together: it was Hogan's first ever, with 11,500 fans in attendance. In May and June 1980, Vince McMahon Sr. booked Hogan in Japan, where he worked for Antonio Inoki's New Japan Pro Wrestling. That's where he first teamed with André, in a six-man tag alongside Dusty Rhodes. Returning to North America for the summer, the idea was to pit Hogan and André against each other for the big Shea Stadium show under the main draw, Bruno Sammartino getting revenge against his former protégé, Larry Zbyszko. Surprisingly, there was no big buildup for the match. André defeated Hogan by disqualification on July 26 at the Spectrum in Philadelphia, a match televised on PRISM Network for the local market only. Besides a few small house show matches, the rest was done through advertising. A taped interview conducted by Vince Jr. with André, which was broadcast on August 9 through WWF's syndicated *Championship Wrestling*, didn't even talk about Hogan and the Shea Stadium match (that interview is famous because they had André stand on a box to look much taller). Then again, it was not the main draw. There was another big stage match between the two, prior to the one at Shea, which was almost as big. It was for Bill Watts's Mid-South Wrestling at the Superdome in New Orleans in front of 30,000 fans on August 2, a week before the contest in Flushing, New York. Again they were not the main attraction. Coming off a huge angle where the Freebirds — Terry Gordy,

Michael Hayes, and Buddy Roberts — blinded the Junkyard Dog, JYD was finally facing Michael Hayes, in a dog collar steel cage match, and that drew all the attention. Hogan and André faced each other in a upper mid-card match that ended in a double count-out.

That night in New Orleans proved to be tricky. In his book, promoter Bill Watts explains that André and Hogan were sent to his show by Vince McMahon, who told him Hogan should lose to André. Watts then claimed Hogan didn't want to put the Giant over — which infuriated André. On the other hand, Hogan said in his book that Watts wanted him to lose to Wahoo McDaniel first and then lose to André later on that same night. Hogan said he refused to lose to Wahoo, saying Vince had told him not to, that he knew he had to job for André, but then Watts told André he didn't want to do the job against both of them. What's hard to believe about that version of the story is that Wahoo lost against The Grappler that same night. The Grappler was a heel being built up to win the title from Ted DiBiase the following month. It made perfect sense for The Grappler to beat Wahoo, an established babyface but not a regular in the territory. And that's the point. Since Wahoo wasn't a regular there, how was it a good thing to pit him against Hogan? And how could Watts have sold Hogan to the fans as a threat to André if he had lost to Wahoo earlier that night? Still, at the time, Hogan and André had not wrestled each other that many times in the northeast. André had started the year with a lengthy tour that brought him from Texas to California, and from Florida to Mexico. He only went back to McMahon's territory in late March, and although not every result from that period is available, most of the known André-Hogan matches end in double count-outs. The rest of them have André winning. Why didn't Hogan want to lose this time? Since Watts's story is a little stronger than Hogan's, an educated guess of what really happened is that a week before the big match at Shea Stadium, Hogan didn't want to lose to André in a big showdown. Then again, it is hard to believe that Hogan would try to pull such a stunt when his bread and butter that year was working with André. What both Watts and Hogan agree on is that André took care of the situation as only André could — and that Hogan paid the price in the ring.

"I went and told André the situation, and he just said, 'I'll take care of it, boss,'" wrote Watts in his book. "I knew what was going to happen when I told André what Hulk had said." André could be persuasive in the ring when he wanted to. Still, the match ended up in a double count-out, perhaps a way for André to avoid a backstage confrontation with Hogan. Between that and the beating he gave Hogan in the ring, it was his way of taking care of the situation. "The only thing I know for sure is the double count-out really did happen; people have talked about it and Hogan often mentioned one time, that André had beaten him real good," said Meltzer.

In any case, they were working together again the very next week, as 36,295 fans gathered at the home of the New York Mets and witnessed André win. "Wrestling André that day was my first really big break in the business," Hogan wrote in his book *Hollywood Hulk Hogan*. All in all, between Sammartino and Zbyszko, who drew the house, and André and Hogan, who captivated the fans, the show was a big success. This latest version of the Showdown at Shea beat the one from 1976, when André had wrestled Wepner, by setting a gate record.

In the actual match, both were made to look strong. After the referee was accidentally knocked out when André body slammed Hogan, Hogan attacked the Giant and ended up body slamming him in return, seven years *prior* to when he body slammed André "for the first time ever." Hogan pinned André, and even though the referee was still down, André kicked out before the count of three. André body slammed Hulk right back, delivered his big splash, and a new referee made the three count, though Hogan clearly kicked out at two. (It wasn't even close.) But the aftermath was more important than the match itself. Blassie gave Hogan a foreign object to put in his elbow pad and he attacked André. Then he body slammed him again before leaving him bleeding in the ring.

The two top matches on the card were voted the best two matches of the year by *Pro Wrestling Illustrated*, with the main event having a slight edge. Thanks to the tape of Hogan attacking and body slamming André, the two of them had a multitude of rematches: Pittsburgh, Boston, and Washington, among other cities, witnessed the spectacle. A few of those matches are noteworthy. During a *Championship Wrestling* broadcast that aired on September 6, Vince McMahon Jr. interviewed André at ringside and was interrupted by Hogan and Blassie. Blassie challenged André to a match the following week, which the big man accepted. In his answer to the challenge, André told a story about taking out Don Leo Jonathan and Jonathan later warning him that one day someone would come along to replace him. This was his way of putting over Hogan. The match, taped in Hamburg, Pennsylvania, on August 20 but broadcast on September 13, only lasted four minutes. After the match ended up in a no contest, Hogan body slammed André and used a foreign object in his elbow pad to bloody André with his Hogan Hammer lariat, similar to what they had done at the Shea Stadium. McMahon interviewed André after the match, who was screaming for Hogan to come back and fight.

"They played that tape everywhere," recalled Meltzer. "I remember my friends saying, 'Did you see that guy who body slammed André?' It was a big deal."

That angle built to a main event at Madison Square Garden on September 22 in front of 21,000 fans. At the time, the match was the only one not televised on the MSG Network that night. In a match guest-refereed by Gorilla Monsoon, Hogan again slammed André but lost the match when he tried to slam the Giant a second time, falling under André's weight. Monsoon did a fast count while Hogan, as it was done at Shea, clearly lifted his shoulder at two. Between the body slams, the screw job finishes, André blading for him, and the double count-outs, a lot was given to Hogan during that feud.

A more conventional rematch happened on August 25 in Montreal. The match was proposed to Brito by McMahon. "I was interested," recalled Brito. "When the Giant came to me and told me not to worry, that the match would happen, I knew from that moment on the match would actually happen." It was announced and sold as the rematch of

Shea Stadium in the local newspapers. Until then, Varoussac wasn't much of a big deal. The trio had started the promotion in April, and the only rivalry of note was Raymond Rougeau against Pierre "Mad Dog" Lefebvre. Dino Bravo hadn't started with the group yet, and they had not been able to sell out the Paul Sauvé Arena. However, starting in May, everything was built to make Hogan and André the first big match in the history of the promotion.

Because of the Giant's French origins, the promotion wanted to build up a story of Hogan, a big American giant, wrestling and beating other French-speaking wrestlers, an angle that played well with a French-Canadian majority audience. On May 5, Hogan wrestled and defeated none other than Édouard Carpentier, who was 53 years old but still very much over with the fans. On June 23, the day before St. John the Baptist Day, Quebec's national holiday, Hogan defeated Brito. Then, on July 14, Bastille Day, France's national holiday, Hogan squashed Carpentier in only 30 seconds! Finally, on July 21, Hogan defeated Jackie Wiecz, Carpentier's nephew and André's former partner . "I was booking at the time," said Brito. "I came up with the idea of pitting Hogan against a few local guys. But I would have never asked Carpentier. He came up to me with that. He knew it was a big match for Jean and he thought he owed one to him for how much he had helped the business in the Grand Prix years." Everything was in place for the biggest match in the short history of the promotion. The publicity for the match was also the biggest the company had generated so far. Mostly created by Régis Lévesque, who was the biggest boxing promoter in town and famous for not letting the truth get in the way of a good story, Hogan was sold to the fans as an undefeated terror from the United States — six foot seven, 330 pounds with a Herculean physique, a real threat for the local hero. Levesque wrote that this match was the one fans wanted to see the most since the Jonathan rivalry. The most astonishing thing written was without a doubt the description of the match at Shea in the *Journal de Montréal*. It said that Hogan suffered his first professional defeat when he was disqualified after interference from Ken Patera when the referee was knocked, and that it degenerated in an all-out brawl with 12 wrestlers needed to pull them apart as Hogan totally lost it. It was also said that the match drew 56,232 fans and lasted 28 minutes.

In those days, there was no way for the local fans to know they were being lied to, and Lévesque was really good at his job. On a Monday evening, August 25, 7,383 fans showed up to see the "Battle of the Giants"; it was the biggest crowd for Varoussac and the first time it had sold out the Paul Sauvé Arena. Less than four months after the match, Varoussac had its own TV deal and hope for the future. "A lot of credit has to be given to Vince Sr. for the success we had in the first year," said Brito. "Without his help, I would've never been able to do what I did with the territory. When I was going to New York, he was helping me figure out the payoffs for his guys. I mean, I was talking to him more than I was talking to Frank!"

André's feud with Hogan was not yet over: it was brought to Japan for Inoki's NJPW for a two-month tour, from October to December 1980. It was Hogan's second tour in Japan. André had been on the first one as well, but they had teamed, not wrestled each other. This time, they wrestled against each other in singles and tag team bouts with each one ending in a non-finish, either a double count-out or disqualification. The tape from September was used again and sent to Jim Barnett's Georgia Championship Wrestling to build a big rematch on New Year's Day 1981 at the Omni in Atlanta. "André and Hogan worked mostly in the northeast but also in major cities all over North America, stemming from that same tape," added Meltzer.

The feud was so hot in 1980 that both André and Hogan were among the top 10 biggest draws of the year, sixth and seventh respectively. They kept feuding until the end of 1980, with a few more matches in early 1981 — until Hogan and McMahon Sr. had a falling-out.

Hogan had been offered a role in the third installment of *Rocky*. Sylvester Stallone wanted a scene between a boxer and a wrestler. Many believed the scene was inspired by the André the Giant versus Chuck Wepner fight from 1976, but in Allentown's *Morning Call* newspaper on

May 14, 1981, an interview with Stallone during the filming of *Rocky III* revealed that the boxer versus wrestler scene was inspired by Muhammad Ali versus Antonio Inoki on that same card. Yet it's hard to believe that the scene where Hogan's character, Thunderlips, throws Rocky over the top rope was not inspired by André tossing Wepner in a similar fashion. In any case, Stallone had called the *PWI* offices when he was looking to cast the part. He spoke to Bill Apter, who sent him pictures of Superstar Billy Graham and Hogan. Casting director Rhonda Young's brother, Pete, was a wrestling fan and Young asked him who he would suggest. Pete Young, who later became Hogan's agent, told his sister about Hulk, and in the end, that's who Stallone chose. Filming was scheduled for April to August 1981, but Hogan was only on set for 10 days in late April. McMahon didn't want Hogan to participate in the movie, saying Hogan had to choose between being a wrestler or an actor. Hogan decided to do the movie and McMahon told him he would never work for him again. So he finished his dates in April, did the movie, and went to Japan. Upon returning to North America in June, he worked a little in Florida before joining Verne Gagne's AWA. And sure enough, his involvement with André would continue.

In the meantime, however, André had moved on to another huge rivalry — one based on his first big injury. The effects of his untreated disorder were finally catching up to him and forced him to take a break from wrestling for the very first time. In the ring, he had faced countless foes, but in real life, only one human being could challenge André the Giant. His name was André Roussimoff.

CHAPTER 17

TO THE GIANT AMONG US

A s the decade advanced, André's health took a turn for the worse, and his life slowly turned into a Faustian tragedy. The real-life figure of Johann Georg Faust, an alchemist, astrologer, and magician from the Renaissance, has inspired plays, movies, and comic books and the legend around him gave birth to the expression "to make a deal with the Devil." Faust was a brilliant intellectual bored with life. Full of himself, he summoned the Devil to gain more knowledge and magical powers and to indulge in all the pleasures of the world. The Devil's representative, Mephistopheles, makes a bargain with Faust to serve him for a set number of years, after which the Devil would lay claim to his soul and Faust would be damned for all of eternity. Although he didn't choose to have acromegaly, André decided not to get any treatment to put an end to it and that was his own Faustian bargain. It gave him fame and all the pleasures in the world, but the ailment slowly but surely took everything away.

In May 1981, after an ankle injury, André had to have surgery for the first time. The operation was discussed at length in the 1981 *Sports Illustrated* in a piece by Terry Todd. It was historic because *Sports Illustrated*, established in 1954, hadn't covered pro wrestling and it was still a few years before Hulk Hogan made the magazine's cover in 1985. "I remember an article on Fabulous Moolah in the early '70s," recalled Dave Meltzer. "But [articles on wrestling in *Sports Illustrated*] were rare. There was also a feature in the '50s on who would win between Lou Thesz and Rocky Marciano. But the André piece was the first article of its size and length on a pro wrestler." As groundbreaking as it was, the article perpetuated the legend of André and gave the reader very little of the person behind the giant. For many years, it was considered the bible on André, but unfortunately as a product of its time, kayfabe was very much in place, and the real stories about André weren't told. The article was Todd's idea. André was, at the time, the most famous wrestler on Earth, and Todd thought there was an interesting story to be told, if he could follow the Giant for a while. Todd, who had a PhD in history and philosophy of education, was a former powerlifter as well as a writer. He had created the Arnold Strongman Classic after being asked by Arnold Schwarzenegger himself to create a strongman contest. Todd got in touch with former wrestling promoter and fellow weightlifter Milo Steinborn of Orlando and detailed his plan, asking him to get in touch with Vince McMahon Sr., which Steinborn did. Todd and McMahon met, and it was agreed that the journalist would join André on the road.

The article, published in the December 21, 1981, issue, not only perpetuated myths but was the source of many tales told and retold ever since — that André's grandfather was also a giant, how he was named André the Giant, and how he moved to Paris before being discovered by some wrestlers — all of which were false or exaggerated. The article also quoted Frank Valois, who said people were afraid to wrestle André, which was true. However, it was not because of his supposedly supernatural strength but because he could be clumsy and dangerous at times, especially early on in his career. The article also downplayed any achievements André had before he was put under the tutelage of Vince Sr. Yet, the biggest myth in the article is that André had left home at 14 and when he returned five years later, his parents recognized him as Jean Ferré, the TV star, not as their son — which is an excellent story but far from reality. Here's one more. In 2017, when Todd was interviewed for the HBO documentary, he still believed that André had his ankle broken in a match. And Todd is not the one to blame here. He wrote what André told him. He couldn't know that the Giant would lie to him in order to protect both his character and the business. For André, it was only the right thing to do. He wouldn't let someone in the locker room who had no business there, and he sure as hell wouldn't talk about his true origins. However, such a credible source made some of these "facts" very persistent — even after the internet changed wrestling, after shoot interviews became a thing, and even after the 2018 HBO documentary.

The 11-page, 8,000-word article, titled "To the Giant Among Us," featured many pictures, but one, in particular, captured everyone's attention: the one with the beer can. In the photograph, the reader could see Todd's hands, serving himself a beer, while André had a can of Molson Canadian in his right hand and it looked like it was a miniature version of a beer can. But it wasn't. It was a regular-sized beer can. The picture wasn't modified at all. Those who believe it was changed using Photoshop should know that the software was created six years after the photo was taken. It got so much attention as the years passed that if you Google "12oz beer can," it's one of the first pictures you find. Todd and photographer Stephen Green-Armytage had trouble finding a way to properly show André's large proportions. In an interview with journalist David Goldenberg in 2015, Green-Armytage said that they took a picture with André's restaurant manager in Montreal and another one in Central Park with a horse, but one needs to know the relative size of something to fully understand how big André was. That's when Todd suggested a beer can. "Obviously we chose an item whose size is familiar to the magazine's readers," he told Goldenberg.

The article did a great job in detailing how difficult regular life was for André, his legendary tolerance to alcohol, and the ankle injury and his need for surgery, which had occurred just before the article. André had a bimalleolar fracture of his left ankle. This is the bony structure of the ankle connecting the lateral malleolus (fibula) and the medial malleolus (tibia). What the article didn't mention was that this type of fracture was very rare for a man of André's age — unless he had a pre-existing condition like acromegaly or another bone disease. The ankle injury was the first payment in André's deal with the Devil.

The hospital had a nine-foot bed to accommodate him but had to get custom-made crutches. Perhaps because wrestlers are used to working with severe injuries, André ended up walking in into Dr. Yett's office. This was quite unusual to say the least. He told the doctor he had been injured in a wrestling match in western New York, but none of that was true. André had actually injured himself. His left ankle had been sprained for some time, and it was bothering him enough that Jackie and Frenchy convinced him to go see a doctor. He had X-rays done, which confirmed he had a sprain. In wrestling, that meant he could keep going. Bob Backlund wrote in his book that everyone was in Rochester, New York, on May 2 for a show where André was supposed to wrestle Killer Khan. Instead, when André woke up, he had broken his ankle and was transported from Rochester to Boston's Beth Israel Hospital. That's not entirely true. In the graphic novel *André the Giant: Closer to Heaven*, author Brandon Easton tells the story that André had injured himself at home. Wrong again. The truth is André was in Florida prior to his injury. On May 1, he wrestled in Orlando, Florida, for Eddie Graham in a battle royal. With no time to go home, he most probably took a red-eye to Boston, where he was scheduled at the Garden on May 2, in a tag team match alongside Pedro Morales against the Moondogs. But when he woke up, got out of bed, and put his feet on the floor, he heard a crack: his ankle was broken. And that's why he went to a Boston hospital. He injured himself in Boston.

Whether he went to the arena to meet with Vince or only called him before he visited the doctor is unknown, but one thing's for sure, Vince and André had spoken by the time Dr. Yett asked him how he had injured himself. André already had a story to plant: he had wrestled in western New York and was injured by his opponent. In the *SI* article, the story was even more dramatic to make André look like an even bigger hero. Todd wrote that André was injured by Killer Khan in a match on April 13, didn't realize he had a fractured ankle, finished the match, wrestled the rest of the month until he was unable to walk anymore, and then went to see the doctor. According to the most comprehensive list of André's matches, that means he would have wrestled more than 10 matches in seven different states on a broken ankle. Of course, none of this was true, but that's the story André told Todd. Only the date of April 13 was right. André and Khan had indeed wrestled that night in Rochester, New York, their last match together before the injury.

On May 2, at the Boston Garden, instead of the scheduled tag match, Pedro Morales wrestled Moondog Rex. Two days later, at Madison Square Garden, André was supposed to team with Tony Garea and Rick Martel against Stan Hansen and the Moondogs. He was replaced by Gorilla Monsoon (Moondog King was subbed by Captain Lou Albano). Prior to the show, it was announced to the live crowd that André had a broken ankle.

It was a great idea to blame that injury on Killer Khan. Though admitting someone had injured André in the ring could hurt the Giant's reputation, McMahon never tried to hide it. It made André more relatable to the fans and made the ensuing rivalry — seeking revenge on Killer Khan — a big success at the box office.

André was never hesitant about fixing his ankle, so the surgery was done right away. Upon André being admitted to the hospital, the news quickly spread through the hospital and everyone, no matter their job, found a reason to visit the room and meet with him in their official capacity. The hospital had to post a security guard on the eighth floor near the elevator to control traffic to his room. André had a lot of visits from friends and business associates, and he even consumed his favorite wine with them right in his hospital room. Orderlies and other staff members who were fans talked to him about opponents and feuds. Even with a real and severe injury, André couldn't escape it: the patient was André the Giant, not André Roussimoff.

BLOOD, SWEAT, AND TEARS MARKED MANY OF ANDRÉ'S MATCHES.

LINDA BOUCHER

IN HIS PRIME, ANDRÉ COULD "FLY" WHEN HE WANTED TO.

After the surgery and back at home in Ellerbe, for the first time in his life, André had nothing to do. He had been working or wrestling non-stop since he was 14, and now, as his 35th birthday approached, he had a cast on his foot. But after a short period of time, Jackie and Frenchy couldn't stop him from being active. He would roam around the sundeck or go out and visit friends around town. Still, it was nothing compared to his regular schedule. He watched a lot of television. Anytime André was at home, he particularly enjoyed watching game shows. *Jeopardy!* and *Name that Tune* were his favorites. On the road or not, André was never too far from a good prank. So when he would watch the original broadcast of *Jeopardy!*, he would remember the answers, watch the rerun with Jackie, and make it look like he knew all the correct answers. Poor Jackie thought he was just good at it until she realized what he was doing.

On June 8, André made a surprise return to the delight of the crowd at the Madison Square Garden, in an interview segment with Vince McMahon Jr., in which he said he was going to be back in three or four weeks. The following night, in Allentown, Pennsylvania, where the TV tapings were held, he did another interview with Vince broadcast on June 13 as part of the *WWF Championship Wrestling* TV show. It's during that interview, in which he said his cast would be removed the next day, that the feud with Killer Khan really started.

Billed as a Mongolian, Killer Khan was, in fact, Masashi Ozawa, from Tsubame, Niigata, Japan. Khan and André had known each other for a long time. When Khan made his debut in the early 1970s for New Japan under his real name, he was one of the boys carrying André's bag to the locker room, a huge honor in Japan. They first squared up on March 3, 1974, in a handicap match, and their first singles match was on November 24 of the same year. They faced each other six years later in Georgia. Khan, whose Mongolian gimmick was given to him by Karl Gotch, started working for the World Wrestling Federation in December 1979. In 1980, he was matched with manager "Classy" Freddie Blassie and began wrestling there full-time. At six foot five and 300 pounds, he was a natural antagonist for André, even more so with Blassie in his corner, since the former wrestler had a history with André from when he was managing Hogan. Khan was being pushed as a threat to both WWF champion Bob Backlund and Intercontinental champion Pedro Morales at the end of 1980 and for the first part of 1981. He lost to André in that April 13 match in Rochester, New York, and then wrestled the two champions quite a few times thereafter. When André's injury happened, Khan was ready to move on to another program.

The angle got on its way on May 20, in Hamburg, Pennsylvania, during a TV taping. After a match, broadcast on *Championship Wrestling* on May 23, Khan and Blassie were interviewed, and that's when the injury was credited to Khan. While the interview was going on, photos of André at the hospital were shown. The following week, André was interviewed to discuss how Khan had broken his ankle. That led to the June dates.

André was telling the truth in his interview when he said he would be back in three to four weeks, as his return was in a house show on June 24 in Norwich, Connecticut. However, rehabilitation wasn't an easy journey for the Giant. It was his first real injury, besides his chronic back pain that had plagued him since his days in France. "He started to have back problems in Paris," said his brother Jacques. "He had missed some matches because of that. The kinesiologist didn't know where to start." All in all, he was out of the ring for close to eight weeks, about the average recovery time for the injury. Still, considering his size and the weight he put on his ankle, it was an impressive recovery. But André being André, he could not wait to get back on the road doing what he loved. Tony Garea said that André used DMSO (dimethyl sulfoxide) to help with the healing and recuperation. DMSO was and still is a controversial drug, especially in the United States. Around André's time though, save for some exceptions, it was legal to prescribe it in only three states. It was one of the most popular medications on the black market. In a 1983 *New York Times* article, it was said that DMSO was "most popular among professional athletes, who use it as a chemical hot-water bottle and contend that it gets them back into play within days of an injury; without it, they say, they have to sit on the sidelines for weeks while nature takes its time in healing." Because of its anti-inflammatory functions, it was used as a liniment, much like antiphlogistine, and many wrestlers used it to treat their daily problems on the road. The product is now used as a liniment in veterinary medicine, among other things for horses. At the time André was injured, it was considered to be something of a miracle cure. It was said it could help with almost any illness and be taken orally or topically.

After a few warm-up matches for André in June and July, the first André-Khan match took place on July 17 in Glens Falls, New York, the first of more than 40 matches the two would have with each other, either in singles, tags or six-man tags and mainly in the northeast, Toronto, and Montreal. Glens Falls hosted the first bout, but Madison Square Garden hosted the first important match between the two, only three days later, in front of a sold-out crowd of 20,091 fans. The match ended with a double disqualification, the best way to set up another match between them. Khan was working André's ankle in all of those matches, playing up the injury angle. On television, the feud continued with André interfering in Khan's matches. Also, in order to put more heat on Khan, he "injured" another wrestler, Rick McGraw, who began wearing a neck brace, and the two continued to wrestle each other on house shows.

The rematch at MSG was held on August 24 in front of another sold-out crowd. This time, André defeated Khan in a Texas Death Match, with Pat Patterson and Gorilla Monsoon as special referees for the bout. "It was not a real Texas Death Match," remembered then *PWI* editor Bill Apter, who was at the Garden that night. "When you think Texas Death Match, you think of blood and a lot of outside stuff. The Garden's Texas Death Matches were completely different. In this particular match, I don't even think there was blood." Blood or not, the match was so heated that it was voted match of the year in *Pro Wrestling Illustrated* — probably based more on the rivalry than the match itself, especially when compared to the second-place match, wherein Ric Flair regained the NWA title from Dusty Rhodes.

The André-Khan feud didn't stop there. It lasted until the very end of 1981, with a lot of Mongolian stretcher matches. Although WWE says those matches were the first stretcher matches in its history, that is also untrue. In 1978, Bob Backlund and Superstar Billy Graham had a couple, which were called Sicilian stretcher matches at the time. The most famous one between André and Khan was held on November 14, at the Philadelphia Spectrum in front of 11,000 fans.

The feud with Khan also crossed territory borders with matches being held in Toronto for Maple Leaf Wrestling and in André's territory of Montreal. On August 17, at the Paul Sauvé Arena, André defeated Khan in front of a very healthy crowd of 7,667 fans with Don Leo Jonathan as a special guest referee. It was a logical scenario for Montreal to bring in André's toughest opponent as the referee while André sought revenge on the man who had injured him. Again, the promotion used Édouard Carpentier to put over Khan before his big meeting with André. Why change a winning formula, right? André and Khan worked very well together, thus the length of their program. In Freddie Blassie's autobiography, Khan is quoted as saying, "We hit each other with very hard chops. If I went loose on André, he'd get mad and give me a good hard one and say, 'Come on! What are you doing? Let's go!'" That type of cooperation in the ring is a sign of respect that also demonstrates how important it was for André to create an aura of legitimacy in their encounters. Khan clearly had a style and a background that André knew very well, which perhaps explains their success together. Those who witnessed that feud claim it was legendary.

It was a good year for André at the box office, thanks to a few matches against Hogan to start 1981 but mainly due to his matches with Khan in North America and abroad. On December 8, André versus Khan was part of a triple main event that drew 11,000 to Sumo Hall in Tokyo, Japan, the first singles match the two had had in Khan's native land in seven years. Although he had missed two months of action, André finished second on the biggest drawing cards list that year, behind WWF champion Bob Backlund. Proof that it was a hot feud, and probably that year's best, Khan finished seventh, the only time he landed on that list, and he was ahead of NWA champions Harley Race and Dusty Rhodes. André and Khan continued to wrestle each other sporadically over the next two years in the U.S., as well as in Japan and Mexico; their last encounter was at the very end of 1983. When interviewed about André for a Japanese magazine, Khan kept protecting the story told at the time, although he admitted that the feud had benefited him too: "I broke his leg in Rochester, New York. Then I had a series of grudge matches with him and made a lot of money thanks to him."

The cast the Giant needed after the operation is, to this day, the largest ever made at the Beth Israel Hospital. It was on display during André's interview on *Late Night with David Letterman* on NBC in 1984 and it's still part of the WWE collection and often on display at Axxess during *WrestleMania* week. Terry Todd, who was inducted into the International Sports Hall of Fame a month before the release of the HBO documentary, passed away on July 7, 2018, just a few months after his last contribution to the legend of André the Giant.

One could argue that André had some of the best years of his career after the successful ankle surgery. André was still the man, no argument there. He knew what he was doing and his body was not yet a handicap. Was the ankle injury the beginning of the end or just a hiccup on his journey? In one final point from the *Sports Illustrated* article, André said that in 10 years, he anticipated only working major arenas but still being involved in a promotion. He clearly had a love for the business, but that vision of his future was also a sign that he was oblivious to how badly acromegaly would damage his body and his well-being in the coming years.

CHAPTER 18

BUSINESS IS BUSINESS

J apan was always good to André, and 1981 was no exception. Aside from his feud with Khan, he had quite a few other memorable moments there that year. WWF and New Japan continued their strong relationship by launching an annual tag team tournament called the MSG Tag League in 1980. (The tournament is now known as the World Tag League.) The tournament was a fixture in the relationship between the two major territories.

André was a key component in four of the first five years of the tournament, before Vince McMahon Jr. pulled his roster out completely when his national expansion in the United States made that deal less attractive. André finished third in 1980 teaming with the Hangman (Quebec's Neil Guay). In 1981, he won the whole thing with René Goulet, defeating Inoki and Fujinami in the finals.

Aside from the tournament, and according to many, André had one of the best matches of his career on September 23, 1981, with Stan Hansen, in front 13,500 fans at Den-En Coliseum, a big tennis stadium in Tokyo. The two had met before, but this match cemented their rivalry and highlighted André's use of the sweet science of wrestling learned in his early years. Just as André liked, the confrontation had an aura of credibility, including Hansen body slamming the Giant to the crowd's stupefaction, the first and only time Hansen did so. It was a style and an intensity of wrestling André didn't display much in North America. A rare thing in Japan, the match started all over again after the two fought to a double count-out, with Hansen winning by DQ. "Inoki versus Kim Duk was the main event after Hansen versus André," said Koji Miyamoto. "But the audience was so excited by Hansen versus André. Inoki versus Duk was very calm, non-exciting circumstances."

Footage from that confrontation was used in Montreal as the Hansen versus André feud headlined wrestling's return to the Montreal Forum on July 26, 1982. Since the two shows André headlined back in 1976, there had been four Stanley Cup finals played and not one single pro wrestling event. But after two years of weekly house shows, a year and a half of television, and two full summers touring around the province, Varoussac was more than ready to take things to the next level. And André was a huge part of that. Since the match between André and Hogan, he had been part of every big card held in Montreal. André and Bravo against Swede Hansen and the Hangman drew close to 6,000 in June 1981. Then there were the two main events between André and Khan. And to cap off the year, on December 28, 8,000 fans, with hundreds turned away, watched the double main event of André against Big John Studd and Bravo versus Abdullah. It was the biggest crowd in Varoussac's history. The momentum continued into 1982, when in April, more than 6,000 saw the rematch between André and Hogan. It was Hogan and André's only match together outside of Japan that year. The Giant being part-owner gave Montreal fans some clear advantages. So when July came along with the big return at the Forum, André was the obvious choice for the main event. The card was well crafted by Brito and his team. It was a wink to the heyday of the 1970s featuring many of André's friends and contemporaries: Grand Prix Wrestling's Dino Bravo, Gino Brito, Mad Dog Vachon, Édouard Carpentier, Gilles Poisson, Blackjack Mulligan, and Yvon Robert Jr. as a special guest referee; and All Star Wrestling's

Abdullah the Butcher, Eddy Creatchman, Raymond Rougeau, and his dad, Jacques. The Giant and Hansen were main-eventing, and there were three other main events that night: the champion Dino Bravo against Abdullah the Butcher, Rick Martel against Billy Robinson, and Ray Rougeau versus Pat Patterson. Adding to all this, Frank Valois, André's longtime companion, was the promoter. For Valois, it was a dream come true to book the Montreal Forum. Fans responded well as 14,175 showed up that night. Five days prior, Varoussac had made its debut at the Colisée de Québec and drew a strong 12,000 fans with a similar line-up. Once again, André was pitted against Hansen. "Montreal always was the best wrestling town you could find, and that is true since Yvon Robert," Valois told the *Journal de Montréal* on the night of the show. "Give the fans a good card, good publicity, and you will sell out." Four months prior, André, in an interview with the same journalist, was quoted as saying, "It will go back to what it was. It takes some big American names, and it will work." Even if he wasn't wrong about it, André must have underestimated his own drawing power and that of some Quebec wrestlers like Bravo, Rougeau, and Martel.

It wasn't surprising to see André and Hansen doing well at the box office. The two liked each other and worked well together. As a matter of fact, his book makes it clear that Hansen was very fond of André:

> I have said this many times over the years: André got Stan Hansen over with the people in Japan. I worked hard, and New Japan promoted me well, but it was my matches with André which got me over. He would occasionally give me some ideas on the match we were doing. I was always excited to work with him. Whenever I met up with André in later years, I always took time to thank him for getting me over, and how I never forgot how he had helped me become a top wrestler in Japan. Even later, when he came to All Japan, when his health was spiraling downwards and he couldn't move around

too well, I would sneak over to his dressing room and thank him personally. He always appreciated it.

Not only did Hansen and André have a business relationship, they were also close friends. Not only would they go out in the Roppongi district in Tokyo, they also shared a passion, both being movie aficionados.

One of my fond memories of André was of the times we went to the movie theater. When we were working for New Japan, we would always leave around nine in the morning for the town we were going to wrestle in that night. New Japan wanted us to get there early so we had time to eat and relax. Since we all rode the bus, we would always be there on time, which was usually around noon. Not having anything else to do in the towns, André and I would go see movies. As soon as we arrived in a town, we would ask around to find out the location of the theater and the name of the movie that was playing. We must have seen more than 200 movies over the years. It was almost impossible for André to fit into a movie seat, so he usually picked up a bench in the lobby and carried it into the theater, placing it in the aisle. The two of us would sit on the bench together, eating peanuts and drinking Cokes while we watched the movie.

The first time they had met in the ring was in 1976 at the Garden in New York, in a six-man tag, but it was a one-and-done. In 1978, they crossed paths more often, especially in Georgia. Booked by Ole Anderson, they were opponents for most of their time there, except in October 1979. On one particular day, they had a show in the afternoon in a small town the promoters only ran when they had a big attraction like André in, and then another show in a bigger town at night. For the afternoon show, André was booked twice: in a battle royal and in a tag match with Hansen against Chris Markoff and René Goulet. André was mad at the office because he had to work three times that day. Usually, Hansen started the match when they were teaming, but André had a plan. "André said, 'Let me start, boss.' Based on what happened during the next few minutes, I assumed he had talked previously with René about being upset with the office, as both could speak French," wrote Hansen in his book. Goulet kicked the Giant in the stomach and André went down to the mat, not his typical reaction to that move, to say the least. And he stayed there for what seemed like 10 minutes. He was getting beat up, Hansen was trying to get him to their corner, but nothing was working. "He refused to move, sell, or do anything," recalled Hansen. "He just laid in the middle of the ring. After six or seven minutes, the people began to boo and make catcalls. Three minutes later, they were yelling really nasty things at André and about the match in general. 'Get up, you fat piece of shit' was one of the milder insults."

After 15 minutes, Hansen took it upon himself to fight the heels outside and told the referee to call for a DQ. The heels went to the back, and as people were booing and throwing cups at the ring, André slowly rolled underneath the ropes, got up, and walked back to the dressing room. As Hansen wrote, "André was a smart guy. He knew what he was doing. His actions that night showed the power he had over his career and position in the business. Nobody and I mean nobody could have done what he did without suffering serious ramifications, but André did. Were his actions good for the overall picture of the wrestling business? No, but he sure took a stand and made a statement." André had a unique way of resolving his problems.

Hansen's in-ring style was part of the reason why their matches were so good. His offense came with intensity, power, and toughness — strong style, to use today's terminology. And since André was a good seller when he wanted to be, it made for a good match. Without a doubt, Hansen was the gaijin, the outsider who hit it off with André the most. When Hansen left New Japan for All Japan at the end of the November-December 1981 tour, he confided in André. The only other ones to know were Bruiser Brody, Pete Roberts, and Hulk Hogan. André smiled and told his friend to go for it. He understood the business. Montreal fans who remember André from his early Grand Prix days and from seeing the match with Hansen in person always had a higher opinion of André's wrestling ability than most fans in North America, especially those who started watching after the national expansion.

With Valois having retired from the road, when André traveled to the territories not handled by Skaaland, he was pretty much on his own, as every promoter was responsible for finding him a suitable companion, usually a young wrestler, to drive him around from town to town. For example, in Portland, Oregon, when Terry Allen was breaking in, he had the biggest car, so he got the assignment from promoter Don Owen. In Tampa, where he wrestled next, he had the same duty. As he explained in his documentary *I Never Quit*, it gave him the rare chance to see the creative side of André.

"I was in Tampa by then; he had an eye for talent, and he could see I was on my way up," recalled Allen. "This was at the height of Tom Selleck becoming hot as Magnum, P.I. I was younger and had shorter hair that wasn't quite as bleach blond, with just a little mustache. I was even wearing the Hawaiian shirt since I was living in Florida and it was the cool thing to do. André said, 'You look like that guy on TV. You should be Magnum T.A.'" According to Allen, the Giant was planning on pushing his name to Vince McMahon Sr. to bring him to New York as that character. Before André could get it done, Magnum went to Mid-South Wrestling instead and exploded, becoming a major star for the NWA. His meteoric rise was cut short only because of a career-ending injury suffered in a car crash.

Not only did André have an eye for talent, he was also very good at finding finishing moves for his peers. André was a creative person with great instincts for the business. Barry Windham, Blackjack Mulligan's son, first met André when he was nine years old. As he grew older, he became André's chauffeur. "Later on, when he came to Florida, I was the one who drove him around," he explained to RF Video. "He liked me because I drove fast and would get him back to the bar quickly. He always enjoyed having someone around who understood him and would treat him the same as everyone else, someone with the same intentions: drink and chase pussy. André was legendary for partying. When I was finally old enough to buy alcohol, I would have to go to the store for André and buy the stuff for him, like three cases of Blue Nun, a German wine, and four cases of beer. He would give me $400, and I would spend every penny of it. He would then drink in the back of the car. He would say to me, 'Drink, boss!'"

Montreal was perhaps the only territory where André drove himself from time to time. And believe it or not, he was considered a good driver. "One time, we were coming back from promoter Stan Marshall's place in Quebec City. I was with my wife and the Giant," remembered Gino Brito. "I had one too many drinks so the Giant suggested he drive. For once, he had not been drinking much. He was driving so well. He was going 50 to 55 miles per hour, just perfect. My wife told me he was a better driver than I was. As for myself, I was in the back seat, not feeling well . . . " Not only was André a good driver, he was good with mechanics too. Once, going to Houston with Rick Martel, their car got stuck on the side of the road. Martel was surprised to see how André was handy under the hood of a car. As a matter of fact, he used to take care of the mechanical maintenance while working at the farm in Molien.

In Montreal, André was always the main attraction, even when he was not in the main event — and that didn't make everyone happy. Apparently, Dino Bravo didn't like to play second fiddle to André. Although Bravo wasn't one of the partners, his success with fans made him consider Montreal his territory. Once, Brito asked Bravo to bring the Giant in his car and Bravo refused. Referee André Roy ended up providing the lift.

"Dino didn't really like the Giant," confirmed Brito. "One time, we were in Beauce [Quebec] and the Giant had his car. I was driving with Bravo. Even if the Giant was a good driver, Bravo thought he wasn't driving fast enough. He was grumpy and started insulting the Giant,

DINO BRAVO AND ANDRÉ HAD A TUMULTUOUS RELATIONSHIP BEHIND THE SCENES IN MONTREAL.

ANDRÉ VS. ABULLAH THE BUTCHER WAS ALWAYS A MATCH PEOPLE WERE LOOKING FOR.

saying he was big and lazy. Then he honked at him repeatedly. That's when the Giant started to accelerate. He was taking those curves, it was unbelievable. Bravo had trouble keeping up with him. I told Bravo to slow down, that he was about to kill the both of us. When we arrived at our destination, Jean told Dino, 'I think I lost you on the road . . .' He knew what he was doing, and Bravo was even madder at him for it!"

Brito remembered often telling Dino to shut up. Aside from the Giant, Dino wasn't fond of Édouard Carpentier either. Quebecers and natives of France have a strange love-hate relationship, and the expression "damn Frenchman" is a very popular one in Quebec. However, for Bravo, it made sense. André was the only wrestler paid more than him in Montréal, and he didn't think André was his equal in the ring. In a business of egos, not even the boss could be spared from the dressing room politics. In 1982, André and René Goulet teamed up for the second straight year in the MSG Tag League in Japan and ended up finishing fifth. Coincidence or not, Dino Bravo was also part of that tournament, teaming with Adrian Adonis. Bravo wrestled against and with André during that tour. The tour ended on December 10, and it was right after that that Gino Brito started to hear from their accountant, Jos Bélanger, that André was looking at selling his shares in the Montreal office. When Gino inquired about it, André said he didn't like controversy. A man of few words, the Giant wanted out rather than to be in the middle of endless arguments over the business. Whether or not something happened in Japan between André and Bravo, or he heard about the complaints and insults Bravo was saying behind his back, will probably never be known. "The Giant wasn't friends with Dino. He wasn't someone Dino esteemed," explained Diane Rivest, Bravo's wife.

Gino bought André's shares and, ironically, eventually sold them to Dino. Even if it meant securing his top star's spot, Gino wasn't too happy about the situation then and is still not happy now. Looking back, having the Giant as a partner in the office when Vince Jr. wanted to go national could have changed his luck and saved his territory from WWF expansion. At the very least, Gino would not have lost his shirt in the adventure. A man of very few public emotions, André was affected by that turn of events more than he let on.

"I never saw him angry at a particular person," revealed his friend Bill Eadie, better known as Masked Superstar and later on as Demolition Ax. "But I was around when he was hurt emotionally after he was removed from his part-ownership of the Montreal area. He was very sad and could not believe that it had happened. He didn't understand why his friends would vote him out. He didn't go into the details, but it hurt him very much."

Still, Brito sticks to his side of the story: no one in the office ever kicked André out. However, Brito remembered the Giant having a favorite saying, one he would repeat all the time: "If something's in my way, I simply walk away from it." For example, if he was talking to someone and someone else he didn't like entered the conversation, he would simply walk away. André didn't like confrontations and was a very sensitive guy, and although he wasn't fond of showing them publicly, he had intense feelings. He was hurt by what people said behind his back. When kids would look at him and laugh, it hurt him more than people thought. That's something the general public never knew: they thought he was a seven-foot-four, 500-pound giant who drank a lot of beer and had a lot of fun while playing cribbage. People don't realize that something as simple as playing cribbage was hard on André sometimes. The pegs were too small for his big fingers and when they were close to one another, his opponent had to move them for him. But he would never complain about discomfort or long travel in those years, as long as he could get some peace and quiet. A behind-the-scenes feud with Bravo was not something he wanted to waste time on.

Yet André finished the year in Montreal on a good note. On December 27, André and Abdullah the Butcher drew 8,232 fans at the Paul Sauvé Arena. Bravo worked just underneath them, teaming with Rick Martel. The bizarre relationship with Bravo continued the following year. Both he and André were scheduled to participate in the first International Wrestling Grand Prix Championship League, a 10-man round-robin tournament similar to today's NJPW G1 Climax. Huge names were scheduled to participate, old and future foes of André such as Big John Studd, El Canek, Killer Khan, Otto Wanz, Dino Bravo, Hulk Hogan, and Antonio Inoki. André finished third with 36 points behind finalists Hogan and Inoki, who both finished with 37 points. Hogan ended up defeating Inoki in the final. Curiously, it was said that Bravo had canceled his appearance because of a reported family problem, and he was replaced by Rusher Kimura. Yet, on April 25, 1983, just prior to the start of the tournament, an angle was shot in Montreal where Masked Superstar, using one of Eddy Creatchman's cigars, burned Bravo's eye. Bravo was escorted out on a stretcher, in a buildup to an eventual rematch — the perfect angle for someone who needed a month off to go to Japan for a big opportunity. However, not only did Bravo not do that tour, but he never returned to New Japan. One can wonder if there is a connection between that and André's departure from the Montreal office.

Although André wasn't a shareholder anymore, and even though Dino Bravo was always telling Gino Brito that they did not need him, André still wrestled in Montreal in 1983. The noticeable difference was in the number of bookings. On Easter Monday, André beat Ken Patera by disqualification in the main event, drawing 16,500 fans. It was, at the time, Varoussac's largest crowd and proof of what Brito was trying to make Bravo understand. Brito wanted to bring the Giant in more often, but Bravo didn't want to hear it. On July 25, back at the Forum, three main events were offered to the fans, with André versus Blackjack Mulligan, Dino Bravo finally getting his big one-on-one revenge match against Masked Superstar, and the Rougeau brothers working Pat Patterson and Pierre Lefebvre. The show was a huge success with 18,394 fans in attendance, beating the April show's attendance. Although he wasn't the lone draw on the event, it's hard not to agree with Brito: André was still a top performer.

From September to December 1983, the Giant only wrestled in Montreal three times. The end of 1983 saw an influx of outside talent — a sign that André's influence had diminished and Bravo's influence had grown. Since Bravo was often working for the AWA, the Montreal office was using more of Verne Gagne's wrestlers and fewer of McMahon's. Still, when André came for the annual holiday show on December 26, he packed the Paul Sauvé Arena, once again facing off against Mulligan with 6,000 fans in attendance (the maximum capacity of the arena had changed). Bravo, on the other hand, had booked himself against the AWA champion Nick Bockwinkel. Times *were* changing. It was André's last match in Montreal for the company he had helped create. He did not come back until 1985. The Giant's definitive split from the Montreal office also meant the end of his personal relationship with Frank Valois. The two men had been, for a long time, like father and son — they would never speak again.

"My dad told me he had access to his bank account to pay the bills and that the Giant wasn't very good with things like paying bills on time," Françoise Valois, Frank's daughter, explained. "As he was drinking more and more at the time, words were said, and the Giant believed my dad had stolen from him. They never spoke after that. Years later, I went to see him wrestle with my daughter and André didn't recognize me. He had slept at my house and celebrated Christmas with my family. It hurt my dad very deeply, but he brushed it off saying that business was business."

Jackie McAuley, however, has another version of that story. "André just thought that he was a much better friend than what Frank ended up being, and André felt betrayed by him," Jackie recalled. "He was betrayed by him. It wasn't about money. That's not what hurt him. He betrayed his trust and his friendship. André could hold a grudge. If he thought someone deserved a second chance, that was alright. But if you betrayed him, that was it. He may work with you, he may speak with you, but he would never feel the same way about you. Or he would avoid you. Or give you that stare where all you want to do is turn around and walk away."

And that's exactly what he did with Valois. "André could walk by Frank and not even look at him," remembered Tony Mule. Neither man talked about it publicly. After André passed away, Valois didn't mention any of that in the interviews he gave. Wrestling can be hard on relationships, even when you become almost like family. The business side is always ready to overshadow the personal side. One day everything is great. Then the next, you stop talking forever. In the brotherhood that is professional wrestling, people sometimes end up resuming great friendships, but Frank Valois and André Roussimoff never patched things up. Almost seven years after André's death, Valois passed away at the age of 77. It was the biggest tragedy in André's life that he never had put his personal life ahead of his career. He didn't even have time to think about it.

CHAPTER 19

A GREAT EXPANSION, BUT NOT FOR ANDRÉ

André didn't know it at the time, but 1983 would be the last year he would tour in the way he preferred. Prior to the Montreal show on September 12, André gave a rare sit-down interview with well-known and critically acclaimed Canadian television journalist Pierre Nadeau.

"In the last four days, here's what my life looked like," said André. "Thursday, I was in Jackson, Mississippi. Friday, I was in Houston. Saturday afternoon, I was in Texarkana, Texas. Saturday night, in Little Rock. Sunday afternoon, in Lafayette. Last night I was in Lake Charles. And tonight I am in Montreal. Often enough, I wrestle nine times a week. Believe me, I live in planes and hotels."

The loop André described wasn't, for once, an exaggeration. He had traveled more than 1,300 miles and spent 20 hours on the road before taking a plane to Montreal. It was just an example of the tremendous amount of time he spent traveling, at a time when entertainment wasn't as mobile as it is today. He didn't have a smartphone to keep him connected to the world or a video game console to play at the hotel. It is no wonder that he drank more on the road than at home. Still, André enjoyed being with the boys. A wrestling locker room felt like a sanctuary for him. Another place André was visiting more and more was television and movie sets, but it wasn't always a home-run like with the *Six Million Dollar Man*. If *B.J. and the Bear*, a comedy series about a trucker and his pet chimpanzee in which André appeared twice in 1979, was a mild success, in January 1983, André had one of his most forgettable television appearances, on *The Greatest American Hero*. Some critics consider it the perfect example of bad 1980s television with no budget. André played a genetic monster actually named the Monster! He had no lines, was dressed in what looked like dirty white pajamas, and wore his wrestling boots. He only appeared for a few minutes at the tail end of the episode. He went toe to toe with the lead character and ended up being put down by a tranquilizer dart. It was a far cry from Bigfoot. In 1982, he had reconnected with Lee Majors in his new series *The Fall Guy*, where Majors played Colt Seavers, a stunt man/bounty hunter. In a wrestling-centric episode, André played a wrestler called Killer Typhoon who wrestled with Seavers's friend, undercover as a wrestler. A rarity for the time, the episode included wrestling lingo, and André's character goes off-script and breaks his opponent's leg, even tossing Majors's character into the crowd for good measure. Although *American Hero* and *The Fall Guy* weren't André's finest moments in Hollywood, they kept his acting career alive.

Hollywood wasn't the only place where André was asked to be on set. Montreal came calling as well in 1982, in one of the very last episodes of *Les Brillant*, a well-known French-Canadian sitcom that aired from 1979 to 1982 and was syndicated for years after its initial run. Both the writer and lead actor had worked with André a decade earlier when he was with Grand Prix. André's character was named Jean Petit, an obvious play on words using his French name Jean Ferré and the Robin Hood character Little John, who in French is called Petit Jean. André, whose character was oblivious to his size and strength, excelled with the episode's physical comedy: every time his character broke something, he would say, "Excuse me!"

Back then, some people thought that André's heavy accent in English meant he was slow or didn't always understand the language. In French, he was very articulate and never gave the impression of having comprehension issues. Still, until *The Princess Bride*, André wasn't given speaking roles in English on television or in movies. In *Micki & Maude*, a Blake Edwards movie starring Dudley Moore, filmed in 1983 and released in 1984, André played a fictionalized version of himself and, for the only time in his career, was credited as André Roussimoff — not André the Giant. In the story, the father of Maude is a wrestler played by wrestler-turned-actor Hard Boiled Haggerty. André, Big John Studd, and Chief Jay Strongbow are part of the supporting cast. While Studd has some lines, André's thick accent prevented him from showing what he could do. Still, the film was a Golden Globes best picture nominee in 1985 and drew $26 million at the box office, not bad for a $15-million-budget film.

In early 1983, on the wrestling front, André worked in the Mid-South territory with a new opponent. A Mississippi native, James Harris was a journeyman who struck gold when Jerry Lawler and Jerry Jarrett created a persona for him: a Ugandan head-hunter with face and body paint named Kamala the Ugandan Giant. In his book, *Kamala Speaks*, Harris reveals he had conflicting opinions about André. It's been established that when you fell on André's wrong side, he could be challenging to work with in many ways.

"I honestly screwed up and pissed André off," wrote Harris about their first encounter. "André grabbed me by the neck and picked me off the mat. I gasped for air under his meaty hooks. He didn't do anything more than throttle me for a minute, but I think he was trying to scare me into making sure I always did everything the right way in the ring."

It doesn't mean André didn't like Kamala. After all, André did give him a big push in Mid-South when Kamala attacked the French giant with a two-by-four and then body slammed him. André even did a blade job to sell the attack. These are not signs of André *not* liking someone. What would make more sense is that André was not impressed with

Harris as a wrestler, at first, and wanted to teach him a lesson. Truth be told, Harris was still green at that point of his career: he had been on the scene since only 1978 and was just starting a new character. That said, Kamala might have overreacted. After that match, he started wrestling with a .22-caliber pistol in his wrestling trunks before settling on a small flat pocketknife. He continued to wrestle with his knife for the rest of his career, even when he was not working with André . . . Nevertheless, things got worse in their second match, perhaps causing the real issue between the two.

A miscommunication led to Kamala taking the Giant down at the wrong time, and André insulted Harris in an unforgivable way. Giants do not like being off their feet. As André was trying to get up, he was cussing up a storm, and as Harris wrote in his book, "André called me a ____." We can only assume he means the N-word. In his account, Harris, angry with the situation, beat up André but still let him win with the planned finish. Right after the match, he left the dressing room without seeing or talking to anyone. The following day, with a magnum .357 in his pocket, he confronted André about the slur. André regretted what he had said. "Oh. Aw, boss. I'm sorry. I don't think sometimes." That's all Harris wanted: an apology. After that incident, they had a good relationship in the ring, as they wrestled each other all over the United States in 1983 and 1984. "After that, I had no more problems with André," said Harris in an interview with *SLAM! Wrestling*. "He respected me, and I wrestled him in Mid-South. Then I went on to World Class out of Dallas with the Von Erichs, and he came down and we did the same thing there. He said to me, 'When you finish up, I want you to come to New York.' So André was responsible for me coming to New York. We did real good after that. André and I worked really well together."

The incident with Kamala was the second time André has been accused of using the racial slur. In 1980 and 1981, André did three tours for New Japan. During one of the tours, while riding on the bus to the next town, he was drunk and used the N-word quite extensively. It woke up "Bad News" Allen Coage, better known as Bad News Brown in the WWF, an African-American wrestler who had won a bronze medal in judo in the 1976 Olympics in Montreal. According to Allen, he asked André to stop but the Giant told him to go fuck himself. So Allen, whose judo background meant he didn't fear anyone, had the driver stop the bus. He got out and called out André, ready to fight. It took Stan Hansen to calm Bad News down and get him back on the bus, blaming alcohol for André's behavior. The following day, Allen and André met by the elevator. For Bad News, it was far from over; he hadn't slept all night. André apologized, adding that some people were insulting Polish people too and that he had Polish heritage. Allen didn't want to hear it. He said he would never do that and André should respect him. There was tension between the two for a few years after that, but according to Allen, when they later worked together in Mexico, they talked and patched things up. These two incidents are the only ones like that ever reported about André. And even then, neither Kamala nor Bad News Allen called him a racist. André worked with numerous Black wrestlers throughout his career, like Ernie Ladd, Bobo Brazil, and Abdullah the Butcher, plus the many others he rubbed shoulders with in the locker room, and these are the only two instances where stories like this have surfaced. Even if the incidents with Kamala and Brown do not put the Giant in a positive light, they show that André Roussimoff was a normal man. He had flaws; he made mistakes.

Both Kamala and Allen found ways to end their beef with André. However, a man who did end up on the wrong side of the Giant was The Iron Sheik. Born Khosrow Vaziri, the Iranian was another Olympian soon-to-be WWF champion making a name for himself during the WWF expansion of the 1980s. In 1982, while on tour in Japan, the wrestlers ended up in a bar, and according to the Sheik, André was drunk, stuck his hand in Sheik's pocket, and ripped his pants. It was the kind of rib André would do, especially if he had a few drinks. Did he do that because he didn't like the Sheik? May we remind you that he once peed on the head of one of his best friends, so who knows? In the end, it didn't matter to the Sheik. He was so mad that he wanted to fight and threatened to open up André with a razor blade, until André offered to buy him a new pair of pants, which he did. That's the kind of dispute that can create a long-lasting grudge. And it did. Sheik claimed that André was drunk and dangerous with him in the ring, while others have said that André did not appreciate that the Sheik's substance-abuse issues were putting him and others in danger in the ring. Many people, such as Nikolai Volkoff, Pat Patterson, Hulk Hogan, and Tony Garea, have confirmed that the two didn't like each other. When André didn't like you, he would let you know in different ways. "He used to like to sit on The Iron Sheik; he just hated the Sheik," Bobby Heenan once said. Throughout the years, The Iron Sheik has become a funny, endearing character that fans today appreciate, but back then, he wasn't anyone's favorite, especially not in the dressing room. We don't like everyone we meet in life, and that was as true for André as anyone else.

Around the same time André had started working with Kamala, he was part of something at MSG that has been replayed over and over throughout the years. In one of the featured matches, André was teaming with one of the most popular wrestlers on McMahon's roster, Jimmy "Superfly" Snuka, against the Wild Samoans. The finish was what made the match. After André hit a big boot to Sika, Snuka, whose finishing maneuver was a splash from the top rope, climbed on André's shoulders to hit his move in one of the most memorable moments in WWE's history.

Though André typically only worked the Garden a few times a year, that changed in the second half of 1982, thanks to the son of Vincent James McMahon — Vincent Kennedy McMahon, or Vince Jr. if you prefer. Vince Jr. had been involved in his father's business for more than a decade at that point. He had done ring announcing, promoting, commentating, and ringside interviewing. Only 37 years old and eager to follow in his father's footsteps, when he heard his father wanted to sell his business, he made an offer to Vince Sr. and his partners to buy Capitol Wrestling Corporation. McMahon Sr. was 67 years old and didn't have anything else to prove in the business. Whether he was aware at the time of the sale that he had cancer is unknown, but he was looking to retire to his home in Fort Lauderdale with his wife, Juanita. And even if he was selling the company he had built from the ground up to his own flesh and blood, Vince Sr. didn't make it a gift to his son. Vince Jr. had to pay top dollar to live his dream.

On June 5, 1982, in New York City, McMahon and his wife, Linda, through their company, Titan Sports Inc., bought Capitol Wrestling from his father and three partners, Gorilla Monsoon, Phil Zacko, and Arnold Skaaland. But there was a twist. Vince Jr. was buying the company for a little more than $1.6 million, and all money had to be paid within a year in four payments. If Titan Sports defaulted on a payment, the company would go back to the four shareholders, along with any money already paid. All parties involved shook hands and, without anyone knowing, it became Junior's company. That same night, at the Garden, 22,000 fans saw WWF champion Bob Backlund lose by DQ to Jimmy Snuka, and André the Giant fight Mulligan to a double count-out. André had wrestled three times at the Garden in both 1980 and 1981, but in 1982, he wrestled six times, three times after the company was sold. In 1983, he wrestled seven times at the "World's Most Famous Arena," and wrestled more times in the WWF territory than any other year prior. Something was definitely going on.

Regardless, requests for the Giant hadn't slowed and André worked in Japan, Mexico, and throughout the U.S. and Canada, as he was accustomed to doing. In the fall of 1983, he even did a lengthy tour for Verne Gagne's AWA. Unbeknownst to him, it would be his last. Gagne had been one of the first promoters to bring him to the United States, yet André had more problems with Gagne than with almost any other promoter. Gagne was not always easy to deal with. Bobby Heenan remembered André not being happy to have to work twice most nights, with a match and a battle royal for the same money. André would often shorten his matches to compensate. Gene Okerlund, who was an AWA interviewer at the time, recalled André having issues with his pay a few times and mooning Wally Karbo in restaurants over it. However, since André didn't like disputes, they would end the night by making up, drinking and telling stories together. In Gagne's defense, most of André's matches were tag team and six-man matches, teaming with his friends Mad Dog Vachon and Rick Martel. The latter remembered André loving Minneapolis as he would stay at the Sofitel, a luxurious French hotel chain, enjoying what he missed most from his native land, the French language and cuisine. "He enjoyed the finest things and loved to help his friends discover them," said Martel.

Martel blamed André for introducing him to Calvados, as well as the French tradition of le trou Normand (drinking Calvados in the middle of your meal to reawaken your appetite). Martel also remembered André entertaining a Northwest Airlines flight attendant he was seeing at that very same hotel one day before a show. He truly enjoyed the presence of ladies. In one of his last matches with the AWA in November 1983, André teamed with Hulk Hogan, before the two of them flew to Japan for a four-week tour.

The Hogan who André teamed with in Winnipeg, Manitoba, in November was not the same man he had wrestled with for Vince Sr. a few years prior. The success of *Rocky III*, which was released on May 28, 1982, and did $270 million at the box office worldwide, had made Hogan a much bigger star. On June 15, 1982, he was on *The Tonight Show* and talked about Hulkamania with Johnny Carson. Hulkamania had started in the AWA and would reach a whole new level in the WWF a few years later. Hogan was also a much bigger star in New Japan at the time. Between his popularity in Japan and in the Midwest, Hogan was the third-biggest draw in 1982 and the sixth in 1983; André, in those same years, finished tenth and seventh. In 1982, even before *Rocky III* was released, Hogan had started a feud with AWA champion Nick Bockwinkel and his manager, Bobby "The Brain" Heenan. By Easter 1983, Hogan was the most popular wrestler in the promotion. On what was dubbed Super Sunday, Hogan won the AWA title in front of 20,000 fans at the St. Paul Civic Center, while 5,000 more watched on closed-circuit TV at the St. Paul Auditorium. It was AWA's biggest gate ever. But Verne didn't think it was the right time to pass the belt to Hogan. In the role of AWA president, Stanley Blackburn entered the ring and told the referee he was reversing the decision because Hogan had thrown Bockwinkel over the top rope behind his back, which, according to AWA rules, meant he should be disqualified. To say Blackburn was the most hated person in the building would be an understatement: fans thought they'd been robbed.

A little more than a month later, on June 1, 1983, Vince Jr. made his last payment to his father and the other partners. He and Linda were officially the sole owners of the WWF. Changes occurred quickly after that. In August, McMahon Sr. officially resigned from the NWA. By then, Vince Jr. had already started to position himself to take over the wrestling world and he had found the guy who would make that possible: Hulk Hogan. In November, he went to Minneapolis to meet with Hogan in secret and signed him to a deal. Not too happy about how he was treated in the AWA, especially with the title, Hogan knew that going back to New York would be a good thing for him financially. Although no one was aware that it would be his last, Hogan wrestled his final match for the AWA on November 14. He left for Japan to work a tour that also happened to feature André and just never went back, even though he was still advertised to appear on some AWA cards. On December 18, 1983, he married his girlfriend, Linda, in a ceremony attended by André and Antonio Inoki, who came to North America for the wedding. Just a few years prior, André's presence would have been surprising. Hogan remembered throwing up on the way to the arena when he knew he was going to wrestle André. On his very first tour in Japan in 1980, Hogan tried to win André over by buying him a case of his favorite wine, Pouilly-Fuissé, for his birthday. But he couldn't keep up with André. Hogan was still recovering from the previous night's binge drinking. Hogan fell asleep, and when he woke up a few hours later, all the wine was gone! Even when Hogan started in Minneapolis, their relation hadn't smoothed out yet.

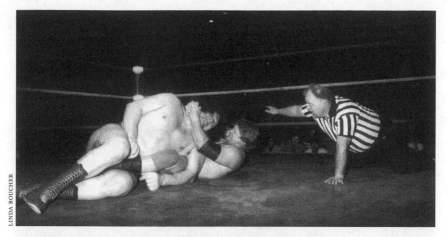

LINDA BOUCHER

STAN HANSEN WOULD BECOME ONE OF ANDRÉ'S CLOSEST FRIENDS.

LINDA BOUCHER

DINO BRAVO, HULK HOGAN, AND ANDRÉ: AN ALL-STAR TRIO IN MONTREAL.

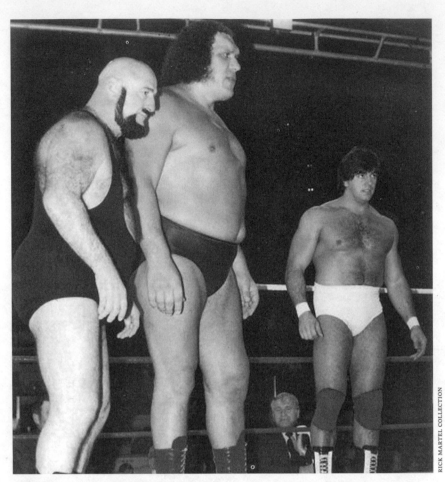

RICK MARTEL AND MAURICE VACHON WERE PART OF ANDRÉ'S FRENCH CONNECTION.

"Before he got married, I was living with Hulk in Minneapolis," recalled Rick Martel, who was friends with both Hulk and André and one of the few who knew about Hogan signing with Vince. "Their relationship was difficult. Every day, Hulk was hoping that André would be in a good mood. My perception was that André had seen Hulk shine in Japan and felt it was inevitable it would carry over in North America. It was not easy for them to find a middle ground."

André was very perceptive to how the business was changing, and he might have seen in Hogan a potential threat to his position. It's also possible that André was only testing him, to make sure he was worthy of taking over. In any case, their trips to Japan over the years helped solidify their friendship, to the point where André was invited to Hulk's wedding. And the more Hogan hung around André, the more he realized André's life wasn't easy. As he wrote in his book,

> People were real mean to him. I used to walk behind him through airports and hear the type of things people would say about him after he walked by. "What a freak of nature" or "What an ugly person" or "God, he walks like a cripple." And André was never, ever comfortable. Even in first-class plane seats, he would have to bend his head sideways because he was touching the air vents. The worst was when we had to fly to Japan because the flight would last 14 hours. André used to worry about having time to go to the bathroom before we got on the plane because there was no way he could fit into the john on a plane.

Flying to Japan was a task for André, and things over there were not always easier. The country wasn't built for someone André's size. Everything was smaller. "The sight of André getting into the back of a Japanese taxi was a funny thing to watch," recalled Stan Hansen. "He would completely fill up the back seat. It was impossible for him to sit in a normal Toyota-sized taxi. He would get in headfirst and crawl to the other side and remain on all fours, and depending on the size of the taxi, he occasionally had to hang his head out the window."

Knowing about his son's plan, Vince Sr. was the one who told his champion Bob Backlund and The Iron Sheik about the title change, which would be held at the Garden on December 26. The finish saw Skaaland throwing in the towel to stop the match as his protégé was locked in the Sheik's submission hold, the Camel Clutch. Ironically, the belt went from one of André's best friends to someone he didn't like . . . because of his road manager! The following night, on December 27, in St. Louis, Hogan made his return to the WWF, this time with a theme song, something that wasn't common at the time: he entered the ring to "Eye of the Tiger" from *Rocky III*. Hogan was the living embodiment of a superhero, an all-American hero. Less than a month later, on January 23, 1984, Hogan subbed in for the announced Bob Backlund, who in the storyline had not fully recovered from the injury he suffered in his title match defeat; Hogan won the title from The Iron Sheik at 5:40. Hogan was the chosen one.

That same night André was teaming with WWF tag team champions Rocky Johnson and Tony Atlas against the three Samoans. Hogan had won his match with a big boot to the face and his leg drop; André won in similar fashion, with a big boot to the face and a big splash. However, that's not what he would be remembered for that night. In a backstage segment following his title win, Hogan was being interviewed by Okerlund when André interrupted and poured champagne on Hogan's head. He shook Hogan's hand and told him he was proud. "The reason André was there for Hulk's celebration was that Vince wanted him there to put over Hulk," said Okerlund. "For André to do that on that night, it validated Hulk's whole championship run." That scene would be replayed over and over throughout the years. The very next day, in Allentown, Pennsylvania, for a TV taping, André was asked by Okerlund what he thought of the new champion. André, a good baby-face, said he was happy for Hogan and acknowledged the fact that he had both wrestled against and with Hogan. But then he said something that, in hindsight, was kind of prophetic. "We never know, maybe someday, I'm maybe going to challenge him too," André said, adding that he preferred to be a Giant than a champion. Little did he know, André was just a few years away from that moment.

Almost four months later to the date, on May 27, 1984, Vincent James McMahon died from cancer at age 69. The funeral was held on May 30, while André was in Japan. For the Giant, it was really the end of an era. The man who had made him rich and made him the world's most famous wrestler had passed away. André had a special bond with Vince Sr., an instant trust that allowed them to work well together and to have good times with each other. Vince Jr. would change the business like no one else had ever done before. As a matter of fact, André, like most of the people involved in pro wrestling at the time, couldn't imagine what Vincent Kennedy McMahon had in mind. Since Vince Jr.'s project was to take over the world of professional wrestling, he didn't want to share his guys with other promoters. That included André. Starting in 1984, with very few exceptions, the days of André traveling from territory to territory, from promoter to promoter, and seeing different friends, were gone. No more AWA in Minneapolis. No more NWA in Charlotte. He continued to travel but only for the WWF, seeing the same people all the time.

"Had my father known what I was going to do, he never would have sold his stock to me," Vince Jr. said in a 1991 *Sports Illustrated* interview. And it's a sentiment André is likely to have shared.

CHAPTER 20

THE WOMEN IN HIS LIFE

J ust a few hours prior to Hulk Hogan winning the WWF World Heavyweight title on January 23, 1984, André was sent to NBC's New York studios for an interview. At the time, David Letterman hosted NBC's *Late Night with David Letterman*, which aired after *The Tonight Show Starring Johnny Carson*. Although it was broadcast at 1 a.m., it was taped in the early evening. Even if the WWF would have preferred to see Hogan interviewed, André was the name people like Carson and Letterman most associated with wrestling — even on the night the Hulkster became champion. Dressed for the occasion, with a nice-looking suit and his size 20 cowboy boots made in Texas, André claimed to have quit drinking beer 14 months earlier and to have recently lost 90 pounds. No one actually remembered him stopping drinking beer completely. When asked by Letterman about the infamous "117 beers in one sitting" story, André said it was true. It was a story he had been telling for years. "Once, I was in a beer-drinking contest in Germany and downed 118," he said when he wrestled in Honolulu for the first time in 1977. "I was so drunk, I couldn't make it through five cases." Ric Flair said he was with him in Charlotte, North Carolina, when André drank

106 beers. Hogan recalled that in Tampa André drank 106 beers in an hour and a half. Mike Graham, Eddie Graham's son, said André drank 156 beers one night in Florida. Ken Patera remembered Dick Murdoch challenging André to a drinking contest at Caesars Palace in Las Vegas. André was known to never back down from a bet. At the end of the contest, André was up to 116 beers.

"Some of these stories have been retold over and over again to the point that it seems like everyone is repeating the same 'André stories,'" wrote Jason Hehir, who made the HBO documentary on André, on Reddit. "Examples being 'the night he drank 100 beers' or 'that time he lifted a car.'" Whether true or not, whether it was the same story retold over and over or different ones, no one will argue against the fact that André drank a lot, more than anyone else in the business. It's probably why in 1984, Canadian brewing company Labatt hired André for a TV commercial. (Both the French and English versions are available on YouTube.) At the time, he was one of the three spokespeople for Labatt Light, alongside fellow French-speaking wrestlers Little Beaver and Mad Dog Vachon.

While André always preferred beer, as he grew older, he needed something stronger for his pain. He also drank screwdrivers, Crown Royal whisky, Pernod, Caribou, a pitcher of Jack Daniel's on the rocks, and Americans, a drink actor Carey Elwes described as a combination of hard and soft liquor, or whatever André felt like drinking, mixed in a beer pitcher. It's notable because Paul Vachon didn't remember André drinking hard liquor when he first came to Montreal in the early 1970s. André's acromegaly was starting to take a toll on his body. Like any true Frenchman, he also drank wine, almost as if it were water. He even told Letterman that he consumed two or three bottles of white wine, during meals, on a daily basis. This lines up with almost everyone's memory regarding his consumption of Bacchus's favorite liquid.

Back in the summer of 1983, André had invited a few of his friends to his ranch: promoters Eddie Graham, Vince McMahon Sr., Jim Barnett, and wrestlers Pat Patterson, René Goulet, Gino Brito, and their respective partners. Brito stayed there for a whole week.

"I never found him to be that big of an eater," recalled Brito. "He ate two eggs and toast in the morning, but with one or two bottles of white wine. He would open two bottles before even having his first glass. He probably drank a minimum of six to eight bottles every day while I was there." Gino also remembered André drinking beer all afternoon while playing cards and capping off the afternoon with a half a bottle of Crown Royal. When it was time for dinner, red wine was a must.

"I would drink maybe 20 beers during the day, but André, he would drink two or three beers for every beer I would have," added Brito, convinced his stay at the ranch gave him heart issues later on in life.

"One day he came to work," recalled Rob Reiner, director of *The Princess Bride*, "and I said, 'What'd you do last night, André?' He says, 'I went to the bar, had a couple of drinks.' I said, 'Tell me, what do you drink? On an average? What do you drink?' He says, 'Well, I had six bottles of wine, three bottles of cognac.' I said, 'Well, you must have been drunk!' He says, 'No, no! I didn't get drunk. A little tipsy, but not drunk!' So at nine in the morning, the nouveau Beaujolais comes out. And André, I'm not exaggerating, he starts drinking. And by the end of the day, I'm not exaggerating, he'd drank 20 bottles of nouveau Beaujolais."

As far as the legend that André could consume so much liquid in one sitting without even going to the restroom, well, it's just that: a legend. Brito remembered that subtly but regularly André would disappear to relieve himself, like any other normal human being. So is every drinking and eating story a myth? Of course not. Many are surely real, but maybe they didn't happen exactly the way they are memorialized today; and perhaps they didn't happen as frequently as legend suggests.

"I saw him finish a case of wine [12 bottles], and I helped him only on a bottle or two, and I didn't witness anything worth noting," remembered Gene Okerlund about André's high alcohol tolerance.

"I remember a lot of nights drinking with the Giant in New York," recalled Paul Vachon, whom André was very fond of because he had been so important to him when he came to Montreal. "Once, while working for Vince, we were doing television somewhere in Pennsylvania, and the

Giant said to me that the liquor store would be closed after his match, so he wouldn't be able to buy us some wine. He gave me some money and asked that I go right after my match. I finished my match, and I started to count the money and there was $200. 'You gave me $200, how many bottles do you want?' 'Buy $200 worth, boss.' That's something like 25 bottles!"

"He would always share the goods with his friends," added Okerlund. "He would drink quite a lot on the road with the boys, but I believe the stories got embellished with time. Forty beers became 80 beers. I am sure that André was a functioning alcoholic though. Yet always the professional, he did what needed to be done and never screwed up. Before the matches, he'd have a bracer or a beer, wine or vodka, but you would never notice."

If in the Grand Prix days, André wasn't drinking before the matches, that was a thing of the past by the 1980s. As the years went by, his pain was growing. Every story seems to indicate that drinking was, in the beginning, entertainment for André, but then he used alcohol to dull his pain, hence drinking hard liquor and before putting some punishment on his body. People close to him, like Okerlund, suggested there was emotional pain to dull as well. Alcohol took care of that, even more than any physical discomfort he might have been feeling. Alcohol was like a mistress to him, a way to escape his life. And once inebriated, André would open up a tiny bit more, providing a different perspective on his life and happiness.

"Maybe it would be better if I closed my eyes and didn't wake up tomorrow. You know, Gino, it's not always a picnic all the time," he told Brito at the ranch. It's clear for Brito there were many emotions bottled up inside his friend. Okerlund had a similar experience. "He would never discuss acromegaly with us. But he actually broke down one day and cried while with me, saying, 'It's not easy to be a giant. People look at me differently.' He was so sensitive."

As far as eating, there's no doubt there were times when André did order everything on the menu. However, he did this to show off and make people laugh. He didn't eat like that at every meal or even every day. For example, at the ranch, he was not the same as he was on the road. "He never really had a large appetite," revealed Jackie. "He was eating what a man his size was expected to eat, which is more than a man the size of Frenchy, for example. I saw him order everything that was on the menu. He could eat like that when he wanted. And he did it because he could." When he was at the ranch for a couple of weeks, he would get up around 8 or 9 a.m., but when he was there just for a few days, he stayed up until the wee hours of the morning and got up in the afternoon. On those days, he wouldn't eat breakfast or lunch. Instead, he would eat fruit and yogurt during the day and only eat a full meal at supper. His routine at the ranch was very different. "He usually didn't drink at all until supper, and then he'd have a bottle of wine, or almost a bottle, because I would take a glass before he would finish it up," laughed Jackie. "Then, on a rare occasion, he would have an after-dinner drink, but that was it. He generally didn't drink that much when he was at the farm. He generally drank iced coffee, and that was pretty much it." In a sense, he was creating his own myth when he was eating or drinking. Witnesses would tell the story to their friends, and those friends would tell it to their friends, and in time, everyone had not only heard but had "seen" André eat every single thing on the menu or drink 100-plus beers.

Luckily, alcohol was his drug of choice. No one ever witnessed the Giant trying drugs, not even marijuana. If drinking made him talk more about how he really felt, drinking and speaking French was the ultimate combination. "We would always speak French together, and when he let you get close, that meant you were important to him," said Brito. "I loved him very much. He wasn't much of a speaker, but he never said anything bad about anyone. You knew it instinctively when something was wrong or unpleasant for him."

The Giant's deep attachment to his native language is something not easy to understand unless you are French yourself. They are very few things when traveling so far from home more enjoyable than to find someone who speaks French. That's why he found his second home in

Montreal. That's why he really liked traveling around the province of Quebec. And that's why he loved going to the French district in New Orleans. Almost every Quebecer who worked with him considered André a friend and most were close to him. Paul and Maurice Vachon, Paul and Jos Leduc, Gino Brito, René Goulet, Pat Patterson, Michel Dubois (Alexis Smirnoff), Frenchy Bernard, Yvon Robert Jr., Tony Mule, and Rick Martel are all examples of that. "Yvon Robert is more than a friend to me, he's like a real brother," André once said. Martel claimed that speaking French meant you were in André's clique right away. No matter where they were, or how long it had been, Paul Vachon was always greeted in French by the Giant. Wrestler Frenchy Martin, who was Dino Bravo's manager in the WWF, was another French-Canadian part of the clique. "He just loved Frenchy because Frenchy would make him laugh so hard," remembered Brito. "His favorite antic was when Frenchy would tap dance, but instead of making the noise with his shoes, he would make it with his dentures!"

"One time, he had me 10 days at his apartment," recalled Martin. "I like having a drink, but after three days, I started to get restless. After four days, someone please call the police! After six days, here's another cognac. After nine days, I started to tell myself that I had to get out of here!"

"The only ones who could keep up with André's drinking were Arnold Skaaland and Pedro Morales," he continued. "He was a good guy, but people didn't understand him. You must also go to the bathroom like everyone else when you're a giant. But everyone wanted to talk to him and touch him. He never had one minute of peace."

Even though André had many French-Canadian friends and drinking buddies, he was generally very lonely. A normal relationship with a woman or settling down to raise a family seemed like an impossibility. He was known to treat women like princesses but was very secretive about it. "He had more than his fair share of conquests," said Paul Vachon. "But he wasn't looking to find the one and settle down. Women were all fascinated by him as they wanted to know if he was big all over. But I never saw him in love. There were always women who wanted more, but he wasn't interested. He had worked with prostitutes back in Paris so getting attention from different women was nothing new to him." Speaking of prostitutes, they had a special place in André's heart. "In Paris, these girls, time and time again, got me out of trouble, they were letting me sleep in their apartments," he told Gino Brito. Once, he was with Brito at the Ritz Carlton in Montreal, when a prostitute came to the bar, crying. She had worked all night and then been robbed of all her money, $700 in total. André took $700 from his pocket and gave it to her, without any more question. More proof of his generosity.

During the Grand Prix days, he went out with Ginette Pélissier, a model from Quebec who looked like Raquel Welch. Known for her TV appearances and for working as a bunny at the Playboy Club in Montreal, the cover girl was frequently seen with André for a period of time. However, she ended up marrying Montreal Expos star Tim Foli in 1974. André did ask a woman to marry him once. "André went out with my sister Rhonda," revealed former wrestler "Cowboy" Bob Orton, Randy Orton's father. "She was working in casinos in Las Vegas. André asked her to marry him, but she said no."

Most of his contemporaries don't remember him bringing the subject up or even having a girlfriend traveling with him. "He loved to have women around, but I don't think he had any romantic line there," said Okerlund. "He had affairs throughout the years. I don't know much more than they did exist. He never talked about it." Tony Mule didn't remember him being a ladies' man when he was in Montreal, but others recalled him always having female companionship. Because of his celebrity status, a new girlfriend was often just around the corner. In his memoir *Accepted*, Pat Patterson told one of those stories.

> We shared a suite on that trip, with two giant, king-size beds. As we were going back up to our room, this beautiful petite girl came out of the elevator and we almost ran into her.
>
> André said, "Excusez-moi."

And she answered right back, "Excusez-moi aussi."

They started to speak a little French together, but I was tired and we were drunk and I pushed André into the elevator.

I was asleep for less than half an hour when I heard noises. I got up to find André dressing.

"Where are you going?"

"Don't worry, boss. Half an hour, then I will be right back."

He came back forty-five minutes later with the French lady. I was in my own bed, mind you, but I had a front-row seat for the rest of the evening. It was quite the sight.

At the ranch, Jackie remembered he brought home only a handful of women. "I would get to the airport and try to figure out which person I was supposed to pick up," she said. "There was one who was very special to him, but it didn't work out."

André himself was clear-headed about these kinds of things. "Naturally, I get propositioned all the time," explained André. "They don't want to know what kind of a man I am. They're mostly interested in the physical adventure. When I go out at night, doing the town, I like to be alone. If I take a girl, they get too excited because they want everyone to notice them because they're out with a giant." Near the end of his life, he met Valerie, a woman from Greenwich, Connecticut, whom he truly loved. She was very important to him, and by all accounts, he was really happy with her, but it was too little, too late.

When André started traveling more in the early to mid-1970s, he became very close with many of the women wrestlers, especially women's champion Fabulous Moolah. Jean Christensen, who had been working in the business in different roles — as a valet, a photographer, part of the ring crew, a seamstress, and a wrestler under the name Trixie Colt — was from Washington State, close to six foot three in heels, and a few years younger than André. André met her for the first time in 1974, and they had an on and off relationship over several years. André kept his personal life private, so it's not surprising that his friends in the business knew little about their relationship. One day, he received news that would change his life: Jean was pregnant. She was surprised because she had been told André was sterile. Acromegaly can cause impotency but not sterility. According to André's brother Jacques, the stories about him being sterile were false. On April 30, 1979, in Seattle, Washington, Robin Christensen was born.

André's first reaction was denial. He may have suspected that Jean was trying to get money from him for a child that wasn't his. However, two years later, André took a paternity test in New York. It was the very first time Robin saw her dad. And the test confirmed what Jean already knew: André was the father. With André always on the road, it was easier for Jean to continue taking care of their daughter. André and Jean didn't want Robin to be raised around wrestling anyway.

"I was not on the road with my dad," Robin said in an interview. "If anything, he had me as far away from that industry as possible. We, unfortunately, did not have that great of a relationship. Mostly because he was on the road so much. Because of that, we never really got a chance to form a relationship."

That became another subject André Roussimoff would shy away from, behind the ever-towering shadow of André the Giant. Some of his peers only learned about Robin after his passing. Robin has known for as long as she can remember. Jean never hid the identity of her father from her. "I knew from day one who my dad was," Robin said. "So, yeah, I totally noticed that he was not around. I knew what he was doing. I knew he was on the road wrestling."

Robin only saw her dad a handful of times, usually at his matches in the Seattle area. "Whenever they came to town, my mom would take me and usually he would come out after doing his thing in the ring and we'd spend time together. I'd sit on his lap," recalled Robin, who is just over five foot ten — tall, but nowhere near a giant. The technology then wasn't what it is today. André didn't have a cellphone, FaceTime, or Skype. There were only landlines and letters. He sent gifts on Christmas and cards for birthdays, but there wasn't much more communication. And because André and Jean didn't have a co-parenting relationship, he didn't want Jean at the ranch. He wanted to see Robin but not her mom, and this complicated things when Robin was young. That said, it was Robin's decision not to go without Jean. Her mom never put pressure on her. Once, there was an agreement that André would send someone to Seattle to pick up Robin and bring her back to Ellerbe. Of course, Jackie was chosen for the task. But once she got there, Robin had changed her mind and didn't want to go if her mom, the only parent raising her, could not go. Robin tried to call him, but he was always on the road. André occasionally called too, but Jean wanted to talk to him first and they'd get into a fight on the phone. By the end of those conversations, André couldn't speak to his daughter — the only reason why he was calling to begin with. Understandably, there was some frustration and resentment from Jean. It's not an easy task to be a single mom. In February 1992, the television show *A Current Affair* covered the court case for child support between André and Jean. André was paying child support, but Jean wanted it increased, and so they ended up in court. André ended up paying $750 a month and in the fall of 1991, $1000. Even if the actual average is half of that today, considering what André was earning as a pro wrestler, and considering Jean had 100 percent custody, the number seems low.

"It's people that he set up around himself. The people that lead him by the nose," explained Jean in that same *Current Affair* story, talking about André's entourage and trying to find a guilty party to explain why André wasn't paying more. "They're only out for their own, what they can get, and they really don't care about this child and they really don't care about his personal life or his feelings." Jackie remembered it differently: "He was paying child support, and then went back because Jean wanted an increase. The amount was set by the court." In that same report, a 12-year-old Robin had mixed feelings about André. "He's kind of a stranger to me. He's my dad, but he isn't," she said, trying to put into words the complexity of her relationship with her father.

His nephew Boris heard about André having a daughter only when he arrived in Canada. In 1992, he was actually at the ranch during the holidays when André spoke to Robin, aged 13, on the phone. "Once again, he tried to connect with me," remembered Robin. "Making small talk about whether it would snow for the holidays; we lived in Washington where it never did. He always asked about my hobbies and interests, things a dad should know." It was the very last time they talked to each other. A month later, he passed away.

Robin wasn't a wrestling fan as a child, and like any child, she didn't like to see her dad getting hurt. Aside from *WrestleMania XIX* in Seattle, Washington, which, ten years after her father's death, Robin, aged 23, wanted to see, Jean Christensen had completely left the business and wasn't watching the product at all. Robin didn't watch wrestling after that for the longest time. She once admitted she hadn't seen *WrestleMania III* in 1987 until years later on the internet. She has now watched a lot of clips of her father's matches online. She knew some of the wrestlers, heard of others, but it was never her world. Jean died in 2008. At the time of her death, she owned a shop in Shoreline, Washington, André's Bodacious Babe Costumes, named after the father of her child.

The saddest part is perhaps that for a good portion of her life, when Robin talked about being André the Giant's daughter, people didn't believe her. Some probably thought she was lying or trying to make herself more interesting than she was. After André passed away, Robin and Jean went to France to meet with members of Robin's family she had never met before. Although it wasn't really talked about within the family, the Roussimoffs knew about her, as André had brought a picture of Robin to his parents. "I wasn't there at the time because I was in Montreal, but she met with our grandmother and the rest of the family," recalled André's nephew Boris. "Everyone was very happy to meet her, even though she wasn't able to speak French."

AS A GUEST AT HIS RANCH, GINO BRITO COULD CHALLENGE ANDRÉ TO PLAYING CARDS, BUT NOT TO DRINKING.

ANDRÉ WOULD HAVE LIKED TO PASS MORE TIME WITH HIS DAUGHTER, ROBIN; HERE SHE POSED WITH HER COUSIN BORIS AND ANDRÉ'S FRIEND, ACTOR CARY ELWES.

FOR GOOD OR BAD, ALCOHOL WAS ALWAYS PART OF ANDRÉ'S LIFE.

Through his lawyers, André had tried to make plans to see her. But it was tricky. André couldn't bring her to a public place like an amusement park like any other dad would do, because it was hard for him to go to these places by himself. "He wanted to spend time with Robin," confirmed Jackie. "The judge thought it would have been a good thing for them to meet in a shopping mall. I told her, 'You don't know what you are asking from that child.' That's why they met at André's lawyer's place in the state of Washington. Since he had kids, they thought it would be a more suitable place."

When she was 10, Robin sent a heartwarming letter to her father, expressing her frustration, the only outlet for closure she ever had. "I wished I could have known what it was like to have a dad in my life," she wrote. "I know you wanted me to join you on your farm . . . but I wouldn't come without my mother. I got the impression it hurt you deeply . . . maybe there was a tiny part of me that wanted to hurt you, to make you feel the loss and pain I dealt with everyday . . . maybe one day we can sit down and just talk. I'd like to know more about you . . . and I could tell you about my life, my school, my friends."

And that's what André wanted as well. He wanted to be there for her and wanted to be a dad. Tim White, a WWF referee who was one of André's most trusted road companions, said time and time again that André cared for her although they didn't see each other, that he wanted to be part of her life, and the fact that it didn't work out hurt him. "That is a very different portrayal than what a tabloid news program wrote before André's death, about him disavowing any knowledge or interest in her, trying to go to court and claim he wasn't the father, and when it came out that he was, never seeing her," wrote Dave Meltzer. And it's not only White or Jackie. From all accounts, he wanted to spend time with his daughter. However, since it's a subject that very few people discussed with André, many questions will always be left unanswered.

"I probably would ask him about his daughter, why he didn't have a closer relationship with her, and how much pain it caused him to be separated from her like that," said Jason Hehir when asked what questions he would have asked André if he had the chance to meet him while making the documentary. "By all accounts, he was a sensitive, caring man to those in his inner circle, so it must have caused him a certain amount of pain."

André was caring and sensitive, not only with grownups but with children too, although children reacted differently to him. Some were afraid of him, some were just mean to him, and others were in awe of meeting such a giant of a man. The wrestling business had always been seen as one big family. Since André was really close to the McMahon family, both Shane and Stephanie, Vince Jr.'s children, have fond memories of meeting André when they were young. André was closest to Stephanie. "I was at home jumping on the trampoline and André walked over to me," recalled Stephanie, now the chief brand officer of WWE. "He held out his hand and I stepped in it, and he brought me up to his cheek and I gave him a kiss on the cheek. So we've had this bond since the very beginning, a very special connection." She first met him when she was only three years old, and she at one time considered him her best friend. Very comfortable around André, she had a unique relationship with him, because even if she was a child, she never treated him like André the Giant. Growing up around the business must have also helped. "I had noticed that everybody always treated André differently, right? And I was a little kid and some people treated me differently, because of who my father was," she explained. "I think that's something we bonded over, because I just knew André as my friend. And it bothered me that people would treat him one way or the other, just because of the way he looked. I just loved him for who he was."

That was precisely the kind of relationship André was looking for with any human being, young or old. People were too easily distracted by André the Giant and very few wanted to know who André Roussimoff was. And Stephanie was able to see the man within the giant. Their relation was so unique that for a long time, it was rumored that André was Steph's godfather. A photo of Stephanie sitting on André's lap in *People* magazine, after *WrestleMania 1* in 1985, may have helped start that story. A few years later, when she was 14, André brought Stephanie to her first dinner date. While André wasn't Stephanie's uncle or godfather, he did treat her differently . . . almost like she was his daughter. And although Stephanie didn't know André had a daughter at the time, those great experiences interacting with another child might have motivated him to connect better with Robin, as she became a teenager herself. Without a doubt, it's a hard thing to explain and it's the reason why Stephanie, although interviewed for it, didn't make the cut of the HBO documentary.

"Here's a guy who barely ever saw his biological daughter but was an uncle-like figure to another little girl of the same age," explained Jason Hehir. "Stephanie had such obvious affection for André, but since we decided to explore his ambivalent relationship with his daughter, it would've really muddled the narrative."

Stephanie wasn't the only kid with a bond with André. "André was very good with children," said Jackie. "There were a lot of wrestlers' children that he was close to. But no one was a substitute to Robin. He really had a desire to get to know Robin and he tried the best that he could. But there's only so much you can do when you're André the Giant, you're restricted a lot." Among those children, he had a similar uncle-like role in Dwayne "The Rock" Johnson's life. "At five, I never knew why people got so excited to see him," wrote Johnson on Twitter. "To me, he was just 'Uncle André.'" Although no legal papers were signed, Bill Eadie and André were close enough that Eadie considered André the godfather of his two daughters. They had made a pact that if anything happened to him, André would step in. André felt deeply honored by that request. Eadie was one of the few men whom André confided in about his wish to spend more time with Robin and to ultimately be a part of her life.

"I fully understand that he couldn't be the father he probably wanted to be," concluded Robin. "I do forgive him for not being there when I wish he would've been, but at the same time you know, the hurt comes back."

CHAPTER 21

SPEARHEADING WWF SUCCESS

I n his effort to take over the wrestling world, Vince McMahon was employing two strategies: buying the local promotion or getting WWF television to air in new targeted markets and run live shows in those same markets. Vince had started this strategy in 1983, just before the company officially became his. It happened in Los Angeles, where promoter Mike LeBell was the first to sell his promotion to Vince Jr. On March 6, 1983, WWF held its first show in L.A., featuring, among others, André the Giant. That pattern repeated itself over and over. Cincinnati in October 1983, San Jose in September, and Detroit in December. Then in 1984, when Vince's strategy became even clearer, it continued: Oakland in April; Minneapolis, Memphis, and Nashville in June; Atlanta, Miami, and Birmingham in August; Kansas City in September; Calgary, Alberta, in November; and last but not least Dallas in December. André was a featured act in every city. Even a year later, when Vince invaded Don Owen's Portland, Oregon, territory, André was Vince's go-to star. This tactic was not implemented in St. Louis, Chicago, Houston, or Toronto, as André was out of town when those invasions started.

WWF's first show in the province of Quebec was held in May 1984 at the Verdun Auditorium, because Vince couldn't get the Montreal Forum. The Verdun Auditorium was where André had had his first match in North America 13 years prior, almost to the day. It would have made sense for him to be on the show; André had been featured in almost every territory that Vince Jr. took over. Many of those territories had been run by promotors that were friends of the Giant. However, the Montreal territory was different. It was his home away from home. Yet, André wasn't in Montreal for that show. So just like in Chicago and St. Louis, Hulk Hogan was brought in instead. We can't know for sure if André would have agreed to do the Montreal show; he was in Japan at the time. That said, the fact André wasn't in Verdun for the second show WWF did there a month later, although he was back from Japan, helps make the argument that it might not have been a coincidence. His friend Gino Brito never asked him about it, and he said it would have been very kind of André to refuse to work Montreal against his company.

In April 1984, André also worked in Texas for Fritz Von Erich (Jack Adkisson) and in Florida for Eddie Graham. Vince had his eye on both markets, so he sent them the Giant. "Like André's visit to Jack Adkisson in Texas, this seemed like a gesture of goodwill to ensure the WWF and Florida remained on good terms," wrote historian Tim Hornbaker in *Death of the Territories*. That said, make no mistake: Vince's goal was always to end up with those territories. Some just took longer to acquire than others.

In the world of technology and television, 1984 was a year of change. Cable TV was becoming much more affordable and accessible, and Vince McMahon wanted to take advantage of that. In May 1984, *Tuesday Night Titans* debuted on the USA Network, and in September, *All American Wrestling* joined it on the airwaves. In July 1984, what became known as Black Sunday occurred: McMahon took over Georgia Championship Wrestling's time slot on SuperStation WTBS, where GCW had stood tall for 12 years, dating back to before it was even on cable TV. McMahon was creating a platform for his stars to be exposed all over the United

States, which had never happened before. Usually, a promotion ran a territory in terms of producing shows and television content only for local television. Someone in California, for example, couldn't watch wrestling from New York. McMahon wasn't the first to try this, but he was certainly the first to enjoy significant success. Still, at that time, the money was in live events and McMahon knew that all too well. "While he did offer full matches on his various telecasts, he usually withheld superstar bouts and his top-running feuds," wrote Tim Hornbaker. "Hulk Hogan, André the Giant, the other upper-echelon talent made TV appearances but only to whet the appetite of eager fans. Thus, if they wanted to see more of their favorite performers, people would have to buy tickets."

While all of this was happening, André's popularity was growing in North America. He had been making trips to Mexico since 1980, though never for more than a few days, and his time there was never as lucrative as his Japanese tours. It was an excellent way to keep him active without overstaying his welcome in any one place. At first, André wrestled for Salvador Lutteroth's Empresa Mexicana de Lucha Libre (EMLL), the oldest wrestling company in the world (now called CMLL). Wrestling as André el Gigante, he teamed with guys like Cien Caras and Mil Máscaras. He also worked for EMLL's opposition, the Universal Wrestling Association (UWA). Unhappy with Lutteroth, promoter Francisco Flores and wrestler Ray Mendoza, along with a financial investor, had started their own company, UWA, in January 1975. Seeing as the grass is always greener on the other side, many wrestlers decided to switch over to the new promotion, including young guys like Dos Caras (Alberto Del Rio's father), Perro Aguayo, and El Canek. The group had a relationship with Vince McMahon Sr., similar to the one McMahon had with New Japan, making it the Mexican promotion André worked for the most. Also, Canek knew André from Japan; the two of them had wrestled on some New Japan cards in 1979. He even was in attendance for André's 33rd birthday party at the Tokyo Hotel with Freddie Blassie, Frank Valois, Victor Rivera, Tony Garea, Chavo Guerrero, Larry Zbyszko, and others. El Canek, whose real name is

Felipe Estrada, was a six-foot, 250-pound masked wrestler who had been wrestling since 1973. In 1978, he had won the UWA World Heavyweight title from Lou Thesz to become the top guy in the promotion. A few years later, he was one of the hottest tickets in lucha libre. By 1980, the heat had died down and some big names were able to work for both promotions. Since André was wrestling in Mexico only a few times a year, he took advantage of that. On February 24, 1980, a UWA card that saw André teaming with Mil Máscaras against Colosso Colosetti and Tiger Jeet Singh in Naulcupan drew 20,000 fans. Five days later, he worked for EMLL in almost the exact same match (TNT replaced Singh), as a part of a triple main event, and drew 16,000 fans. Both companies were healthy, and André was a big star. "Nearly every show he did, large or small, was sold out or was close to it," explained wrestling historian and lucha libre expert Matt Farmer.

Mexico had been good for André: most of his matches were six-man affairs and a lot easier on his body. But with Vince Jr. wanting him to be WWF-exclusive, André's visit to Mexico on February 12, 1984, was his last for eight years. On that day, he wrestled for UWA's ninth-anniversary show at the famous El Toreo de Cuatro Caminos, located on the border of Mexico City and Naucalpan. It was UWA's weekly venue, and the promotion averaged 10,000 fans every Sunday. André main-evented the show against Canek in front of 20,000 fans (some reports stated about 25,000). He was working as a rudo, a heel, but that wasn't always the case for him in Mexico. "In Mexico, the line between the heels and faces could be more blurred than they were in the U.S. and Canada," said Farmer. "Against Canek, André would be heel, but when he went to the smaller buildings, it was usually as a technico [babyface]." On that night, André was definitely a rudo, trying to rip off Canek's mask to the point where fans could see his hair. André even brutalized the luchador outside of the ring. Canek, however, won the match two falls to one, the last one via DQ. He also added his name to the list of wrestlers who had body slammed André. The Giant knew he would not be going back to Mexico, and it was the right thing to do for Canek and UWA. To this day, Canek has a lot of respect for André and for what that did for his career. "To face 'El Gigante' in my country was one of my biggest accomplishments," said Canek to the *Jornada Deportes*.

That year, André appeared in the sequel to *Conan the Barbarian*, called *Conan the Destroyer*, which was filmed in Mexico and featured Arnold Schwarzenegger and Wilt Chamberlain among others. It's probably the least-known role in his silver-screen career. Not only was he not promoted, but he is uncredited and he didn't have a speaking role. He was completely covered up by prosthetics to play the monster Dagoth. The makeup was worse than when he had played Bigfoot, making him totally unrecognizable even to wrestling fans. Looking back at the brief fight he had with Conan (played by Schwarzenegger), it's easier to make the connection today than back then, as the creature moved like André and slapped Conan around, much like André's in-ring repertoire. It was on the set of *Conan* that the famous picture of André, Arnold, and Chamberlain was taken. The movie was released in the summer of 1984 and while it made more money than its budget, it was a disappointment compared to *Conan the Barbarian*. There would never be another Arnold-featured sequel.

Always having an eye for talent, André had pushed the Freebirds — Michael Hayes, Buddy Roberts, and Terry Gordy — to Vince in the summer of 1984. The Freebirds represented rock 'n' roll, entering the ring to Lynyrd Skynyrd's "Freebird," and the WWF was in its Rock 'n' Wrestling era. Cyndi Lauper celebrated with them at ringside on one occasion. The trio made their debut with the WWF, but they didn't stay long. One night, André was, as usual, drinking and playing cards when the trio showed up. Hayes was intoxicated and having trouble walking. André took one look at them and yelled, "He's drunk! He's messed up." André was mad since he had put his reputation on the line for them. He told them they were fired, only about two months after their debut. "When the Freebirds protested that André was unable to make such a decision, André countered, 'We'll see tomorrow if you're gone or I'm gone,'" recalled Bret Hart. "The next day the Freebirds were gone. So I guess André could fire you."

Toward the end of the year, on November 13, 1984, at the Mid-Hudson Civic Center in Poughkeepsie, New York, André shot one of his most famous angles. With S.D. Jones, he battled Ken Patera and Big John Studd, who were backed by their manager, Bobby Heenan. What made this unforgettable was the fact that the bad guys cut the Giant's famous hair! They snipped the signature afro that added a few extra inches to his already intimidating height. "It was the greatest angle I was ever involved with," recalled Patera, adding that it was all André's idea. "We met Vince and George Scott, who was the booker at the time. We were sure this thing was going to be hot."

Aside from the "Killer Khan breaking his ankle" storyline, it was probably the most heat that had been put on André's opponents. It wasn't always easy to find ways to generate sympathy for him as everyone believed the Giant was untouchable, but this certainly worked. And it was a very creative way to create a personal issue for André. This had never been done, and his hair was as much a part of his persona as his giant status. Not since his early career in France had people seen André with short hair, so it was definitely something new. Perhaps it was a way for him to reinvent himself. Since he was not traveling to other territories anymore, he needed an ongoing story to be relevant on the road. The promotion needed him on deck ready to draw everywhere. It was perfectly timed, just before a tour in Japan, explaining his sudden absence from the WWF. André was very smart with his career and understood the business very well, and this is another good example of that.

Pretty much like NXT did until just recently, back in 1985, WWF taped approximately a month's worth of television programming in one night. However, since the shows were only an hour long and you rarely had two true superstars facing each other, stories were told at a much slower pace — unlike today, where you have at least seven hours of programming every week, plus monthly PPV events. In 1985, André's revenge against the Heenan family was still an active storyline. The company had started running more than one live event a day and needed other programs aside from the main one, which included Hulk Hogan and the WWF World title. Ironically, McMahon quickly realized that although Hogan was the biggest draw ever, he, like the Giant, couldn't be brought in too often in the same markets, as he did not draw as well the second or third time in a row. So although André wasn't getting any younger, or healthier, he was still very important as a proven commodity. In both 1984 and 1985, André was among the top 10 drawing cards in pro wrestling. In the WWF, he was only behind Hogan and whoever Hogan had worked with on a regular basis during that year.

Looking for revenge against Studd and Patera, André worked a lot of tag team matches or six-man tags. With the expansion of the WWF now in full swing all over North America, traveling by car was becoming less frequent and flying became the norm for talent. A typical week during that feud looked like this: February 22, in Detroit with Junkyard Dog as a partner; February 23, in Pittsburgh against Patera; February 24, in Minneapolis with Mad Dog Vachon and Rocky Johnson against Studd, Patera, and Orndorff; then Vancouver, Edmonton, and Calgary over the next three days, teaming with either Tony Atlas or Pat Patterson. It was a tough schedule for a regular-sized wrestler, let alone André. He was used to working in the same territory for a few days, or a week, driving from town to town. Flying was never easy on him. And while no one is ever truly comfortable in a plane, imagine what it was like for André. He couldn't fit in the small lavatories, and some flights were very long. Faced as he was with so many flights, he became miserable. He had lost the camaraderie of riding to the next town with his friends and drinking as much as he wanted.

The climax of the feud with Studd and Patera was scheduled to be a one-on-one match between André and Studd at the biggest wrestling extravaganza in the history of pro wrestling, something called *WrestleMania*.

WWF's TBS programming wasn't as successful as Vince thought it would be, and he eventually sold the time slot to Jim Crockett Jr.,

ANDRÉ AND HOGAN AT SHEA STADIUM IN 1980.

FREDDIE BLASSIE SERVED AS AN AGITATOR IN THE FIRST FEUD BETWEEN ANDRÉ AND HOGAN.

GEORGE NAPOLITANO

IN 1982, JEAN FERRÉ VS. HULK HOGAN IN MONTREAL FOR ONE LAST TIME.

LINDA BOUCHER

EVERY PLACE WAS A GOOD ONE FOR ANDRÉ TO HAVE SOME WINE, EVEN AT THE HOSPITAL!

LONGTIME FOE DON LEO JONATHAN CAME TO REFEREE A MATCH BETWEEN ANDRÉ AND KILLER KHAN IN MONTREAL.

PAT PATTERSON AND GORILLA MONSOON RAISED ANDRÉ'S ARMS AFTER HIS WIN AGAINST KILLER KHAN.

FEZZIK, IN *THE PRINCESS BRIDE*, WAS ANDRÉ'S ULTIMATE ACTING PERFORMANCE THAT MADE HIM IMMORTAL BEYOND THE SQUARED CIRCLE.

IN THE AWA, WITH MANY OF HIS FRIENDS AND FOES, SUCH AS OTTO WANZ, HULK HOGAN, RICK MARTEL, MAD DOG VACHON, KEN PATERA, SHEIK ADNAN, GENE OKERLUND, BOBBY HEENAN, VERNE GAGNE, AND BILLY ROBINSON.

THE IDEA OF ANDRÉ AS A CHALLENGER WAS SET ON HOGAN'S FIRST NIGHT AS WWF WORLD CHAMPION.

AT THE *WRESTLEMANIA I* AFTER-PARTY, ANDRÉ WITH A YOUNG STEPHANIE MCMAHON.

ANDRÉ WITH TIM WHITE, WHO BECAME HIS HANDLER AND, MORE IMPORTANTLY, HIS FRIEND.

IT'S ON THE SET OF THE PIPER'S PIT THAT ANDRÉ AND HOGAN OFFICIALIZED THEIR MATCH AT
WRESTLEMANIA III.

DURING HIS FEUD WITH JAKE THE SNAKE, EVEN IF HE WASN'T THE SAME WRESTLER HE USED TO BE,
ANDRÉ WAS STILL ABLE TO ACT.

THE FAILED BODYSLAM ATTEMPT WAS A HUGE PART OF THE STORY OF THE MATCH AT *WRESTLEMANIA III*.

EVEN IF HE DIDN'T WRESTLE, ANDRÉ WAS VITAL TO THE FIRST ROYAL RUMBLE ON THE USA NETWORK.

LIMITED IN HIS CAPACITIES, ANDRÉ COULD STILL DISH IT OUT AT *WRESTLEMANIA III*.

ANDRÉ SELLING THE WWF WORLD TITLE TO TED DIBIASE MIGHT HAVE BEEN ONE OF THE BEST STORYLINES IN WWF HISTORY.

THE UNDISPUTED BOSS OF THE WWF, WORLD CHAMPION AT LAST, BUT FOR LESS THAN TWO MINUTES.

ANDRÉ'S LAST HURRAH: WWF TAG TEAM CHAMPION WITH HAKU, AS THE COLOSSAL CONNECTION.

ANDRÉ WAS AFRAID OF NO ONE BUT DAMIEN, JAKE "THE SNAKE" ROBERTS'S PYTHON.

TURNING ON BOBBY HEENAN AT *WRESTLEMANIA VI* WAS THE BEST WAY FOR ANDRÉ TO RETURN AS A FAN FAVORITE.

ANDRÉ HAD TO USE CRUTCHES FOR HIS LAST FEW APPEARANCES IN THE WWF.

ANDRÉ'S LAST TV APPEARANCE WAS WITH WCW; HERE SITTING WITH BRUNO SAMMARTINO AND DUSTY RHODES AT THE AFTER-PARTY.

ONE OF ANDRÉ'S LAST PICTURES, WITH HIS MOTHER IN FRANCE AFTER HIS FATHER'S FUNERAL.

for a reported $1 million. McMahon used that money to realize an idea he had at the end of 1984. While he and Linda were on a Caribbean vacation, McMahon had a stroke of genius. Inspired by the boom of the Rock 'n' Wrestling era, thanks to WWF's association with MTV and Cyndi Lauper earlier that year, Vince wanted to create an event where pop culture and pro wrestling would share the stage. "I just thought it was the next logical step for us," McMahon said in the book *30 Years of WrestleMania*. "Hollywood had the Oscars, the NFL had the Super Bowl, and so forth."

He and Linda poured every dollar they had into the show, scheduled for March 31, 1985, at Madison Square Garden. McMahon and his close allies — a group comprised of Pat Patterson, George Scott, Jim Barnett, Ed Cohen, and Howard Finkel — worked on making the night a memorable one for fans all over North America, as the show would be shown on CCTV. Finkel, inspired by the 1960s' Beatlemania, was the one who suggested the name "WrestleMania." Aside from drawing cards such as André, Hogan, Roddy Piper, Jimmy Snuka, The Iron Sheik, Paul Orndorff, Junkyard Dog, and Ricky Steamboat, the show would also feature Lauper, Billy Martin, Liberace, Muhammad Ali, and Mr. T. The latter was the only one who would wrestle, teaming with his *Rocky III* co-star, Hulk Hogan.

It was only natural that André would be booked in a battle of the giants, and Studd was the perfect opponent. They had known each other for 12 years, as they first met in Verdun back in 1973, when Studd was wrestling under the name Chuck O'Connor. Billed at six foot 10 (although he was a few inches shorter) and over 300 pounds, Studd was a big man and had been feuding with André for the past two years. In fact, in 1983 and 1984, when McMahon was invading so many different territories, André versus Studd was a good way for the WWF to win over new fans. Even the fact that *Wrestling Observer Newsletter* readers had voted the rivalry between André and Studd the worst of 1984 didn't prevent the feud from continuing and the match from happening at *WrestleMania*. It was the right call.

When *WrestleMania* was announced, aside from the tag team main event match with Hulk Hogan and Mr. T versus Roddy Piper and Paul Orndorff, one of the main matches was the $15,000 Body Slam Challenge between Studd and André. It was a gimmick Studd had been doing in WWF since 1982, when Freddie Blassie managed him. Money was offered to anyone who could body slam Studd. Of course, no one was successful, giving Studd the opportunity to boast about it, saying no one could ever slam him. André would then accept the challenge, but Studd, grabbing the ropes or aided by Blassie, avoided getting slammed and dubbed himself "the true giant."

In an often-forgotten fact, André had vowed to retire if he was unable to slam his opponent at *Mania*. On the March 22 episode of *Tuesday Night Titans*, a WWF talk show hosted by Vince McMahon himself, André and Vince added another reason for fans to care about the match. In the buildup to the match, McMahon told André that Heenan wanted him to put up something since they were putting up $15,000. André first tried to avoid the question, saying he had already put up his hair. But Vince kept coming back to it. André was having none of it, saying he didn't have to put up anything. It escalated to the point that André acted as if he was getting annoyed while McMahon pretended to be agitated about not getting an answer. That's when McMahon said that people might call André "yellow" if he didn't change his mind. In the middle of the interview, André stood up and violently grabbed Vince by the tie and said no one called him that and stormed off the set. Vince, looking really upset, threw a coffee cup, as they went to a commercial. After that, Lord Alfred Hayes, Vince's sidekick on the show, said that during the commercial, André had accepted Heenan and Studd's challenge and put his career on the line. These kinds of promos were something new. It was great to watch as a fan: you could feel the discomfort on the set, thanks to the great acting by both André and Vince. It is considered to be the first, or one of the first, worked shoot promos done by WWF. That said, André was not always easy to interview. French announcer Marc Blondin remembered that André was impossible to anticipate when shooting an interview and he always needed to be alert to avoid getting hurt when working with André.

Everything had been done to make the match more interesting to fans. For Studd, the match was even more important. "Big John Studd idolized André," recalled Ken Patera. "He had taken so many steroids and growth hormones that he was many inches taller and a hundred pounds heavier in the seven or eight years between our first meeting and our angle with André." But Studd didn't just idolize André: he wanted to be André. And that's why, according to many of their colleagues, André didn't like him. "Big John Studd was another guy André didn't like much," said Jason Hehir. "Studd stepped over the rope to get into the ring. No wrestler except André stepped over the top rope. There was only one giant in professional wrestling and André went out of his way to prove that to Studd." At *WrestleMania*, André convincingly won by slamming his nemesis in a 5:54 match where Studd was never allowed to put the Giant in any danger of losing. The crowd loved it, especially when André opened the bag of cash and made it rain on the live crowd at MSG. Bobby Heenan was supposed to steal the bag of money from André and run to the dressing room before André could give away the money to the fans as he promised he would. But right after the match, André told Heenan to let him have some time with the bag.

"So he reaches into the bag, grabs two or three big handfuls, and starts throwing it to people in the audience," recalled Heenan. "People were going nuts . . . I ran in the ring after two or three throws and grabbed the bag. André let me have it, because if he wanted to empty the bag, he would have. I went back with the bag and saw Vince. I thought, 'Oh man, am I in trouble! I didn't get the bag back quick enough.' But he never said anything to me and never said anything to the Giant." Aside from a few rematches, the feud with Studd was pretty much done with that send-off.

After *WrestleMania*, André's schedule got a bit lighter. Leading up to *WrestleMania* it had been grueling, even for André, who was used to being on the road all the time. It was the kind of schedule that made other wrestlers quit the company because they couldn't take it anymore. On top of that, André was in more pain than ever and further payments were about to come due for all the success, pleasure, and money that acromegaly had granted him so far. His belly was getting bigger and he was moving more slowly than he ever had. This was only natural — his only workout was wrestling, and he didn't expend as much energy in his matches as he once had. The back pain he experienced was slowly robbing him of the small pleasures of life.

André went to New Japan for a month-long tour in May and June of 1985. That tour was mostly tag team matches with some singles tournament matches. The boys were traveling by bus to most shows, and the company had designed a unique seat for him on the bus a few years earlier. "New Japan built a special, larger-than-normal seat on the bus for André," remembered Stan Hansen. "Next to the seat was a large, blue, Japanese-style trashcan. It was always filled with large bottles of Kirin, Asahi, or Sapporo beer that were covered in ice. The first thing André did when he got on the bus was open a beer, and no matter how long of a trip it was, he drank almost constantly. When he got back onto the bus after the matches, he would continue where he left off."

Although he wasn't in his prime, André managed to have a 12-minute match with Antonio Inoki, drawing 11,474 fans in Tokyo. This was the second-biggest crowd of the tour, behind only Inoki and Hulk Hogan two days later. On that tour, André rekindled his friendship with Tony St. Clair, who had come over from England. The two of them hadn't seen each other since 1969, but they were back to being friends like nothing had changed. The wrestling business is like a big family, and friendships never really end. At least not with André, who once more remembered those who had helped him when he was starting.

"Visually he was totally different," recalled St. Clair. "His full head had grown out. The curve in his back. Much heavier. But personally — naturally, I could talk to him properly in English — he was still the same person that I first met. We played rummy or cribbage and we would play for days, with only a few hours of sleep. And he also told me about his daughter."

Upon returning to the United States, André appeared on the "Body Shop," a talking segment hosted by the future governor of Minnesota, Jesse Ventura. The Giant said he had gained weight and was now at 520 pounds, the weight he was later associated with. Whether true or not, it was fitting for his next program, as he entered into a feud with King Kong Bundy, the master of the five-count. King Kong Bundy's gimmick was that he was so big and so strong that he would ask the referee to count to five instead of the regular three, adding insult to injury to his fallen opponent. Bundy was not a giant, but he was a big man, billed as more than 450 pounds, with a different morphology. That made him a natural opponent for André. They had crossed paths before in Texas, but now Bundy was going to replace Patera as Studd's partner. He had joined the Heenan family after first being managed by Jimmy Hart. Despite the potential in their rivalry, Bundy didn't have fond memories of André from working for the Von Erichs in Dallas.

"André didn't like me," said Bundy. "I was the top heel in Dallas when we first met. At the end of the week, I shook his hand, said thank you, and said it was a dream and an honor of mine. Mind you, I am 24 and just a kid, and as I turn around, I said, 'Guess I'm ready for New York.' That pissed him off. He was a prick. He was the scariest man in the business, not for what he could do to you in the ring but what he could do to you professionally. He could just say the word and you would be done."

That said, Bundy stayed with the WWF for three years and was in a big angle with André. In fact, the storyline called for André to be injured by Bundy's devastating avalanche splash, where he would splatter his opponent, dropping all of his weight on him. André even did a stretcher job, as it was said Bundy broke the Giant's sternum. However he felt about Bundy from first working with him, the Giant didn't block Bundy or nix the program with him. Business was important to André, and Bundy was a brand-new opponent for whom he could sell convincingly. They had a major feud, with a main event at the Garden and two matches on WWF's newest television show, *Saturday Night's Main Event*. Aired on NBC and created by McMahon and Dick Ebersol, an NBC executive who had developed *Saturday Night Live* with Lorne Michaels, the show was taped in advance and aired at 11:30 p.m., the time slot usually assigned to *SNL*. Instead of having a star and a jobber work against each other, the idea was to showcase matches between stars, like at a live event. It marked the return of professional wrestling to network television for the first time since the 1950s. The first *Saturday Night's Main Event* in May 1985 did an 8.8 rating and 26 percent audience share, more than almost any *SNL* episode that season. That show didn't feature André, but the second and third shows, in October and November 1985, included the Giant and his feud with Bundy. On October 5 (taped on the 3rd), André and Tony Atlas, managed by Lou Albano, defeated Bundy and Studd by DQ, with Heenan in their corner. The following month, it was the same match with the same ending, but Hogan replaced Atlas. The shows did 8.3 and 6.8, respectively.

Bundy remembered that after their match at the Garden in September of that year, André came to his dressing room to thank him — a change of attitude in Bundy's eyes. The rivalry with André elevated Bundy, and he headlined *WrestleMania 2* the following year. During that time, in response to Bobby Heenan, André was given Lou Albano as a manager, as McMahon was trying something new to keep the Giant fresh. Albano had been red hot with Cyndi Lauper the year prior.

"It was mass production, like an assembly line when I was in New York . . . We recorded interviews for each specific market," recalled Gene Okerlund. "It got to the point where we would do a hundred interviews a day. Each of them was three-minutes long, so 12 to 14 hours a day for me, at least once a week. When André could not find Lou Albano, who was managing him at the time, he would do them himself. So he came up, and we started to talk, and I asked where Lou Albano was. 'He is in the back room, and he is drunk.' We kept that, and it aired!"

In the end, a babyface manager is never as effective as a heel manager, and needless to say, the combo of André and Albano didn't last long. Still, Albano and André were part of an animated television series called *Hulk Hogan's Rock 'n' Wrestling*, broadcast on Saturday mornings on CBS from September 1985 to October 1986. It featured the animated adventures of some WWF wrestlers including Hogan, Piper, The Iron Sheik, Junkyard Dog, and others.

Also in the fall of 1985, André returned to Montreal for the first time since 1983. Although he and Dino Bravo had not been on the same page, two years later it was water under the bridge. Like all other major wrestling markets, Montreal and Quebec City were on the shortlist for Vince McMahon's takeover. But the territory was not that easy to claim. Even though the WWF had been on a local TV station for a couple of years, McMahon was not able to secure dates at the Montreal Forum, the biggest arena in the province. The people in charge of the Forum were satisfied with Varoussac, now called International Wrestling, and chose the local promoters over the WWF. So McMahon went to Quebec City, where International didn't have the same success, having only drawn 3,000 fans to a show in June. McMahon held a show in July and came back in August, this time with the Giant in the main event against Studd. Both shows drew 10,000 fans, as the crowd was really happy to see one of their all-time favorites back in town. The following week, McMahon was finally in Montreal. In an unprecedented move, WWF ran joint shows at the Montreal Forum with International Wrestling. It was the only way Montreal Canadien president Ronald Corey and GM Serge Savard agreed to give McMahon dates. Although André had been in Quebec City the week before, he was leaving for Japan right after and could not be a part of WWF's first-ever event at the Forum. But the show didn't need him since it was the rubber match between the Rougeaus and the Garvins, one of Montreal's hottest feuds ever. In September, André was back in North America, working Bundy at the Garden the same night WWF did its second joint show at the Forum. At the third show, in October, André was not booked although he was in Quebec City two days later, wrestling Bundy. Finally, on November 15, 17,822 fans showed up to the Forum to see the return of the Giant, who was still called "Géant" Jean Ferré there, once again versus Bundy. The match lasted only five minutes and was reportedly not good by any measure. It was the last time André worked for his good friend Gino Brito's promotion. The next time he came to the Forum, it was solely for the WWF. Starting in February 1986, WWF was able to take over the Forum.

In another unprecedented move, WWF and International Wrestling made a trade. McMahon gave back Quebec City and its Colisée to Brito in exchange for the Montreal Forum. It was the beginning of the end for International. That same month, the Rougeaus left for the WWF, and by the fall, Rick Martel, Dino Bravo, and King Tonga were all gone too. In the summer of 1987, International Wrestling, the only promotion André ever held shares in, filed for bankruptcy.

By that time, André was living in North Carolina and working out of what was called the New York office, most of his family was in France, and his daughter was in Seattle. But André was never that far from Montreal. Still, as his match in his former hometown showed, he had slowed down in the ring. André Roussimoff was in more pain than ever, while André the Giant was becoming a shell of his former self. Was retirement an option? Perhaps a full-time move to Hollywood? The following years would provide the answers.

PRO WRESTLING ILLUSTRATED

BIG JOHN STUDD AND ANDRÉ HAD A RIVALRY IN AND OUT OF THE RING.

LINDA BOUCHER

KING KONG BUNDY WAS A DIFFERENT OPPONENT FOR ANDRÉ, AS HIS PHYSICAL ATTRIBUTES WERE STARTING TO FAIL HIM.

CHAPTER 22

SHOOTING IN JAPAN

n the mid-'80s a Rhode Island native by the name of Tim White started working for the WWF as a vendor. While at the merchandise booth at live events, he befriended Arnold Skaaland. At the time, "The Golden Boy" was still traveling with André whenever he was in the northeast. His son, George, had begun wrestling, so he had another reason to stick around. But Skaaland had turned 60 at the beginning of 1985 and didn't want to be on the road as much. Arnold saw White as reliable, someone who could take his place alongside André. Eventually, Skaaland introduced him to André — but before the two could even have a drink, they got off to a rocky start. Because White had just started working for the company, Chief Jay Strongbow, one of the backstage agents, asked him to make copies of the matches for that night's card so he could put them in the locker room. White made the copies and thought, since he was working for the WWF, he could just walk in the locker room . . . Well, at the time, that was a big no-no. Kayfabe was still prevalent and not everyone was welcomed into the dressing room, whether you were working for the company or not. As White passed through the curtains, André was playing cards with Tito Santana. Not recognizing the small bearded man, André yelled, "Get out!" Instead of leaving immediately, White started to explain that he was working for the company, which didn't help his case. André repeated himself one more time: "I said get out!" As he yelled, he pushed away the card table and rose. That's when White left — after angering the Giant. It took a lot of convincing from his good friend Arnold for André to include White in his inner circle. But André didn't hold grudges over these kind of things for long. For him, it was all about teaching a lesson to guys who were still green, whether in or out of the ring.

That André was playing cards in the back wasn't surprising. He loved to play card games. On December 28, 1985, a show in Buffalo, New York, was canceled because of a severe snowstorm. Before that decision was made, André was at the building ready to play cards. But for some reason, he didn't have a deck with him. "André was miserable without a deck of cards," remembered Lanny "The Genius" Poffo. "So I gave a girl who was at the arena $10 and asked her to go and get me a set of Bicycle cards, the best deck of cards at the time, and to keep the change. When she came back, I went to André and said, 'Voilà!' He started crying and said, 'Merci beaucoup, monsieur!' Moreover, he gave me a kiss on both cheeks, like the French people do. He started calling me boss after that." That's quite the outburst of emotion from a man who usually kept his feelings to himself. Mostly alone that day, with most of his regular card players missing, and without a show to perform between Christmas and New Year, he found a friend in Poffo and his touching gesture..

Eventually White started riding with André and Skaaland; as they traveled, Skaaland taught White the ropes, showing him what needed to be done for André on the road. Soon enough, André agreed to travel with White, who became André's driver and road manager, succeeding Skaaland and Valois in the role. It was also around this time that a change in André's mode of transportation made his life a little easier. The office had found a business in Long Island that customized vans. They took all the seats out and put in a captain chair for him. They installed a television, a car phone, and a fridge to keep beverages cold.

There was also a pop top to allow extra head room for André in what came to be known as the "André van." He could watch movies and drink while on the road. (André had had a similar van in Montreal, procured by Gino Brito's brother-in-law who owned a car lot.) When they were in California, for example, White had to rent an RV so André would be comfortable. André would give White a list of people he wanted to travel with, guys like Gorilla Monsoon or Pedro Morales. "The WWF travel office would ultimately call them Big Bear and Little Bear as code words in order not to attract too much attention to their travel plans," recalled Backlund. In 1986, since he was on the road with André all the time and was a trusted employee, Strongbow suggested to McMahon that White act as a referee. The Chief himself taught White how to ref and he started soon thereafter. He became a full-time road agent with André and a part-time referee, until André left WWF, at which point he became a full-time referee, a job he had for two decades.

In the ring, André had renewed his feud with Big John Studd in Australia, where the WWF was doing its second tour, the first with André in the line-up. André had gone back to Australia in the early 1980s after the dismantlement of the WCW. His friends Ron Miller and Larry O'Dea had promoted a few independent shows, and André wanted to give them a hand, as he had done for his friend Yoshihara in Japan. It was during the WWF Australian tour that the Rougeau brothers started with the company, putting a nail in International Wrestling's coffin. André and Studd found themselves together again in April, when WWF held *WrestleMania 2* on April 7 in three different cities: New York, Chicago, and Los Angeles. At the Rosemont Horizon (now the Allstate Arena), located in the Chicago suburbs, the main event featured the British Bulldogs winning the tag titles from Brutus Beefcake and Greg Valentine, but the attraction was without a doubt the WWF versus NFL battle royal. Chicago was the right town to hold such a match, as the Chicago Bears had won their first Super Bowl two months earlier. Football and pro wrestling have always had a tight history, with retiring players moving into wrestling. But this was two active Bears who were chosen to participate. Rookie sensation and defensive lineman William "The Refrigerator" Perry and pro-bowler Jimbo Covert got the call, while a third, Tom Thayer, was approached and interested, but ultimately wasn't invited to the press conference and didn't wrestle. Six NFLers in total were part of the match: Russ Francis, a pro-bowler who was the son of Hawaii wrestling promoter Ed Francis; Ernie Holmes and Harvey Martin, two Super Bowl champions who were the only ones retired from football; and another rookie sensation, Atlanta Falcons' Bill Fralic. Fralic took the most advantage of the press conference, held on March 25, when he talked trash about André. "I guess the only way André could hurt me is if someone pushes him over and he falls on me," he said, referring to André's lack of mobility in recent years. Chicago Bears legend and Hall of Famer Dick Butkus and Ed "Too Tall" Jones, who was a legitimate six foot nine, were the special guest referees, while wrestling and football legend Ernie Ladd was the special guest announcer. WWF had asked all-time great Joe Namath to be the special announcer, but he declined the invitation.

In a rare occurrence for the time, they did a complete rehearsal of the match since non-wrestlers were involved. George Scott and Pat Patterson were in charge of laying things out. On the way back to the hotel, Ernie Holmes was bragging a lot about how tough he was. No one said anything, even if that was the most annoying thing a guest can do among a bunch of wrestlers. Finally, André had had enough and told the former defensive tackle, "You talk too much, you know what I mean?" Holmes and everyone else fell silent. On the wrestling side, legends Bruno Sammartino and Pedro Morales, Big John Studd, The Iron Sheik, King Tonga, and Bret Hart and Jim Neidhart were among the many who completed the 20-man field. The last two men to make their entrances were "The Fridge" and André, the clear favorite. Fralic's statement wasn't that far from reality as it was hard not to notice André's balance issues as he stayed in a corner, using the ropes to help him stay on his feet. He also relied on working with his old nemesis Big John Studd whenever possible — he might not have liked him, but he knew he could trust him. Russ Francis, who had wrestling experience and had worked for his dad in Hawaii, seemed to be gunning for André on several occasions and was the last football player eliminated. André had selected The Hart Foundation to be the final two with him. They were good workers and they could make him look good. André explained to Hart what he wanted the finish to be, but Bret had something else in mind. It was a move they often did. Hart would whip Neidhart in the corner, he'd reverse it and send Hart in for a tackle. But instead, André would give him a big boot.

"André thought about it while his huge fingers worked the laces tight," wrote Hart in his book. "The dressing room was suddenly quiet. I saw a frozen face on Tom's [Dynamite Kid] face, and I wondered what I'd said wrong. Then André smiled and said, 'Yeah, boss, I like that better.' A few minutes later, Tom told me that it was unheard of for anyone to suggest the slightest change to André." André, with his unconventional yellow trunks and yellow boots, double head-butted them, eliminated Neidhart with a big boot, and sent Hart flying to the outside on his partner. The king of the battle royals was victorious. "The NFL players were really good guys and respected what we did," recalled Jim Neidhart. "They all couldn't believe how big André the Giant was."

Following that match, they ran an angle on television where Bobby Heenan petitioned WWF storyline president Jack Tunney to ban the Giant from competing because he failed to show for a tag team match against Heenan's guys, Studd and Bundy. Heenan finally succeeded at the end of May, announcing on commentary that André had been suspended. In reality, they needed to explain André's long absence as he was going to spend three months in Japan. Japan was the only place where he could see some of his friends not in the WWF, like Dick Murdoch, Bill Eadie, Canek, and Tony St. Clair. Mostly working in tag teams, André kept his feud with Inoki ongoing and was still able to draw decent crowds. But none of that came close to the most important story coming out of that tour.

Formed in 1984 by Hisashi Shinma, a former New Japan booker who was expelled from that promotion, the Universal Wrestling Federation was built around Akira Maeda, who had a background in karate. Trained by Karl Gotch, Maeda had started wrestling for New Japan in 1978. The company was a shoot-style promotion, which meant matches were still scripted but looked more like an MMA fight than a scripted wrestling match. The company even had a working relationship with the WWF, since Shinma had known McMahon for years. Maeda worked in New York and was billed as the WWF International Heavyweight champion. However, the UWF was short lived and closed down in 1985. Maeda went back to New Japan. "Maeda decried pro wrestling for not being a true sport and in his youth often had outbursts at fans, wrestlers, and reporters regarding such a thing," wrote Dave Meltzer. "Maeda's statements about wrestling and American wrestlers in general often led to a lack of cooperation in those matches. It was well known in those days that Maeda's matches would be phenomenal against the Japanese, but largely nothing with Americans."

On April 29, 1986, Maeda was booked against André in a match refereed by Frenchy Bernard. "Maeda wanted to play along with the New Japan style, but Seiji Sakaguchi [co-founder of NJPW and booker at the time] wanted to rib him, and put André out there opposite him," recalled former company board member Akehiko Age in 2014. Well, one can wonder about who got pranked here: Maeda, André, Inoki, or the fans.

The match didn't start like a usual pro wrestling match. Both were observing each other and circling, as you would see in a modern UFC fight. The first move of the match was a stiff kick to the leg from Maeda, playing on his shoot style. Then, as he tried a leg takedown, André caught him in a double arm underhook and used his weight to bring the Japanese star down to the mat, immobilizing him. After a rope break, Maeda whipped himself into the ropes and as he was running toward André, the Giant hit him with a stiff forearm, sending Maeda hard on the mat. That was the first move of the match that made onlookers think the ordeal was real. "We were just so curious. I was Fujinami's attendant at the time, and we were gathered around the monitor with Inoki, Sakaguchi and their attendants," recalled *Wrestling*

Observer Newsletter's Hall of Famer Masakatsu Funaki. "I was excited but could tell in the first five minutes something was up." They kept wrestling and every time they would both stand up and just stare at each other, André couldn't wipe the smirk off his face. They clearly didn't like each other's styles. André turned a lock-up into a full nelson and dropped his massive weight on the Japanese wrestler's back, using his body to teach Maeda how to cooperate. André was an expert in using his body to his advantage, but he didn't have the same strength he once had. Both up again, Maeda threw three stiff kicks to the back of André's left leg, where André was well protected by the weight he had put on in recent years. Needless to say, André didn't sell any of this offense. Although they didn't look like worked kicks, Maeda didn't aim at André's knee, meaning he was probably still working. André then let Maeda grab his arm and the latter took advantage of it by sending André to the mat hard with a single leg takedown.

As mentioned before, André didn't let just anyone take him off his feet. In this case, Maeda had not asked permission and André responded by trying to gouge out Maeda's eye with his big thick fingers. Maeda turned that into an arm bar. Oddly, he got up and dropped an elbow — straight from his pro wrestling repertoire — and after André tried a rear naked choke, Maeda applied the arm bar once more. Either Maeda wasn't able to lock it in or didn't apply enough pressure. André's arm was never in any real danger, but it looked like it was stiffer than a usual pro wrestling hold. During that second arm bar, André stopped selling and yelled at Maeda, "Let go of my hand!" After having worked on it for close to two minutes, Maeda released the hold and got up. André wasn't used to being on the mat for that long anymore and had a lot of trouble getting back up. He had to use the ropes in the corner. Maeda brought André back down on his back with a takedown. André choked him from his back, and once again, they both got up as André said something to his opponent. Throughout the match, André tried to communicate with Maeda, either trying to bring the match back to pro wrestling or expressing his discontent. Maeda threw a dropkick, a sign he was still trying to work, but André brushed him off and didn't sell it one bit. Clearly, he hadn't appreciated being brought down to the mat so often and for so long. So what did Maeda do? Another takedown. If it had been an MMA fight, Maeda would have been ahead in points.

André was sweating profusely by this point and they were only half-way through the match. Maeda put him down again with a single leg takedown and tried to move André toward the middle of the ring. But André didn't help him and André's weight was just too much for Maeda to move, so he went to the mat and continued working the leg. André used his other foot and kicked Maeda right in the face with the heel of his boot. That's when the match really started to unravel. For several minutes, all they did was circle each other. Maeda threw some worked kicks, but André couldn't care less about selling them. Maeda didn't know what to do. At that point, he stopped and put his hands on his waist. André didn't try any offense either. Maeda amplified the intensity and the frequency of his kicks, but André was done collaborating. So Maeda started to kick his left knee instead of the upper thigh like he had at the beginning of the match. Maeda was sizing up his opponent: he was clearly in shoot mode. Whatever was going on, it got the attention of Antonio Inoki, who walked to ringside. At the same time, Maeda's kick to the knee made André lose his balance as he held himself on the ropes. Another kick almost brought the Giant down as André barely kept his balance. André was losing his patience and turned his back to Maeda, who kicked him behind the knee again. André retreated to his corner and spoke with his manager, Wakamatsu, while Maeda had an animated discussion with Inoki. Both were showing signs of impatience. After two more takedowns, André stayed on the mat, shoulders down, daring Maeda to pin him. Maeda then looked at Kantaro Hoshino, an older New Japan wrestler at ringside, and asked if he could take him out, but Hoshino said no. Out of respect for André, Inoki the promoter stepped in the ring and ended the match. After the bell rang, Maeda finally covered André, but André got his shoulders up, even if the referee wasn't counting the pin. The match lasted 26 minutes — almost all of it painful to watch.

"The awkward affair where Maeda grew ever more frustrated with an immobile, uncooperative, and arguably intoxicated André has gone down in history as one of Japan's most famous 'cement matches,' a Japanese industry term for a wrestling match that breaks the fourth wall into a real and often embarrassing struggle," wrote author Chris Charlton. Perhaps an André the Giant from another era would have been able to do something with Maeda. The match could have been a wild contest. But with his weight, back problems, and lack of balance, he probably did as much as he could do without risking injury. Maeda and André were on opposite sides of a tag team match a month later, and that was the last time they faced each other. In November 1987, Maeda broke Riki Choshu's (another wrestler who once body slammed André) orbital bone with a kick and was fired from the company. He reopened the UWF, this time with more success. Despite all this, he ended up being a major name, named *Wrestling Observer*'s wrestler of the year in 1988, promoter of the year in 1989, and a charter member of the *Observer*'s Hall of Fame.

That tour was the last time André worked with New Japan. The relationship between New Japan and WWF had terminated at the end of October 1985, though André, who had always worked under a different deal, was afforded one last tour. Despite having his last match on June 20 against his old nemesis Inoki, a four-minute match that the Giant won by count-out, the match most remembered by fans happened three days earlier. On June 17, New Japan ran a TV taping in Nagoya, headlined by André and Inoki. At nine minutes and 30 seconds of an IWGP League semi-final match, Inoki submitted André with an arm bar, on his way to winning the tournament. Not only was it a rare loss for André, it was the only recorded submission defeat of his career. André was leaving the territory and did the right thing by putting over Inoki. He was not the same André Inoki had brought to Japan a decade earlier. But still Inoki loved and had the utmost respect for André. He was good to André. He had put him over and protected him as much as he could. He brought him to Brazil and, even as late as December 1984, had brought him to the Philippines, where Inoki versus André drew 23,000 fans. André had always been well booked and protected.

In August 1985, when Bill Eadie (Masked Superstar) and André were booked on a tour for New Japan, they were offered something they didn't expect. "When we arrived, the first day, we were approached with the idea from the office to become the new and better Machine tag team," revealed Eadie. "Each night, the manager would challenge his former team to a fight. He and the New Japan company were burying his former team, saying they were cowards and telling the fans we were superior. The gimmick was just supposed to last during the tour. I think the fans enjoyed it."

To understand the story better, we need to go back in time. Junji Hirata had started his wrestling career in New Japan in 1978. Four years later, he moved to Calgary to work for Stampede Wrestling, where he created a new masked character, Super Strong Machine. He came back to New Japan in 1984 and brought his newest persona with him. Wrestling as Strong Machine #1, he started teaming with Yang Seung-hi, who worked as Strong Machine #2, both managed by wrestler-turned-manager Ichimasa "KY" Wakamatsu. Soon enough, there would be a Strong Machine #3 and #4, all part of the Machine Gun Army faction. But at the beginning of the summer in 1985, Wakamatsu turned against the first two Machines and was looking for a new tag team. So André, for the first time in years, wrestled under a name other than André the Giant or Jean Ferré and, for the first time in his career, wrestled under a mask. Spoiler alert: it's very hard to hide a giant under just a mask, let alone André the Giant . . . "Of course, all the fans knew who we were!" said Eadie. Managed by Wakamatsu, who was carrying a megaphone at ringside, the pair wrestled the likes of Inoki, Sakaguchi, and Fujinami.

Fast forward to a year later: André was on his way back home from his last tour of Japan when he stopped in Austria to work Otto Wanz.

The match saw Wanz body slam the Giant. André was back in the U.S. for only a brief time, as he was scheduled to film *The Princess Bride* in September. "Vince had heard about the Machines gimmick and decided to use it in the U.S. for a short time as a fun little gimmick," explained Eadie, who didn't want to do it at first. "André asked me to do it and I wasn't interested in going back into New York, to be honest. So I went back up as a favor to him." Putting a mask on André seemed like a different idea, and surely WWF saw the possibility in marketing the gimmick. After all, the company did release a T-shirt and a poster featuring André under the mask. And since André was still "suspended," it gave the WWF another reason to bring him back under a hood. Also, André was talking about retirement because his back was in so much pain. There was no point in bringing him back as André the Giant for a month or two. If he was going to retire, his last match would have been, fittingly, winning a battle royal at *WrestleMania 2*. Moreover, as Giant Machine, André did not wear his traditional wrestling trunks but a singlet, with a single strap, which hid the back brace he now needed to wear when wrestling. "His health was getting worse," remembered Tim White. "It was getting harder and harder for him to move. And he would never say how bad things were."

Although today almost everything related to André, including that character, is seen through the lens of nostalgia, the reality is that André never really got over as Giant Machine. He wrestled a handful of matches against the same opponents from the Heenan family that he had been working with before. There was no real emotion or reason for the fans to attach themselves to the character, aside from the comedy Heenan provided by complaining that Giant Machine was in fact André, which everyone knew anyway. They even flew Gene Okerlund to Japan to tape interviews with Super Machine and Giant Machine. It didn't help. The story ended with Big Machine (Blackjack Mulligan) replacing André, who left to shoot *The Princess Bride*. They even had Hulk Hogan as the Hulk Machine and Roddy Piper as the Piper Machine for six-man competition after André left. In November, Big and Super Machine were beaten by Bundy and Studd. It was Lou Albano's last match as a manager and the end of the Machines.

Meanwhile, André was already playing another role.

ANDRÉ LOVED HIS TIME SHOOTING *THE PRINCESS BRIDE* AND WAS CRITICALLY ACCLAIMED IN HIS ROLE OF FEZZIK.

DOING AN INTERVIEW WITH ANDRÉ WAS NOT ALWAYS EASY. ASK MARC BLONDIN, HERE WITH ANDRÉ AND FRENCHY MARTIN IN FRANCE.

PAIRING BOBBY HEENAN WITH ANDRÉ GUARANTEED NO ONE WOULD CHEER FOR HIM.

CHAPTER 23

A GENTLE GIANT!

In 1986, very few professional wrestlers had turned to acting. Mike Mazurki, who had wrestled in the 1930s and who founded the Cauliflower Alley Club, was the first wrestler to make a foray into that world. Hard Boiled Haggerty wrestled for 20 years and acted for 20 more. And Harold Sakata, a former Olympic medalist who wrestled as Tosh Togo, played Oddjob in the third instalment in the James Bond series, *Goldfinger*. Yet, none of these men were hugely popular wrestlers like André. Although he had acted in *Rocky III*, Hulk Hogan was still a few years away from having a prominent film role. And it was decades before Dwayne "The Rock" Johnson became the biggest action star in Hollywood.

And then, in 1987, André was given the role of Fezzik in *The Princess Bride*.

The Princess Bride was an adaptation of the late William Goldman's original 1973 novel of the same name. "I had two little daughters," recalled Goldman, who was already a revered author, in an interview with *Entertainment Weekly*. "I said, 'I'll write you a story. What do you want it to be about?' One of them said a princess and the other one said a bride. I said that'll be the title."

The film rights had been bought by 20th Century Fox for half a million dollars and Richard Lester was set to direct it in the 1970s. But the project fell into oblivion with a Fox executive turnover and Goldman repurchased the rights. Director Rob Reiner's passion for the book brought the project back to life 13 years later, and the search for Fezzik the Turk Giant started. Even in the 1970s, Goldman had wanted André to play the part. "I had no idea who should play Fezzik if the movie ever actually happened," recalled Goldman. "Then one night on the tube there, André was wrestling. He was young then, I don't think much over twenty-five. I screamed, 'Helen, my god, look, Fezzik.'"

So André was the first name brought to casting director Jane Jenkins. According to her, she contacted WWF and was told André was wrestling in Japan during the dates proposed for filming. WWF added he would be paid $5 million for that tour. "They asked, 'Will you pay him five million dollars?'" remembered Jenkins. "And I said, 'I don't think so! That's like half the budget of this movie!'" André wasn't being paid that, as the most he ever got in Japan was just little under $10,000 per week. Although New Japan did have a tour in November and December 1986, an educated guess is, at the time the company was asked, WWF didn't want to lose one of its main stars for several months. Perhaps Vince McMahon Jr. remembered when his father told Hogan he had to choose between being a wrestler and a movie actor. In any case, the production met other people such as Richard Kiel, who had played Jaws in multiple James Bond movies; Kareem Abdul-Jabbar, who was a fan of the book; Lou Ferrigno, the Incredible Hulk; and Carel Struycken, also seven feet tall and suffering from acromegaly. But no one was available or quite right for the part. At the last minute, WWF told Jenkins that André's booking was canceled in Japan and that he would be in Paris visiting his family. Reiner left right away for Paris to meet with him. "And that's how we wound up with André at the eleventh hour," said Jenkins. "And he was absolutely perfect!"

"We all knew André because we'd seen him wrestling," recalled Reiner. "But I had no idea if he could act. We met him at a hotel in Paris, and when we walked in, the manager said, 'There's a man waiting for you at the bar.' So we walked into the bar, and it was literally like Fezzik was described in the book. It was like a landmass sitting on a barstool. He came up to our hotel room to read. We had a three-page scene for him to audition with, and I didn't understand a word he said!"

The filming for the movie was going to take place in the same town for 15 straight weeks, something a world-traveler like André could have found challenging. "I do it, boss," answered André, before adding, "You want me to play these three pages for fifteen weeks?" André thought those were his only lines! After being told he would have more lines and be in a lot of scenes, his answer didn't change. André was in. "So he leaves — and he was a really sweet guy — and I turn to Andy and say, 'Oh, my god. I don't know if he can do this or not.' But he was perfect for the part. He looked exactly right." Reiner decided to go all in and to record every line of the script exactly the way he needed them so that André could study for his part. André studied so hard and delivered each line just the way the director had envisioned it, that the production didn't need to loop him (recording lines of dialogue in a studio after the end of principal photography). According to Reiner, André's ring instinct made him a natural actor, always spot-on in his performance. He also considered André an important piece of the puzzle, without whom he couldn't have made the movie.

The movie was shot in Ireland, an incentive for André as he could visit his home country whenever he had downtime. "He came to visit us often," remembered Boris. "He would travel with a driver in a Rolls-Royce. They would cross by ferry boat, and one time the exhaust broke getting off the boat in France. They drove like that up to Molien, making an enormous amount of noise on the four-hour run!" Not fazed by the noisy ride, André simply asked his nephew to help the driver get to Labeda's garage so he could get the car fixed. Labeda was a childhood friend, whom André played cards with until his death. Deep down,

André was a simple man from a small village in France. Filming that movie gave him the chance to be that man once again. "When he was filming *The Princess Bride*, he was at home and was working hard on his part," remembered Jacques. "He'd tell us, 'I have to read. I have to study this book.'"

The Princess Bride was the perfect project for André to show he could be a good actor — not just in the way he delivered his lines but through his body movements and facial expressions. The story is about a young boy, sick and missing school, being told the fairy tale of Princess Buttercup and her true love, Westley, a farm boy destined to become the dreaded Pirate Roberts. The young boy is played by Fred Savage, just before he became the star of the television show *The Wonder Years*, while Peter Falk, better known as Columbo, played his grandfather and the narrator of the story. Much like in a wrestling storyline, the Fezzik character starts as a villain because of the evil influence of the Sicilian Vizzini, who behaves much like a wrestling manager, making him do his bidding. Slowly, Fezzik turns into a hero, becoming an ally to the main character, Westley. Much like André, Fezzik always has a good heart. Fezzik is vital to the story because he rallies the three heroes together after they first fight each other. Fezzik also finds a way to help bring Westley back to life with the aid of Miracle Max, played by Billy Crystal.

Details from the book that were left out of the final movie script are eerily similar to André's life. Fezzik was a good person but very uncomfortable with his differences, going back to his childhood. His size made him a natural at wrestling and led Fezzik to tour the world from Europe to Asia, mirroring André's career. One of Fezzik's famous lines from the movie is "I don't even exercise!" That line was perfect for André, as that was true for most of his life. If that wasn't enough, Fezzik, even if he was undefeated in wrestling, still wasn't happy after joining the circus, and when alone at night in his tent, would also cry about how different he was. Fezzik was a character André was passionate about. It was almost like the fairy tale story of his own life. In later years, he was so proud of the movie, he would carry a VHS copy and play the tape endlessly to his friends at home, in the bus while on tour in Japan, and in his hotel room on the road. In fact, he would order room service for whoever stayed to watch the movie, an incentive for many of his colleagues. It was a rare occasion but here André Roussimoff shone more brightly than André the Giant — even if the credits list him as André the Giant. He was much more than his wrestling persona and in this film delivered a charming performance that felt genuine to movie aficionados. Also, the fact that the movie kept André for such a long period in the same place allowed him to get comfortable with another group of people, other than wrestlers. For the man behind the giant, that meant a lot.

"I don't want to call him a tragic figure because he was not. He was filled with enjoyment of life and love for other people," expressed Chris Sarandon, who played bad guy Prince Humperdinck. "He enjoyed being around us, and I remember clearly André saying he enjoyed being around us because he didn't feel like he was different. Because we were all a little nuts." André played gin rummy on the set with Andy Scheinman. Being at ease with a group of people and playing cards with them, it must have really felt like a wrestling locker room for André. For most of the people on set, meeting him for the first time was like stepping into a fairy tale. A world where this giant was your friend.

"Rob came to me at the studio so I could meet André," recalled Mandy Patinkin, who played the third hero, Inigo Montoya. "He was there sitting on that couch like a landmass just like Bill Goldman described it. I never saw anything like that, and I lost my breath. I had to get it together, he was my partner in the film, and we had to bond. He took a picture with my family but my favorite part is that he had his hands on top of my son Isaac's head."

André also had opportunities to show his true self, a generous, gentle giant. Robin Wright, better known for the role as Claire Underwood on Netflix's *House of Cards*, played Buttercup, or, if you prefer, the Princess Bride. She was overwhelmed the first time she met André — she knew nothing about him. But he showed her she didn't have to be afraid: "He would keep me warm by putting his giant hand over my head as it was freezing cold where we were shooting. He was the sweetest." Wallace Shawn, who played Vizzini, was afraid of heights. But André promised him everything would be alright, that he would take care of him. "André was very kind that day," he said. "I was physically tied to him during the part of the film that was the most terrifying to me. He had a flask of cognac in his costume that he offered me. I declined because it was sort of dizzying up there anyway."

One of the most challenging things for André was that he needed back surgery. He looked the part and could act the part, but what would have been easy for him years earlier was now difficult. "Because André could not handle any weight on his back everything needed to be rigged," recalled Patinkin. "Robin, Wallace Shawn, and I were sitting on bicycle seats so that no weight was on André even if he was to pull us in the story."

"André couldn't fit on a horse, he was too heavy," said Reiner. "We had guide wires from the ceilings." It wasn't just his back — André's knees were giving him a lot of trouble too. "I always thought that the hard part would have been his performance," continued Reiner. "But the wrestling was the hardest thing for him." The myth that André was strong until the end of his life remains, but it wasn't his reality. In fact, he was so physically compromised by this time that he couldn't even catch a 115-pound woman. "There's a scene where I'm supposed to fall from the castle and he catches me," explained Robin Wright. "And they had to put me on cables so that he had no weight on his arms." Granted, there might be an explanation for that. Close to 75 percent of acromegaly patients develop carpal tunnel syndrome. Carpal tunnel is a common condition that occurs when one of the major nerves to the hand is squeezed or compressed as it travels through the wrist. One of its symptoms is weakness in the hand and arm, which could explain the difficulty he had filming that scene — as well as explain some other diminished-strength stories that have circulated about André over the years.

Getting André to the set wasn't easy: he could not use traditional means of transportation. The production ended up providing him a four-wheeler

ATV similar to what he had at his ranch, but it was a decision they came to regret. André convinced Cary Elwes (who plays Westley) that it was easy to drive, even for a first-timer. André was persistent, so Elwes tried and the inevitable happened. "Cary pretended he was fine. I could see that he couldn't walk, and André, it was his fault," recalled Reiner. But André faced no repercussions. Probably too happy to have cast the perfect person for the part, the production ignored some of André's habits. On the night of the table reading, where the cast assembled for the first time to go through the script together, André passed out in the hotel lobby. He had found the hotel's wine cellar. No one from the Dorchester Hotel or from the production could move him. When they finally gave up, they pulled a rug over him and put up velvet ropes around him. But André was able to make up for those moments, making sure he left a good impression on everyone. During filming, he was always charming and always laughing. And André being André, he once put a stop to a scene after one of his legendary episodes of flatulence . . .

"Once, André had one of the most monumental farts any of us had ever heard," wrote Elwes in his book. "Now, I suppose you wouldn't expect a man of André's proportions to pass gas quietly or unobtrusively, but this particular one was truly epic, a veritable symphony of gastric distress that roared for more than several seconds and shook the very foundations of the wood and plaster set we were now grabbing on to out of sheer fear. It was long enough and loud enough that every member of the crew had time to stop what they were doing and take notice."

Laughter ensued, as no one in the scene could stay in character, even if every trick in the book was used. Reiner was ultimately able to get Elwes to stop laughing after pointing out that it was probably happening to André quite frequently and it might not have been that funny to him anymore. Quickly catching his composure, he went to talk with André and apologized. "It's okay," he replied. "My farts always make people laugh . . . That was a big one, wasn't it?"

New to his on-set coworkers, André's flatulence was legendary in the wrestling world. "André so enjoyed flatulence," recalled Vince

McMahon. "When he passed gas, it was an event!" Not only did he enjoy it, he even had a special position. "That was his trademark. And he had a real knack for lifting his left leg," remembered Gene Okerlund. "I would see him go into the launch position," continued Tim White, "and I'd say, oh my god, here it comes. You've never heard anything like it."

Believe it or not, sometimes his farts would get André in trouble, especially if he was on a plane. "To see the pilots, you know, almost like somebody got smoke in their eyes," said Hogan. "I'm like, you're gonna wreck the plane, André, you can't fart like that in your pants. And the pilots would be GD this, F that, never, never on this plane again!" At least, the pilots could retreat to the cockpit. But in an elevator, you had nowhere to hide. And farting in an elevator at full capacity would really make André laugh. It was one of his favorite pranks, and he could make it last. Sometimes, it would even be a finishing move. "During one match, I had with André, he sat on me in the corner and he farted on me," Greg Valentine said. "I told the referee, 'Count me down, my shoulders are on the floor! Get him off me!'" Not only could they be almost lethal, they were very noisy. "It was like an explosion!" remembered Pat Patterson. "Like a deep roar kind of thing. It would rumble!" added McMahon. However, Okerlund perhaps summarized it the best: "Well, they were loud. Big man, big fart!" André loved farting so much that when his body would not cooperate, he would use a fart machine to make the noise while in an elevator, for example, just to get a laugh and a reaction.

Elwes, who considered André a good friend even after filming of *The Princes Bride* concluded, got closer to André than anyone else on set. They would sit and talk during their downtime. André showed Elwes pictures he kept in his wallet. Some were of himself with celebrities like Muhammad Ali, others were of his youth. Some were from London, walking down the street or lifting a car. Although he also told some exaggerated stories to Elwes, he opened up to him in a way he wouldn't normally. He told Elwes how difficult it was for him to deal with constant attention. And while he loved wrestling in Japan, he was not a fan of the attention he generated or the Japanese legend that touching or rubbing a giant brings good luck. However, André Roussimoff was still André the Giant when it came to pro wrestling and keeping the oath of omertà on wrestling's secrets. He never admitted to anyone that wrestling was in fact sports entertainment. "The only topic you could not get André to budge on was whether or not wrestling was fake or rehearsed in any way," said Elwes. Mandy Patinkin echoed his coworker: "I'll never forget, I was having lunch at the commissary at Shepperton with André, Rob, and Andy. And I was busy trying to connect with him because we had to be partners for the next four months, and I wanted to bond as quickly as possible. We were all chatting away, and at some point, during the lunch, I said, 'So this wrestling thing, it's obviously all fake, right?' And the conversation just stopped on a dime. And André looked at me and said, 'What do you mean?' And I went, 'It's all planned, right? It's all fake?' And he said, 'NOOOOO, BOSS!' And he was serious."

"He seemed very humble at that table and very much wanted us to believe him and to take him seriously," added Patinkin. "He wasn't playing games. I didn't feel I was being schmoozed by him. Ever."

That might be why André was so happy with the experience. The acting world offered hope: the chance to give his body a break, to be with a group of people who accepted him, and to make decent money. André was generous with his co-stars, as he usually was with people he liked. "During a break in his shooting schedule on the movie, he chartered a truck and took the ferry across the channel back to his homeland, ostensibly to see his folks," continued Patinkin. "When he returned though, he arrived back on the set with a crate of pâté, cheese, foie gras, and a crate of fine wine. The crew, who already loved him, worshipped him after that."

The filming lasted until December 1986. Its original release was scheduled for July 31, 1987, as a major summer blockbuster. However, due to ongoing editing, it was pushed back. While everyone who worked on *The Princess Bride* felt they had made a good, funny, heartwarming, and memorable movie, the studio wasn't sure how to promote it. It finally saw limited release on September 25, in only nine theaters in New York and

Los Angeles. The wider release came on October 9, Columbus Day weekend in the U.S. and Thanksgiving weekend in Canada. André attended the world premiere on September 18 at the Toronto International Film Festival, but he was too big to fit in a regular theatre seat. He was seated on an orange vinyl bench designed to accommodate his size. The movie had won the festival's people's choice award and received good reviews, but that didn't translate into box office success. It made almost $31 million (close to eight million tickets sold) in gross revenues in 11 weeks, good enough for the 41st position of films released in 1987. The timing of the movie was perhaps an issue, as big hits like *Dirty Dancing* and *Fatal Attraction* were still going strong. The movie did not find its audience in theaters, though it ultimately earned twice its budget. The studio had selected a silhouette of Fred Savage and Peter Falk for the poster instead of promoting the sword fight, the princess, the pirate, or the Giant. It branded it as a kid's movie, alienating a large chunk of its possible audience. In France, where the movie was finally released on March 9, 1988, it sold only 560,000 tickets. However, the critics were very good to it and one in particular noted André's performance, saying he was great, loveable, and a born actor.

The wrestling audience would have probably supported it more if André was not a heel by that point. In 1987, it was still the old mentality that a heel was supposed to get booed, not praised as a movie star. Instead, it was at best timidly promoted by WWF on its *Superstars* television show. In Montreal, André's fame helped get the movie promoted in the *Journal de Montréal* and *La Presse*, but instead of focusing on his work in the film, the articles focused on his wrestling career and his condition as a giant. Even if André mentioned his real name in them, André the Giant overshadowed André Roussimoff once again.

Patinkin and André were on *Good Morning America* on September 30 to promote *The Princess Bride*. Again, the movie came second to wrestling, though Patinkin convincingly argued that André did a fantastic job as an actor. André knew how to promote himself and made sure to say the right things in front of a new audience. "If they got a part for a giant, I'd be ready," he said, talking about acting roles he could do.

Two weeks after the Toronto festival, there was a screening at the New York Film Festival, with the whole cast present. After the event, André invited his new friend Cary for a nightcap, which the actor gladly accepted. They went to one of André's favorite places, P.J. Clarke's on Third Avenue. It was the kind of place André loved: a small, intimate bar, where celebrities were just part of the family. Elwes remembered that the place went silent when André came in. "It's really not possible for you to make a subtle entrance, is it?" he asked André. The Giant smiled and said, "Not always. But it's okay. They know me here." Only staying an hour or so, the duo went bar hopping all over Manhattan. As usual, André refused to let Elwes pay for anything. After a few bars, Elwes started noticing that a man seemed to be following them everywhere they went. So André looked at the guy and simply said, "Oh, don't worry about him." Turns out the man was a cop.

According to the story André told Elwes that night, one time, he was bar hopping in town, had one too many drinks, and as he was waiting for his car, he fell asleep and collapsed . . . on another customer! A very surprised customer! After that, the NYPD decided to send someone to follow André every time he was in town. "They said it was for my own safety," André told Elwes, who didn't question it since André wasn't usually inclined to tell those stories. That said, it wouldn't be the first time André lied or exaggerated a story. But Elwes might be right. Somehow, that one sounds legit.

Elwes was not the only one who took a liking to André. "I just loved being around him," said William Goldman. "I am starting my fifth decade of movie madness, and he was by far the most popular figure on any film set I ever knew. A bunch of us — Billy Crystal, I think, was one — used to spitball about doing a TV series for André so that he could cut down the 300-plus days a year of travel wrestling required. I think it was going to be called something like *Here Comes André!* and it was going to be about a wrestler who decided he'd had enough and got a job as a babysitter." In 1998, Billy Crystal co-wrote the movie *My Giant*, which was inspired by his time with André.

The way André left his mark on the cast and crew of *The Princess Bride* makes you wonder what might have been for him if his body hadn't become a burden. He did a commercial for Honeycomb cereal and did a fine job. Selling it as a big breakfast — one fit for a giant — André was surrounded by kids in the spot. His facial expressions were atypical, childish, and very funny. And on January 6, 1991, he was featured in an episode of the second season of a TV show called *Zorro*, about the famous masked vigilante, on the Family Channel. Filmed in Madrid, Spain, André played Nestor Vargas, the big brother of an accused bank robber. He had lines in that role, but the show wasn't much of a success. Wrestlers Jesse Ventura and Roddy Piper also guest-starred on the show in 1990 and 1991.

Then, in July and August 1992, in Richmond, Virginia, he filmed what would be his last movie, *Trading Mom*. The movie, featuring Sissy Spacek and Anna Chlumsky, who had just starred in *My Girl*, revolved around Spacek's kids trying to replace her while learning a valuable lesson about love. André played, you guessed it, a giant but didn't have many lines. It was reminiscent of his television appearances from the 1970s and 1980s. The movie was eventually released in 1994, so unfortunately André never got to see it. The movie was not very well received and brought in a little more than $300,000 at the box office. To be honest, his performance would not have inspired more acting offers.

Except for those roles, nothing really materialized after *The Princess Bride*. What had originally made him so interesting for casting directors, his physical attributes as a giant, were deteriorating. By the time of *Trading Mom*, he was walking with a cane and a severe limp. He also looked at least 10 years older than he actually was. Nevertheless, not too long before he died, he was offered a role in *Jack and the Beanstalk*. "He was really excited about that, and I was picking on him, asking him which part they wanted him for," recalled Jackie.

The Princess Bride was a tough act to follow. Its legacy has become another way André will live forever. Merchandising for the movie exploded in popularity, from T-shirts and Funko Pops, to trading cards and so much more. It's one of those few properties that generates more money today than it did in its original release. VHS rentals and sales turned the film into a massive success. Much like *The Rocky Horror Picture Show*, theatrical screenings of *The Princess Bride* see audience members attending in costume and reciting lines together. It has become a cult classic and it still has fans from all walks of life, from President Bill Clinton to the late Pope John Paul II to mobster John Gotti. Its Rotten Tomatoes rating is 94 percent, while the site listed it as the 14th-best romantic comedy of all time. "It's the perfect fairy tale," summarized Billy Crystal. "It makes you feel good. It makes you miss your childhood. It makes you want to have someone read stories to you again."

André was ready to tell the world a whole other story. A story he would be hated for by fans in the U.S. and Canada for the very first time. His biggest story ever.

CHAPTER 24

BIGGER, BETTER, BADDER!

B y the time he started filming *The Princess Bride*, André must have thought his career was all but over. He desperately needed a back operation, and there was no guarantee he could return to the ring afterward.

"André had pretty much cashed in his chips," remembered Vince McMahon. "He was in the U.K., filming *The Princess Bride*, so I went over to talk to him, and he was not feeling well. His back was really, really bothering him. He was all hunched over. He was pretty much ready to give up the business. He wasn't sure if he was going to retire to France or just what he was going to do." So McMahon pitched André the idea of doing the biggest match of his life. "The Pontiac Silverdome is the biggest stadium in the world, it's 93,000 seats, and I want you to headline with Hogan," McMahon explained. It was a great opportunity: André would have his name attached to the biggest wrestling show of all time. And McMahon had an almost foolproof plan: not only was it a covered stadium, but Detroit had become a real stronghold for the WWF, packing houses every time they were in town. Of course, André would have to turn heel, because there was no way McMahon would have turned Hogan, and a babyface versus babyface match wasn't an option. There were still a lot of obstacles with André's health, and even Pat Patterson was unconvinced they could get the match done when the idea was first brought up.

At this point, reality and fiction collided. André's back operation was always reported as having taken place just after the *Princess Bride* shoot and before *WrestleMania III*. That's the story in the original A&E documentary and the way it was presented in the more recent HBO documentary. It's also the story in *A Legendary Life* and both of the biographical graphic novels. Vince McMahon has gone on record multiple times telling it this way, and it is what is commonly believed. That said, information coming from André's working permit paperwork was uncovered in the research for this book, and it indicates clearly that the operation to relieve pressure from marked spinal stenosis took place on July 21, 1987 — almost four full months after *WrestleMania III*. The operation was performed by the famous orthopedic surgeon Patrick England at the Cromwell Hospital in London. The confusion over the timing might stem from the fact that the consultation and decision to go ahead with the operation was made after *The Princess Bride* wrapped. Tim White's recollections seem to indicate four months were needed to get everything ready.

"They had to cut his back open and widen the spine, which was a very, very tricky operation," said White. "I was told it took three or four months to assemble the operating room because they needed bigger scalpels, they needed bigger everything." They would basically need to build everything from scratch to work on André, as nothing they had was to his scale. It would have been very difficult for him to recover fast enough from an operation at the end of 1986 to be back wrestling in March 1987. Why the real surgery timeline was not revealed will probably never be known. Nevertheless, the timing of the operation is another myth in need of proper perspective.

As before any other operation to relieve pressure on joints, André needed to get in better shape and lose some weight. Even for the sake of participating in the match, he needed to do that. Vince McMahon offered to let André train twice a day at his Connecticut home gym, which was as big as any gym you could find at the time. André would start early in the morning on only a few hours of sleep. André might have been serious about it, but at the same time, he was in a hurry to finish so he could celebrate the workout with a 9:30 a.m. beer. McMahon tried to get André to drink protein shakes, but André didn't like them because they made him fart.

The buildup to the match against Hogan began on November 29, 1986. An interview from London aired announcing that André's suspension had been lifted and that he was coming back to the World Wrestling Federation. In December, the first seed of his heel turn was planted. Jack Tunney confirmed André's reinstatement, adding the Giant wasn't at his hearing, but Bobby "The Brain" Heenan was. Which could make sense since it was Heenan who had pushed for the suspension. Interviewed by Jesse Ventura and asked about how André got reinstated, Heenan told "The Body" it was none of his business. The same question was asked by Jake Roberts on the "Snake Pit" and André said it was a mystery. On the January 17, 1987, edition of *WWF Superstars*, the "Piper's Pit" segment hosted by "Rowdy" Roddy Piper saw an over-six-feet-tall trophy given to Hulk Hogan to mark his three-year reign as champion. Footage of the dressing room celebration from January 1984 after Hogan had won the championship, showing André pouring champagne on his head played as Hogan accepted the honor. According to many, McMahon was already planting the seed of the idea that André would be the ultimate opponent for the new champion. André then appeared as a surprise and Piper introduced him as Hogan's best friend. André simply told Hogan that three years as champion was a long time, shook his hand, and left the set. Hogan sold the handshake as if André had actually hurt him.

The following week, another presentation was scheduled. A smaller trophy was given to André to celebrate his undefeated record. Almost perfectly timed, after a few words by the Giant, Hulk Hogan walked in to hand him the trophy — and unwittingly to take the spotlight away. André walked off, leaving the trophy behind. Hogan tried to explain it as André being the model of modesty, even if he and Piper knew something was off. The only thing missing here were the words "to be continued."

The buildup was terrific. The following week, heel announcer Jesse Ventura was on set with Piper. He said he knew about what went down with André's reinstatement. Ventura and Piper both agreed to produce André and Hogan the following week on the "Piper's Pit" set in order to address the issues they had been having and get to the bottom of what was happening. There was no need for André and Hogan to do interviews that week since Ventura and Piper, two of the best talkers in the history of the business, got the storyline going. It led to arguably one of the best segments ever put on by the WWE.

Airing February 7 from Tampa, Florida, Piper was the first one to make good on his promise when Hogan showed up on the set. He was soon followed by André with none other than Bobby Heenan. Heenan was the most hated person in the WWF at the time. The Heenan family (Bundy and Studd) had been a thorn in the Giant's side since the national expansion, and during André's suspension, Heenan had been cast in the same light toward Hogan. There was nothing worse in wrestling at the time than to be aligned with Bobby Heenan, and so this was the perfect way to turn André heel. At first, André did not speak as Hogan expressed how he couldn't believe what he was seeing. It was a great promo that put André over in the process. Heenan confirmed he was André's new manager and explained his motivation. As Hogan tried to plead his case, he reached out and grabbed his friend by the shoulders. That's when André boomed, "Take your hands off my shoulders. I am here for one reason. To challenge you for a world championship match in the *WrestleMania*!" Hogan couldn't believe it. His best friend and mentor, a role model, now thought a wrestling belt was more important than their friendship. To make sure Hogan understood, André ripped off his yellow Hulkamania T-shirt. In later years, Hogan explained that when André tore his shirt, he was trying to put Vicks VapoRub in his eye to help him cry faster and sell the emotion. Fate or luck, as André did that, he also broke Hulk's necklace and drew blood from Hogan's chest. The fake tears didn't matter anymore. The following week, Hogan appeared one more time on "Piper's Pit" and accepted the challenge with an emotional "YESSSSS!" which sparked joy in the live crowd.

Those "Piper's Pit" segments sold out the Pontiac Silverdome and drove PPV orders. Nothing else mattered. If wrestling storytelling was taught in school, this would be the textbook. Nothing was left to chance. At house shows before André's heel turn made it to TV, André was announced against Intercontinental champion Randy "Macho Man" Savage. But in every town, including Montreal, it was said he had left his place to Ricky "The Dragon" Steamboat. In fact, André only wrestled one time during the whole buildup to *Mania*. It wasn't necessary for him to do more. The interviews alone created interest. At the contract signing, broadcast on February 28, Heenan demanded a new championship belt be commissioned — one that would fit André. André remained silent. To add more reality to the angle, Jack Tunney called André "Mr. Roussimoff." Hogan blamed Heenan for André's change of heart. "If you wanted a title shot, all you had to do was ask me," he said. "I would have given you anything, man. André, you were bigger than the world title to me."

After they both had signed, André answered Hogan: "You think I tell you everything you know in professional wrestling. But I didn't. And believe me, *WrestleMania III* will be your last lesson." André started to speak in French to Hogan. "Et ça va vraiment me faire plaisir de le faire, crois-moi. Parce que pour la dernière fois . . ." *And I'm really going to like doing it, believe me. Because it's the last time . . .*

"Speak to me in English when you talk to me!" yelled Hogan. "As far as I'm concerned, it's not signed in ink; it's signed in blood!" To which André responded, "You want me to speak in English . . . I will speak in the ring at *WrestleMania*. Au revoir!"

Everything about the buildup made perfect sense. Although André was very good in these segments, Heenan was by far a better talker and was the right choice to speak for André, considering the importance of the angle. Plus, André liked Heenan. "He realized the Hogan match would be his last big match and he asked Vince for me to be his manager," said Heenan. "Because he trusted me. He wanted to make his money on the way out."

What North American fans likely did not realize was that André had been a heel in Japan for 17 years by that point. He knew how to be an efficient heel, what to do, and how to work. The only match André wrestled in leading up to the show was a battle royal on *Saturday Night's Main Event*, which drew a monster rating of 11.6, the biggest audience that show had ever reached. Taped on February 21 at the Joe Louis Arena in Detroit, Michigan, and broadcast on March 14, Hogan and André dominated the match. They were the only two who eliminated all the other opponents. Gorilla Monsoon suggested a blade job to Lanny Poffo, as a way to sell André's signature head butt, and when Poffo did it, it made André look even more deadly. Poffo was stretchered out to put over the new monster heel even more. In the middle of the match, Hogan and André had what everyone was waiting for: a face-to-face confrontation. After exchanging a few blows, the heels attacked Hogan and the babyfaces jumped on André. In the footage of the match, you can see André's back brace peeking out from his singlet. He was also using the ropes to keep his balance. Then André picked Hulk up by the hair and head butted the back of Hogan's head. Next, he easily threw the champion over the top rope — as quickly as he had dispatched Poffo. While André was being distracted by Hogan being pushed back to the dressing room, the remaining eight competitors in the ring pushed him over the top rope. Perfectly booked by Pat Patterson, a new heel was emerging . . .

Publicity was strong everywhere they went, including in Montreal. On February 27, in the afternoon before a house show at the Forum, a press conference was held at the Ritz Carlton Hotel, where André was staying every time he was in town. The event included an appearance by Géant Ferré (as he was still called in Montreal). After all, *WrestleMania III* was going to be shown on massive screens in two more locations in the province aside from the Forum, the Colisée in Quebec City and the Centre Georges-Vézina in Chicoutimi. One hundred and fifty-seven more locations would be added across the continent where PPV was not yet available. The *Journal de Montréal* hyped the event, and like the WWF, it completely ignored the two wrestlers' history in the city. The article stated that a rematch could be signed for August 10 at the Olympic Stadium. Although such a thing never came close to materializing, it would have had a good chance to beat all the records in terms of gate and attendance in the city. There was so much interest, 15,000 people showed up at the Forum and the result of the match made the front page of the newspaper the day after *WrestleMania*.

The location for *WrestleMania III* was ideal. At the time, Detroit was one of WWF's strongest markets. Now a yearly tradition, it was the first time fans from around North America traveled to attend *WrestleMania*. Conveniently located in Pontiac, near Detroit, the venue was close to other strong markets like Chicago and Toronto, where WWF had drawn 64,100 fans for the Big Event at the Exhibition Stadium the previous year.

Like many things in André's life, the biggest match of his career was not without its own legends and myths. First off, the attendance. WWF and Vince McMahon wanted to break the attendance record at the building, no matter what. And although it was a record-breaking attendance at the time, 93,173 tickets were not sold — as WWF lore has been repeating for years. It's been hyped so often that many, including wrestlers who were on the show, believe it to be an indisputable fact. But it's hard not to challenge the WWF's headcount. After all, stadium officials estimated the capacity at 88,000 three weeks before the event. Dave Meltzer got access to the real paid attendance through local promoter Zane Bresloff and later confirmed his finding through WWE's internal records. The reality was closer to 78,500 paid to be in attendance. If you count comp tickets, as well as everyone working there that night, including the wrestlers, you can add several thousand more "in the stadium." Pat Patterson, who started in front of hundreds of people, still has trouble wrapping his mind around the fact they drew such a house, no matter what the real number is. Even *Mad Magazine* poked fun at it. In 2014, they joked, "When the immortal Hulk Hogan become the first man ever to body slam the 7-foot-4, 520-pound André the Giant before 93,173 fans to hand the big man the first loss of his career, it set the all-time record for the most lies in a single sentence!"

Leading up to the match, the question was whether or not André was ready to let Hulk Hogan beat him. And so, yet another myth was created. Truth be told, none of the boys in the back knew the finish; no one but Pat Patterson, Vince McMahon, Hulk Hogan, and André knew what was going to happen. Over the years, conflicting stories have emerged, creating even more folklore.

"I worked on that match day-in and day-out, making sure they were in a good mood," recalled Pat Patterson in an interview for RF Video in 2018. "André, we had to take care of him, we had to make sure he wouldn't get hurt. André would say, 'Hogan, if I feel bad, I am going to kick the shit out of him.' I would tell him to stop saying that. He was just trying to joke around. But that would get Hogan nervous too. André was just messing with him. However, at that time, Hogan didn't know that. André played a game that he was in a bad mood all the time with Hulk. André worked him. He was so good at that. There was no doubt in my mind it would happen. André was winking at me."

Vince McMahon shared pretty much the same opinion. "Hogan would not say anything to André, like, 'Hey, are you going to do this job for me?' He had too much respect for André to come out straight and ask him. Instead, he would beat around the bush. 'Hey, boss, what are we going to do?' 'I will tell you later,' André would answer. Well, later never came, and Hogan kept coming to me. 'Oh my god, am I going to win this thing?' 'Yeah, yeah, yeah,' I kept saying. 'It's all set.' Finally, I got Hogan in my room the night before the event, and that's when André let him know what was going to go down. After André told Hogan what he was going to do, there was a big hug and all that kind of stuff. And there we go."

That meeting either never took place, took place with André and Vince only, or Hogan completely forgot about it, because not only has

Hogan never mentioned it, he swears he has no recollection of it what-soever. As requested, Hogan wrote a match synopsis, leaving André and Vince to decide upon the finish. "I don't know if they were ribbing me," said Hogan on Chris Jericho's podcast. "Around 2 or 3 p.m. Vince said, 'I think you need to go talk with André.' I am sitting next to André, who's in a lot of pain with two quarts of Crown Royal already ingested. That was nothing for him. He's handing me a drink, and when he's not looking, I am dumping it because I can't start drinking now. Just before going in the ring, he said, 'Don't worry. I will take care of you.' I didn't know going in what that meant."

Tim White remembered André being the same as usual, stopping for beers on the way to the stadium. "Hogan was sweating the whole day," said White. "I think André was holding court, like, 'Know this. Before I make you the guy, remember that I'm the guy and always have been.'"

Édouard Carpentier, who was the French-language play-by-play announcer that night, had clear memories of the mind games. "André was drinking a lot. On that day, he had promised not to drink. But he had bought his wine bottles. He was looking at Vince while drinking his wine, mocking him. I asked him why he was drinking since it was a big match, and he told me it was none of my business. No one knew he was drunk in the ring that night." It's unlikely André was too drunk to perform in that match, but he would have been unable to perform while sober because of the pain.

"My clearest memory of that match was the pain André was feel-ing that day," recalled Raymond Rougeau. "I asked myself, 'How was he going to pull it off?' Just moving was hard for him. I was eager to see what they were going to be able to do. He wasn't drinking for no reason. Each time I saw him, I could see the pain in his eyes. I think he should have retired after that match."

The day of the event, he was in better shape than a year prior, but nowhere near what he once was. Nonetheless, between the training, the shakes, the alcohol, and the brace for his back, he was able to proceed. The back brace was the reason why he used the same singlet he did as

Giant Machine — ring attire he would keep wearing for the rest of his career. About 10 minutes before the match, André told Vince McMahon that he wanted Joey Marella, the son of Gorilla Monsoon, to be the referee. He then got on the cart with Bobby Heenan, prepared to meet his destiny, while being pelted with trash. Bob Uecker, Mister Baseball and future WWE Hall of Famer, was the special guest ring announcer.

Hulk Hogan walked to the ring, the personification of the irresistible force, and on that night the only wrestler not to use a cart to reach the squared circle. André was waiting for him in the middle of the ring, the ever immobile object ready for the inevitable clash. Guest timekeeper Mary Hart from *Entertainment Tonight* rang the bell. Right off the bat, Jesse Ventura called it the biggest match in the history of professional wrestling.

After just a few seconds, Hogan crumbled under the Giant, trying to slam him. The referee counted to three and André raised his arm in victory. But as he got to three, Hogan had lifted his right shoulder. Although he was in no position to see that, Marella told the timekeeper that it was a close call but only a two-count. That controversy would later be used to sell rematches and, as hard as it seems to believe, was more than likely just an accident. Hogan's job at that point was to sell André's attacks and show people he was in serious trouble. Hogan did a masterful job.

When André missed one of his famous head butts, hitting the turnbuckle instead of the Hulkster, Hogan finally took over. But it was just a short-lived reversal, and André halted Hogan's comeback with a big boot to the face. This is a classic heel move. Called a hope spot, it's designed to offer fans a light at the end of the tunnel but then bring them crashing back down on the roller coaster of emotions. Limited as he was and showing signs of being out of breath, André enveloped Hogan in a bear hug. Hogan was trying to support André as much as he could, making sure the Giant could rest a little and straighten his back. Hogan sold it like he was going to pass out, building to his classic comeback: the moment when he would "Hulk up," just seconds from being defeated. He almost got the Giant off his feet after a few shoulder blocks, but André cut him off one more time with a big chop, followed by a big boot that sent Hogan to the outside. Hogan was doing most of the work, bouncing off the Giant and letting André unleash all of his trademark offense. But Hogan ducked one of André's head butts and the Giant hit the ring post, knocking himself silly. They got back in the ring, and André finally went down after a clothesline. As Hogan Hulked up a second time, the crowd went crazy. Then came the body slam people would say was heard round the world. It wasn't the first time André had been slammed — we know that's far from the truth, but in the reality WWF had created, it *was*. Hogan hit his finishing move, the leg drop, to beat André in the middle of the ring and keep his precious world tile. The crowd reaction was amazing — because the fans believed what they saw and felt so many emotions. As André and Heenan exited, they were pelted once more by debris. Hulk Hogan celebrated with his classic "Real American" theme and posed. "When Hogan body slammed André the Giant . . . There isn't a more iconic moment out there in our sport," said current WWE Superstar Braun Strowman.

Guy Hauray typically joined Carpentier for the WWF's French commentary, but that night they were joined by Frenchy Martin and French promoter Roger Delaporte. For the French-language markets of Quebec and France, there was even a commercially released VHS tape of the event. After so many years abroad, Delaporte reminded the fans that André had started in France and had worked for him when he started, while Hauray said that Jean Ferré was called André the Giant but was indeed French. Guy Hauray had a lot of influence back then as the vice-president of European operations with WWF. That also included finding broadcast partners for French-speaking Africa. Selling André as a genuine French superstar was an essential part of that. *WrestleMania III* was broadcast on Canal + in France, a paid channel, which meant it only reached a tiny number of viewers. While Gorilla Monsoon was praising Hogan, and Jesse Ventura, toning down his heel character, had mixed feelings about the result of the match, on French commentary, no one was on Hogan's side. "I didn't see the Giant losing this one," said Delaporte. "Me neither," answered Carpentier. "It seems to me like the referee did a fast count," added the promoter. "I agree," said Hauray. "It's true. The referee did a fast count," concluded the heel Frenchy Martin.

Despite all the talk of André not doing the right thing, the Giant was all business. He knew why McMahon had booked the match, and he knew what it meant for both Hogan and his own legacy. "The fans are going to remember me losing a lot more than if I was to beat him," André told Carpentier after the match. According to what he told Carpentier, it was a way for André to link his own legacy to the one Hogan was building. The match itself has become as legendary as André and Hogan individually, and André was proud of it and his role in it.

Some consider it one of the best matches in the history of the WWE. Some others, like the readers of the *Wrestling Observer* in 1987, voted it the worst match of the year. "This wasn't the worst match I ever saw, but it threatened to be at times," wrote Meltzer in April 1987, criticizing the workrate. "André was even worse than I expected. Everything done except for the first non-slam and the final slam was poor. I'll have nightmares about this one. But who can complain? In one day, this match did more business than every Buddy Rogers versus Johnny Valentine, Pat Patterson versus Ray Stevens, Lou Thesz versus Karl Gotch, Ricky Steamboat versus Ric Flair, and Jack Brisco versus Terry Funk match combined. And that's something to think about." Meltzer was right. Aside from the 78,500 paid fans generating $1,599,000 in ticket sales, closed-circuit drew 450,000 fans and $5.2 million, and there were yet another 450,000 PPV buys, making it the biggest pro wrestling event of the time. It held the biggest indoor wrestling crowd record until *WrestleMania 32*, in Dallas, finally surpassed it in 2016, and it's still the third-largest crowd in WWE history. Hogan and André were both paid $750,000 for the match, with André earning a $250,000 bonus for doing the job.

"That match was truly the passing of the torch from André to Hogan," said Meltzer. "It is also the most important match in modern wrestling history. The match between Hogan and Piper in 1985 came when the war had just started. But in 1986, Jim Crockett Promotions was still number one in some markets. The difference was that Ric Flair and Dusty Rhodes couldn't draw 30,000 people. The André-Hogan match solidified WWF as number one."

Over the years, some narratives make it seem as if André's career and life ended shortly after that match, capping off a legendary journey. While that may make a better story, it's not true, and during the last five years of his life, there were many other significant career highlights.

EVERYBODY'S GOT A PRICE FOR THE MILLION DOLLAR MAN, EVEN ANDRÉ!

ANDRÉ USED THE ACT OF TYING HIMSELF UP TO THE ROPES SINCE ALL THE WAY BACK IN HIS EARLY DAYS IN JAPAN.

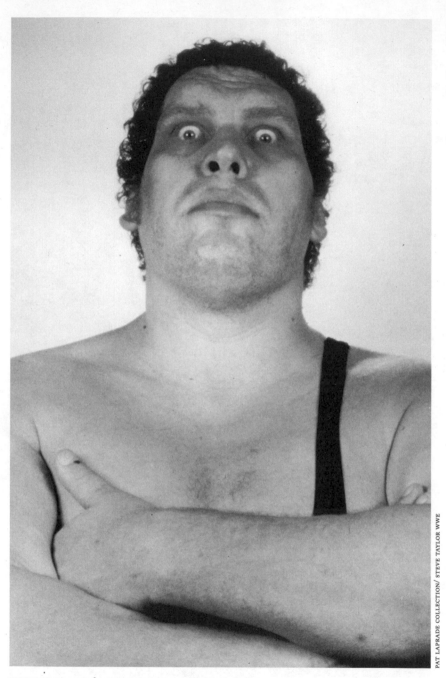

THE LOOK OF ANDRÉ COULD BE REALLY SCARY SOMETIMES.

CHAPTER 25

THE FOUNDATION OF WWE PPVS

After *WrestleMania III*, André still desperately needed back surgery. In fact, he might have had the first documented case of spinal stenosis in pro wrestling. Spinal stenosis is the reduction of the space within the spine, which can put pressure on the spinal cord. It usually occurs in the cervical (neck) area or the lumbar (lower back) area. It has ended the in-ring careers of "Stone Cold" Steve Austin and Sting. It's also strongly suspected that ignoring it or not detecting it in time led to the deaths of Mitsuharu Misawa and El Hijo del Perro Aguayo, both in the ring.

The main cause of this ailment is wear and tear, which make wrestlers prime candidates for it. Every in-ring bump puts their bodies through a small trauma. Most patients are diagnosed with it in their 50s and osteoarthritis sets in. Pro wrestlers are prone to herniated disks with multiple traumas to their spine every time they hit the mat. These are major contributing factors for the condition to be diagnosed before the age of 50 in a wrestler. Cervical stenosis (which Sting and Austin have) causes numbness or weakness in one or more extremities, neck pain, difficulty walking or balance, and, in some cases, bladder or bowel issues. André was suffering from lower back pain, and his symptoms of numbness, tingling, and weakness in his foot or leg, pain or cramping in one or both legs and the standard back pains, are consistent with the condition. On the doctor's note submitted to the immigration department in order to renew his U.S. working papers, it was clear that this set of symptoms was secondary to his acromegaly. It's also suggested in that same doctor's note that André's stenosis was of skeletal origin. Around that time, André had gone through another growth spurt. His forehead had become more prominent and his extremities were getting bigger and larger. Since his bones couldn't get any longer, they simply got larger. In cases like his, the secretion of growth hormone enlarges and deforms the bones and ligaments, resulting in the widening of the thoracic and lumbar parts of the vertebral column, while narrowing the spinal canal. Most people experience back pain at one time in their life, but we can only imagine the pain André was suffering after years of mostly enjoying the benefits of acromegaly.

The consulting orthopedic surgeon, Dr. England, suggested a lumbar decompression from L1 to S1, preserving the mid-line structures. He was hopeful it would give André relief from pain without affecting the stability of his spine. A decompressive laminectomy (removing part of one or more vertebrae as well as bone spurs and ligaments if needed) took place on July 21, and a 14-day hospital stay was scheduled. For what is considered a common back surgery, André's hospital stay was close to three times as long than that of a regular patient. Nothing was ordinary for André. In fact, doctors only performed the surgery after trying a brace and different kinds of anti-inflammatory medications, including steroids, had proven ineffective. André was also given an epidural injection, straight in the spine, that could be compared to taking 200 Motrin at once. When that didn't help, surgery was his only option. He kept the operation hidden from almost everyone, including his close friends and family. As his nephew Boris noted, he came from an era where you needed to protect your parents from such things. The surgery, which was performed at the Cromwell Hospital in London, England, went well.

André began to take painkillers afterward — medicating himself in a way he never had before.

Since *WrestleMania III* and before the surgery, André had wrestled just once, on April 28, in a taping for *Saturday Night's Main Event*. He teamed with Hercules against Hogan and Ken Patera. During the broadcast, there was an interview with Heenan and André in which they claimed Hogan had actually been beaten in the first few seconds of their *WrestleMania* match, but due to poor officiating, André had been robbed of the title. Heenan claimed the title should be awarded to the Giant or a rematch should be scheduled.

André made his first appearance after the surgery on August 22 at the Garden. He was presented to the crowd and walked halfway down the aisle before retreating to the dressing room when fans didn't react positively. Many believed he should walk away from the business at this point. But he wasn't ready for that — he wasn't prepared to listen to retirement talk. He wanted to be in the dressing room with the boys and to play cards with his friends, even if his position and role would slowly be reduced. He kept appearing at different events, mostly TV tapings, and usually as a corner man for the Heenan Family, as he wasn't ready to wrestle yet. The most physically demanding role he had was refereeing a Junkyard Dog versus Harley Race match on October 23 at the Bercy Stadium in Paris. The Bercy in Paris is pretty much like the Forum in Montreal or the Garden in New York. It was André's first time in a ring in France in more than 16 years, and he couldn't even wrestle. If only he could have, it would have been the perfect night for his return. He got cheered when he appeared in front of the crowd but booed by the end of the match. Televised on Canal +, the event drew 12,000 spectators for a show headlined by three French-Canadians, the Rougeau brothers against Dino Bravo and Greg Valentine.

A month later, WWF was ready to launch a new PPV, and the Giant would be a huge part of it. It was scheduled for November 26, Thanksgiving night. As the company's second annual PPV, it was an extremely important event for the WWF. McMahon and his team had to find a way to surf on the André-Hogan rivalry, while protecting André, who was not able to wrestle in a singles match yet. André and Hogan were seen as vital for WWF business at the time, and their presence sealed the deal with the different PPV providers. Called *Survivor Series*, the concept was to establish a PPV where only multi-man elimination matches would be showcased. André wouldn't have to do all the work. Hogan teamed with Paul Orndorff, Don Muraco, Ken Patera, and Bam Bam Bigelow while André teamed with One Man Gang, Butch Reed, Rick Rude, and former foe King Kong Bundy, managed by Bobby Heenan and the Doctor of Style, Slick. The last one to make his way to the ring, André was announced by Heenan as the "uncrowned heavyweight champion, and the next heavyweight champion," still playing on that *WrestleMania* two-count storyline. André didn't wrestle much. He did a lot of posing and outside interference, much like he had done on the road the previous few months.

However, it was important for André and Hogan to be in the ring together at one point, and when they finally were, the crowd went crazy! Hulk slugged the Giant multiple times, but then André's partners pulled Hogan to the outside, and he was counted out. The crowd was not happy, but the table was set for a rematch. Bam Bam Bigelow eliminated André's two remaining partners, and then André took out Bam Bam with a double underhook suplex. This was a wise move since there was a way for André to do that suplex and fall on his knees, therefore protecting his back. After André had won the match, Hogan came back to get revenge and hit him with the championship belt. André didn't fall on his back but instead to his knees and slowly exited the ring, always making sure to protect his back. Backstage with Bobby Heenan, an ecstatic and sweaty André made the challenge for a rematch with Hogan.

PPV technology was about to change the way wrestling promotions drew money, and how workers would get paid, and everybody wanted their share. WWF's arch-enemy, Jim Crockett Promotions, under the banner of the NWA, was about to present its first PPV event, *Starrcade*, also on Thanksgiving night. It was well known within the industry that a show on Thanksgiving night was a tradition the group had since 1983. And that alone started a PPV war. Vince McMahon threatened the PPV carriers choosing *Starrcade* over *Survivor Series* that he would not allow them to carry the next *WrestleMania*. Since *WrestleMania III* had done record-breaking numbers, almost every carrier chose WWF over JCP. However, at the end of the day, cooler heads prevailed and even those who chose *Starrcade* were also allowed to carry *WrestleMania*. It was a gamble at the time, and McMahon used his leverage to fight his competitor. In the end, *Survivor Series* did 350,000 PPV buys, close to 20 times more than what *Starrcade* did.

André finished the year wrestling in Europe, losing by count-out to Otto Wanz in Bremen, Germany, on December 19 for a very lucrative payday. Accompanied to the ring by Baron von Raschke, it was André's first singles match since *WrestleMania* and the operation.

The year 1988 started with a big angle. On the January 2 episode of *Saturday Night's Main Event*, André replaced Heenan at ringside for a match between King Kong Bundy and Hogan. After Hogan defeated Bundy, André attacked him from behind, hitting his traditional head butt while pulling Hogan's hair. He then strangled the champion, again from behind, his large hands closing tightly around Hogan's neck. McMahon loved this image: fans could see André's sadistically evil facial expressions, as well as Hogan's selling the attack. To make André even stronger, the British Bulldogs came in and tried to get André off Hogan, but the Giant no-sold them and threw them out of the ring. Four more babyfaces were sent, but again André didn't react to their attacks. "Hacksaw" Jim Duggan finally arrived with his 2x4, and when he hit the Giant in the back the piece of wood almost broke in half. André stood tall but distracted; the other wrestlers got Hogan out of the ring. This set up the next step in the Hogan-André rivalry.

In fact, McMahon and his booker Pat Patterson had known exactly where they wanted to go with the Hogan-André angle since *WrestleMania III*. They wanted to find someone capable of playing a cocky, arrogant guy, who thinks he can buy anybody and anything. That person would have a huge role in the Hogan and André feud. And they found it in Ted DiBiase. However, McMahon didn't even tell DiBiase what his gimmick would be before he signed his contract. He didn't want to give away a good idea if DiBiase didn't sign with the company. Coming from the Mid-South territory, DiBiase had already worked for the WWF, for only a short stint back in 1979. DiBiase signed and started in the summer of 1987. He was given the nickname "The Million Dollar Man" and a bodyguard named Virgil. The gimmick was working well, and after *Survivor Series*, DiBiase revealed that he had plans to buy the WWF World title from Hogan. Of course, the champion refused the offer. That's when, the week after the first *Saturday Night's Main Event* of the year, DiBiase purchased André's contract from Heenan. The idea behind the storyline was that if DiBiase wasn't able to buy the championship from Hogan, he would sign the one individual who could actually beat the champion — André. The Giant would then give DiBiase the title, proving that everybody had a price for the Million Dollar Man. Since André was unable to wrestle most of the time, DiBiase could do what Heenan couldn't: he could wrestle. And as André's health began to improve, they could work tag team matches.

On January 24, in Hamilton, Ontario, at the first *Royal Rumble*, André and Hogan signed a contract to wrestle in a rematch on February 5, live in primetime for an NBC show simply called *The Main Event*. The *Royal Rumble* wasn't yet a PPV but a special presentation on the USA Network meant to offset JCP's PPV *Bunkhouse Stampede*. Later that year cable companies settled the rivalry for the two promotions: they were told not to schedule big shows against each other anymore. Too much money was being left on the table. Still, it was another critical show and, like *Survivor Series*, an entirely new concept at the time. André and Hogan appearing on the show, even if they weren't wrestling, was key to generating interest for the new event. A good recap aired with footage from *WrestleMania III* and led up to the contract signing, which focused on the near-fall in the first few seconds of the match. The storyline was that André had agreed to win the championship and then sell the title to

Ted DiBiase. André's body language during the segment was excellent, and he teased not signing the contract. He eventually put pen to paper, and as Hulk was distracted by DiBiase, André slammed the Hulkster's head on the table and flipped it over him. The simple scenario was very effective, especially in an era where you did not see things like a contract signing on a regular basis. *Royal Rumble* earned an 8.2 rating, the biggest on the USA Network at the time, thanks in major part to the Hogan-André feud.

Everything was now set up for the February 5 rematch. According to Bruce Pritchard, who was on the creative team with Pat Patterson, Indianapolis was selected as the venue because it was a good market for the WWF, it was already on the schedule, and the Market Square Arena looked very good on television. The show was scheduled at 8 p.m. on a Friday, instead of 11:30 p.m. on a Saturday. Ever since the deal with NBC for *Saturday Night's Main Event*, Vince McMahon was hoping to get back in primetime on national television, a first since the 1950s. Dick Ebersol, who was not with NBC at the time but was still partnering with WWF on big shows, was pushing for it as well. André had a hard time adapting to the new reality of what the WWF was becoming, a worldwide television show with a large production. Gone were the days when only wrestling people had a say in the business. Rick Martel remembered that the wrestlers were not big fans of the way television production people claimed ownership of the product. They all felt it was their work in the ring that was the selling point, not the packaging imposed by the broadcaster. André was not impressed and he wasn't a big fan of Dick Ebersol at first.

"People outside of the business would get him to lose patience faster," revealed Okerlund. "André would listen to Vince. Ebersol started to tell him what to do, and André didn't buy into it. It was time for André to get ready at the Gorilla position and Ebersol was giving all these instructions . . . do this and that and don't do that. André told him, 'Fuck you!' and walked right by him, straight to the ring, the way he wanted to. He violated Ebersol's authority as the executive producer of the show. It wasn't a rib. He just didn't like the guy. He recognized his authority, but he just didn't want to do it. If he didn't want to do it, he just would not do it. You can talk to Pat Patterson or any other agents. If he felt it was a bad idea, he would find a way to slip around it." That said, André and Ebersol ended up finding mutual respect as Pritchard remembered them hanging together after shows from time to time.

The presentation was pretty much like a boxing match or a UFC fight today with a little bit more showmanship. André looked in better shape than he had at *Survivor Series* and appeared to be in less pain than at *WrestleMania III*. He had a look in his eyes — the match mattered to him. Early on, Jesse Ventura on commentary saluted the choice of Dave Hebner as referee, instead of *WrestleMania*'s referee Joey Marella, still playing that angle. Taking his time and enjoying the moment, the Giant was also buying time, knowing full well he couldn't perform to his old level. DiBiase and Virgil were at ringside and provided something extra, creating a different dynamic than at *WrestleMania III*. During the nine-minute affair, many moves were designed to make the match easy on André's back. At one point, Hogan went to the top rope, and André picked him up for a body slam, the perfect camouflage to help him slam Hogan with minimum effort. Near the end of the match, Virgil interfered as Hogan was about to land his leg drop. Once he finally hit it, there was no referee to count the pin since Hebner was reprimanding DiBiase's bodyguard. Hogan started arguing with Hebner, until André got back up and grabbed Hogan from behind and hit him with a series of head butts to the back of the head. André then used a double underhook suplex, protecting his back like he did with Bigelow at *Survivor Series*, and covered Hogan. Then the unthinkable happened. The referee started counting. Hogan clearly lifted his left shoulder after the count of one. Yet the referee proceeded to count to three. Pandemonium ensued. Hogan tried to explain that his shoulder was up, but Hebner was not having any of it and brought André the belt.

Contrary to all expectations, and just as Bobby Heenan had predicted, André the Giant became the 14th WWF World Heavyweight champion. Hulk Hogan's 1,474-day reign, to this day the second-longest behind only Bruno Sammartino, was over. Right after the match, "Mean" Gene Okerlund interviewed the new champion on the ring apron.

"This is not a surprise," said André. "I told you I was going to win the world tag team championship. And now I surrender the world tag team championship to Ted DiBiase."

Yes, André said "world tag team championship." Twice.

Was it the booze? Was it the language? Was it the fatigue? No one knows, and no one said anything to the Giant. "That slip of the tongue by André in Indianapolis was the kind of thing that would be over-looked because of who he was," remembered Okerlund. Once again, no matter how hard he may have been to deal with or whatever concerns there were about his health or ability to perform, he was still André. That carried a ton of respect.

Hogan was actually the reason for the title change. He was taking a break to film *No Holds Barred*, and his wife, Linda, was pregnant with their first child. (Brooke was born on May 5.) But André couldn't go on the road as champion and work a schedule like Hogan and the men before him did. That said, with less than two months until *WrestleMania*, he could have kept the title and main-evented the show with Hogan or with someone else. Instead, the plan was to protect the Giant and leave him undefeated. Selling the title to DiBiase was the perfect solution. So, although the Million Dollar Man had the belt around his waist, the seg-ment was far from over. As the heels were leaving, a second referee, who looked exactly like Dave Hebner, appeared in the ring. When Hogan saw that, he grabbed both referees by the throat. Then the fake Dave Hebner beat the hell out of the real Dave Hebner, letting Hogan know who was responsible for his loss. Hogan then picked the fake Hebner up and press slammed him to the outside, at the feet of André, but over the heads of DiBiase and Virgil, who were supposed to catch him.

The first Dave Hebner, the referee for the match, was in fact his twin brother, Earl. Like his brother, Earl had been a referee for several years, working for Jim Crockett Promotions. Dave had asked McMahon about getting his brother a job, as he wanted to wind down his referee schedule and work more as an agent. During the conversation with Vince, Dave mentioned Earl was his identical twin brother, which prompted McMahon to hire him. The latter actually worked as late as January 24, on that *Bunkhouse Stampede* PPV, but everyone was asked to keep this a secret, including Jim Crockett Jr. Earl injured his right shoulder after being thrown from the ring and missed several weeks, although he ended up working for the company for more than a decade and is perhaps the most widely known ref in WWE's history. The first WWF explanation for the resemblance between the two refs was plastic surgery, but the company eventually settled on the twin referees story and that one of them had been bribed.

At the end of it all, André was the world champion for just one minute and 48 seconds. It's still the shortest WWF championship reign on record. "This one finish goes down as the best of all time," claimed Bruce Pritchard.

The idea to showcase the rematch from *WrestleMania III* on national television was put together in October 1987, a month prior to *Survivor Series*. The whole team — including people from accounting, creative, marketing, and promotion — were brought into the loop at the same time. It created an interesting situation as many more people than usual knew Hogan's reign would come to an end and that a tournament to crown a new champion would follow at *WrestleMania IV*. Because of that, information was leaked and it created a good buzz. Now people wanted to see how they were going to beat Hogan or if it would really happen. Like Eric Bischoff asking Tony Schiavone to give away the results of Mick Foley winning the WWF title, leaking the information that André would beat Hulk helped ratings. "We didn't know that at the time," said Pritchard. "It was a happy mistake."

"All I can say is that I hope whoever came up with that finish got a nice bonus," wrote Dave Meltzer. "They got the title from Hulk Hogan without having him do a job. André wasn't hurt. *WrestleMania* was set up. And most of all, they ended the show with an angle so bizarre that it diverted everyone's attention away from the few weaknesses in the show.

'And that was a stroke of genius, because doing a screw job title stealing from a babyface as over as Hulk Hogan could easily escalate into an out of control situation."

The show was a huge success. It drew 33 million viewers for a 15.2 Nielsen rating. That year, the NBA finals had 21.7 million viewers and the World Series had 34.5 million. It's still the biggest rating pro wrestling has ever achieved in North America. Considering the advent of the internet and how television has fragmented the audience with so many channels, it is unlikely to ever be beaten. It was not just a phenomenon in the United States. Ratings were as good in the Montreal market as the show was broadcast in French, live on TVA, with more people watching wrestling than hockey that week. *Pro Wrestling Illustrated*'s readers voted the match their 1988 match of the year. It is difficult to argue for the sheer scope of the event. It also made André and DiBiase the most hated men in wrestling that year. DiBiase was shown with the belt a few times in the days that followed. Teaming with André against Hogan and Bigelow, and then in singles matches against Bam Bam, he defended his newly purchased title. A match was even announced for March 12 in Philadelphia between DiBiase and Hogan for the WWF Heavyweight championship. However, on the February 13 episode of *WWF Superstars*, Jack Tunney decided the title would be vacated and a 14-man tournament would take place to decide the next champion at *WrestleMania IV*, just as the plan had been drawn up back in October. André and Hogan, as previous champions, got a bye to the second round — where they would face each other.

Between February and *WrestleMania IV* at the end of March, André was on the road teaming with DiBiase against Hogan and Bigelow. Some of those main events, in Minneapolis and Montreal, for example, were part of a tour to honor Mad Dog Vachon, who had recently lost a leg in an accident. It was the busiest schedule André undertaken since 1986.

"Tim White, Virgil, and I would travel together," remembered the Million Dollar Man. "I enjoyed being with André. Besides eating and drinking a lot, we did everything first class. He loved champagne, and one night he ordered a hundred-dollar bottle of Dom Pérignon. Before the night was out, we had gone through 10 bottles!" As usual, André never let anyone else pay, not even DiBiase, whose expenses were reimbursed by the WWF when he played the Million Dollar Man outside the arena to sell the character as legitimate. Vince McMahon believed the rubber match between Hogan and André was going to sell the next *WrestleMania*. The publicity was centered on that match. The table was set, and everyone was working toward the plan. "André was losing weight just to feel better," recalled Pritchard. "There was always concern about his back and his health in general, but there was no concern he wouldn't be at *WrestleMania IV*."

However, *WrestleMania III* was going to be a tough act to follow. It was impossible to draw a bigger crowd or deliver a more significant match. But the idea was always to do something different and unique. Basil DeVito, WWF director of promotions, explained in his book that he was approached in January 1988 by Mark Grossinger Etess, the president and COO of the Trump Taj Mahal casino hotel in Atlantic City. Etess offered to bring *WrestleMania* to the Boardwalk Hall, adjacent to the main sponsor, the Trump Plaza, much like major boxing shows. He even pitched them an idea to turn the event into a whole weekend of activities, ultimately leading to what we know today as WrestleMania Axxess. WWF had something new and got a lot of publicity from the Trump name at the time. That's why there are pictures of the now-President Trump holding the WWF title between Hogan and André. Again, the event was filled with celebrities. One of them, Bob Uecker, was part of one of the lasting highlights of the show: André choked him during an interview segment. The way Uecker sold it has become an iconic moment — one that's been replayed over and over.

André had already made an appearance with DiBiase for the Million Dollar Man's first round match against "Hacksaw" Jim Duggan. André had been feuding with Duggan for a few weeks, ever since he'd blasted André with his 2x4. The brackets of the tournament were such that if DiBiase won his quarterfinal match against Don Muraco, he would face the winner of André and Hogan — smart booking, as either could win. A Hogan-DiBiase match in the semifinals would make sense. But a DiBiase-André match would as well. André could have just walked away and given the Million Dollar Man the victory. DiBiase won his match, and, returning the favor, both he and Virgil were in André's corner for his match midway through the show. André seemed full of energy as he jumped Hogan right away, interrupting his entrance. For the first few seconds, he looked like the André of old. Gorilla Monsoon, on commentary, even said he looked awesome and probably meant it. Near the end of the match, as the Hulkster was about to slam André once again, DiBiase ran into the ring to hit Hogan with a chair while referee Joey Marella was distracted by Virgil. Then both André and Hogan hit each other with a chair in front of the referee for a double disqualification. The match lasted only five minutes and 22 seconds, the shortest of André and Hulk's three encounters. After running off DiBiase and taking care of Virgil, Hulk came back and body slammed the Giant.

This resulted in DiBiase getting a bye straight to the final, where he met with Randy "Macho Man" Savage. André, who was in DiBiase's corner, wasn't doing much outside of the ring until Savage got on the top rope, looking to jump down on his opponent lying on the concrete. André stepped in front of DiBiase and dared Savage to jump. Instead, Savage made the call to ask his valet, Miss Elizabeth, to go back to the locker room for help. As one could expect, she came back with none other than Hulk Hogan. It wasn't the first time that Elizabeth had reached out to the Hulkster for help. She had done the same thing on an October episode of *SNME* in the debut of the Mega Powers, the nickname given to the team of Hogan and Savage, the company's top two babyfaces. The crowd exploded when Hogan arrived and sat at ringside. Even if they were not wrestling in the main event, André and Hogan were still a huge part of it. Not only did Hogan interfere when André attacked Savage through the ropes, but he clobbered DiBiase's back with a chair while the referee was distracted by André. This gave Savage the win and the WWF World title. The next big WWF rivalry was set up.

Hogan and Savage would face each other at *WrestleMania V* in one of the best storylines ever produced by the company.

Although the CCTV was hurt by a free JCP special, *Clash of the Champions*, on TBS the same day, the PPV buyrate was stronger than *WrestleMania III* at 650,000. Between the PPV numbers, CCTV, and the fans in attendance at the Trump Plaza, *WrestleMania IV* generated more revenue than the event had in 1987. Right after *WrestleMania*, André left for a European tour. When he returned, he renewed his feud with Jim Duggan and his trusty 2x4, which was billed as an equalizer. The feud culminated at the Garden on July 25, 1988, when André and Duggan main-evented in front of 11,500 fans. "Wrestling André was a thrill of a lifetime," recalled Duggan, who had wrestled André back in 1979 in Hawaii. "The biggest thrill of my career was to pull up in front of the Madison Square Garden and to see my name on the marquee versus André the Giant!"

A month before, also at the Garden, André had wrestled Bam Bam Bigelow. Young, big, and athletic, Bigelow had upside and huge potential. But he was also known for bragging a lot. And every time the Giant would wrestle him, he made sure Bigelow knew he didn't like him. "He tried to kill me by stepping on my head a few times," exaggerated Bigelow in an interview. Still, Bigelow knows he might have been at fault. "In our business, he was a classic. He was the Giant. I guess he felt I was getting too cocky." After the match, Bigelow left the company without finishing his scheduled dates and didn't return until 1992. Many reasons have been reported for his departure. Knee problems, McMahon not letting him be present for the birth of his first child, and André roughing him up at the Garden. In the match, it was obvious André didn't want to sell for him. He even kicked him in the face at one point. (André was still the man in the dressing room in 1988, and gaining his respect was still important.) According to DiBiase, he was in the dressing room when Bigelow stormed in after the match, grabbed his bags, and said he quit. When André arrived, he said, "I taught him a lesson." When Bigelow returned to the company, he told DiBiase, who was now his manager, that it was the best thing that ever happened to him because he had a horrible attitude and needed to be set straight.

Another wrestler André didn't like was Randy Savage. Well, he mainly didn't like one aspect of Savage. "He hated Randy Savage. Hated him with a passion. Whenever I would see Randy was wrestling André, I used to laugh," remembered Hogan on the HBO documentary. "Randy was always worried about how André was gonna beat him. Randy would wait till the very last minute, you know, and he'd be all taped up and he'd have baby oil all over him and Randy would come in, 'Oh excuse me, André, uh, big brother, you know, uh, what do you think, uh, we're gonna do out there in the ring tonight?' André would look up at him, playing cards, he'd go, 'No baby oil, GET OUT! Get out, no baby oil!' And then I'd watch the match and André would just get in there and just beat the hell out of him, just pull his hair out. I'm like oh my god, he just beat Randy to death!"

This story was confirmed by Savage's own brother, "The Genius" Lanny Poffo. "The story of André hating the fact my brother Randy was putting too much baby oil on his body is true," confirmed Poffo. He remembered asking his brother if he could make an exception for André, to which Savage responded, "What the fuck are you talking about! No exceptions!"

"Randy was not a big guy for his time, so he relied on three things: his clothes, his body, and his tan," continued Poffo. "He owned a tanning bed and was working on his body and his tan a lot. André's gimmick was to be a giant, and Randy's was baby oil. André saw this as a lack of respect. But Randy liked André. Yet André was really making Randy's life miserable. He would surprise him with potatoes [stiff shots]. Randy was stubborn. The more André didn't like it, the more baby oil Randy was putting on. And André would be over friendly with Liz to piss off Randy!"

"He almost killed Savage one night in one of the main events," recalled agent and former wrestler Blackjack Lanza. "Savage is lying down, and André just kept sitting on him and jumping on him, just beating the hell out of him. He got disqualified, which saved the championship, and afterwards Savage told him, 'This isn't the way to get me over.' And André just said thank you and he left."

Although some could say André was being difficult and didn't have to rough Savage up, again it was a question of respect. Imagine being a giant and being covered with your opponent's baby oil after your match. Most hotel rooms were not equipped for a guy André's size and taking a shower was almost impossible for him. Cleaning himself properly was hard enough as it was; imagine having to remove that much baby oil. "André had a great deal of trouble getting a comfortable night's sleep or even taking a hot shower in the little tub/shower combos that those places had — so he preferred to just stay up most of the night drinking," wrote Bob Backlund in his book. André, being a proud man of few words, never explained to Savage the real reason behind his hatred of baby oil. Savage didn't understand and thought André was just being difficult.

Six days after the Garden match with Duggan, André wrestled a returning Hulk Hogan, back from filming *No Holds Barred*. In a major live event called WrestleFest 88, on July 31 at the County Stadium in Milwaukee, André and Hogan squared off in a steel cage match, the first and only cage match the two ever competed in. Originally rumored to be at *WrestleMania IV*, that match was only promoted locally and never used in storylines. A cage match provided the cover for André losing without getting pinned as the goal was to exit the cage to win. Back with his former manager Bobby Heenan, who had managed André a few times throughout the years, André was still very much hated by the live crowd of 25,866 fans. No better or worse than their three other encounters, the 10-minute match saw Hogan escaping the cage after André had tied himself in the ropes trying to escape the cage himself. The tying-himself-on-the-ropes spot was used a lot by André at the time. But that wouldn't be the last featured singles match between André and Hogan. They had two more: one on August 7 in Greensboro, and one on October 23 in Atlanta. Although those matches were not presented on a big stage, they were significant since they were held in cities in the heart of JCP's territory. McMahon was sending his big guns to take over that part of the wrestling map.

Through August, André mainly worked on top against WWF world champion Randy Savage, with many of the matches drawing at least 10,000 fans. Those matches were to set up Hogan's return as Savage's partner at an event called *SummerSlam*. The WWF was launching another PPV spectacle and they were ready to use the rivalry between André and Hogan one more time. In the main event of the show, held on August 29, 1988, the Mega Powers, Hogan and Savage, with the lovely Elizabeth in their corner, were scheduled to face the Mega Bucks, André and DiBiase, with Virgil and Heenan in theirs.

"André was a great friend. Most people didn't know he wrestled in pain," said DiBiase. "There were times when we walked to the ring together, and he would have his hand on my shoulder to keep himself balanced. In the ring, I basically did all the work. André was very limited. Still, we had a great tag team against Hulk Hogan and a variety of guys."

It would be André's last main event for a major WWF show and it seemed fitting it was held in the home arena of Madison Square Garden. Like most of the WWF storylines at the time, the buildup to that *SummerSlam* main event was done masterfully. After being attacked by DiBiase and André, Macho Man challenged both men to a match with a partner of his choosing. A special guest referee was announced, and it was heel commentator Jesse Ventura, a man who fans thought could be bought by the Million Dollar Man. Of course, Savage chose Hogan, the only man who could make a difference with the odds so heavily stacked in the bad guys' favor.

It was a good match, full of theatrics, based more on the personalities in the ring than on pure athletic ability. André didn't wrestle much. He choked Hogan and made Savage's life miserable. He also made a big save toward the end, trying to get a count-out win for his team. However Elizabeth distracted Ventura as she unleashed her team's "secret weapon," taking off her dress to reveal her panties. Savage double ax-handled the

Giant, who was thrown to the outside, and then dropped his elbow from the top rope onto DiBiase before Hogan landed his big leg drop for the win. The show was a huge success. The Garden was sold out and it did 400,000 buys on PPV.

For the rest of 1988, most of André's matches were championship bouts against Savage, though there were a few others, like on October 7 at the Bercy Stadium in Paris. It was the first and only match André had at home for WWF. The Junkyard Dog was his opponent, and as a true heel, André pinned him with his feet on the ropes. When he was called by the name "André le Géant," he requested that his name be said in English to make sure the crowd booed him. Friends and family made the trip to see him wrestle what would be his last match in France. For some, like his nieces and nephews, it was the only time they saw him in the ring. His father was also there, which was important for André. He had always wanted his parents to see him do what he had become famous for; he once sent his parents a VHS player and tapes of his matches.

A month later, on November 7, André was representing WWF at a boxing event at Caesars Palace in Las Vegas promoted by McMahon. It was McMahon's first foray in promoting boxing through Titan Sports, and it was for Sugar Ray Leonard's third return to the ring, against WBC light heavyweight champion Donny Lalonde. Heavily promoted at *SummerSlam*, at which the Giant had been one of the main perform- ers, André sat in the crowd with other celebrities — because that's what he was, a major celebrity. Along with Whoopi Goldberg, Bob Dylan, Natalie Cole, Chuck Norris, Howie Mandel, Bruce Willis, Mike Tyson, Muhammad Ali, Joey Bishop (who had interviewed André on *The Tonight Show*), Joe Theismann (with whom André had done the NFL publicity stunt), and Donald Trump, who was sitting right next to him, André watched Leonard win the title in what was considered as a minor success for McMahon. Another movie star at the event was Sylvester Stallone. When asked by the press if Rocky Balboa against André the Giant could happen in *Rocky V*, Stallone nixed the idea. *WrestleMania V* was better suited for André anyway.

SummerSlam was the last PPV built on André and Hogan's feud. Between *WrestleMania III* and *IV*, *Survivor Series*, *Royal Rumble*, the February 5 *Main Event* on NBC, *SummerSlam*, and some other big shows, that feud is arguably the most important in WWE's history. It was the backbone in the creation of three PPV events, the match that drew one of the biggest live attendances as well as the biggest TV rating. All at a time when WWF was still at war with the last surviving territory of note. The feud was the foundation of WWE's pay-per-views. It would be another five years before a fifth regular PPV saw the light of day.

The feud also made André a rich man. He was the third-best draw in wrestling in 1988, tied with Flair right after Hogan and Savage. He made millions of dollars that year. (Anywhere between two and five million, depending on who you believe.) But money wasn't everything. He was 42 years old and had been wrestling for 22 years. The clock was ticking on both his career and his life.

By the end of 1988, he was starting to be used less often. He still worked some main events, but his role wasn't as important, as *Royal Rumble* 1989 would indicate. Still, 1987 and 1988 were two of the most important years in WWE's history, and the Giant was a huge part of it. Even if the story is tidier to pretend André's career ended in 1987 after his defeat at the hands of Hogan, the fact is it was only the beginning of something bigger. And even if his workrate wasn't the same, 1988 was his last real hurrah in the world of professional wrestling.

CHAPTER 26

OFF
CAMERA

Things would never be the same. André wasn't ready to quit, but he was aging and McMahon had milked his feud with Hogan as much as he could. André was no longer headlining *Saturday Night's Main Event*. Nor was he working the Garden shows. On the first *Royal Rumble* PPV, the man who once was the king of the battle royals entered at number three and exited at number five. After he eliminated Demolition Smash, his good friend Ronnie Garvin, and Jake "The Snake" Roberts, André eliminated a fourth participant: *himself.* After being eliminated, Roberts came back to the ring with his python Damien. Playing up a fear of snakes, André threw himself over the top rope while running away from the reptile. André and Roberts had been feuding since the October 25, 1988, episode of *Saturday Night's Main Event.* After a match between Roberts and Bobby Heenan's protégé "Ravishing" Rick Rude, André came to the rescue of his friends. He head butted Roberts a few times, before the latter came back to the ring with his python. André was not the wrestler he used to be, but to his credit, he could still act. He played the role of someone with ophidiophobia very well. He looked scared to death, screaming for Heenan to do something. After

Roberts threw Damien at the Giant, André had a heart attack that left him unconscious. Of course, it was all part of the story. That's all it took to book *Survivor Series 1988*, when André and Roberts captained their respective teams. Damien was a huge part of that storyline, as André would sometimes refuse to wrestle if the snake was anywhere close to the ring. Like with André's feud with Duggan and his 2x4, a prop was utilized to keep things entertaining for the crowd. After *Survivor Series* and *Royal Rumble*, the next logical step was *WrestleMania V*, which was again held at the Trump Plaza in Atlantic City.

Roberts, a second-generation superstar, was one of the most memorable wrestlers of the period. Aside from his finishing move, the DDT, no one could ever forget the sight of the six-foot-five wrestler standing on top of an opponent with a giant python named Damien in his hands. André knew him from back in 1979 when Jake was just starting out as a referee and was assigned to drive André around. They shared a mutual respect — until André found out about Jake's substance abuse issues. "André didn't like Jake because Jake was a big-time drug user," recalled Vince McMahon. "So Jake was on his back, André stepped on Jake's hair, and then takes Jake's arms and pulls him up, literally pulls his entire body off the mat. Meanwhile, he's stepping on Jake's hair, pulling it out by the root." Pulling hair wasn't the only thing André would do to Jake. He also farted on Jake in the ring. But according to Roberts, they made up at one point.

"He was pretty busted up. If I needed him to go down, it was supported by one or even two ropes," Roberts recalled. "I had a great time. I did play a lot of cards with him. We had a little problem the first time we wrestled as he completely guzzled me. He ate my ass up and didn't give me anything. I went back to the dressing room and had completely lost my mind as I screamed at him. I must have been high. The screaming was about if you are going to work like that, we are fucked, we are not going to make a goddamn nickel with that idea. Sometimes he would test people, and that's what it was with me. After that he looked at me and smiled, 'Now we have bonded, and now we make money.' If you didn't fight André when you were in the ring, like really fight, he would punish your ass."

Roberts was a great talker, the perfect storyteller to dance around André's physical limitations. The wrestling was secondary to the story of the Giant battling the snake handler. André's rival from the first *WrestleMania*, Big John Studd, was also back in the mix, returning after two years. Now a babyface, having won the latest *Royal Rumble*, he was the guest referee on April 2 at *WrestleMania V*. The match wasn't much. At that point in time, André was more effective at live events: there was still something to seeing the Giant in person. Near the end of the match, Ted DiBiase came ringside and stole Damien. Meanwhile, André attacked and choked Studd. But Roberts finally got his snake back and scared André off. Roberts was declared the winner by disqualification. The match served two new storylines, as DiBiase would feud with Roberts, and André would renew his feud with Studd. They feuded for two months, but André was still not a fan of Studd. Studd started to get paranoid, as the gossip around the dressing room warned him that André was going to beat him up. André was just stirring the pot, having fun roughing him up a little bit every night and feeding the other wrestlers the story of his dislike of Studd. It might be called bullying now, but in 1989, especially in the context of a pro wrestling locker room, it was nothing more than a guy who didn't like someone deciding to have fun with it. However, that's not how Studd saw it.

"Vince, I can't do it. I just can't get in there. I'm scared to death of this man, he's going to kill me," Studd told McMahon.

"No, he's not. He's just working you; he's playing with you."

"No, you don't understand, I heard it from the boys, he's really going to kill me. I can't do it. I'm quitting. I'm quitting the business."

And so in the afternoon of June 6, 1989, in Madison, Wisconsin, where he was supposed to wrestle André, Studd quit. After a few matches on the independent circuit, he was diagnosed with a tumor in his chest. On March 20, 1995, he died from liver cancer and Hodgkin's disease at the age of 47. According to his friend Superstar Billy Graham, his use of human growth hormone — which he took to be a giant like André — could have triggered the tumors he developed.

André could hold grudges. If you were on his bad side, it could last forever. It all depended on the issue. André was not a fan of Bret Hart when they first met in Calgary, but it was all different once the two had started working exclusively for McMahon. The week after *WrestleMania V*, WWF did a tour in Italy, and André worked with Hart in Milan. Calling the whole match in the ring, André took most of the match, defeating Hart with an elbow drop. Although he had very little offense, Hart had fond memories of his time in the ring with André.

"In truth, André was a great worker — I never felt a thing," recalled Hart. "After the match, he told me that he'd specifically requested to work with me at least one time because he considered me to be a great wrestler. It meant more to me than he would ever know."

"I remember that André put me in a headlock . . . and I felt very small, even though André's touch on me was light as a feather," wrote Backlund in his book. "André was very good in the ring — he took care of you and worked harder on that than most wrestlers because he was so big that he was worried about inadvertently hurting people. But André was a gentle giant who had very delicate touch in the ring unless he was trying to make a point."

Back at the ranch, André had a meeting with someone who would make him very happy in the final few years of his life. Enter Darol Dickinson, general manager of Dickinson Cattle Co., a family business that raised Texas longhorns. He became so important over the next few years that he was asked to speak at the Giant's funeral. At the ranch, André had Hereford and Angus cattle, but the land at the ranch in Ellerbe was not really conducive to such demanding species. While traveling or waiting in airports, André read articles about longhorns. He had met a private pilot for an Arabian sheik while in France, who had his own herd of Texas longhorn back in the United States. André called Frenchy Bernard and told him they were going to raise Texas longhorn.

Frenchy contacted Dickinson and explained that André was going to wrestle in Colorado Springs and wanted to talk with him. André invited him and his family to attend the event. There must have been 15 of them, and André took the time to meet everyone and was very friendly. "His awesome size was astonishing," said Dickinson. "It took a few minutes for me to get over that." André told him he had milked cows as a kid and was very interested in raising Texas longhorn. They went through pictures of cattle together as André selected the ones he wanted, like a proud rancher. Over the years, André would purchase three truckloads of cattle from the Dickinson ranch. André was happy with his investment. "They gave my property a special distinction along the highway," explained André. "People enjoyed stopping along Highway 73 and photographing them. I was very proud of Frenchy's cattle sales income too."

On the wrestling front, Hillbilly Jim had taken Studd's place through the first part of the summer, until McMahon made other plans for André. His next opponent was different. André was still protected, not even losing by pinfall against Savage, then the world champion. But starting in July 1989, André's next rivalry was against The Ultimate Warrior. Warrior (Jim Hellwig) was a bodybuilder-turned-wrestler with a Superman-like body who wore face paint. He had started with WWF in 1987 and was still somewhat inexperienced. Warrior had just lost the Intercontinental title to Heenan family member Rick Rude at *WrestleMania V*, so it was only fitting he would get a feud with someone from the same stable. He was being groomed as the successor to Hulk Hogan, who had just regained the WWF World title at the same *WrestleMania*. McMahon needed someone who could claim victories over the Giant. So André was asked to make the Warrior.

The way live events matches were booked, Warrior would defeat André in quick matches. Like, really quick. Most matches lasted just under a minute, with Warrior hitting a few clotheslines and then his big splash for the win. But André didn't like Warrior and wanted to spend as little time as possible with him in the ring. According to Bret

Hart, it was André who asked for the matches to last less than a minute. But fans were not ready for it. He was the Giant and he was legendary. They felt cheated by the whole scenario. Yet, as a result, Warrior has the most pinfall victories in history over André. One of those wins was in Anchorage, Alaska, in front of a sold-out crowd — the first time WWF held a show there. Just as in the mid-1980s, André was used to promote the company in a new territory. In fact, André was working in his 49th and final state; he never wrestled in Wyoming. To help spark the rivalry on television, André even wore face paint to mock the Warrior — but one thing was never shown on TV . . . and that was André being defeated in seconds. The feud didn't go over well with some WWF employees either. George "The Animal" Steele, who was an agent for their first match, thought people would not buy the result. He remembered telling Vince McMahon that it was killing the Giant and that it didn't even help the Warrior. He was told they were going to shove the program down the fans' throats until it worked. It took three months for the Warrior to get over working with André. It worked to some degree, even if it was voted worst feud of the year by *Wrestling Observer* readers.

Warrior didn't seem to understand that hitting someone with a clothesline didn't have to be stiff to look real, even with someone as big as André. So every night, Warrior would go full speed with his clothesline and hit André as hard as he could. Every night, André made a groaning sound Bobby Heenan could hear at ringside and become visibly irritated by the way Warrior was working. And every night, Warrior was told to slow down. One night, when the Warrior dashed forward with his clothesline, André waited for him with his hand clenched into a fist. The Warrior ran into it and was literally knocked out. The following match, Warrior's clothesline was very soft, and André made it look like it was the most devastating clothesline ever. André then looked at Heenan and said, "He's learning!"

As he had demanded many times before, André wanted his greener opponent to show respect. "The boss was trying to teach Hellwig how to work," explained McMahon. After the incident, Warrior tried to make it up to the Giant. "He learned how to treat the boss, every night coming in the locker room with a nice bottle of wine," McMahon continued. "That was his way of showing respect for André, so that André didn't kill him." It didn't mean André was pleased about working with him. Clearly, he was there to put someone else over, which was a new role for him. That said, something else was bothering André, maybe even more than losing to Warrior on house shows.

"A disgruntled André wasn't happy about being left off the *SummerSlam* card in favor of a Black bodybuilder and actor called Tiny Lister," said Bret Hart. In fact, the main event of *SummerSlam* that year had been Hulk Hogan and Brutus Beefcake against Randy Savage and Tiny Lister, a.k.a. Zeus. Lister was the antagonist for Hogan in the movie he had filmed the year prior, *No Holds Barred*. The movie was going to be released on June 2, 1989, and it gave McMahon the idea to have Zeus, a six-foot-five, 300-pound non-wrestler work a match. André, who didn't have much respect for people not in the business presenting themselves as wrestlers, thought he should have been the one teaming with Savage. And a few years prior, he would probably have been. Perhaps he was also a little mad about not being in the movie, when so many of his friends, like Bill Eadie, Stan Hansen, and Jos Leduc, were.

So it's with that state of mind that André wrestled on August 21, a week before *SummerSlam*, at the Five Seasons Center in Cedar Rapids, Iowa. He faced the Warrior in the main event of the show, in another crushing 30-second defeat. That's also when André had the most public episode of his legendary moodiness. Ben Hildebrandt, a five-foot-eight, 175-pound cameraman from local television station KCRG, who had grown up watching wrestling and André the Giant, was taping a WWF feature for a KCRG newscast. Hildebrandt was given permission to film anything he needed from ringside and was even given a piece of paper outlining all the match finishes for the evening. André and Warrior were main-eventing the show and just before the match, Mel Phillips, the ring announcer, told Hildrebrandt he couldn't film the main event.

The cameraman asked if he could tape the ring entrances for André and Warrior, as well as the bell to start the match before turning his camera off, and was told yes for both. As we know, the match didn't last long.

"I was walking away from the ring with my camera turned off when out of the corner of my eye, I see André crawling under the ropes," said Hildebrandt. "And he's coming right at me yelling, 'I want the camera, I want that camera!'" André grabbed the cameraman's shoulders and took a swing at the camera, missed it, and hit Hildebrandt on the side of the face instead. The cameraman clung to his camera with both hands to make sure André wasn't going to break it. They fought for the camera for a few seconds, before security got there. "I had never been in a fight in my life. I was like, 'I do not get paid enough for this,'" recalled Hildebrant. "It is the dumbest assignment I have ever taken!" Policemen were called and André was arrested at 10 p.m. and charged with simple assault (having the general intent to cause pain or injury) and third-degree criminal mischief, an aggravated misdemeanor. Criminal mischief means that you have ruined someone else's personal property. In André's case, this was a broken camera cord, an estimated loss of $300 for the television station. If the damages had been over $500, André could have been subject to a two-year prison sentence and up to $6,250 in fines.

"The policemen were pressing me," revealed Hildebrandt. "They were telling me, 'You might want to press charges, you're a bright boy, you decide.' The reality was that I was a 23-year-old, who was making $12,000 a year and who, I thought, had just broke a $23,000 camera. When I sat down with the promoters and policemen to press charges, the promoters were livid." Sgt. Jerry Potter politely convinced André to come to the police station without resisting, and since no handcuffs could fit him, he was brought in without restraints, though Potter had planned to use leg shackles on André's wrists. "He was real cooperative, but when he saw the leg shackles, he put his hand on my shoulder and said, 'You're not going to put those on me,'" recalled Potter. "He smiled, and I figured he was kidding, but I got out of the way. That guy could have pinched my head like a pimple." Even in a serious situation, people were impressed by his presence. The police station was not equipped to weigh or measure André accurately, so the report stated he was seven foot four and 520 pounds. André's handprint was taken, as well as the traditional mugshot.

André was released on a $1,285 bond and never spent any time behind bars. By 10:33 p.m., he was already gone; the next morning, he left town. "In most cases, a person found guilty of these offenses will be fined or given a deferred judgment, which, in Iowa, is like going on probation," said Linn County district attorney Denver Dillard to *Pro Wrestling Illustrated*. "There's a lot of notoriety to this case because there's a seven-foot-five wrestler involved, but it happens on a fairly common basis among normal people."

Meanwhile, Hildebrandt and WWF promoters viewed the footage at the KCRG studios that night and proved that he had not filmed anything he wasn't supposed to film. One of the promoters said the camera spooked André. "Like what is he, a racehorse or something?" asked Hildebrandt, not believing what had just happened. Hildebrandt said André may have reacted so strongly because he thought he had taped the match, which would have violated WWF copyright. The only thing that could have spooked him was the idea of his loss being broadcast, especially considering his state of mind at the time. André was clearly in the wrong. If he had kept his cool, the situation would have been taken care of behind the scenes, with some footage being destroyed, if necessary. Instead, André panicked and overreacted. And, just as Tim White and Dick Ebersol had learned, when André thought an outsider should not be somewhere, he got really aggressive, really fast. Hildebrandt went for X-rays at St. Luke's Hospital and, fortunately, nothing was broken. Still, he wore a neck brace, claiming he had a history of lower back problems and that he was in tremendous pain the following day. In the long run, he ended up being fine. Hildebrandt's lawyer had three theories on why André did what he did: he didn't want to be seen losing so quickly on TV; he was really drunk and therefore extra angry; or the whole thing had been planned by the WWF to get André in the news.

On August 31, André and Titan Sports Inc. were sued by Hildebrandt for compensatory and punitive damages. The lawsuit read, "His rage in having to lose the match together with his misguided zeal to enforce the Titan policy culminated in an unscripted explosion of violence against the plaintiff." It also said that Hildebrandt was videotaping some matches but had agreed not to tape the main event as per ring announcer's instructions. After an unsuccessful attempt to move the case to federal court, a non-jury trial was held a year later, on August 20, 1990, with André's presence being waived. On September 26, 1990, André was found guilty of criminal mischief for causing $183 damage to the camera but was acquitted of assault. Judge Robert Sosalla said, "Roussimoff's publicity rights do not justify his use of force, but evidence showed the wrestler did not mean to harm the photographer." On November 6, as André was working in Japan, he received the amount he would have to pay: a $100 fine and $233 in damages to the television station. Hildebrandt walked away with a small amount of money that came directly from André but had to sign a non-disclosure agreement.

The amount André had to pay was nothing compared to what he was earning at the time, as he was still main-eventing shows. André and The Ultimate Warrior main-evented *Survivor Series* on November 23. The Warrior team, including Jim Neidhart and The Rockers (Shawn Michaels and Marty Jannetty), defeated André's team consisting of Haku, Arn Anderson, and Bobby Heenan, replacing the suspended Tully Blanchard. Since the match was on television, André wasn't pinned in 30 seconds but was counted out instead. André was protected, but clearly his role was once again to put over the Warrior. Two nights later, on *Saturday Night's Main Event*, Warrior faced André for the Intercontinental title he had won back at *SummerSlam*. They wrestled for close to eight minutes before André was disqualified. The match was at least eight times longer than they were used to, and there's little wonder why it was voted worst match of 1989 by *Wrestling Observer* readers. It also solidified the theory that André had lost it in Cedar Rapids because he didn't want any of his 30-second jobs to be on TV. "It makes perfect sense," said

Hildebrandt 30 years after the fact. "And I held no animosity toward him." The very few times André and Ultimate Warrior wrestled each other on television, the matches were booked differently.

That match marked the last time André wrestled on *Saturday Night's Main Event*. It was a disappointing way to go out for a man whose feud with Hogan helped draw the biggest rating *SNME* ever. Although André was glad that the storyline had come to an end, the series of matches helped build the Warrior character, and for months they main-evented the shows Hogan wasn't on, allowing the WWF to have two strong groups on the road. Or they co-main-evented with Hogan on bigger shows. André only worked twice at the Garden that year, both times against Warrior. The first match, in September, was a nine-minute contest in which he was defeated by DQ. The second was on October 28, and André lost in less than 30 seconds. Ironically, Warrior defeated him with a big splash, the same finish André used on Buddy Wolfe during his very first match at the Garden. It also marked the only pinfall loss André ever suffered at the Garden.

But since the match was televised on the MSG Network, McMahon had found a way to protect the Giant. As he would generally do, Warrior came running to the ring as his music played. In this case, his music never stopped, the bell never rang, but still Warrior hit André with a few clotheslines before finishing him. After the pin, André took the mic and protested to the referee, in vain, that the bell never rang and the loss should not count. It was as close to a clean win by pinfall he could have gotten. It also marked the last time André ever main-evented a show at the Garden. Two months later to the day, he had his very last match in the building. From 1973 to 1989, André had wrestled 63 times — almost half of them multi-man matches — at Madison Square Garden. His record shows 53 wins, five losses (one against The Ultimate Warrior, three by DQ, and one in a tag team match in which he wasn't pinned), and five draws (DDQ or DCO). Thanks to his feud with The Ultimate Warrior, André finished eighth among the biggest draws of 1989. It was the last time he made that list.

"André was so over as a talent. That made it easier," remembered Warrior. "Whatever limitations he had for his size or his aging, they were not disadvantages at all. Because he was so over in a way, the matches that I had with him were set up to get The Ultimate Warrior over even more. When André the Giant let me put him in a bear hug and he squealed like a pig, that meant something. He never did anything that he would not want to do. I was very honored."

It's also against Warrior that André did his final match in Montreal, at the Forum on October 20. Every time he wrestled at the Forum in those last years, whether or not he was in the main event, he ended up being one of the most talked about wrestlers on the show, and his matches were the real draws. Even in the end, he was drawing decent crowds, with 12,342 fans watching him against Roberts in January and close to 10,000 in attendance to see him against the Warrior in August, in a match that lasted less than a minute. Seven thousand fans watched his final match, an 11-minute loss by disqualification. For the hardcore fans, it must have been way too long. But those who appreciated the nostalgia were just happy to see more from "le Géant" Jean Ferré, as he was still called in the province of Quebec. He was no doubt still the best draw in Montreal after Hogan. André made one last appearance at the Montreal Forum on August 16, 1991, as a corner man for the Bushwackers. Because of the way things happened, he never had a chance to promote his last match in Montreal, which, if publicized as such, would have been a much bigger deal. Especially since his good friend Gino Brito was the local promoter for McMahon.

It was the end of an era for André. The Montreal Forum had seen him wrestle Don Leo Jonathan three times in a feud that opened the door to the New York territory and made him the superstar he was. Montreal was his home away from home, perhaps more than Ellerbe because of the common language. Whether he was ready or not, André's career was drawing to a close.

CHAPTER 27

THE
END
OF AN
ERA

"**W**ill André the Giant ever leave the ring? Or is the veteran wrestler a workaholic who won't stop until he's destroyed all those around him — including himself?"

It was an interesting question Troy Moon posed in the *Pensacola News Journal* on October 23, 1989. Everyone could see the Giant wasn't the same. And it wasn't just hardcore fans but sportscasters as well. Some referred to him as the "once-legendary" André the Giant, while others were decidedly meaner. "Some things definitely should not be recycled, and André the Giant is among them," wrote Richmond, Indiana, *Palladium-Item* columnist Bob Matthews. And even if *Wrestling Observer* readers thought he should retire, voting him the most embarrassing wrestler of 1989, André himself wasn't ready. Being around the boys still gave him too much pleasure.

At the very end of his feud with the Warrior, he started teaming with Haku. Also known as King Tonga and later on as Meng, Haku was born in the Kingdom of Tonga and trained in Japan. Prior to coming to the WWF in the mid-1980s, he had been a star in Montreal working for International Wrestling. He was a great worker and a good partner for

André — he could carry a match all by himself. On house shows, they started working with the team of Demolition, Ax, and Smash. Ax was André's friend Bill Eadie; Smash was Barry Darsow, who had worked for Crockett before replacing Randy Colley as a member of Demolition. Wearing face paint reminiscent of the hard rock band KISS and sporting studded black leather jackets, they were WWF's answer to the Road Warriors. They had won the tag team belts at *WrestleMania IV* against Strike Force (Rick Martel and Tito Santana), before losing to the Brain Busters (Arn Anderson and Tully Blanchard) after a 478-day reign — the longest tag team title run at the time. It was a win André had contributed to, as he had been ringside with Heenan. But Ax and Smash had won the titles back in October 1989. In 1989, Bobby Heenan's family, arguably one of the biggest heel stables of all time, consisted of the Brain Busters, the Brooklyn Brawler, Rick Rude, Harley Race, Haku, and André. With Anderson and Blanchard both having left the company, it made sense to have another team from the Heenan family to feud with the champions. Therefore, the team of Haku and André, known as the Colossal Connection, was put together.

Then the unthinkable happened. On December 13, 1989, they defeated Demolition to become the WWF tag team champions, when André pinned Ax in less than five minutes. The match aired on the syndicated show *Superstars of Wrestling* on December 30. It was a way to keep the Giant fresh and give him something the fans cared about, as Demolition was among the most popular wrestlers on the roster. It was a valiant attempt to give some credibility back to André.

On paper, the pairing looked like it would work, and like it should prolong André's career. André and Haku both had great respect for each other. Haku remembered offering to carry André's championship belt on the road, in order to not bother André with the extra luggage. "Boss, no," answered André, "you carry yours, and I will carry mine." He might not have been the same wrestler he once was, but he still had his pride. They almost exclusively worked Demolition in return matches all over the country. The matches were better than most of André's recent feuds since Haku was carrying the load, but André's work was not getting any better. To be fair, no opponent could have changed that. "He was banged up a little, but we could work around any of his limitations," recalled Eadie. "He was suffering from back issues but never complained at all. He was the same person, but as performer, and as we get older, none of us are the same. He loved the business and I feel he just wanted to be around it for as long as he could."

More proof of his love for the business can be seen in an encounter with Lex Luger. Although Luger had never worked with André before, or even shared the same locker room, he remembered being approached by the Giant at the airport. André insisted Luger jump into the airport cart with him on his way to his plane, and he talked with Luger even though he was working for WCW at the time. André was wrestling savvy, something he was not necessarily known for outside of the wrestling world.

The whole program with Demolition was about them getting a rematch at *WrestleMania VI*. That's why, in the 1990 *Royal Rumble* match, the four of them faced off, with Ax and Smash double teaming André and eliminating him. It would be André's last *Royal Rumble*. Had this PPV come earlier in his career, he probably would have won the whole thing. Instead, many fans don't even remember him working a *Royal Rumble* match. Coming in at number 11, he was in the ring with some people he appreciated, such as Eadie, Bret Hart, and Dusty Rhodes. At that point in time, it was all about playing cards, being with the boys, and having fun. Dusty was probably one of the guys André had the most incredible stories with. One time in Atlanta, André was with Heenan, Rhodes, Michael Hayes, and some other guys in a bar owned by "Mr. Wrestling" Tim Woods. There was a woman there with big breasts and André asked to see them. She took off her bra and issued a challenge to André. She told him that if he'd go across the street to the Crystal Club, where there was a wooden horse on the roof and put the bra on the horse, she'd show him. André took the challenge. He took a ladder, climbed on the roof, mounted the horse, and tried to put the bra on the horse's head! "He just looked like King Kong!" recalled Hayes. Seeing the Giant up there, someone called Rhodes. "You need to come over here and get him down off the horse," Dusty was told. "I'm thinking, 'What is he doing on a horse?' He was just up there trying to fix the bra, laughing and having the biggest time," recalled Rhodes.

Of course, since it was his creation, Pat Patterson booked the *Rumble* match, and he too had shared so many experiences with André that he could make a book out of the stories. "One time, André was so out of it . . . we walked into the lobby of the hotel at 3:30 in the morning, and he passed out in front of the coffee shop," remembered Patterson. "We're trying to get him up, but there's no way we can. So I took his wallet, I took his watch, and left him there. The manager said he had to open the place at six o'clock for breakfast. I said, 'Call AAA, there's nothing we can do . . .'"

Even though André's schedule was lighter, sometimes Heenan would actually sub for him with Haku. After five months together, Haku and André became close. On one occasion, a meeting with his daughter, Robin, was canceled — and Haku witnessed the Giant in tears. If he liked you and let you get close enough to him, he would open up.

Aside from Demolition, the Colossal Connection also defended the titles against The Rockers and The Hart Foundation. On March 24, 1990, they even faced Hulk Hogan and Big Bossman, as WWF was trying to build Bossman as a top babyface. It was André's very last match against Hogan. The rematch with Demolition was scheduled for *WrestleMania VI* at the SkyDome in Toronto, in what would be the most well-attended *WrestleMania* since André faced Hogan in Michigan. Three short years after *WrestleMania III*, André was still in a championship match but relegated to going out second on a 14-match card.

"It was strongly rumored he'd be done after the big Japan tour that was coming right after *WrestleMania VI*," recalled Bret Hart. "André seemed pained, sad, and longing for the good old days. He was pale and sickly, and many of us wondered whether he was trying to drink himself to death."

André never tagged in. He interfered a few times, looking very slow. Haku did all the work. That was actually André's idea. Again, showing his generosity, he knew his time with WWF was at a close. That spelled the end of the Colossal Connection, so he wanted Haku to look good and be in position to have a decent storyline following the end of their team.

"I guess it was meant to be a short run. I was surprised that we went all the way into *WrestleMania VI*," Haku said. "André never tagged in. It is exactly what André had wanted. We were going to be having our last match together. He wanted me to be strong, you know? It was our last match, and he didn't know whether or not I was going to end up being a babyface, but at *WrestleMania VI* he told me to carry the match and to keep going. That was what he wanted me to do."

"André certainly was on the decline, so he needed Haku badly as a partner," said Howard Finkel. "André's skills were starting to deteriorate. His in-ring presence was always there, but his skills were limited at best."

In a similar scenario to that of their December match, André was holding Smash, ready for Haku's superkick, but this time Smash ducked and Haku hit the Giant right on the kisser. André fell onto the ropes and into his tied-up spot. With the Giant immobilized, Demolition pinned Haku to become tag champions for a third time. Even then, André was protected. Getting pinned in front of 64,000 fans and hundreds of thousands watching at home still wasn't an option. Bobby Heenan, the catalyst in turning André heel three years prior, was going to be just as crucial in bringing him back from the dark side. While the Brain chewed André out and poked him on the chest more times than anyone else had ever dared, André tried, in vain, to explain he had been hit by his partner. That's when Heenan slapped André's face. That slap was one slap too many. The Giant grabbed his manager by the collar and slapped him back multiple times. And just like that, André was once more a babyface.

Even if his work in the ring was poor and he had trouble keeping his balance, he hadn't lost his timing; he was excellent in that exchange. The crowd went crazy and gave him a standing ovation as he left the ring. Older fans were hoping the André of old was back. In reality, André and Vince were no longer on the same page, and there was no plan for him other than to end his career as a babyface. Some athletic commissions had refused to clear André in recent months, and it was becoming harder and harder to book him with confidence. No matter how much McMahon and his team wanted to have the boss around, it was becoming unsafe for him to be in the ring.

Whether or not it would be his last match, André was always up for a good prank. On the same show, Bad News Brown and Roddy Piper were facing off in a singles match. Piper was wearing half-blackface. "The reason I painted myself half black was more the meshing," said Piper in an interview. It was a different era. Although he had agreed to it, Brown, an African-American, didn't particularly like the idea. After the match, Piper was given a special clear solution to take off this black paint. But André and his old friend Arnold Skaaland, who was still around and played cards with him every time he came to the matches, had replaced the solution with water. Unable to remove the paint without scratching his skin raw, Piper had to make peace with the fact that he had to travel looking like that, and that also meant crossing back into the U.S. "The way I got the black off was that I had to sit in the sauna," said Piper. "Took me about a month of rubbing this stuff off. But what am I going to do? Go beat up André?" he added, laughing.

Being in the second match on the show had its benefits. It meant André could drink, play cards, and prank while waiting for everything else to end. He had received a lot of love from the fans and the same from his peers.

On top of being one of the best in the ring, Bret Hart is also a very talented cartoon artist. Since he knew it would be one of André's last matches with the company, he had worked on a special cartoon for the Giant, a montage of every name wrestler who had worked in the WWF since the early 1980s. Before his match, he passed around the drawing for all the wrestlers to sign and brought it over to André. "André grasped it in his big hands and turned it over in order to sign it too," remembered Bret. "I stopped him and said, 'It's for you, boss. That's you there, right in the middle, carrying everyone on your back.'" André got emotional. He didn't expect such a nice gesture from his friends. Fighting back tears, he thanked Bret. It was a gesture André never forgot.

Although many believed this was André's farewell to the WWF, he had a few matches left with the company. On April 13, he wrestled in front of his largest Japanese crowd ever at a show called Wrestling Summit in the Tokyo Dome. The stadium, built for the Tomiuri Giants baseball team, had opened in March 1988 and was the turf in a three-way war between NJPW, UWF, and AJPW, which all wanted to showcase events in the biggest venue Tokyo had to offer. When Jim Crockett Promotions was sold to Ted Turner and became World Championship Wrestling in 1988, All Japan distanced itself from the group. WCW turned to New Japan instead, while All Japan entered into an arrangement with the WWF. UWF had done a show there in 1989 and drew 60,000 fans. NJPW had done 63,900 fans in February 1990. So it was now AJPW's turn. Two months earlier, when New Japan ran its show, the planned main event of Ric Flair versus Keiji Muto was canceled because of Flair's problems with WCW. So Inoki asked Giant Baba for help; the result was that the companies worked together for the first time since the late 1970s. It now made sense for Baba to seek Inoki's help. But to make things even more special, the show also showcased his new partner, the WWF. For the first time, the three biggest promotions in the world were collaborating. And although it may have not been a big deal for fans in North America, historically speaking, it was for the wrestling world. However, planning for the show turned into a hot mess.

"This was really Baba's show, but Vince's people wanted to take over and they disagreed on everything," said Dave Meltzer. "New Japan didn't want any part of it. You could tell the week of the show that there would never be another. But it's historical, All Japan, WWF, and New Japan all on the same show. I don't think anyone today understands how big that was."

André, who had never worked for All Japan, was returning to Japan for the first time since 1986. His match was indeed special, as he teamed with Giant Baba against the WWF tag champs, Demolition. The match had been set up back in February in Phoenix, Arizona, of all places. Ax and Smash interrupted an altercation between André and Baba and challenged them to a match. If Randy Savage against Genichiro Tenryu, The Ultimate Warrior defending the WWF World title against Ted DiBiase, and Hulk Hogan wrestling Stan Hansen were the top matches, then André and Baba teaming was something unique. Baba was 52 years old and lacking mobility too, but the match was a novelty draw. They beat Demolition in a non-title affair that lasted only six minutes, as there was no way such a legendary team could lose in Japan. When André tagged in, he received a huge pop from the crowd, who were seeing him perform for the first time as a babyface. Japan was one of the few markets where he had not been overexposed. Darsow has said that wrestling the two legends, in front of 53,743 fans, was his favorite match ever. André was so happy to be back in Japan that he went out with Eadie and Darsow that night, got drunk, and fell down the stairs at a restaurant. It took him two hours to finally exit the premises.

André, in the end, was conflicted about Vince McMahon and the WWF. He was not pleased to be put on the shelf, yet he knew he wanted to do different things that couldn't happen if he continued working for the WWF. To be fair, McMahon had all the reasons in the world to force out André. He took care of the Giant as long as he could, was patient with him, and even gave him a title run at a time when most would have already put him on the sidelines. André had made both Vince and Vince's father a lot of money, and in return, André was also very well paid. But he was 44 with a body that hurt so much he couldn't do what he used to in the ring, and McMahon needed to push younger talent. Plus, he really didn't want André to look bad; and although it was probably already way past that, it needed to stop.

"André's body was breaking down. He could not perform. So we slowed things down for André in the latter years," explained Vince McMahon. "But eventually it does catch up with you and your career is over and it's difficult for someone to accept." It was especially difficult for someone like André. So there were natural feelings of resentment toward McMahon.

Things were so cold between André and Vince that in between Japan tours, André made two appearances, on October 11 and November 11, for the newly created Universal Wrestling Federation. Herb Abrams created the company in September 1990 and had a deal with SportsChannel America, a national group of regional sports networks owned by Cablevision which operated it as a joint venture with NBC. Abrams had hired former WWF guys like Paul Orndorff, Brian Blair, Ken Patera, and Bob Orton Jr. — guys André had known for years. Abrams had also hired former WWWF champion Bruno Sammartino as his color commentator. At the Reseda Country Club in Los Angeles, André recorded four segments in total. Two interviews with Lou Albano, in a segment called "Captain's Corner," saw André put over the promotion as the place to be. And he also recorded two promos. It was a way for André to work in the U.S., and perhaps a way to get back to the WWF. And somehow it worked.

The segments aired in late November but André never wrestled for the company. By the time the UWF was on TV, or shortly after, André got himself a new deal with WWF. The plan was for him to appear in January 1991. In a television segment that aired on December 9, the first 20 participants of the 1991 *Royal Rumble* match were announced, including André. However, that announcement didn't last long. On December 23, an interview with André aired: he said he didn't mind having Hogan or the Road Warriors in the *Royal Rumble*, as he would win the match no matter what. However, only seven days later, during a Mr. Perfect match, Vince McMahon, on commentary, said that André would not be able to compete in the *Royal Rumble* due to an injury sustained in Japan. Although it was true he had wrestled in Japan, the story was more complicated than that.

"It was health issues. It was the thought that we're not going to get André beyond this," explained Bruce Pritchard. "Maybe we do one where he wins, but health issues just weren't going to allow him to be able to compete in it. Even bringing him out at number 30 wouldn't have been pretty."

That *Royal Rumble* match is the closest André was to ever squaring off with The Undertaker. Billed at six foot 10 and 309 pounds from Death Valley, The Undertaker would have been the perfect opponent for André in his prime. To this day, it is a fantasy match fans talk about. And fans are not the only ones who wanted it to happen. Mark Calaway began portraying the Undertaker character in November 1990 and by 1991, André already saw something in him. He even had an idea for a match. Calaway, who would become the locker room leader years later, just as André had been, shared his story of the Giant:

> I never got the chance to wrestle André. By the time that I got there, his health was really in decline. André didn't like big guys either — he loved me, thank goodness. But for most big guys, he thought they were arrogant or bullies or whatnot. Anyway, he liked me, and I guess we always think we got one match left in us. He'd come in, and he's André the Giant. Biggest star that's ever been at that time in wrestling, a worldwide phenomenon. And he was always the first guy in the locker room. He was always there. He would love to sit there and play cribbage, and I'd come in and say, "Hey boss, how are you doing today?"
>
> He'd say, "Good. You know, one day, kid, me and you. I have this idea."
>
> "Oh really, boss? Tell me about it."
>
> And he'd never tell me. I asked Tim White all the time, "Did he ever tell you?"
>
> "I would ask, and he'd never tell me."
>
> He was old school. He didn't want anyone else to do it because he thought he was going to get to a point where he could get back in the ring, and we could do something that would be a big deal. No one knows what it was, but you know, he ended up passing away, and he

never let me know. I wonder to this day. Man, I bet it
was good.

At the time, the winner of the *Royal Rumble* didn't have an automatic
championship match at *WrestleMania*, although that's what happened
here, as Hogan won the *Rumble*, and ultimately won back the title on
March 24 in Los Angeles, at *WrestleMania VII*. That *WrestleMania* was
also André's official return with the company. "Mr. Perfect" Curt Hennig,
now part of the Heenan family, was defending the Intercontinental title
against the Big Bossman. As Bobby Heenan was about to take an unfair
advantage over the challenger, André came to ringside to the surprise of
everyone in the crowd. The fans were going nuts and started chanting
the Giant's name. He might have been too old to wrestle, but he was a
legend and that still meant something. After Haku and The Barbarian
interfered for the disqualification, everyone but Heenan took a shot from
André. They all sold — oversold would be a better word — for the Giant.
Even if they were three-on-one and the logic dictated a gang beatdown,
it wasn't going to happen. André demanded respect — and even the
booking sheets gave him what he'd earned. As they were retreating to
the dressing room, Bossman raised André's hand, but the latter switched
things around and raised Bossman's hand instead. He knew why he was
there and even if he was the more over of the two, he didn't want to
steal Bossman's spotlight. Unbeknownst to anyone, it was André's last
WrestleMania moment. Even if he walked naturally to the ring, as he was
battling the Heenan family, he had kept a hand on the ring apron to keep
his balance. He also looked out of breath going back to the locker room.
His skin was greyish, not the pinky rose it had been at the event a year
earlier. In retrospect, it looks like a clear physical sign that something
was wrong.

A week later, he officially broke all ties with Heenan and became a
storyline free agent. WWF then recycled the plot in which every manager
made a play for the hottest talent, a scenario that was very successful
with Randy Savage and Bam Bam Bigelow. Every week, a manager was

turned down in humiliating fashion by André. In the parking garage, "The Doctor of Style" Slick was thrown in the trunk of a limousine with André sending him to New Jersey. In a restaurant, Mr. Fuji got his face shoved into a cake. In a bar where André was drinking with his friends Arnold Skaaland and Pat Patterson, Sensational Sherri tried to seduce him. She promised him anything he wanted but was turned down and spanked for her troubles.

That left "The Mouth of the South" Jimmy Hart. Hart tried to convince Gene Okerlund that he had signed André. When André showed up, Hart went to meet him and André put his arm around Hart's shoulder. It actually served two purposes: making the fans believe André had signed with Hart and helping André walk to the ring. Still playing the Giant, he got in the ring stepping over the top rope like he had always done. When asked by Okerlund if he had signed with Hart, André, with his rasping voice, replied with a loud "NO!" to the delight of the fans in attendance. Hart lost it so André grabbed him by the collar. However, Hart's protégé Earthquake attacked André's left knee with Hart's famous megaphone. Earthquake was John Tenta, a former sumo wrestler from Vancouver, Canada, billed at six foot seven and 468 pounds. He continued his attack while André sold his knee perfectly. Those managers' vignettes and the angle with Earthquake proved that André, even if he was too frail to wrestle, was still good at acting. Whether it was for a funny skit or to sell an injury, André always had a good sense of timing.

That said, selling a knee injury wasn't difficult: André actually needed an operation. The angle legitimately explained the time off André was going to have to take. It was a flashback to the Killer Khan storyline, which had been a success, and perhaps there was hope that André could work one last match at a major event, despite Pritchard's comments. But André was 44 with a body savaged by acromegaly and a life in the ring. If there was a shot at one last successful angle, it had to be soon after surgery, and Earthquake was a good candidate to be his opponent.

Just before beginning that angle, André had been part of a WWF tour in the United Kingdom. He mostly managed The Rockers or the

Bushwackers, but he did wrestle one match. On April 26 in Belfast, Northern Ireland, in the main event, André teamed with Shawn Michaels and Marty Jannetty against the Orient Express and Mr. Fuji. It was WWF's Irish debut — and a nod to the past, when André was brought in to juice a new market.

Pairing André with The Rockers was odd, considering André's hatred for the youngsters. Back then, The Rockers had a lot of heat backstage because they were immature and cocky. After a false start with the company in 1987, they got a second chance in July 1988. They were told to mingle more with the boys and to shake hands with them. So at their first TV taping, they saw André in the locker room. He was playing cribbage with Arnold Skaaland. And while he played, everyone would come to shake his hand. All the top guys like Hogan, Savage, Roberts would come and ask, "How you doing, boss?" They would all come to pay their respects to him. "Hogan may have been the main event guy on TV, but André was the main event in the locker room," wrote Shawn Michaels in his book, who described the scene like André was the Godfather.

When Michaels and Jannetty went to shake his hand, André didn't even look at them. For almost three years, every time The Rockers and André were on the same show, they would extend their hands, but André didn't acknowledge them once. Rick Martel remembered that when André gave someone the silent treatment, it was so intense that it became uneasy for everyone. After a while, Jannetty stopped trying and accepted the fact that André had heat with him. The first time they had to work with André was during that European tour. In those days, especially with someone like André, few words were said before a match. So André hadn't spoken to The Rockers yet. After the match, the heels shook André's hand, as it is custom to do so after a match, and finally André shook hands with his teammates. That night at the bar, André invited Michaels for a beer.

"Yes, sir," Michaels fired back, before whispering, "I know you don't like us."

"When you first came in, I didn't like you. But after that, you're okay."

"But you never shook our hands?"

"After that, I was just ribbing you," André said, laughing.

It might have been a long, drawn-out process, but it was his way of getting respect from a rookie. The locker room was his home and he was the leader, the boss, the don.

"He was kind of the leader, a dressing room general if you will," added Raymond Rougeau. "He was respected because he never complained. When he said something, it meant something. If someone was bringing the dressing room down, he would set him straight by telling him how lucky he was to be here. He was a silent presence that demanded respect . . . The boys would not act the same around him, including [notorious pranksters] the Bulldogs. They would never try to play ribs on him."

André had knee surgery in June at the River Oaks Hospital in Flowood, Mississippi. It was performed by Dr. Gene R. Barrett, who had a reputation among wrestlers as the best knee surgeon in the country. This hospital stay was completely different than the one 10 years prior. Back then, he had been keen to meet with staff, sign autographs, and talk to people; now it was a complete 180. He wanted privacy, and both the hospital and WWF made sure no one could get close. But it didn't mean his peers had forgotten about him. At the hospital, he received a giant "get well soon" card, with a drawing of André's knee in a cast, signed by the majority of the roster and Vince McMahon. André was so moved by it, he kept the card at home until his passing, and it's now housed at the Rankin Museum in Ellerbe. André was back on house shows by June 23, managing his old foe Jake Roberts in matches with Earthquake. (Perhaps Dr. Barrett had cured his fear of reptiles while fixing his knee.) Walking with crutches, he stood in the corner, not doing much, but he was able to work big arenas like he had in the old days. On July 1, he was in Roberts's corner at the Garden and had a faceoff with Earthquake after the match. WrestleFest '91 was on July 14, in front of 19,000 fans at Busch Stadium in St. Louis, and André was in Jim Duggan's corner, as the Glens Falls, New York, native was subbing for Roberts.

The next day, a *Prime Time Wrestling* episode aired in which André was interviewed by Sean Mooney. André, walking with crutches, claimed that he was two or three months away from a return and that the doctor had to remove two bone spurs almost the size of golf balls from his knee. He had noticeably regained a lot of the weight he had lost from earlier that year, and his ankles were also swollen. It was a very frustrating time for him as deep down he knew it was a major setback.

While André had his problems, Vince McMahon and Hulk Hogan also had theirs: that same year Dr. George Zahorian had been found guilty of selling steroids without medical purpose to some WWF wrestlers. On July 16, Hulk Hogan appeared on *The Arsenio Hall Show* and famously lied, saying he had only taken steroids once in 1983 to rehabilitate a torn bicep. It was a scandal that had spared André, who had taken them only once for rehabilitation purposes. André never fit the steroid profile. Some newspapers even pointed that out, saying everyone but André could be on Zahorian's list. As a matter of fact, André was named on another list when Midway Airlines took a full-page of advertising in the *Chicago Tribune* with the following:

> André the Giant
> Imelda Marcos' Shoe Closet
> Your Mortgage
> Uncle Arv's '68 Caddy
> Midway Airlines
> One of these is a lot bigger than you think.
> As for André the Giant, um, André, buddy, you can take a little joke, right?

He sure could, especially one that said he was not as big as fans thought — when he was probably at his heaviest.

But back to wrestling: anyone who found themselves in the ring with Earthquake had the benefit of André at ringside. Guys like Bret Hart, Jim Neidhart, Davey Boy Smith, Kerry Von Erich, and Greg

Valentine were all managed by the Giant. But Earthquake's main opponent was Jake Roberts, especially since he'd "killed" Jake's snake Damien. The plan was to bring André back to the ring, teaming with Roberts at *SummerSlam*, against The Natural Disasters, Earthquake and Typhoon, formerly known as Tugboat. It was even mentioned in the WWF magazine's *SummerSlam* preview edition. It was a match that would have made sense, since André could have let Roberts work the bulk of the match as Haku had done in Toronto. Again, reporters and journalists doubted the premise. Especially those who had seen André work in Japan in recent months. "Earthquake and Typhoon will be a heel tag team called the Natural Disasters," wrote Meltzer. "This leads to an inevitable feud with André the Giant and Jake Roberts, which is a natural disaster." However, by July, the idea was nixed and André started appearing in the Bushwackers' corner. André knew them from back when he wrestled in New Zealand in 1972 and from when the Kiwis wrestled for Grand Prix. In Montreal, André had taken them under his wing and made sure they were looked after.

It was then announced that at *SummerSlam*, on August 26, 1991, at the Garden, André would be in the Bushwackers' corner against The Natural Disasters. That night, the once-powerful André had to walk to ringside with crutches and stay in the aisle. Except for pointing his crutch at Earthquake, he was a non-factor in the affair, and the Bushwackers were easily beaten by the monstrous duo. As the Natural Disasters were about to attack André, the Legion of Doom, Hawk and Animal, made the save. André could barely get a few crutch shots in on Earthquake for revenge. André's salary for that show was $8,000, more than each of the four men who had actually wrestled and as much as Jimmy Hart, who worked two more times that night.

And that's as close as André came to returning to action in the WWF. *SummerSlam* was his last WWF appearance in North America. His last match with the company was a battle royal on May 10, 1991, in Long Island. Five weeks after SummerSlam, he was sent to Europe to be in Davey Boy Smith's corner against Earthquake. He still had his crutches and didn't look anywhere close to being ready for a comeback. McMahon didn't need to send André to Europe — even if Hogan wasn't part of the tour, André was not there to sell tickets. Instead, it was as close to a retirement gift that André would get after 18 years of work for the McMahons. He was able to be part of shows in big arenas in front of large crowds. He went to England, Spain, Belgium, and as if his life wasn't a fairy tale story already, he finished up his career where everything had started for him — in his native France. The show featured a battle royal in the last match of the evening, but André wasn't part of it. The King of Battle Royals had been dethroned. "The Giant" Jean Ferré was no more. The WWF's giant was gone.

ANDRÉ IN ONE OF HIS LAST PROMO SHOTS WITH THE WWF.

ANDRÉ, TOWARD THE END OF HIS LIFE, WITH JACKIE, JANINE JONES, AND FRENCHY BERNARD.

ANDRÉ ALWAYS TRIED TO TAKE CARE OF HIS MOTHER, MARIANNE, AND HIS FATHER, BORIS.

CHAPTER 28

LIFE
AFTER
THE WWF

With newfound free time, André went back to the ranch to his Texas longhorns. When the writing was on the wall with the WWF, he'd brought in Darol Dickinson to stay with him for a few days. André wanted to pick his brain. A wrestling neophyte, Dickinson remembered that André wanted to lose weight and was trying to follow a diet. They ate chicken breasts and salad, and the Giant mostly drank diet soda. Unfortunately, the dietary changes didn't last long. Even if André was taking this business venture seriously, it was also a reason for him to have fun with his friends. Dickinson remembered André inviting people over for a BBQ party every time a calf was getting branded. Every cow at the ranch had a branding that was so bad, it looked like a birthmark. The brand was actually the name of the ranch, AJF: A for André, J for Jackie, and F for Frenchy. André and his friends were so bad at branding that one time, he asked Dickinson to send his ranch foreman to do it properly. Wrestling was easy for the Giant compared to that! Even though André didn't share many personal stories, Dickinson remembered him genuinely enjoying himself, working with animals. The ranch had everything to make André's life comfortable. He had a huge chair and a giant television set, where he loved to watch *The Princess Bride* and talk about his experiences on the set. Sleeping seemed less comfortable — André snored louder than anyone Dickinson had ever heard. "It was like sleeping in a den with a bear," he said. "It never stopped, and I just gave up sleeping early in the morning."

Despite the snoring, Dickinson wasn't André's only visitor. "Frenchy told me when he picked me up at the airport that he was just dropping off one of André's lady friends who had been staying there with him," recalled Dickinson. "When I went back home, Frenchy dropped me at the airport and then he was picking up a different lady friend who would be coming to spend a few days with him."

André's career in the WWF was over, but it didn't mean he was ready to hang up his boots and singlet. In short order, he traveled back to Japan. André had stopped working for New Japan in 1986 and by the 1990s, Inoki's promotion wasn't an option for André anymore. The wrestling style had evolved and there was no place for a guy with André's limitations. But the people running New Japan were happy to help him, however; the Giant had been good to them for more than a decade and that hadn't been forgotten. Sometime after the Wrestling Summit at the Tokyo Dome, the president of New Japan, Seiji Sakaguchi, met with Giant Baba.

"Sakaguchi asked Baba to bring André back to Japan," explained Meltzer. "He'd always be able to draw money and All Japan always booked one pure comedy match per show, largely to give Baba a place on the tour, and the idea of Baba and André as a tag team would be a nice touch. It's a famous story in that it marked two competing promotions, one asking its competition to use a major drawing card because they had so much respect for what the man had accomplished." Again, there was always something special around André, even when he wasn't at the peak of his career. Baba also had a soft spot for André. As a giant himself, he could relate to André's numerous difficulties. Plus, the team of Baba and André had worked at the Tokyo Dome, so why not try it for a whole tour?

André had worked a match for All Japan three days after the Tokyo Dome show, but that was just a one-shot deal. André made his official debut on an All Japan tour named Giant Baba 30th Anniversary Giant Series, at the very end of September 1990. He ended up working mostly six-man tags with Baba and Rusher Kimura, but on September 30, at Korakuen Hall in Tokyo, André teamed with Stan Hansen against Abdullah the Butcher and none other than Baba himself. It was billed as Giant Baba's 30th anniversary special match, since his first match was on September 30, 1960.

As odd as it sounds, Baba didn't win the match. André went over on Abdullah with an elbow drop, the finish he mostly used at the time. It was also the first time the two of them were on opposite sides in a match other than a battle royal. It was too late for André and Baba to have a singles match, which would have been a much bigger deal for Baba's 30th anniversary. That match, in the 1970s or early 1980s, would have been huge. It's arguably one of the biggest missed opportunities of André's career. The Giant was brought back to Japan in November for All Japan's tag team tournament, the Real World Tag League. André and Baba wrestled the likes of Terry Gordy and Steve Williams, the Funks, and Dynamite Kid and Johnny Smith. They were protected, winning most of their matches or losing by forfeit. Following that tour, André came back to All Japan in April 1991 for a short stint, before going back in November for the 1991 Real World Tag League tournament, teaming once again with Baba. This time around, they wrestled guys like Jumbo Tsuruta, Mitsuharu Misawa, Toshiaki Kawada, Mitsuo Momota (Rikidozan's son), Kenta Kobashi, Johnny Ace, Abdullah the Butcher, as well as André's friends Mighty Inoue and Stan Hansen. Every show drew at least a few thousand fans, but the last was in front of a sold-out crowd of 15,900 at Budokan Hall. Even if most of André's matches were mid-card, he was still wrestling in front of big crowds.

"People loved him like a god over in Japan," said Johnny Ace, better known to WWE fans today as John Laurinaitis. "Near the end, he and Baba were tagging up, and they loved that. It was an attraction. Baba was not in good shape either, but the sight of the two of them in the ring and the history about what they both brought to the business, it didn't matter. The fans had such an appreciation and respect for what they did in the business."

It was no longer about what André could do — and it had been like that for a few years — but about what he represented. Being a wrestling legend was keeping his career alive and Japan was the perfect place for André to get respect and appreciation from the fans.

"I had the chance to wrestle André a couple of times in Japan," recalled Mick Foley, who wrestled as Cactus Jack in the 1991 Champion Carnival tour in April, "and even at a time and age he was really starting to struggle physically, he still had this aura of invincibility, especially among the Japanese fans."

After another short Japanese tour at the beginning of 1992, André spent most of April and May working in Mexico, where he hadn't been since 1984. For UWA, he mainly wrestled in six-man tag team matches alongside former rival El Canek. During that tour, he worked against guys like Kokina, who would become better known as Yokozuna; Dr. Wagner Jr.; and 2 Cold Scorpio, who wrestled there as Black Scorpio.

"It was a true pleasure to wrestle a true legend," remembered Scorpio. "My first reaction was that he was old and slow, and it was going to be easy. I remember him getting his hand around my neck, and he backed me up into the corner. He hit me on the top of my head, and it felt like a redwood tree fell on top of my head. I never was hit that hard by an old man."

In reality, André was only 46. He clearly didn't feel too old or that he was finished with wrestling. In fact, he made changes to his gear. For the Mexican tour, his look was different: he went into the ring sporting a red singlet with a slightly larger shoulder strap, red boots, and a red knee pad on his left knee. His hair was also longer, but not quite as long as when he first became famous in the 1970s. On this same tour, he made peace with Bam Bam Bigelow and Bad News Brown, who worked south of the border as Buffalo Allen. Working with Bad News led to the most talked about story of André's return to Mexico.

"It's me, Kokina, and Bad News against Dos Caras, Canek, and André," said Bam Bam Bigelow. "André was a big drinker, and he was drinking Clamato juice and mezcal all day. During the match, André does his spot where he sits on the guy, on Allen, and he shits all over him! Diarrhea running down his neck and the smell from a distance was unbelievable! Every time he tried to lift himself or move, it would start again. Nastiest, funniest, and grossest thing ever!" The incident was not taped and the match Bigelow talked about has never been found in any of André's records. Yet it doesn't make the story untrue. "True story," confirmed Bad News Brown. "This is the last time I saw André alive. He shoots me across the ring and he says, 'Big ass, boss!' And he gives it to me and so everything went! Right in the corner and he just let go and it's all over me. I fell out of the ring and I'm about to puke. I didn't take off my boots or nothing, I went in and just jumped in the shower. I felt sorry for the guy, I mean, he was just sick, that's all. But that's a true story."

Whether it was his drinking or a stomach bug, or a combination of both, it wasn't André's finest moment. And the tour in general was far from his finest work in the ring. In some matches, he was barely able to get on the ring apron because there were no ring steps to help him. He also started to step in the ring between the second and third rope, instead of his over-the-top-rope signature move. It was sad to witness — especially knowing how much pain he was in at that point.

After another short tour in Japan, André made a special appearance at a spot show run by Bobby Fulton on July 4, in Pembroke, North Carolina. Jim Cornette remembered the sight of the biggest star of the past 20 years suddenly entering the building through the back door just before show time. About 400 people at the National Guard Armory got to see André that day for $8 each. The town was only 55 miles from Ellerbe. It was an easy drive to make that Independence Day, and an opportunity to see his French-Canadian friend Ivan Koloff. The crowd gave his short appearance a great reaction, but Cornette also recalled something a little more disturbing. He noticed that André's socks were red, pink, and white and seemed to sparkle. He thought it was a little odd — until he realized André was not wearing any socks. His ankles were discolored; his body was deteriorating. At his size, if he could not stand, he would be shackled to a life of misery, unable to wrestle and see his friends. For the past few years, Tim White had been pushing him in a wheelchair at airports to try to relieve some of the stress on his legs. Perhaps Scorpio was right: André, at 46, was broken.

It was not surprising to see André doing something for the locals. He was good for his community. He appeared at Lions Club events, gave generous tips to local retailers, and spoke out against a nuclear waste company and their efforts to place a nuclear waste dump in Richmond County.

His next wrestling appearance baffled many, but no one more than Vince McMahon. On September 2, WCW presented *Clash of the Champions 20*, from Atlanta, Georgia, celebrating 20 years of wrestling on TBS. The show, which aired live on the Superstation, started with an old archived interview of the voice of wrestling at the time, Gordon Solie, and none other than André the Giant. Just an archived interview — no big deal, right? But there was more. Seconds later, in front of the Center Stage Theater, the two hosts, Tony Schiavone and Missy Hyatt, welcomed the same two men, Solie and the Giant. André, on crutches, didn't say much, only that he was happy to be there. A lot of his friends were at the event —Dusty Rhodes, Jim Barnett, Harley Race, and other acquaintances like Bill Watts, Bruno Sammartino, and Jake Roberts. Even baseball legend Hank Aaron was there. Later on, during the broadcast, Teddy Long was conducting interviews in the VIP room. Standing next to Solie and André, who was now sitting on a stool, Long interviewed a couple of former wrestlers. During that minute-long segment, André didn't say one word — he just smiled, laughed quietly, and had fun with Solie. He was like an afterthought, put there just to make sure that if someone had missed the opening of the show, they wouldn't miss seeing André on a WCW broadcast. For WCW, it was a big deal. The management team, who were rarely seen, made sure to get their pictures taken with the Eighth Wonder of the World.

Nevertheless, André may have made a mistake with that appearance. It was four years since the first *Clash of the Champions* went head to head with *WrestleMania*, but WCW was still the main rival of McMahon and his WWF — even more so now that multi-millionaire Ted Turner was the owner. Former WWF wrestlers like Rick Rude, Ricky Steamboat, Paul Orndorff, Davey Boy Smith, and the Nasty Boys were now working for Turner. Ric Flair had just returned home after a quick two years with the WWF.

"When André showed up on Ted Turner's broadcast, it was just such a shock," recalled Shane McMahon. "I remember my dad called André and said, 'Boss, I've just gotta say that you really hurt my feelings. After everything, to see you with a competitor really hurt.' I think André apologized."

It was a slap in the face for McMahon. He expected it from Bruno Sammartino, since the Italian Stallion had been vocal about his discontent with the WWF. But from André? It came as a surprise. What was André thinking? Was he trying to get back to the WWF, pulling a stunt like he had done with UWF? Or did he just want to be with the boys, with people he hadn't seen in a long time?

"In the later days, André drank even more and internalized even more," explained McMahon. "He wasn't on the road anymore, so he felt like he had no value. I think that really got to him. André had an ego and a good one. When it looked like he no longer had any value, I think that weighed on him more than anything else."

That WCW stunt was his final U.S. TV appearance.

André went back to Japan in October to work the 20th anniversary Giant Series, which also celebrated All Japan's 20th anniversary. On the last match of the tour, on October 21, in front of 16,300 fans at Budokan Hall, André, Jumbo Tsuruta, and Terry Gordy defeated Baba, Stan Hansen, and Dory Funk Jr. It marked the second and last time André and Baba wrestled against each other. It was also All Japan's 100th consecutive Tokyo sell-out. André was brought back for the Real World Tag League in November, although he wasn't used in the tournament. He only worked six-man tags, going over every single time. On December 4, the last day of the tour, André teamed with Giant Baba and Rusher Kimura to face Masanobu Fuchi, Motoshi Okuma, and Haruka Eigen in front of another

16,300 fans at Budokan Hall. André barely took part in the actual match, although he pinned Okuma. The match was right in the middle of the event, fourth of an eight-match card. Even André's biggest fans likely had to question how much longer Baba would have been able to feature André, despite the fact that all three opponents sold for him like he was still the fearsome Frenchman from 22 years ago on his first Japanese tour. He won the match by sitting on his opponent, keeping his balance by holding on to the top rope.

"It was not a pretty sight. Each tour he grew progressively worse," explained Meltzer. "However, out of loyalty, probably more than anything, since his shows were doing sellout business without André, and André's price tag (probably in the $15,000 per week range) was no doubt the heftiest ever for a wrestler working in the third match on a card, Baba continued to book him."

It was his last match.

Wrestling Observer readers had voted André the worst wrestler of the year in 1989 and 1991. His run in Mexico combined with his matches in Japan also landed him that title in 1992. "In a league by himself. Very sad. He's still over, though," wrote Meltzer. The team of André and Baba, which was voted worst tag team of the year in 1990 and 1991, finished third in 1992. Fans were embarrassed by his performances. And even if André had made a lot of sacrifices to be able to perform like he did throughout the years, these fans and experts were telling him what Vince McMahon had tried to tell him when he stopped using him.

The October 21 six-man match between André, Gordy, and Tsuruta against Hansen, Baba, and Funk was voted the 11th-worst match in the world in 1992 by *Wrestling Observer Newsletter* subscribers. That very same match was voted fourth-best in Japan that same year by *Weekly Pro Wrestling*'s readers. A clash of stylistic preference between wrestling fans, maybe — but the Japanese had, at the time, a keener appreciation of nostalgia and legendary acts. As Meltzer wrote, André was still over in Japan, although his performances were very far from what they had been in the '70s.

"He was totally broken down," recalled Missy Hyatt from her meeting with André in Atlanta. "I was in disbelief about how André was still getting booked in Mexico and AJPW at that point. I thought, 'Did André need the money that badly?' Having matches in which you have to hold yourself up with the ropes for balance and getting by on just his height would do nothing for me if I was a paying fan."

Hyatt echoed what many fans thought at the time, and perhaps still do today. But it was not about money. André thought wrestling was all he had, or at least it was all he knew. Even as his body was deteriorating, he couldn't imagine himself doing anything else. Perhaps he was right. Retirement would have bored André to death. He knew how that worked: once retired, he would no longer see his friends. As strong as they can be, wrestling friendships don't always survive the business. That's why it was important for André to invite some of his friends to the ranch from time to time. Besides wrestling, the only other thing André had was his daughter and family back in France, and he had not seen them as much as he had wanted to. Some would say he had neglected them because of wrestling.

In October 1992, André's nephew Boris, 26 at the time, came to live in North America. Like his uncle, he chose Montreal for his new life. André had been a hero to him for having the courage to leave his country to chase his dream. He wanted to do the same. So he sent André a letter letting him know how to reach him in Montreal. André, ever the proud uncle, because his nephew crossed the river as he was would say, called Boris and invited him to spend the holidays with him in North Carolina. André didn't want to go to France that year after traveling so much to Japan. Still, it didn't mean André didn't want to have a good time. So he invited Boris, Jackie, Frenchy, and some other people to a restaurant for Christmas. They went there in a limousine and didn't wait one second in line. André wanted to have a good time and he succeeded in making everyone laugh by ordering 12 T-bone steaks, one at a time. This stay at the ranch gave Boris great insight into the man his uncle truly was.

"What made him happy was that everyone around him was happy," Boris said. "He made sure that we had everything we needed. He loved to play pranks and laugh."

At the time, André was considering selling the property in Ellerbe and moving to Hawaii. It was something he had had in mind for a while, since it would put him between Japan and Seattle, where Robin resided. It also indicated he wasn't ready to quit wrestling yet, although Hawaii is a perfect place to retire. The weather probably would have helped with the pain in his joints. The house at the ranch had many stairs and was not suitable for him anymore. The work on the farm was starting to weigh on him. Robin was also getting older and it would be easier for him to spend time with her without having to shield her from the attention he attracted everywhere he went. Tim White also visited his friend during that holiday season. Boris knew him from France as White visited with the family many times, just like Frank Valois had done back in the day. In fact, in the late 1980s, when André was working for the WWF, the company stored a ring in a barn just across from the Roussimoffs in Molien: they would use this ring while touring in France and other European countries.

André and Boris had a very good time together. When the holidays were over, they promised to see each other again. On January 10, Boris had a message from André on his home answering machine in Montreal. André had to leave for France as his dad was not feeling well and he wanted to see him. The Giant arrived with just enough time to see his father at the hospital.

"He had a hemiplegia and was slightly paralyzed on one side," recalled André's brother Jacques. "We couldn't understand much of what he was saying. He had had a stroke, had Parkinson's disease and prostate cancer. He had not been sick before the last three or four years of his life." On January 15, 1993, Boris Roussimoff Stoeff passed away at the age of 85.

"It was a shock for [André]," said Hortense, André's sister-in-law. "I believe that's what finished him." André decided to stay to attend the funeral and to be home for his mother's birthday on the 24th. He also wanted to enjoy his time with friends and family since he hadn't been home for Christmas. Realizing the importance of family and perhaps feeling the burden of guilt, at his father's funeral, he invited Antoine and Hortense to North Carolina, offering to pay for their trip. While in France, he spent his time commuting between Paris, Ussy-sur-Marne, and Molien — he employed the same driver he had used during *The Princess Bride* shoot. In Paris, he stayed at Hotel de la Tremoille, a five-star place downtown known for having welcomed many celebrities. In Ussy-sur-Marne, his favorite place was le Café de la Marne. There, he spent his time playing cards with his brother Jacques, his childhood friend Jacques Poulain, and some other friends like Hubert Leloutre. André Roussimoff was home, and he could finally take some time away from being André the Giant. On January 27, he played cards and drank beer at the coffee shop in Ussy-sur-Marne. Those with him have said he looked tired and was experiencing back pain — they didn't know this because he told them but because of the way he leaned up against the wall. Jacques Poulain left around 11 p.m. André stayed with his brother for a little while longer before going back to Paris. He promised to return the following day.

As usual, he got back to his hotel after midnight, he took the elevator to room 108 and went to sleep. On Thursday morning, January 28, his driver was back to pick him up around 9:30 a.m. But André didn't answer the phone. It was unusual, because André always answered the phone. His driver thought he was perhaps a little tired, so he decided to let him rest. The driver and the doorman tried again at 11 a.m. and then at noon — but there was still no answer. In the meantime, André's mother and his sister-in-law Hortense were waiting: André was supposed to have lunch with his mother at noon. Around 3 p.m., the driver called again. No answer. Around the same time, Hortense called the driver, and he told her he would go to the room to see what was going on. The driver and Noël Mateos, the doorman, under the supervision of the hotel's director, went upstairs and knocked on André's door. André didn't answer. They hesitated but realized they had no other choice but to break into the room.

When they got there, André was lying on the bed, not breathing. It was too late.

CHAPTER 29

A LEGEND
IN AND
AFTER
HIS DEATH

E ven in death, the legend that had devoured André's life conspired to complicate matters. Removing his body from the hotel room seemed impossible, due to his size and weight. One idea was to use a lift or some equipment used to move furniture and to get him out from the room's balcony. However, as much for the hotel's reputation as for André's, that would not have been a tasteful exit, and it would have been very public. The only feasible option, as gruesome as it sounds, was to break one of his arms in order to get him through the door. It wasn't more tasteful, but it was more discreet.

The death certificate listed André's time of death as 6:20 p.m. on January 28. This was the time a doctor confirmed the death. However, from almost all reports, André passed away on January 27, the day that is still commonly used as his date of death.

When we review his final night, that turns out to be inaccurate. André stayed in Ussy-sur-Marne until late evening on the 27th. According to the hotel doorman, he arrived way past midnight, between 12:30 and 1 a.m. His friends and brother saw him for the last time on the 27th, but his driver and the hotel staff saw him in the early hours of the 28th. Of course, it was Paris time, which was six hours later than Eastern Time in North America. So when it was January 28 at 1 a.m. in Paris, it was only January 27 at 7 p.m. in New York. That said, since André was only discovered dead on the afternoon of the 28th, by the time it became news, it didn't make sense for the 27th to be reported. The explanation resides in the first story published. On January 29, at the Garden in New York, WWF held a show and did a 10-bell salute memorializing André's passing. "I'll never forget the shock in MSG when they announced his passing, leading to a massive André chant," remembers journalist Mike Johnson. The promotion was the first to break the news. The first printed story came from the Associated Press and was published on January 30 by many newspapers in North America. In the story, there was a quote from Frenchy Bernard saying, "He visited his family on Wednesday, then returned to his hotel room where he died." The story then said that "the exact date of his death was not immediately known." Since Wednesday was the 27th and the article did not mention that he had gone back to his room after midnight, people assumed he had died on the 27th. Without confirming all the details, some reporters wrote that André had died on the 27th. On the 31st, some newspapers added that André had been cremated in France and his ashes were brought back to Ellerbe — which was not true either.

André wanted to be cremated, but there was no crematorium in France large enough for him. Even in death, his body was difficult to accommodate. His family, especially his mother, firmly refused the option of cutting him up in pieces for the cremation to occur in France. His body had already been mutilated enough. They finally found a crematorium that could take care of him in Pinehurst, North Carolina, near his home. "André's mother didn't want the body to be brought back by itself," explained Jackie. "So my sister and I flew there, and we were back on the Monday. That's when I met his siblings and his mother. The mother wanted to have André buried in France and she could have, if she would have agreed to have André cremated. His ashes could have been buried in France. But he was adamant that he was to be cremated. While he wanted to have his ashes spread in Ellerbe, it wasn't restricted to just

THE ONLY ROUSSIMOFF AT THE FUNERAL, HIS NEPHEW BORIS WAS HOLDING THE FRENCH FLAG.

ANDRÉ'S FUNERAL: WE CAN RECOGNIZE WAHOO MCDANIEL, PAT PATTERSON, IVAN & NIKITA KOLOFF, RANDY SAVAGE, DIAMOND LIL, FABULOUS MOOLAH, FRENCHY BERNARD, HULK HOGAN, VINCE MCMAHON, AND MAE YOUNG.

HULK HOGAN WAS ASKED TO DELIVER A EULOGY AT ANDRÉ'S FUNERAL.

FRENCHY WITH ANDRÉ'S CUSTOM CASKET THAT WAS DISPLAYED AT THE FUNERAL EVEN THOUGH HIS BODY HAD BEEN INCINERATED.

that, because he was traveling a lot and knew he could have passed away anywhere. The chances of him dying in Japan or Europe were very high." However, it was not an easy task to bring his body back home. Jackie had to figure out the flying route to make sure the planes had large enough cargo space for the 300-pound custom oak coffin. When she finally arrived in North Carolina, a friend offered to transport the coffin in his pickup truck since no hearse was large enough.

André's death was covered by almost every news outlet in North America. Whether it was the *L.A. Times*, *Washington Post*, *New York Times*, or *Sports Illustrated*, his death was news for weeks, with in-depth articles by columnists who remembered his heyday. In cities like New York, Montreal, and Ellerbe, André got more comprehensive coverage. Especially in Montreal, where he was never forgotten, all the major papers ran stories and tributes. Sadly, in his native France, there was very little coverage of his passing. Only a small blurb was published in *Le Figaro* and *L'Équipe*, full of mistakes and offering the same old tales. Wrestling's popularity in France had waned in the mid-1970s and only rebounded at the end of the 1980s, missing André's best years. Even if the French WWF commentators were talking about André, the press didn't pick it up. Many wrestling fans in France didn't even know André the Giant was one of their own. Ussy-sur-Marne papers covered the passing of its most famous son, taking the time to speak with his family. Still, at home, it was minimal coverage for such a global star.

Following the show at the Garden, WWF did 10-bell salutes to André on many of their house shows, with the last one occurring on February 1 at the Manhattan Center in New York, on the fourth episode of *Monday Night Raw*. In Mexico, at the UWA 18th anniversary show on January 31 at El Toreo in Naucalpan, they had a moment of silence. With his recent presence in the country, the news of his death made the rounds in the media. In Japan, the news of his passing was a major item in every newspaper. On February 1, New Japan had a classic 10-bell salute in Tokyo with Antonio Inoki and Seiji Sakaguchi holding André's picture in the ring. On January 31, All Japan held a similar ceremony.

André's funeral took place on February 24 at his ranch in Ellerbe. It was a dark time for pro wrestling. Kerry Von Erich committed suicide on February 18 and Dino Bravo was murdered on March 10, making him the third major WWF name to die before the age of 50 in a seven-week period. The funeral was a formal affair, open to family, friends, and people from the area who knew André. Among those in attendance were Vince McMahon, Hulk Hogan, Randy Savage, Brutus Beefcake, Pat Patterson, René Goulet, Tim White, Terry Todd, Darol Dickinson, his physician Dr. Rankin Jr., Ivan Koloff, Nikita Koloff, Wahoo McDaniel, Fabulous Moolah, and Mae Young. His nephew Boris was the only family member in attendance. The family in Molien had already held a small ceremony on February 5, and his name had been added to the family tombstone. Sadly, many wrestlers from the province of Québec were not there: Gino Brito, Rick Martel, the Vachons, and Frank Valois, a clear proof that his relationship with André had been broken. The funeral program featured a nice poem about a traveler coming home, which was exactly what André was. In between his birth and death in France, he had toured the world more times than he had ever imagined possible. Hulk Hogan was one of the speakers, alongside Tim White, Terry Todd, Dr. Rankin, Jackie, Frenchy, and Darol Dickinson. The people who eulogized him had all been chosen by André himself.

"I did not understand why my friendship with him meant that much to him," said Dickinson. "As we spent four or five days together my whole life, I could not comprehend why he would put me in there with Hulk Hogan. I don't think I did a very good job. There were a lot of people there who knew him much better than I did."

The André the Giant character had always cast a huge shadow over André Roussimoff, and it even showed in the funeral program, where there was no mention of his real name. André's ashes were spread by riders on horseback on his ranch in a flag ceremony that included the United States, France, North Carolina, and the Confederate flag, since North Carolina had been part of the Confederate States of America during the American Civil War. Associated with racism as it is, Boris (who carried the French flag) was uncomfortable and he didn't believe his uncle would have approved. He thought a Canadian flag would have been more appropriate. A local police helicopter provided security, and locals respected the grief of the celebrities on hand. A lot of André's female friends were at the funeral. They were very fond of him. "There was that blond lady that wanted to talk about André with me," remembered Dickinson. "She would fly in and meet him at matches. She poured her heart out to me about André. She was broken-hearted about André's passing. There was a bunch of other women there who felt just like she did. They were like the ex-wives club, sort of. They all felt a close connection to him. He liked them all." Except for a Japanese contingent and Dave Stubbs from the *Montreal Gazette*, no other journalists were present. (Stubbs's article was the only one to mention his real date of death.)

André had made quite a bit of money during his career, especially after WWF's national expansion. Not only had he been paid for performing, but he received royalties from tapes, PPV shows, T-shirts, and action figures. Today, an original LJN action figure of André in its package sells for more than a thousand dollars. While André made millions during his 26-year career, he was also a big spender. Not only did he drink a lot, he was generous with his money. So it's hard to estimate how much he had left when he passed. Aside from some money he directed to Jackie and Frenchy, André left everything to Robin. His lawyer, also his financial advisor, liquidated everything, including the ranch. Robin was only 13 at the time, and she could only access the money when she reached the age of 30 in 2009 — 17 years after his passing. "In the mid-1980s, André updated his will, and he wanted Robin to inherit the money when she was 40 years old," explained Jackie. "And the lawyer said that's a long time. But André didn't want Jean to get a hold of Robin's money and blow it all. He wanted her to have some security. That's when they agreed to 30." The house was sold at auction. When it was sold again in 2013, it was still called the former home of André the Giant. The ranch was sold to Frenchy and Jackie. Two years later, they got divorced and both eventually remarried, but they stayed friends. On September 16, 2013, Frenchy died at the age of 77.

Surprisingly, aside from a suitcase with some personal effects and a pair of shoes that his brother Jacques retrieved from the hotel, André didn't leave anything for his mother or his family. "He took care of his parents, the best they would let him, when he was alive," said Jackie. "He wanted to buy them a new house, but they wanted to stay where they were. He paid for modern plumbing at the family house. He was very generous to them when he was alive, but I don't know why he didn't leave them anything."

CHAPTER 30

A
GIANT
LEGACY

Things move fast in the world of wrestling. The day before André passed away, on January 27, the WWF held a press conference in Las Vegas to announce the top three matches at *WrestleMania IX*. One of them was The Undertaker against the new giant in town — Giant Gonzales. (In the May 1993 edition of the WWF's magazine, Gonzales was already nicknamed "The Giant.") The show must go on as they say. Nevertheless, Gonzales didn't replace André in the collective wrestling consciousness. Even if this book tells the truth behind the myths, one must not forget that these myths are what created André's legacy, and although André died in 1993, his legacy has continued, and he has remained part of popular culture.

In 1989, aspiring artist Shepard Fairey started a street art movement with a few stickers on which you could read "André the Giant has a posse 7'4" 520 lb." "The sticker had no meaning but existed only to cause people to react, to contemplate and search for meaning in the sticker," explained Fairey, who strangely enough had no interest in wrestling. Shortly after, a guy saw the sticker on the street and thought it was fresh. So he put it on his baseball cap. Incredibly, Fairey saw that guy and his baseball cap at a party. It gave the young creator an idea. He stylized and cropped André's face and added the word "OBEY." The inspiration and the font of the lettering came from the 1988 John Carpenter movie *They Live*.

"I realized very quickly even though the subject was silly, it was spreading in a very underground mysterious way," said Fairey about his campaign, which kept André in the minds of so many who were not even wrestling fans. "I had a feeling that it would be like-minded people perpetuating it." André's estate didn't go after Fairey's art because of fair use, a doctrine in the law in the United States that permits limited use of copyrighted material. Moreover, he has since replaced the original picture and removed the name André the Giant. Still using obeygiant.com as his website, Fairey gained more notoriety for designing the famous Hope poster of Barack Obama in a street art campaign meant to inspire people to vote.

Shortly after André's passing, Vince McMahon decided to create the WWF Hall of Fame with André as the first inductee. In the beginning, it was nothing like the current ceremony that fills arenas every year. On the March 22, 1993, episode of *Monday Night Raw*, the announcement was made by Howard Finkel and a video package aired. The following year was the first time a ceremony was held. For the next three years, a ceremony was held in a hotel the same weekend as a WWF PPV. Friends of André like Arnold Skaaland, Pat Patterson, and Vincent J. McMahon were among the inductees. The Hall of Fame then took a long break before finally coming back in 2004 in conjunction with *WrestleMania XX*. Since then, a ceremony has been held in a big arena the weekend of *WrestleMania*. Although André wasn't honored the same way many of his peers are today, he has the distinction of being inducted in the inaugural class and is the only one to be inducted alone.

In 1995, André's name resurfaced but not in the WWF. In the spring of that year, Hulk Hogan, who had left WWF and had started with WCW in the summer of 1994, was booked in feuds that echoed his with The Ultimate Warrior and André the Giant, with other wrestlers playing their roles. At Slamboree in May 1995, WCW introduced wrestler

Paul Wight, showing brief glimpses of him during a match between Hulk Hogan and Randy Savage against Ric Flair and Vader. At the Bash at the Beach event in July, Wight showed up wearing a shirt like the one André used to wear and threw it at Hogan. Hogan claimed it was actually André's shirt. Other skits followed, in which Wight was said to be André's son. WCW dressed him and styled his hair like André's. Hogan said he could feel the presence and strength of André in his "son." Although there were rumors at the time about naming Wight "André the Giant Jr.," Eric Bischoff is adamant they weren't serious about doing that. "There was a lot of goofy ideas bouncing around at the time, but at no time was there any consideration billing him as André the Giant Jr.," explained Bischoff. "I don't think Hulk Hogan would have wanted it. You know, Hulk Hogan has a lot of respect. Still to this day, when you talk to him about André the Giant, within three to four minutes, he will start tearing up. I don't think he would have gone quite that far in trying to name him André the Giant Jr., but we definitely wanted to draw the connection with him and André the Giant. That is a fact."

Ultimately, Wight was simply named "The Giant," a subtler nod to André. Discovered by Hulk Hogan, Wight was young enough to be André's son, born on February 8, 1972, when André was 25. Like André, Wight also suffered from acromegaly. Hogan immediately saw the potential of replicating the success of his feud with the original Giant. In his first official match, at Halloween Havoc on October 29, at the Joe Louis Arena in Detroit, Wight defeated Hogan for the WCW World Heavyweight title. Detroit instead of Pontiac, Joe Louis Arena instead of the Silverdome, WCW title instead of WWF title — nothing was a coincidence. Even the match itself looked like the one André and Hogan had in 1987. "Nobody spent a lot of time trying to camouflage the fact that we were just basically ripping off that idea," explained Bischoff. "There were no nuances or subtleties in ripping it off." But most of the fans didn't buy into the storyline and the idea of billing Wight as André's son was dropped. Wight himself had mixed feelings about it. "It was awkward. It was very awkward because Hogan and Bischoff came up with this idea and that's why Hogan latched on to me right away," Wight explained. "That's why I got a career and opportunity. I'm thankful that he noticed me.

"To go as the son of André, yeah, it gave me credibility with the fans," Wight continued. "It was kind of a real crappy trick to play on the fans because everybody loved André so much and it cornered me into a position because I still have fans that come up to me to this day that tell me how much they loved my dad."

It was also something Robin wasn't thrilled about, although she understood it was just a gimmick. In February 1999, Wight signed a 10-year deal with the WWF, once more inviting comparison to André. Twenty years later, Wight is still working for the WWE and will soon star in a situation comedy on Netflix. Even though he's had a long and successful career, he's never achieved what André did.

"Wight never got to be close to the level of stardom André was," explains Meltzer. "Wight could do more in the ring, but since he was on TV every week, he became ordinary. André was kept fresher and more like an attraction. Also, having seen both live, André had a better presence." That presence can be explained by André's physique, as Wight and him were not built the same way. "Wight is a tall guy," continued Meltzer, "but André had a weird thickness, probably because of acromegaly. His body structure was completely different. His legs were not that long as compared to people that height and were absolutely massive, as were his hips and butt. His torso was enormous, both unusually long compared to his legs, and thicker and wider than pretty much anyone ever as far as a not completely blubbery chest, back, and shoulders. Just because of his proportions and thickness, he was probably the most physically intimidating wrestler ever."

In 1997, a playable character in the fighting video game *Street Fighter III: 2nd Impact* made its debut. Named Hugo, the character was designed as an homage to André. His fighting style was pro-wrestling based and his intro animation was based on the *WrestleMania III* match. In 1999, A&E aired a 45-minute documentary titled *André the Giant: Larger than Life*. Produced by ESPN's Chris Mortensen, it got good reviews and was the first in-depth piece on André's life. It did a 2.7 rating and the replay did 2.0, one of the highest-rated shows ever on the network. André's real life was always a matter of interest, not only for wrestling fans. Every year since WWE resumed its Hall of Fame in 2004, the company makes sure to remind everyone that André was the first inductee. He is also part of every "Then. Now. Forever." video along with other WWE legends. WWE uses the videos to open its television and PPV broadcast. In 2009, a biography by Michael Krugman was published by WWE Books. *A Legendary Life* almost entirely focuses on André's WWE career, with descriptions of his most well-known matches and storylines. In 2011, Jason Segel, from *How I Met Your Mother*, performed a sketch on *Saturday Night Live* playing André, where he was choosing an ice cream flavor; the parody was a mix between André's distinctive voice and the Fezzik character from *The Princess Bride*.

At the WWE head office in Stamford, Connecticut, there's only one wrestler showcased in the lobby: André the Giant. A statue of André is displayed most of the year alongside an exhibit where you can compare your hand size to André's handprint. Built in 2013 for WWE Axxess, the statue is also showcased there every year. Because of its close likeness to André, Tim White couldn't stop staring at it when it was first shown to him. Aside from the Hall of Fame, another yearly event happens during *WrestleMania* weekend because of André. On the March 10, 2014, episode of *Raw*, *WrestleMania XXX* host Hulk Hogan announced that WWE was establishing the André the Giant Memorial Battle Royal in honor of André's legacy. Battle royals were often included as part of the *WrestleMania* line-up, but it wasn't a yearly tradition like it became after 2014. The winner of the match gets a trophy with a statue of André on top of it. Tim White had the honor of escorting the 50-pound and five-foot-tall trophy from Axxess to the Mercedes-Benz Superdome on the day of the show. Cesaro became the first winner, defeating Big Show, the odds favorite because of his similarities to André. In fact, Big Show won the match the following year. Since its inception, over 70 individuals, including basketball great

Shaquille O'Neal, have participated in it. Unfortunately, the winner of the match doesn't always get a push, which has made some experts question the significance of the match. The match serves two purposes: to give 30 wrestlers a chance to perform on the biggest show of the year and to honor one of the all-time greats, the King of the Battle Royals — and that alone should be sufficient.

Also in 2014, a graphic novel by Box Brown called *Life and Legend* was published and went on to become a *New York Times* bestseller and was translated into three languages. Very well received, it brought back so many questions about the man behind all the legends in André's life. A year later, a second graphic novel was published, *Closer to Heaven*, with Robin's collaboration. That same year, the Rankin Museum of American Heritage in Ellerbe opened a small exhibit on André with items provided by Jackie.

Aside from a mural painted in 2018 on the wall of le Café de la Marne, André's favorite place, there's nothing else in his hometown of Molien. There's not even a street named after André, while there is one named after Samuel Beckett. Fictions based on André's meeting with Beckett were released in 2017. The Sky Network in the U.K. produced an episode of *Urban Myths* about André's relationship with Beckett, depicting fictitious events between André, his dad, and Beckett. There was also a play off-Broadway called *Sam & Dede, or My Dinner with André the Giant*, that ran in March 2017. André is also featured on Pro Wrestling Tees branded T-shirts, packaging, and marketing materials, and he's one of the top 10 selling legends. "He is so well liked by everyone in the industry and so well recognized by non-wrestling fans," explained CEO Ryan Barkan, who founded the store located in Chicago in 2010. "There are very few wrestlers who went mainstream and André was definitely one of them." And finally, in April 2018, a documentary directed by Jason Hehir aired on HBO to critical acclaim, bringing a whole new understanding and interest in the man behind the character. A new generation of fans learned more about someone they had only heard about. The film had become the most-watched documentary in HBO Sports history

ABOVE: ONE OF THE MOST FAMOUS TATTOOS OF ANDRÉ, ON BLUE MEANIE'S ANKLE.

LEFT: THE ONLY STATUE IN WWE'S HEAD OFFICE, IT IS ALSO DISPLAYED AT WWE AXXESS.

QUEBEC TV PERSONALITY KEVIN RAPHAEL AND AUTHOR PAT LAPRADE AT THE HBO DOCUMENTARY PREMIERE IN L.A.

EVEN IF THE CHARACTER OVERSHADOWED THE MAN, ANDRÉ ROUSSIMOFF COULD STILL BE FOUND SOMETIMES.

with seven million viewers, won the *Wrestling Observer Newsletter*'s best pro wrestling documentary award, was released on DVD, and is available on the WWE Network.

In recent years, YouTube and Facebook accounts celebrating the Giant have shared photos and videos of André with fans from all over the world. A popular page is run by Chris Owens, a Midwest resident who was just seven years old, in 1981, when he became André the Giant's biggest fan. He started by collecting wrestling magazines, but today his collection is invaluable, and his research has given fans and historians access to footage, articles, documents, and pictures never before seen. Always fascinated about legends and what hides behind them, he had made it his mission to ensure that André's whole story stays alive. Owens's way of remembering André is through collecting.

For others, that fandom is immortalized with tattoos of André. One of the most famous tattooed fans is wrestler Brian Heffron, better known as the Blue Meanie. "André the Giant headlined the first show I ever attended in 1982," said Heffron, who got a tattoo of André sitting on planet Earth a few years ago. "After the match, as he was leaving, I was able to pat him on the stomach. I swore I would never wash my hand again, and it was the coolest thing in the world. Ultimately I had to wash it but still. I just love him.

"But the reason why I became such a big André the Giant fan is because as a kid I grew up severely asthmatic," continued Heffron, who wrestled for ECW and WWE. "During lunch, my grandfather would come to school with my ventilator machine so I could take my medicine. The other kids were watching me like I was an outsider. When I learned more about André, I learned that he felt like an outsider everywhere with people making comments. I latched on to this, I always enjoyed his work, but personally that story made me relate to him. It made me love him even more. He lived his life in a fishbowl and I kind of felt the same way as a kid."

Because of all this, it comes as no surprise that André's career is seen as legendary more than 25 years after his passing and his name still resonates with younger fans. The WWE still uses his image on trading cards, action figures and video games. In particular, they did a wonderful job in making his *WrestleMania III* match with Hulk Hogan the centerpiece of their mythology. It has made André even bigger and more important to wrestling history — if such a thing was even possible. In many cases, it has made older fans forget about the slow degradation of his work after that match.

Over the years, André's accolades mirrored the great career he had, including the fact that he overcame being a giant to end up being one of the best. He was ranked sixth by author John F. Molinaro in his book about the best 100 wrestlers of all time. Larry Matysik ranked him 24th in his book about the best 50 wrestlers of all time. Historian Steve Yohe conducted a survey among wrestling historians and that list, considered one of the most credible, ranked André eighth. Greg Oliver and Steven Johnson listed André as the seventh best babyface of all time in their book *Heroes and Icons*. The *Wrestling Observer Newsletter*'s Hall of Fame is often seen as the most reliable source, and André was a charter member when it was created in 1996. He's also in the Pro Wrestling Hall of Fame and the Quebec Wrestling Hall of Fame. Speaking of his second home, in a survey conducted for the Quebec version of *Family Feud* in 2011, 20 years after his last appearance in Montreal, André was the sixth-most remembered wrestler. He's also statistically considered a top 15 draw in the history of wrestling and top 10 draw in Quebec.

It's safe to say that his legend will be protected for years to come. Future generations will remember him after many others will be forgotten.

WHAT ABOUT ANDRÉ ROUSSIMOFF?

André the Giant's legacy and image will live forever in a multitude of ways. But what about André Roussimoff?

André Roussimoff became André the Giant, relegating the man who played the part to an observer role in his own life. He played a role 24/7 for over 25 years.

"He had kind of a bad hand dealt to him in life, but he handled it as best he could, which I think was pretty damn good by the way," said Gene Okerlund. "The thing I always respected about André is that he played the role of a giant without trying to be what he was not. When he didn't win, it was an accident that made him legendary in that role."

Tim White remembered a person not afraid of anything, who loved wrestling, and who wanted to go out there and enjoy life every single day. "He felt wrestling was his love, and people in that locker room were his family," said White. "He was a proud guy, and he didn't want to say goodbye." It breaks White's heart today thinking about the times he had to push such a proud man through airports in a wheelchair. In the HBO documentary, he broke the hearts of the millions watching with his feelings of guilt for not having been with André until the end. André was not a legend to White, he was his friend.

The irony is that even surrounded by so many of his peers and even more of his fans, in the end, André was a lonely man. With his wonderful qualities and with his flaws, he was a man who wanted to live life to the fullest. Because like in a wrestling match, he knew his outcome in advance. He always had his guard up to protect wrestling and to protect himself from people who wanted to take advantage of his fame and fortune. In later years, his patience was almost nonexistent. He had become a heel and didn't have to cater to fans anymore. The pain was enough to make anyone irritable. Combined with years of being an oddity, it's not surprising he didn't always leave a good impression. Once, on a plane, Michael Jackson's parents wanted his autograph and André categorically refused.

"I've learned to handle things differently," said Wight, who, like André did, lives in a world that was not built for him and who can't hide behind a cap and a hoodie. "I engage people. I make them laugh. André went the other way with it. André was kind of bitter. He didn't want to sign autographs. He didn't want to deal with people. He didn't want to deal with the attention. There are two ways you can deal with that. Some days I don't want to deal with people, so I stay home. I know I'm going to be a grumpy ass, so I stay home. I don't want people to have a bad day by interacting with me." Unlike Wight, André didn't live in a world where fans were a cellphone away from taking a picture or posting an Instagram story. Considering his legendary drinking, it was better that way. And even if he was smiling and didn't complain, you might well ask: how can someone be truly happy and drink that much?

"It's a terrible shame he had to go through so much pain," said Rick Martel. "After traveling all over the world, he was able to come home to France and enjoy what he truly loved for the last few days of his life. It's poetic justice, in a way. It helped me accept it. I will always remember the smiling person he was when we first met."

Other dear friends like Bill Eadie, Bob Backlund, Hulk Hogan, and Bret Hart were all sad to see him go. "I was in Japan at the time and not able to get to his funeral," said Eadie. "You never expect things like this to happen. He was way too young to die. I think about him frequently. I miss his friendship."

"I think of him often and was saddened by his untimely death," wrote Bob Backlund. "I will always think of him as a special man. To me, he was a giant . . . not just in size, but in heart and character. I miss him."

"I pictured him walking through the Pearly Gates with a big smile on his face, for once not having to duck, saying, 'Hello, boss!'" wrote Bret Hart. "There would never be another giant like André."

"The wrestling world lost a titan," wrote Hogan, "a guy that would never be replaced. I lost a friend."

His passing affected wrestlers widely. Lou Thesz, considered by many to be the greatest wrestler ever, was very sad about André's death. "Lou adored André, he thought the world of him," said Charlie Thesz, Lou's widow. "Lou enjoyed his company a lot. It really broke his heart when he heard about André's passing. He had a genuine respect for him."

André's relationship with Vince Jr. was not like the one he had with Vince Sr. In Vince Sr., he saw the man who had made him famous worldwide and who let him wrestle in all those territories. The younger McMahon, he may have felt, restricted him, cut him off from all the fun he was having. Some said it was also a question of trust. André and

Vince Sr. had never signed anything — it was all about the bond of a handshake. But Vince Jr. had to make André sign a contract. In any case, Vince Jr. was aware of André's feelings toward him and he offered a transparent take on his relationship with André when interviewed for the HBO documentary.

"I was responsible for the fact that business was good, and everyone else was going on without him," McMahon said. "André more or less wanted to blame me, you know, and resented me a bit, because he knew the business was gonna go on without him. I think André resented that a little bit too, that his time was up, dammit, you know? And yet I was gonna continue on, and sometimes it could even be situations whereby, 'What, you used me?' No longer when I was in André's presence, no longer was it this loving, warm, admiration that we had for each other. It wasn't there."

Still, when he was asked if André's passing affected him more than other deaths, McMahon's answer was very emotional. "Oh god," he said with watery eyes, before pausing for a few seconds. "He was special."

The Roussimoff family in France and his nephew Boris, who lives in the Montreal suburbs, remembered André for who he really was. A man who enjoyed life. They were the ones who saw André the Giant the least but who had privileged access to André Roussimoff. He was the same person who grew up with them, and they were the people with whom he could simply be himself in the last few days of his life.

"We surely miss him. We all miss him, there's no doubt about that," said his brother Jacques. "Even now, he's always in our thoughts. To me, he was my brother, he was my big brother."

For Jackie and Frenchy, it was also like losing a family member. However, upon André's death, there was a lot on Jackie's shoulders. "When he passed away, I just felt like I was being asked a million and one questions. And having to make a million and one decisions," she expressed. "But I miss him every day. I miss his sense of humor. He was a terrible prankster. He got me several times."

To his daughter, he was always only André Roussimoff. "Maybe had he lived longer, I might have had a closer relationship with him," Robin said. "Perhaps he would've attended my graduation, or been proud of my successes. I'll never get to really know who he really was as a person. His persona hasn't really touched me. When I saw him, he was dad. He was truly the gentle giant."

Whether he was André Roussimoff or André the Giant, whether he was the brother or the uncle, the friend or the father, André created memories for everyone he met. He imprinted our consciousness, and that turned him into someone unforgettable. André didn't care about that, however. His physique made him famous but also very sad. "If I could take your place for a week, I would give you everything I had," André once told Tim White. And even if he wouldn't show it, being on the road all the time wasn't easy on him. "It's difficult wherever I go," he said. "They don't build anything for big people. They have everything for blind people, for crippled people, for some other people, but not for big people. So we have to fit in there and it's not too easy all the time." That was the duality of his life. The wrestling business was made for him, but life on the road wasn't. He never had the surgery that would have allowed him to live longer, out of fear of losing what made him special to the wrestling business. He thought he was trapped. When asked about his future, André had a simple answer.

"I live day to day, and I don't think about the future. You never know what might happen tomorrow."

ACKNOWLEDGMENTS

First, we'd like to say *merci beaucoup* to André's family, starting with his nephew Boris, without whom this book would not have been possible. André's brothers, Antoine (and his wife Hortense) and Jacques were also very helpful and provided us with invaluable information about André's time in France.

Thanks to Jackie McAuley, who lived with André for more than a decade. She was a tremendous help throughout the process, providing us with hours of her time.

Pat's work as field producer for the HBO documentary on André is the main reason why this book was able to see the light of day. To HBO, Bill Simmons, director Jason Hehir and his team, Jake, Matt, Sari, Bob, Jon, Thomas, and Alex: thank you.

Thanks to Stan Hansen for agreeing to write the foreword. We know André meant a lot to you. Your help was very much appreciated.

Chris Owens, the number one André the Giant collector, shared not only his knowledge but also part of his collection, including a list of matches that was invaluable throughout the writing of this book. Chris, thank you; there's a lot of you in this book.

Also, a huge *arigato* to Japan's wrestling historian Koji Miyamoto and his son Takaya. Not only did Koji tell us all the stories about André's time in Japan, but he and his son translated pages and pages of information, material that had never been translated before. You both contributed to this book more than you think.

To the community of wrestling historians, people such as Greg Oliver, Dave Meltzer, Phil Lions, Vern May, Bradley Craig (the England chapter would not have been possible without your help), Bob Plantin (*merci pour les infos sur Dédé en France*), Dave Cameron, George Schire, Markus Gronemann, Matt Farmer, Mike Steele, John Lister, Chris Charlton (for some translation as well), Gernot Freiberger, Mike Lano, Ronald Grobpietch, and Tim Hornbaker: a warm thank you.

Over the years we've had the chance to become close with many of André's friends, such as Gino Brito, Raymond Rougeau, Jacques Rougeau Sr., René Goulet, Pat Patterson, Gilles Poisson, Neil Guay, Rick Martel, Paul Leduc, Tony Mulé, and Paul Vachon. When interviewed, Vachon told us: "You know, if André had met you, he would have liked you guys and probably told you all of these stories himself over a beer!" It was both validation and motivation. To them, and all of André's friends in the province of Quebec, thank you for sharing your stories.

Attempting to name everyone who helped us with this book is a recipe for disaster, but we decided to try anyway. We're sorry if we forgot anyone:

Adnan Alkaissy, Alexandre Lépine, Ben Hildebrandt, Bill Apter, Bill Eadie, Bob Orton, Brain Blair, Chris Harrington, Christophe Aigus, Darol Dickinson, David Bixenpan, Diane Rivest, Ed Lock, Eric Bischoff, François Poirier, Gene Okerlund, Geoff Brown, George Napolitano, Gerry Brisco, Greg Valentine, Guillaume Lefrançois, Gilbert Wehrle, Grant Zwarych, Guy Hauray, Jacques Poulain, Jay Slack, Jean Brisson, Jim Stevenson, J.J. Dillon, John Cosper, John Dzafarov, Jonathan Plombon, Keith Elliot Greenberg, Lanny Poffo, Larry Hennig, Luc Poirier, Marc Blondin, Marc Mercier, Mary Fries, Michèle Valois, Michelle Léon, Mike Mooneyham, Missy Hyatt, Nathalie Dubail-de-Rooij, Noel

Mateos, Pascale Valois, René Duprée, Richard Vicek, Réjean Tremblay, Rodger Brulotte, Ryan Barkan, Shazza McKenzie, Steve Ogilvie, Stu Saks, Suzanne Robert, Thierry Fonteyne, Tony Garea, Tony St. Clair, and Yan O'Cain. Please know we appreciated your contributions more than words can convey.

We'd also like to thank every person who contributed their own memories or experiences with André, whether in books, newspapers, or films. These valuable archives brought us closer to the man behind the myth.

Finally, we'd like to thank everyone at ECW Press, but more precisely our editor Michael Holmes, for the extraordinary opportunities afforded to us, and for his trust and confidence over the years. We wouldn't be where we are right now without you. Between the two of us, this is our fifth book with ECW, and hopefully it won't be the last. Thanks also to Tony Stabile, for reviewing our work and cleaning it up. We'd also like to salute the team at Hurtubise, our new French publisher, led by André Gagnon, Alexandrine, and Arnaud Foulon. We always felt this was worthy of a dual release and you guys made it possible. Merci!

In closing, writing a book like this is fun, but hard — especially on family and friends. In this regard, a loving thank you for their support to Monique, Françoise, Alessandra (Sempre!), Zakary, Elayna, Jean-Krystophe, Gabriel, Samuel, and all of our respective friends.

In our first book, *Mad Dogs, Midgets and Screw Jobs*, on Montreal's wrestling history, we were unknowingly promoting some of the myths surrounding André's life and career because we hadn't done the extensive research and interviews we would later undertake. We quickly learned from our mistakes and realized that writing a definitive biography would be a giant task — pun intended. Therefore, we left behind the larger than life image of Jean Ferré we had from our childhood and put everything we had into this book to make sure the facts were right, the tales were debunked, and, mostly, that someone who didn't have the chance to see André in person would understand how unique he was — why he was one the most historical figures in professional wrestling, and why he truly was the eighth wonder of the world.

We're hoping we have succeeded.

Pat & Bertrand,
January 2020

REFERENCES

Aside from the references cited below, we have benefited from access to the archives of CBC, Radio-Canada, Tele-Quebec, TQS, Bibliothèque Nationale de France, l'Institut national de l'audiovisuel de France, and les Archives Nationales du Québec.

BOOKS

Abdul-Jabbar, Kareem, and Raymond Obstfeld. *Becoming Kareem: Growing Up On and Off the Court*. Little, Brown Books for Young Readers, 2017.

Al-Kaissy, Adnan, and Ross Bernstein. *The Sheikh of Baghdad*. Chicago: Triumph Books, 2005.

Apter, Bill. *Is Wrestling Fixed? I Didn't Know It Was Broken*. Toronto: ECW Press, 2013.

Backlund, Bob, and Rob Miller. *Backlund: From All-American Boy to Professional Wrestling's World Champion*. New York, Sports Publishing, 2015.

Boesh, Paul. *Hey, Boy! Where'd You Get Them Ears?* Houston: Minuteman Press Southwest, 2002.

Birkholz, Peter. *When Wrestling Was Rasslin'.* Houston, 2012.

Blassie, Fred, and Keith Elliot Greenberg. *Listen, You Pencil Neck Geeks.* New York: Pocket Books, 2003.

Brown, Box. *Andre the Giant: Life and Legend.* New York: First Second, 2014.

Brown, Craig. *One on One.* London: Fourth Estate, 2012.

Charlton, Chris. *Eggshells: Pro Wrestling in the Tokyo Dome.* Japan: Amazon digital services, 2018.

Charlton, Chris. *Lion's Pride: The Turbulent History of New Japan Pro Wrestling.* Japan, 2015.

Devito, Basil V., and Joe Layden. *WWF Wrestlemania: The Official Insider's Story.* New York: Harper Entertainment, 2001.

DiBiase, Ted, and Tom Caiazzo Ted DiBiase: *The Million Dollar Man:* New York, NY: Pocket Books, 2008.

Dillon, James J., Scott Teal, and Phillip Varriale. *"Wrestlers Are Like Seagulls": From McMahon to McMahon.* Hendersonville, TN: Crowbar Press, 2005.

Dinkinson, Darol. *Filet of Horn II.* Barnesville: Filet of Horn Publishing, 2011.

Duncan, Royal, and Gary Will. *Wrestling Title Histories* (Fourth Edition). Waterloo, ON: Archeus Communications, 2000.

Easton, Brandon, and Denis Medri. *Andre the Giant Closer to Heaven.* San Diego: Lion Force Comics, 2015.

Eclimont, Christian-Louis. *Catch L'Âge d'or 1920-1975.* Paris: Huginn et Muninn, 2016.

Ellison, Lillian, and Larry Platt. *The Fabulous Moolah: First Goddess of the Squared Circle.* HarperEntertainment, 2002.

Elwes, Carey, and Joe Layden. *As You Wish: Inconceivable Tales from the Making of The Princess Bride.* New York: Touchstone, 2014.

Esposito, Phil, and Peter Golenbock. *Thunder and Lightning: A No-B.S. Hockey Memoir.* Toronto: McClelland & Stewart, 2004.

Flair, Ric, Keith Elliot Greenberg, and Mark Madden. *To Be the Man.* New York: Pocket Books, 2004.

Goldman, William. *The Princess Bride: S. Morgenstern's Classic Tale of True Love and High Adventure.* New York: Harvest Book, 2007.

Gross, Josh. *Ali vs. Inoki: The Forgotten Fight That Inspired Mixed Martial Arts and Launched Sports Entertainment.* Dallas: BenBella Books, 2016.

Hansen, Stan, and Scott Teal. *The Last Outlaw.* Gallatin, TN: Crowbar Press, 2011.

Harris, James, and Kenny Casanova. *Kamala Speaks.* WOHW Publishing, 2015.

Hart, Bret. *My Real Life in the Cartoon World of Wrestling.* Toronto: Random House Canada, 2007.

Hart, Jimmy. *The Jimmy Hart Story.* Toronto: ECW Press, 2004.

Heenan, Bobby, and Steve Anderson. *Bobby the Brain: Wrestling's Bad Boy Tells All.* Chicago: Triumph Books, 2002.

Hogan, Hulk, and Michael Jan Friedman. *Hollywood Hulk Hogan.* New York: Pocket Books, 2002.

Hogan, Hulk, and Mark Dagostino. *My Life Outside the Ring.* New York: St-Martin's Griffin, 2010.

Hornbaker, Tim. *Capitol Revolution: The Rise of the McMahon Wrestling Empire.* Toronto: ECW Press, 2015.

Hornbaker, Tim. *Death of the Territories.* Toronto: ECW Press, 2018.

Jarrett, Jerry, and Mark James. *The Best of Times.* USA: CreateSpace, 2011.

Kenyon, J Michael, and Scott Teal. *Wrestling in the Garden, volume 2: 1940-2019 — The Battle for New York: Works, Shoots & Double-Crosses.* Gallatin, TN: Crowbar Press, 2019.

Korderas, Jimmy. *The Three Count.* Toronto: ECW Press, 2013.

Krugman, Michael. *Andre the Giant: A Legendary Life.* New York: Pocket Books, 2009.

Lageat, Robert, et Claude Dubois. *Des Halles au Balajo.* Paris, 1993.

Laprade, Pat, and Bertrand Hébert. *À la Semaine Prochaine, si Dieu le Veut!* Montréal: Libre Expression, 2013.

Laprade, Pat, and Bertrand Hébert. *Mad Dogs, Midgets and Screw Jobs.* Toronto: ECW Press, 2013.

Laprade, Pat, and Bertrand Hébert. *Mad Dog: The Maurice Vachon Story.* Toronto: ECW Press, 2017.

Laprade, Pat, and Bertrand Hébert. *Maurice Mad Dog Vachon.* Montréal: Libre Expression, 2015.

Lawler, Jerry, and Doug Asheville. *It's Good to Be the KING... Sometimes.* New York: Pocket Books, 2002.

LeBell, Gene, and Bob Calhoun. *The Toughest Man Alive.* Santa Monica: HNL Publishing, 2003.

Lister, John. *Have A Good Week... Till Next Week.* England 2018.

Matysik, Larry. *The 50 Greatest Professional Wrestlers of All Time.* Toronto, ECW Press, 2013.

McCoy, Heath. *Pain and Passion: The History of Stampede Wrestling.* Toronto: CanWest Books, 2005.

Michaels, Shawn, and Aaron Feigenbaum. *Heartbreak & Triumph.* New York: World Wrestling Entertainment, 2006.

Michaels, Shawn, and David Thomas. *Wrestling for My Life.* Grand Rapids: Zondervan, 2015.

Molinaro, John F., Jeff Marek, and Dave Meltzer. *Top 100 Pro Wrestlers of All Time.* Toronto: Winding Stair Press, 2002.

Mooneyham, Mike, and Shaun Assael. *Sex, Lies and Headlocks.* New York: Broadway Books, 2004.

Mulligan, Blackjack. *True Lies and Alibis: The Blackjack Mulligan Story.* Groveland, FL: Headlock Ranch, 2008.

Murphy, Dan, and Pat Laprade. *Sisterhood of the Squared Circle.* Toronto: ECW Press, 2017.

Oliver, Greg, and Steven Johnson. *Pro Wrestling Hall of Fame: Heroes & Icons.* Toronto: ECW Press, 2012.

Oliver, Greg. *Pro Wrestling Hall of Fame: The Canadians.* Toronto: ECW Press, 2003.

Orr, Bobby. *Bobby: My Story in Pictures.* Penguin Random House Canada, 2018.

Patterson, Pat, and Bertrand Hébert. *Accepted: How the First Gay Superstar Changed the WWE*. Toronto: ECW Press, 2016.

Piper, Roddy, and Robert Picarello. *In the Pit with Piper*. New York: Berkley Boulevard Book, 2002.

Race, Harley, and Gerry Tritz. *King of the Ring*. Champaign: Sports Publishing L.L.C., 2004.

Ross, Jim, and Paul O'Brien. *Slobberknocker: My Life in Wrestling*. Sports Publishing, 2017.

Rhodes, Dusty, and Howard Brody. *Reflections of an American Dream*. Champaign: Sports Publishing L.L.C., 2005.

Rougeau, Jean. *Johnny Rougeau*. Montreal: Éditions Québecor, 1982.

Robinson, Jon. *Creating the Mania*. Toronto: ECW Press, 2018.

Santana, Tito, and Tom Caiazzo. *Tales from the Ring*. Champaign: Sports Publishing L.L.C., 2008.

Sarrault, Jean-Paul. *Fais-le saigner*. Montreal: Logiques, 1993.

Schire, George. *Minnesota's Golden Age of Wrestling*. Minnesota: Minnesota Historical Society Press, 2010.

Sullivan, Kevin. *The WWE Championship: A Look Back at the Rich History of the WWE Championship*. New York: Gallery Books, 2010.

Shields, Brian. *30 Years of Wrestlemania*. Indianapolis: DK publishing, 2014.

Thesz, Lou, and Kit Bauman. *Hooker: An Authentic Wrestler's Adventures Inside the Bizarre World of Professional Wrestling*. Norfolk: Lou Thesz, 1995.

Thornley, Peter. *Kendo Nagasaki and The Man Behind the Mask*. London: The Man Behind the Mask Ltd, 2018.

Toombs, Ariel Teal, and Colt Baird Toombs. *Rowdy: The Roddy Piper Story*. Canada: Random House, 2016.

Vachon, Paul. *The Rise and Fall of Grand Prix Wrestling*. Laval, QC: Impressions Prioritaires, 2009.

Vachon, Paul. *The Territories and Japan*. Laval, QC: Impressions Prioritaires, 2009.

Vachon, Paul. *When Wrestling Was Real: Memories and True Stories, "The Early Years."* Laval, QC: Impressions Prioritaires, 2009.

Vicek, Richard. *Bruiser: The World's Most Dangerous Wrestler*. Gallatin, TN: Crowbar Press, 2016.

Watts, "Cowboy" Bill, and Scott Williams. *The Cowboy and the Cross: The Bill Watts Story; Rebellion, Wrestling and Redemption*. Toronto: ECW Press, 2006.

WEBSITES

Acromunity: www.acromunity.ca

Ancestry: www.ancestry.com

Association des médecins endrocrinologues du Québec: www.ameq.qc.ca

Assymcal: www.assymcal.org

Carenity: www.carenity.com

ClubWWI: www.clubwwi.com

Cagematch: www.cagematch.net

CBS Sports: cbssports.com

The Dan Gable International Wrestling Institute and Museum: www.wrestlingmuseum.org

Doctissimo: www.doctissimo.fr

History of WWE: www.thehistoryofwwe.com

Kayfabe Memories: www.kayfabememories.com

Legacy of Wrestling: legacyofwrestling.com

Maple Leaf Wrestling: http://mapleleafwrestling.blogspot.com/

Mid-Atlantic Gateway: www.midatlanticgateway.com

Newspapers: www.newspapers.com

Le portail des maladies rares: www.orpha.net

Pourquoi docteur?: www.pourquoidocteur.fr

Santé sur le net: www.sante-sur-le-net.com

SLAM Wrestling: http://slam.canoe.com/Slam/Wrestling/home

Sports Reference Olympics: www.sports-reference.com/olympics

Société Canadienne du cancer: www.cancer.ca

World Wrestling Entertainment: www.wwe.com

Wrestling Classics: www.wrestlingclassics.com

Wrestling Observer: www.wrestlingobserver.com
Wrestling Title Histories: www.wrestling-titles.com

NEWSPAPERS AND MAGAZINES

The Boston Globe
The Burlington Free Press
The Des Moines Register
The Detroit Free Press
Le Droit
L'Écho du Saint-Maurice
Échos-Vedettes
L'Équipe
Green Bay Press-Gazette
Honolulu Star-Bulletin
The Indianapolis Star
Le Journal de Montréal
Le Journal de Québec
Los Angeles Times
The Lowell Sun
Le Lundi
La Marne
The Minneapolis Star
The Montreal Gazette
New York Times
Le Nouvelliste de Trois-Rivières
The Orlando Sentinel
La Patrie
The Press and Journal
La Presse
The Richmond County Daily Journal
San Francisco Chronicle
Le Soleil (Québec)

Le Soleil (Saguenay)
Sports Illustrated
Télé-Presse
Télé Radio Monde
Toronto Star
La Tribune (Sherbrooke)

SPECIALIZED MAGAZINES AND NEWSLETTERS

Catch
Inside Wrestling
Le Journal de la lutte
Le Livre de la Lutte (magazine)
Lutte et Boxe
Main Event: The World of Professional Wrestling
Pro Wrestling Illustrated
La Revue de lutte professionnelle du Québec
The Ring Wrestling
Sports Review Wrestling
The Wrestler
Wrestling Monthly
The Wrestling News
Wrestling Observer Newsletter
Wrestling Revue
WWF Magazine
WWF Programs

TV SHOWS, MOVIES AND DIGITAL CONTENT

André the Giant. Directed by Jason Heir. HBO. USA: 2018.
André the Giant — Larger than Life. Written and produced by Chris
    Mortensen. A&E. USA: 2000.
André the Giant Facebook page

André the Giant YouTube channel

The Big Show: A Giant's World. Directed by Kevin Dunn. WWE. USA: 2011.

Miki & Maude. New Japan World, Directed by Blake Edwards. Columbia Pictures. USA: 1984.

Obey Giant. Directed by James Moll. Hulu. USA: 2017.

The Princess Bride. Directed by Rob Reiner. USA: 1987.

RF Video

Six Million Dollar Man. Directed by Richard Irving. Universal Television. USA: 1973.

Something Else to Wrestle with (Bruce Pritchard and Conrad Thompson)

World Championship Wrestling (Australia 1964-1978) Facebook page

Wrestling Observer Radio (Dave Meltzer and Bryan Alvarez)

WWE Network

At ECW Press, we want you to enjoy this book in whatever format you like, whenever you like. Leave your print book at home and take the eBook to go! Purchase the print edition and receive the eBook free. Just send an email to ebook@ecwpress.com and include:

- the book title
- the name of the store where you purchased it
- your receipt number
- your preference of file type: PDF or ePub

A real person will respond to your email with your eBook attached. And thanks for supporting an independently owned Canadian publisher with your purchase!